A
WORKING
WOMAN

A

WORKING
WOMAN

The Remarkable Life
of
Ray Strachey

JENNIFER HOLMES

Matador
9 Priory Business Park,
Wistow Road, Kibworth Beauchamp,
Leicestershire. LE8 0RX
Tel: 0116 279 2299
Email: books@troubador.co.uk
Web: www.troubador.co.uk/matador
Twitter: @matadorbooks

ISBN 978 1789016 543

British Library Cataloguing in Publication Data.
A catalogue record for this book is available from the British Library.

Printed and bound by CPI Group (UK) Ltd, Croydon, CR0 4YY
Typeset in 12pt Minion Pro by Troubador Publishing Ltd, Leicester, UK

Matador is an imprint of Troubador Publishing Ltd

For my grandsons,
Finlay, Edmund and Ralph

Contents

List of Illustrations   ix
Preface   xiii
Acknowledgements   xvi
Abbreviations   xviii

PROLOGUE   1

PART ONE: Foundations   3
CHAPTER ONE: *Divided Loyalties: 1887-1900*   5
CHAPTER TWO: *The New Girl: 1900 –1905*   28
CHAPTER THREE: *'Hurrah for Ray!': 1905–1906*   41

PART TWO: The Young Suffragist   57
CHAPTER FOUR: *Embracing the Cause: 1905–1908*   59
CHAPTER FIVE: *Apprenticeship: 1908–1910*   74

PART THREE: Wife, Mother, Feminist   101
CHAPTER SIX: *Ending and Beginning: 1911*   103
CHAPTER SEVEN: *Mrs Strachey: 1911–1914*   119
CHAPTER EIGHT: *Wars and Peace: 1914–1916*   136
CHAPTER NINE: *Triumph! 1916–1918*   152

PART FOUR: Building a Better World   165
CHAPTER TEN: *Aftermath: 1918–1920*   167
CHAPTER ELEVEN: *'A Reckless Woman': 1920–1923*   185

PART FIVE: Progeny   205
CHAPTER TWELVE: *A Mother's Place? 1924–1930*   207
CHAPTER THIRTEEN: *Fame without Fortune: 1927–1931*   231

PART SIX: Working for Women   257
CHAPTER FOURTEEN: *Hard Times: 1931–1935*   259
CHAPTER FIFTEEN: *Keeping Calm and Carrying On: 1935–1940*   284

EPILOGUE   311

APPENDICES   317
A: *The Whitall and Smith Families*   318
B: *The Costelloe Family*   319
C: *The Strachey family*   320

Notes   321
Select Bibliography   365
Index   379

List of Illustrations

All illustrations (including Ray Strachey's paintings) are © National Portrait Gallery, London, except where otherwise specified. Photographers/artists are stated where known.

In text

Figure 1: Mary Costelloe (née Smith, later Berenson), 1885

Figure 2: Benjamin Francis Conn ('Frank') Costelloe, circa 1886

Figure 3: Pearsall Smith Family, 1894

Figure 4: Ray Costelloe (later Strachey) and Karin Costelloe (later Stephen), 1898

Figure 5: Kensington High School circa 1900. UCL Institute of Education Archives, GDS/13/11/14

Figure 6: Hockey team at Kensington High School. The Women's Library @ LSE, 7BSH/6/1, Box 14

Figure 7: 'I Tatti' (home of Bernard and Mary Berenson), 1909

Figure 8: The motor accident as sketched by Ray Costelloe in her diary, 2 July 1905, reproduced with permission of The Camphill Village Trust Limited and courtesy of the Lilly Library, Indiana University, Bloomington, Indiana (H. W. Smith Collection, Bound Volume 36)

Figure 9: Geoffrey Scott, early 1910s

Figure 10: John Maynard Keynes (later Baron Keynes) by Gwen Raverat, circa 1908

Figure 11: Newnham Suffrage Caravan, 1908. The Women's Library @ LSE, 7BSH/5/2/04, Box 11

Figure 12: Ray addressing a meeting (or preparing to) during the Newnham Suffrage Caravan tour, 1908. The Women's Library @ LSE, 7BSH/5/2/04, Box 11

Figure 13: Press cutting from *Denver Post*, 31 October 1908. The Women's Library @ LSE, 7BSH/5/2/7, Box 12

Figure 14: Postcard of Court Place, Iffley [private collection]

Figure 15: 96 South Hill Park (front) [author's photograph]

Figure 16: 96 South Hill Park (rear) [author's photograph]

Figures 17 and 18: The workshops set up by the Women's Service Bureau of the London Society for Women's Suffrage to train women in oxyacetylene welding for aircraft manufacture. The Women's Library @ LSE, 7BSH/6/3-4, Box 14

Figure 19: Catherine Marshall, 1916. Courtesy of Cumbria Archive Centre (Carlisle), DMAR/10/1

Figure 20: 'Durbins' (home of Roger Fry) by Ray Strachey, and by Oliver Strachey, 1916

Figure 21: Ray Strachey in her Rover, mid 1910s

Figure 22: Inez Ferguson. Courtesy of the archives of the National Federation of Women's Institutes

Figure 23: Press cutting from *Our Home* April 1920. The Women's Library @ LSE, 7BSH/5/2/2, Box 11

Figure 24: The Mud House (originally Copse Cottage) in 1923. Courtesy of the Lilly Library, Indiana University, Bloomington, Indiana (H. W. Smith Collection, Box 18)

Figure 25: Election poster, 1922. The Women's Library @ LSE, 7BSH/5/2/2, Box 11

Figure 26: Christopher Strachey; Barbara Strachey; Ray Strachey by Elliott & Fry, 1922

Figure 27: John Strachey; Barbara Strachey, 1924-1925

Figure 28: Postcard showing Ray Strachey with Dame Millicent Fawcett and her daughter and sister after Royal Assent to the Equal Franchise Act 1928. The Women's Library @ LSE, TWL/2002/329, Postcard Box 03.

Figure 29: 4 St James's Square [author's photograph]

Figure 30: Ray Strachey (née Costelloe) with her grandson Roger. Biblioteca

Berenson, Villa I Tatti – The Harvard University Center for Italian Renaissance Studies, courtesy of the President and Fellows of Harvard College

Figure 31: Ray Strachey, 1938-1939

Figure 32: Photographic etching of Ray Strachey on the plinth of Gillian Wearing's statue of Dame Millicent Fawcett in Parliament Square [author's photograph]

Plate section

Plate 1: Mary Costelloe (later Berenson); Ray Costelloe (later Strachey), 1887

Plate 2: Mary Anne Costelloe (née Conn); Benjamin Francis Conn ('Frank') Costelloe; Ray Costelloe (later Strachey), circa 1895

Plate 3: Bernard Berenson, circa 1900

Plate 4: Hannah Smith (née Whitall) (Mrs Pearsall Smith), circa 1892

Plate 5: M. Carey Thomas, by Theodore C. Marceau, 1910, courtesy of Bryn Mawr College Special Collections

Plate 6: Ellie Rendel, circa 1908

Plate 7: Alys Whitall Russell (née Pearsall Smith); Bertrand Russell, 1907

Plate 8: Adrian Stephen; Karin Costelloe, September 1914

Plate 9: Oliver Strachey, 1911

Plate 10: Pippa Strachey, circa 1920

Plate 11: Julia Frances Strachey, circa 1913

Plate 12: Ralph Strachey by Henry Charles Spink, 1910

Plate 13: Ray Costelloe (later Strachey), 1889

Plate 14: Ray Costelloe (later Strachey) and Karin Costelloe (later Stephen), circa 1896

Plate 15: Ray Costelloe (later Strachey), 1908

Plate 16: Ray Strachey, 1911

Plate 17: Portrait of Ray Strachey by Simon Bussy, 1912 [private collection]

Plate 18: Photo of Ray Strachey used in her election material, 1922 and 1923. The Women's Library @ LSE, 7BSH/6/1, Box 14

Plate 19: Ray Strachey, 1928

Plate 20: Ray Strachey, 1936

Plate 21: Studio portrait of Ray Strachey by Ramsey and Muspratt, Cambridge, circa 1939. The Women's Library @ LSE, 6WEF/07/11, Box FL493

Plate 22: Edgar Algernon Robert Gascoyne-Cecil, by Bassano Ltd, 3 February 1920

Plate 23: Nancy Astor, Viscountess Astor, by George Charles Beresford, 22 December 1920

Plate 24: Mary Agnes Hamilton, *Illustrated London News*, 24 December 1932, p.1024

Plate 25: Oliver Strachey by Gilbert de Beauregard Robinson, 1930s

Plate 26: Mary Berenson with her daughter Ray, granddaughter Barbara and great-grandson Roger, 1935. Biblioteca Berenson, Villa I Tatti - The Harvard University Center for Italian Renaissance Studies, courtesy of the President and Fellows of Harvard College

Plate 27: Olav Hultin. Courtesy of the Lilly Library, Indiana University, Bloomington, Indiana (H. W. Smith Collection, Box 18)

Plate 28: Roger Hultin with Wolf, 1938. Biblioteca Berenson, Villa I Tatti - The Harvard University Center for Italian Renaissance Studies, courtesy of the President and Fellows of Harvard College

Plate 29: Oliver Strachey by Ray Strachey, circa 1925

Plate 30: Barbara Strachey by Ray Strachey, circa 1926

Plate 31: Julia Frances Strachey by Ray Strachey, 1925-1937

Plate 32: Lytton Strachey by Ray Strachey, circa 1925-1930

Plate 33: Roger Fry by Ray Strachey, late 1920s or early 1930s

Plate 34: Wolf Halpern by Ray Strachey, mid-1930s

Plate 35: Karin Stephen by Ray Strachey, 1925-1937

Plate 36: Adrian Stephen by Ray Strachey, late 1920s or early 1930s

Plate 37: Adrian Stephen by Ray Strachey, late 1920s or early 1930s

Plate 38: Virginia Woolf by Ray Strachey, 1938

Plate 39: Bernard Berenson by Ray Strachey, 1925-1937

Plate 40: Grace Worthington (née Thomas) by Ray Strachey, 1925-1937

Plate 41: Dorothy Bussy (née Strachey) by Ray Strachey, late 1920s or early 1930s

Plate 42: Simon Bussy by Ray Strachey, late 1920s or early 1930s

Plate 43: Janie Bussy by Ray Strachey, late 1920s or early 1930s

Plate 44: Ray Strachey by Ray Strachey, circa 1926

Plate 45: Ray Strachey by Ray Strachey, 1930s

Plate 46: Ray Strachey by Ray Strachey, 1930s

Preface

Who was Ray Strachey? When she died in 1940, she was a nationally known figure. Since then she has been remembered as the author of a classic history of the women's movement, *The Cause* – still an invaluable source of information and lively quotations for writers on women's history – but has otherwise slipped into the shadows of history, her life and achievements of continuing interest mainly to feminist historians.[1] Within that limited sphere, she has been discussed (often with amused nods in the direction of her supposedly eccentric private life) as a suffragist, as a fighter for women's employment, as the biographer of Millicent Garrett Fawcett and as a historian of the movement in which she played a leading role. Her other public roles – as novelist, journalist and broadcaster – have received little attention.

Within the world of women's history, Ray Strachey has evoked mixed reactions. While her abilities and achievements have been widely acknowledged, her abundant self-assurance and personal ambition have not been universally popular, and her goodwill has been questioned. She has been portrayed as a trouble-maker and habitual intriguer. Her role in the split between the 'patriots' and the 'pacifists' in the National Union of Women's Suffrage Societies (NUWSS) in 1915 has attracted criticism, as has her decisive role soon afterwards in ending the NUWSS partnership with the Labour Party. In her private life she has been accused of being a cruel stepmother, a less than enthusiastic wife, and an overfond mother. Her sexuality has been the subject of debate, her financial extravagance censured, her lifestyle somewhat inconsistently mocked for its austerity. Yet her family, friends and staff were devoted to her and the tributes paid on her death suggest that she had become a much-loved heroine for generations of women. Who, then, was the real Ray Strachey?

'She was a wonderful mother.'[2] This was the sentence which more than any other decided me to write about Ray Strachey. The author of this verdict, Ray's daughter Barbara, had been my original intended research subject. She had been a friend of the philosopher Isaiah Berlin, so my work on his letters had led me to the convoluted story of Barbara's two marriages, an intriguing biographical topic, I thought. But as I started to investigate Barbara's background, I kept finding my attention wandering to her mother Ray, who achieved so much in her public life at the same time as propping up vast numbers of family and friends. Her usual tag of 'feminist and writer' hardly does justice to the wide range of her public and private roles. For many women a successful public life has been achieved at the expense of their family; how had Ray been able to balance the two? What made her tick?

Once I had decided to transfer the focus of my research from Barbara to Ray, the research process proved more complicated than expected, as I had somehow overlooked the fact that most of the family papers were now in the United States. But after two substantial research trips to Bloomington, Indiana, I had harvested what felt like an entire archive of photographs of correspondence and diary entries (in truth just a fraction of the Lilly Library's holdings on the Pearsall Smith family). Together with the records in this country of Ray's public life, they demonstrated that over the years since her death Ray's achievements had been diminished, her personality and motivation distorted. The more I delved into Ray's life, the more misinformation and cloned error I discovered in previous accounts. Her own words have all too often been turned against her out of context to give a quite false impression.

Her public persona was admittedly misleading and the paradoxes in her character and behaviour difficult to explain at first encounter. Was she a conservative or a social reformer, an imperialist warmonger or an appeaser, a devious manipulator or deeply honest? How did her taste for the dramatic relate to her commitment to rationalism, common sense and moderation? How does one reconcile her harsh verbal criticisms with her habitual kindness in action, her awareness of her own abilities with her capacity for passing credit for her achievements onto others? A complex personality with an essentially private and self-contained inner core lay behind Ray's façade of ebullient self-confidence. Her emotional reticence, so frustrating for a biographer, meant that I had to read her silences: what Ray did not say was often as important as what she said.

I became convinced that to understand Ray it was necessary to explore her relations with men, particularly her father and her husband and, more widely, the male feminists inside and outside Parliament who had helped the cause of female emancipation. It became clear that she had been deeply influenced by a number of men who scarcely rate a mention in previous accounts of her life and that her success as a feminist had much to do with her ability to communicate with and convince men in general, not by flirting (never her style) but by empathy and rational argument. Ray Strachey was a feminist not because she regarded women as different and in need of special treatment but because she saw little difference between the sexes: it was hence both logical and sensible for men and women to have the same rights, opportunities and responsibilities.

After nearly a decade of digging into Ray Strachey's life and times, my admiration for what she achieved for women remains considerable. There is no doubt about her status as one of the most important feminists of the early twentieth century. But I admire even more the way she lived her own life. She could so easily have remained a spoilt brat, as in many ways her mother did. Instead, she took the differing sets of values offered by her father, mother, grandmother and in-laws and crafted her own synthesis from them. 'We've got to put our teeth into ourselves', Ray advised her erratic daughter, and watching Ray follow her own advice has been one of the most interesting aspects of my research.[3]

Jennifer Holmes
September 2018

Acknowledgements

This book is based on my dissertation for a DPhil in Biography at the University of Buckingham, supervised by Professor Jane Ridley, and I owe her a massive debt for her teaching on the craft of biography and her guidance on my own work.

My research has been facilitated by the extraordinary helpfulness of a large number of archivists and librarians. My thanks go to the staff (present and past) of the Lilly Library, Indiana University, Bloomington, Indiana (especially David K. Frasier); the Women's Library (both at its former location in the London Metropolitan University and its new home at the LSE); the London Library; the British Library; the National Portrait Gallery; the National Archives, Kew; the Berenson Library, Villa I Tatti (Harvard University Center for Italian Renaissance Studies, Florence); Cumbria Archive Centre (Carlisle); the University of Reading (Special Collections); University College London (Special Collections); the Institute of Education, University College London; the National Records of Scotland, Edinburgh; the Schlesinger Library, Radcliffe Institute, Harvard University; Bryn Mawr College Special Collections; Newnham College Archives, Cambridge; Lady Margaret Hall Archives, Oxford; the Churchill Archives Centre, Cambridge; the Imperial War Museum, London; Fernhurst Archives; the archives of the National Federation of Women's Institutes; and the Albert and Shirley Small Special Collections, University of Virginia Library, Charlottesville.

For permission to include quotations and images I am grateful to the Camphill Village Trust (the copyright-holder for the unpublished writings of Ray Strachey and many members of her family); the Lilly Library, Indiana University; the President and Fellows of Harvard College; the National Portrait Gallery, London; the Carnegie (UK) Trust; Bryn Mawr College Special Collections; the Institute of Education, University College London; Cumbria Archive Centre (Carlisle); the archives of the National Federation of Women's Institutes; Peter Lofts; and the current holders of the copyright in Simon Bussy's paintings.

I am most grateful to Veena Raleigh for her kindness and hospitality at the Mud House after a serendipitous meeting. My thanks go too to my colleagues on the University of Buckingham course in Biography who made helpful suggestions and offered useful material from their own research.

Finally I must thank my family and friends (especially Kate, Alison and Patsy), who have advised and supported me (and endured with tolerant good humour endless conversations about Ray Strachey) during the many years that this book has been in the making.

Abbreviations

BB	Bern(h)ard Berenson
BL	British Library
BV	Bound Volume
EFF	Election Fighting Fund
ER	Elinor Rendel
GC&CS	Government Code and Cypher School
HWS	Hannah Whitall Smith Collection
ILP	Independent Labour Party
IWSA	International Woman Suffrage Alliance
LCC	London County Council
LNSWS	London and National Society for Women's Service (from 1926)
LNU	League of Nations Union
LSE	London School of Economics
LSWS	London Society for Women's Suffrage (1907–19)
	London Society for Women's Service (1919–26)
MWW	Mary Whitall Worthington
NAWSA	National American Woman Suffrage Association
NCAC	National Council Against Conscription
NUSEC	National Union of Societies for Equal Citizenship
NUWSS	National Union of Women's Suffrage Societies
RC	Ray Costelloe
RS	Ray Strachey
UCL	University College London
UDC	Union of Democratic Control
WAAC	Women's Army Auxiliary Corps
WEF	Women's Employment Federation
WL	Women's Library
WSPU	Women's Social and Political Union
VAD	Voluntary Aid Detachment

"*And do you think, Ray, that if you had it to do, you could manage the universe?*"

"*Yes, I rather think I could.*"

Mary Berenson's memory of a conversation with her teenage daughter, Ray Costelloe, recorded in her 'Life of Ray Strachey'.

Prologue

When Generalfeldmarschall Albert Kesselring, commander of the German forces in Italy defending the Gothic Line against the advancing Allied troops and recent recipient from his grateful Führer of the Knight's Cross with oak leaves, swords and diamonds, established his headquarters in one of the splendid villas outside Florence during the summer of 1944, he left undisturbed one of the villa's existing inhabitants. The villa's owner, the art expert Bernard Berenson, American by nationality but Lithuanian-Jewish by birth, had taken sanctuary with a friendly diplomat the previous autumn, accompanied by the woman with whom he and his wife had lived in a longstanding *ménage à trois*. They left without taking – or even revealing their nearby destination to – his ailing wife: moving Mary Berenson would have been difficult and trusting her discretion impossible.

The bedridden old lady was clearly no threat to the Third Reich, despite her American nationality. When Wehrmacht officers first moved into the house, she was evicted from her suite of rooms on the first floor, with its charming loggia overlooking the garden. It took four soldiers to hoist her considerable bulk – evidence of a life-time's gluttony – on a chair up to the attic flat previously occupied by her husband's companion. There she was cared for by several nurses and a small remnant of the Berensons' large staff. Villa I Tatti fared better under occupation than many of the surrounding properties, though the German officers' enthusiasm for soaking in generously filled baths eventually drained dry the house's water supply. The magnificent art collection and library which Bernard and Mary Berenson had built up over four decades had been largely dispersed or hidden: what remained of the villa's former glories were its wide view over the Arno valley and the imaginatively designed though now neglected gardens sloping down the steep hillside.

Mary coped with the alien intrusion into her home by putting her remaining energies into completing the project which continued to give her life a purpose. The death of her beloved elder daughter Ray in July 1940 had prompted not the hysteria her family and friends had expected, but calm resignation and a determination to leave a record of her daughter's life and achievements. The family had always been assiduous letter writers, so Mary could turn to a mass of preserved correspondence for factual information, supplemented by her own (not always accurate) memories. Day after day Mary reread her daughter's letters and committed her life to paper; the happy past was a more attractive place to live than the distressing present. Mary's strength was failing and anyhow an objective assessment would never have been within her compass. Her aim was unambiguously to glorify her daughter's memory, and her portrayal contains barely a hint of criticism and no indication of emotional turbulence. Having failed to mould Ray into the person she wanted her to be during her lifetime, Mary found the transformative process easier after Ray's death.

At times the biography she produced is little more than a sequence of freely edited quotations, all tending to back up her conviction that her daughter was a 'serene, good-tempered, humorous, joyful, hopeful, helpful, selfless, wise and competent woman, a companion who radiated happiness and sympathy'.[1] The picture which emerges from Mary Berenson's 'Life of Ray Strachey' is of a near-saint who enjoyed a perfect marriage and an untroubled relationship of mutual devotion with her mother. The reality, to which Mary remained blind throughout her life, was far more complex and far more interesting.

PART ONE

Foundations

CHAPTER ONE

Divided Loyalties: 1887-1900

... a mother's first and most sacred duty is to her children; and I cannot feel that anything will really prosper that involves the neglect of them.[1]

Only weeks after the end of a war which had shattered cultural assumptions as well as lives, the general election held in Britain on 14 December 1918 bore witness to changing attitudes. For the first time the electorate included women – nearly eight and a half million of them – and seventeen female candidates were standing. There had been little time for women to find seats since the introduction six weeks earlier of legislation allowing them to become Members of Parliament. Those who succeeded included stalwarts of the women's suffrage movement such as former suffragettes Christabel Pankhurst and Emmeline Pethick-Lawrence, and non-violent suffragists Charlotte Despard and Margery Corbett Ashby, as well as prominent Trade Unionist Mary Macarthur. But when male MPs discussed which of the women candidates were best suited to join them, their choice fell on a young mother, half-Irish, half-American, who had only recently burst onto the political scene. As the Liberal MP F. D. Acland reported, 'in discussions with fellow MPs of the women "who really ought to be in the next Parliament", we all put "Mrs Strachey" at the top of the list'. [2] Ray Strachey did not succeed on that occasion, nor in two later attempts to enter Parliament, but her capacity for persuading men to back her brand of feminism continued to play a key role in her tireless championing of women's interests.

Rachel Pearsall Conn Costelloe was born on 4 June 1887, appropriately enough in Westminster, at 40 Grosvenor Road (later the birthplace of Labour MP Tony Benn and now the site of Millbank Tower). Known from birth as Ray after an aunt who had died in childhood, she was the first child of ill-matched parents. Ray's father, Benjamin Francis Conn ('Frank') Costelloe, was a restlessly energetic, deeply religious Irish Catholic, raised in Glasgow in a middle-class family. His brilliant educational successes at school and university in Glasgow and at Balliol College, Oxford (where he was influenced by Benjamin Jowett and Thomas Hill Green), led to a career as a barrister (supplemented by political and religious journalism), a commitment to social reform, and political ambitions as a Radical Liberal. Despite some social failings, such as a tendency to express his views too vehemently and at excessive length, he seemed destined for success.

On a trip to the United States in 1884, at the age of thirty, Frank Costelloe met and fell in love with Mary Pearsall Smith, the daughter of a wealthy family of Philadelphia Quakers. Mary's parents had followed unusual religious paths from their Quaker origins to achieve international fame as Evangelical preachers. Robert Pearsall Smith's reputation, self-confidence and religious faith had never recovered from an unfortunate incident with a female disciple in England some years earlier; but his wife Hannah Whitall Smith remained well-known as a religious speaker and writer. Only three out of their seven children survived to adulthood. Mary, her brother Logan and her sister Alys became all the more precious to Hannah, who developed a child-centred theory of parenting unusual at that time: children should be given whatever they wanted, young people knew better than their elders and (after marital disillusionment had produced a fixed dislike of men in general) daughters were far more worthwhile than sons.

Twenty-year-old Mary, tall with red-gold hair, was adored and indulged by both her parents. Although good-humoured (except when complaining of her frequent physical afflictions), intelligent, and anxious to further her education, she was self-willed, manipulative, and supremely confident of getting her own way. Opposition or the exercise of authority over her made her rebellious: what Mary wanted, Mary got. Impressed by Frank's intellect, earnest sincerity, philanthropic and political intentions, and his certainty that 'the foundations of the world were the four corner stones of God, Duty, Free-Will and Immortality', she entered into a trans-Atlantic correspondence and soon agreed to marry Frank Costelloe.[3]

Mary's horrified family, particularly Hannah, objected to Frank's religion and lower social status. Mary, at the time a student of philosophy at the Harvard Annex (which later became Radcliffe College), was subjected to a barrage of letters pointing out the evils of Catholicism, the dangers for the wife in a mixed marriage, the unimpressive financial position of her intended, as well as (over and over again) his social failings. According to Hannah, Costelloe lacked both the 'air of refinement that comes from refined breeding' and 'the true instincts of a gentleman'.[4] Mary stood firm.

The engaged couple eventually overcame the resistance of Mary's parents, though Hannah, with her strong dislike of husbands, never became enthusiastic about her daughter's choice. Hearing Costelloe give a political speech in Glasgow, where he hoped to find a Parliamentary seat, did, however, produce a favourable impression, for his advocacy of Temperance, Women's Rights and Moral Reform matched Hannah's views exactly. On 3 September 1885 Frank Costelloe and Mary Pearsall Smith were married in Oxford, immediately after Mary's baptism into the Catholic Church. After a lavish reception in Balliol College, the new Mr and Mrs Costelloe returned to Frank's (unsuccessful) political campaign in Scotland and thence to their leased house in Westminster.

40 Grosvenor Road was convenient for Parliament but hardly a prestigious address, surrounded as it was by a mixture of commercial premises, poor quality housing, a none too respectable public house, and, a few houses to the west, the ominous bulk of Millbank Prison:

(Figure 1) Mary Costelloe as a new bride in 1885.

(Figure 2) The barrister: Frank Costelloe c. 1886.

when the Costelloes moved in, one of its inmates was Rebecca Jarrett, a former prostitute and procuress who had helped W. T. Stead in his exposé of child prostitution and like him been imprisoned. (Frank Costelloe, active in the Vigilance Association and often their legal representative, was an enthusiastic supporter of Stead.) The narrow, tall, deep, red-brick house, in a recently-constructed terrace, consisted of ten rooms over four floors above a basement, and backed onto workmen's cottages and Mowlem's stone yard. The house's main glory was its ever-changing view of the river at the front.

Money was tight for the young couple.[5] Mary's expectations exceeded their income and they were forced to rely on support from her parents, who therefore felt free to intervene and criticise as they pleased, particularly when in 1888 the Pearsall Smiths moved permanently to London, to a house just four doors along from their beloved daughter. Nevertheless, the early years of the marriage appear to have been happy, even if the absence of quarrels mainly resulted from Frank's forbearance. Frank adopted the Pearsall Smiths' Quaker speech – 'thee' instead of 'you' – and tried to live up to their requirements. Mary threw herself into her husband's activities. The charms of working in the slums with Henrietta Barnett soon palled, but taking on a public role in the Women's Liberal Association and other reforming bodies was more to her taste.

Both parents were delighted at the birth of their 'strong and vivacious' daughter in June 1887, and Frank Costelloe earned praise from his mother-in-law for staying with Mary during a difficult and painful delivery.[6] But Mary found motherhood less rewarding than Hannah had done, and given her husband's demanding workload, the help he expected from her with it, and the growing list of good causes seeking her services, was unenthusiastic when she became pregnant again only a year after Ray's birth. Resentment at the pressures placed on her by their way of life built up. After the birth of the second Costelloe daughter in March 1889 (officially named Catherine Elizabeth, but always known as Karin), Mary had a major breakdown. Members of the Pearsall Smith family in every generation suffered from manic depression (bi-polar disorder), including Robert, and although Mary was not one of those worst affected, the combined impact on her of natural susceptibility, marital disharmony and apparent post-natal depression made her wretched.

It was a particularly unfortunate time for Frank Costelloe, whose attempts to enter Parliament were persistently unsuccessful, to find his political niche. January 1889 saw the birth of the London County Council (LCC). The Radical Liberals (Progressives, as they were known in London) took control, promising a dramatic improvement in London's local government. The new Council of 126 members was full of idealistic, forward-looking, self-sacrificing men who were prepared to devote long hours without pay to the task before them. Costelloe was one of them, narrowly elected as one of the two members for Stepney. He soon became one of its leading influences, as chairman of the important Local Government and Taxation Committee, responsible for policy on revenue, and as one of the Council's political driving forces. By 1893 Beatrice Webb, who with her husband Sidney (Frank Costelloe's friend and fellow-councillor at the LCC) lived next door to the Costelloes, could claim: 'The Council is really run by various groups of county councillors circling round the three officials – the chairman, vice-chairman and deputy chairman – of the Council. Of these the most prominent are the group who

direct the parliamentary and political policy of the County Council –
Costelloe, Sidney, Benn.'[7]

Mary never shared Frank's enthusiasm for his 'beloved Council.'[8]
She was capable of recognising that 'he is so much *better* than I. He
does what he ought and doesn't go about following out his own whims
and desires regardless of the moral law'; but she found self-sacrificing
goodness more admirable than exciting – and excitement was what
Mary craved.[9] She found it in a slight, faun-like young man she had
first glimpsed at Harvard.

Bernhard Berenson was by birth a Lithuanian Jew whose family
had emigrated to Boston when he was a child. The family struggled
financially but nevertheless young Bernhard was educated at Boston
University and Harvard, acquiring a passion for culture and a
reputation for brilliance well before he had decided how to spend his
life. A grand tour of Europe, during which he encountered Giovanni
Morelli's iconoclastic approach to the attribution of paintings, made
him an aspiring art expert, with a particular love for the Italian
Renaissance.[10] He became a close friend of the Costelloes.

Mary quickly responded to Berenson's idealisation of culture. Their
days in art galleries in August 1890 – and the correspondence they
started soon afterwards – gave Mary a new interest in life: she became
determined to study art herself. Partly from Frank's influence, Berenson
became a Catholic. It is not clear who made the first amorous move –
Berenson later claimed that it was Mary – but in the spring of 1891,
when Berenson was a house-guest at 40 Grosvenor Road, he and Mary
became lovers.

Soon afterwards Mary devised the idea of spending a year in
Florence as Berenson's pupil with a view to developing a career for
herself as an art expert. Despite Mary's continuing complaints about
their way of life, Frank appears to have had complete faith that the
relationship between Berenson and Mary was platonic, simply that of
master and pupil. And he was seriously worried about Mary's mental
health: she had talked at length of her fears that she would inherit
the mental problems to which her family were prone. Despite the
opposition of her parents, Mary remained adamant in her intentions.

A medical diagnosis of acute exhaustion and the recommendation that Mary spend a year abroad settled the matter.

Friends marvelled at Frank's acceptance of Mary's departure in August 1891. Sidney Webb clearly thought him naive and over-trusting:

> C[ostelloe] still thinks and trusts it will be all right; asserts that she has not the faintest idea or intention of leading any but an independent life; and that any move on *his* [Berenson's] part towards anything else would bring about disillusionment at once. C. is playing a very magnanimous game: he has just sent her authority to sign cheques on his account! And talks of taking the children out to her in Florence. As he says, it is not worth playing unless he plays to win *completely*, to have her return to him wholly and spontaneously– for which he still hopes, though he does not hide from himself the immense danger she is unconsciously running.[11]

Frank agreed that both children could spend several months in Florence with Mary, but as she admitted to herself, only Ray was of real interest to her:

> if he wants to keep Karin I shall make no objection, because she is really too little to learn Italian, whereas Ray will learn it so that it will be as natural to her as English [...] then I will see the Angel too, without whom I am only three quarters happy. Sweet little Seraph – I wonder why I love her so?[12]

Mary returned to London at the beginning of December for a fortnight, then took the children out to Florence. By January she was feeling the strain, complaining to her diary that:

> Every girl ought to be made to spend six months taking care of little children before she marries. She would then think twice before having children of her own!! The nurse came at 11!! Children restless all night and I terribly unhappy at being absent from B.[13]

In January 1892 the arrival of Hannah eased the burden of childcare (though presumably not Mary's solitary state at night) and Hannah's residence in the household for a month undoubtedly lent some respectability to her daughter's circumstances. Although Mary and Berenson maintained separate households, in close proximity, they were constantly in each other's company and their relationship was easily deduced (less socially risky in Florence, where so many expatriates enjoyed unconventional sexual liaisons, than in London).

The children stayed in Florence until May, but Mary was not always with them. While Ray and Karin remained in the care of the nurse and an American friend, Mary and her tutor-lover pursued their art study tours of Italy. Ray seems to have taken a dim view of this further abandonment, as Mary recounted to Hannah in March:

> Ray gave me a severe reproof today. She said she never thought of people who were away. So I said foolishly (one is foolish with a sweet child) "wouldn't thee think of me if I was away?" "No," she said decisively, "Dear me, that is hard luck!" I said, "when I would be thinking of thee all the time." "Well, what did you have me for?" she asked – and the question was unanswerable.[14]

But even the amount of time Mary did spend with her children was too much for Berenson, not a child-lover, who objected to 'the general tendency of children to engulf the personality of the mother – at any rate her intellect' and came to regard Ray as 'a rather detestable specimen of humanity'.[15]

Frank was successfully re-elected for the LCC on 6 March 1892, this time for Chelsea, where he had also been selected as the Liberal candidate for the forthcoming general election. When Mary brought the girls back to London in May, she announced that her return to London was to be temporary and that she wanted to end her marriage, preferably by divorce, and take custody of the children (or at least Ray – she would apparently have traded custody of Karin for a divorce). She was intent on preventing the children from being brought up as

Catholics: after studying the historical role of the Roman Catholic Church, both she and Berenson had now turned against it. The strained goodwill that had so far been maintained between Frank and Mary broke down in bitter arguments and mutual recrimination.

Mary could not instigate a divorce herself; admitting to adultery with Berenson and allowing him to be named as co-respondent would have put her lover's hopes of building up a career in the art world into grave jeopardy. As a Catholic, Frank was firmly opposed to divorce. And although, thanks to the legal battles fought by Caroline Norton earlier in the century, the law was now more sympathetic to the mothers of young children in cases of separation, there was no doubt that, given Mary's behaviour, a court would uphold their father's claim to custody and choice of his children's religion.[16]

Frank lost the election on 5 July and turned his attention to ensuring that Mary could not remove the children from the jurisdiction of the British legal system. The eventual separation agreement (apparently not ratified by a court) provided that the girls should remain in the custody of their father and be educated as Catholics; Mary was allowed limited access, in return for a promise not to damage Costelloe's career or reputation; Hannah retained 'the right to the children for a while'.[17]

Mary, used to getting her own way, was forced to accept that she faced a clear-cut choice between her life with Berenson and life with her children (though Berenson's reaction to her children might have suggested this already). She chose Berenson and her intellectual life, but the shock and disappointment of not being able to have everything she wanted was long-lasting. Over the following years Mary's letters and diaries reflect her inner conflict, but nowhere suggest that she ever contemplated putting the interests of her children first. In her diary she acknowledged that:

all that is personal in me, all that means self-development, real education, knowledge, enjoyment, is with Bernhard. With Ray I could not help sinking to a mere instinctive motherhood – that is, with Ray and without Bernhard. Yet, even knowing this with certainty, the struggle against the chains of womanhood – the *inside* chains – is a terribly hard one[18]

and

The children simply tire me to death, and leave nothing interesting to be said. [...] my meat and drink has become the possibility of escaping to impersonal interests, and at every moment I am pulled down into the most revoltingly sordid and to me almost heartbreaking worries – this and that going wrong with the children's bringing-up – too burdensome to tell anyone about.[19]

To Berenson she protested:

if thee *should* get to hate me, or not want me, and I came back here, not even the children could in the least make up, not for thee, but even for the life thee has given me, almost as free as life can be from what is sordid and mean.[20]

Even to the children themselves Mary was open about her preference. In January 1893 five-year-old Ray received an unusual admission from her mother:

I love thee dearly, dearly, my precious Ray … I love thee more than anybody else in the world, except myself. [...] It is the fashion for people to think that they love other people better than themselves. And *sometimes* they do, but it is very rare. People as young as I am, very seldom do … Now that I have found studying of my own I really like to do, I do not want to give it up in order to stay with thee all the time. If thy father would let me have thee always with me, I should be perfectly happy…But he wants you in London. So I go away, and only come home now and then, so that I can go on with my studying.[21]

Hannah Whitall Smith was appalled both at her daughter's behaviour and at the iniquities of a legal system which did not allow her to get away with it, and she feared losing contact with her grandchildren. Intent on trying to persuade Mary to return to her maternal role, over the following years she took every chance to paint the children's lives without her in the blackest possible colours. The faintest suspicion that all was not well in Ray's life led to an anguished letter from Hannah to Mary, an angry letter from Mary to Frank, a letter of restrained politeness from Frank to Hannah asking her not to interfere or explaining that she had misunderstood the situation and a complaint from Hannah to Mary about Frank's response.

Single parenthood was not easy for someone as busy as Frank Costelloe. Reliable servants were essential – yet the Pearsall Smiths soon started complaining that his first choice of nursemaid, who had been with the girls since their mother's departure, was mistreating Ray (their favourite). She was eventually replaced, but running battles over the girls' upbringing continued between their father and maternal grandmother (and with their widowed paternal grandmother, a frequent and demanding presence in Costelloe family life). The allegiance of the current nursemaid or governess in these battles was a prize trophy. Mutual suspicion was rife, and at the back of everyone's minds was the knowledge that if Mary once took the children to Italy it would be difficult if not impossible to force her to return them.

Gradually the children settled into a pattern of life in which they spent holidays and many weekends at a rented cottage in Fernhurst (Sussex), and attended kindergarten, then school, while in London. The children saw their grandparents almost every day, and Hannah played an active role in their lives. She started the custom of reading to them every evening – progressing from fairy stories to tales of adventure – took them on outings, bought their clothes and, when relations with Frank allowed, acted as his advisor and assistant in major matters such as choosing a new governess.

As the children grew older, Hannah organised activities for them in London to give them the outdoor life she thought healthy for children: she regularly took them rowing in Battersea Park, despite her increasing immobility from rheumatism, and in the cold winter of 1897 endured chilblains so that the girls could learn to skate in

(Figure 3) The Pearsall Smiths in 1894: a disunited family?
(l. to r. Alys, Logan, Robert, Hannah, Karin, Mary, Ray)

Regent's Park. For the children, their grandparents' house was a place of total indulgence. Hannah encouraged them in the belief that she would meet all their wishes, buy them anything they wanted, feed them every kind of dietary treat, and clear up after their games. 'I delight in there being absolutely no ceremony between us, and no manners either', Hannah admitted in 1897, and at nine years old, Ray was quite clear on the distinction between the two houses in Grosvenor Road: 'We have plenty of morals at home, and we come in here for sprees!'[22]

Mary's absence from the daily routine of family life endowed her with glamour in Ray's eyes. She wrote to her daughters daily and entertainingly, and swept into their lives once or twice a year to become the ring-leader in many of the wilder activities at Fernhurst, more like an elder sister than a mother. As a five- and six-year-old, Ray seems to have gone through a stage of idealising her, confiding to Hannah that 'Mother is the most beautiful person in all the world'.[23]

Frank's country cottage was close enough to Friday's Hill House, the Pearsall Smiths' leased property, for there to be frequent contact between the two households, and, particularly for the month or so when Ray and Karin were in the charge of their mother, the girls spent much of their time playing in the extensive grounds and woods of the 'big house'. Ray's lifelong love of swimming started at Friday's Hill when Mary paid to have a stream through the woods dammed and a brick-lined pool made. When Ray was ten, a carpenter built for them, at the edge of the woods, a hut made out of boards, which was immediately dubbed the 'Fort'. The children then put hours of work into camouflaging it and digging a deep 'moat' around it crossed by a plank drawbridge, the withdrawal of which could keep out invaders. Ray was the leader in this work – other children sometimes complaining that she was a slave-driver.

From 1897 the sisters' main playfellows were their American second cousins. Grace Worthington (Mary's cousin) had attempted to enforce celibacy on her husband and consequently been divorced for desertion. Short of money, Grace brought her two sons and a daughter to England and settled near the Pearsall Smith enclave on Grosvenor Road. From then on, the five children were constantly together, particularly during regular Thursday evening gatherings in Hannah's house where the fun only stopped for a sumptuous tea, with a typical menu consisting of 'asparagus, macaroni with cheese, shrimps, macaroons with cream, Swiss roll, grapes, apples, pears, bananas, chestnuts, sweets and *marrons glacés*'.[24] Karin paired up with the middle Worthington child, Mary – always known as Pug – and they became inseparable, isolating Ray from her sister.

Frank was often away on legal work and over-stretched when at home but nevertheless he was an active parent and clearly close to his children. Hannah recounted to Mary that one day at Friday's Hill they met Frank walking back from the station and took him in their carriage to a nearby common where 'Ray had a lovely time guiding her father and Karin all through the heather. I must confess that Frank *does* play with them very nicely. They had great adventures, and Ray was supremely happy'.[25] When his work schedule allowed,

Frank took the children to the seaside in England while they were young and on holidays in Europe as they grew older, admitting to his absent wife how important his daughters had become to him and how much he missed them when they were apart.[26] His attempts to instil some form of self-discipline in the girls – politeness and care for their belongings, for example – were often undermined by Hannah's indulgence and her indignation when her granddaughters were not allowed to do exactly as they wanted.

In accordance with Frank's Radical sympathies, and to broaden his daughters' social experience, in 1895 he sent them to a Board school across the river in Lambeth (probably St Mary's Infants' School on Lambeth Road), to the horror of the Pearsall Smith family and their nursemaid, who deplored the 'ragged clothes, […] awful accent and […] rough bad manners' of the other pupils.[27] Hannah objected, too, to the school's academic demands: 'Ray's lessons continue to be outrageous[…] I assure thee I do all I can to make her slur them over and chance it. Her brain would be hopelessly strained if she had really to learn them.'[28] The outbreak of head-lice which Ray suffered in March 1896 was the final straw for Hannah, who successfully redoubled her efforts to get the girls moved to another school.

(Figure 4) 'Devout little Catholics, they seem to enjoy their religion': First Communion, Christmas Eve 1898.

In September 1896 Ray and Karin became pupils at a prestigious Catholic Convent School in Chepstow Villas, Bayswater, run by the Sisters of Sion, where the educational emphasis was as much religious as academic. As children, Ray and Karin seem to have relished Catholic traditions and rituals. Hannah described her grand-daughters as 'devout little Catholics, [who] seem to enjoy their religion' and despite her very different religious outlook she came, through their experiences and attitudes, to see good points in Catholicism.[29] Outside school Mary pressed for dancing lessons (which

Ray hated); Frank took them to museums and concerts and often spent what free evenings he had setting the girls mental problems (to the horror of Hannah, who fervently believed that time out of school should be devoted to play).

Frank's health was suffering, for which he blamed the strain Mary had put him through. Insomnia, severe influenza and an 'incurable eczema-like affliction' all struck him in 1894–5.[30] Nevertheless he was re-elected to the LCC that March, this time for Bethnal Green. Mary, too, had constant health problems; a minor gynaecological operation in 1896 was briefly misinterpreted as an abortion by Frank, and for some weeks Mary faced the prospect of losing all contact with her daughters. Her reaction (to Berenson) was characteristically self-absorbed and free from any consideration of what was best for her children:

> I had a truly torturing night, unable to sleep, going over in anticipation all the pains of tearing Ray and Karin from my heart. I am really prepared for the worst; and have thought a great deal, too, that maybe it would be like a surgical operation and restore real health. We should be married and live where we chose.[31]

By then Mary's first flush of enthusiasm for Bernhard Berenson had cooled, and she had embarked on a pattern of (mainly short-term) entanglements with young men, running in parallel to her relationship with Berenson.

Frank's mother died in September 1897, followed by Robert Pearsall Smith (increasingly alienated from Hannah and hence from his children) in April 1898, while Ray was in quarantine at 40 Grosvenor Road for a mild case of scarlet fever. Neither grandparent seems to have been much mourned. In that generation Hannah was always the dominating figure, and her contempt for the husband who had sought greater comfort with other women than his wife was prepared to offer – combined with her deep-seated belief that death was always to be welcomed as the gateway to glorious eternal life – produced a callous-seeming response to Robert's death which shocked even her children (and horrified her daughter Alys's husband, Bertrand Russell).

In contrast, illness in her granddaughters brought out all Hannah's fierceness and concern. She clashed with the family's doctor over his insistence that Ray be isolated during her bout of scarlet fever. Hannah bewailed his edict that Ray should be 'shut up for three weeks with a strange nurse, and nobody who loved her near' and condemned his unsympathetic response as 'the most cruel speech I ever heard' which 'showed he was not fit to have the care of a child'. Ray, however, saw no hardship in isolation and appears to have much enjoyed the chance to read in peace. Always a voracious reader, during her weeks away from school she worked her way through many of the novels of L.T. Meade and Mrs Juliana Ewing. Hannah's solicitude for an ill granddaughter, and the selection of treats she brought to entertain or feed the patient, made any illness, as Ray later recalled, 'a time of delight'.[33]

The girls' nursemaid, Hannah's ally in disputes about the children's upbringing, was in 1898 replaced by a young governess from Munich, Therese Fürholzer, a devout Catholic fresh from a convent. 'Fraülein' (or 'Terry' as she became known to her charges) was insecure, and sensitive to criticism. Fortunately Hannah's initial fault-finding and countermanding of the instructions Frank gave her gradually subsided, and over time Terry became a vital member of the household.

Ray's father was as busy as ever. As well as his legal practice, LCC commitments, journalism and Catholic activism, he had in 1897 taken on further voluntary activities as a founder member of the Committee of the State Children's Association, and as a newly-elected member of the London School Board. Because the teaching of religion in schools was contentious, and Costelloe's Roman Catholicism made him deeply suspect to Progressive Party members, he had been forced to stand – in the teeth of fierce public criticism from his own party – as an Independent Roman Catholic Progressive. This latest role was time-consuming and onerous but he approached it with characteristic energy, at once joining a campaign – opposed by his own party – to provide school meals for starving children.

Permanently overworked, Frank Costelloe relied on short breaks from his demanding workload to recover his strength. But the trip he took to Rome with Ray and Karin at Easter 1899 left him even more exhausted. Instead of relaxing, he was hard at work on articles for the *Daily Chronicle*. On returning home he started to suffer from pain in his right ear, so acute that he could only sleep sitting up. This marked the beginning of a constant battle with illness, both physical and mental, exacerbated by an unexpected by-election in East St Pancras, the constituency where he had been defeated in 1895 but for which he remained the Liberal candidate.

The intense ten day campaign before the election on 12 July, during which Costelloe made nearly a hundred speeches, would have drained the energies even of a man in good health. Liberal successes elsewhere had raised hopes that this would be Costelloe's moment, and his supporters were confident of victory. The result was a crushing disappointment: Frank significantly reduced the Conservative majority but still lost. In his final speech Costelloe blamed the vested interest of the licensed victuallers who were fiercely opposed to Liberal Party pro-temperance policies (but others considered that his Catholicism was a more important factor). One newspaper report described the defeated candidate walking sadly away from the Vestry Hall where the count took place 'accompanied by his daughter'.[34] It was probably Ray, who had already seen her father in action at the LCC, who witnessed his Parliamentary hopes turn to despair and public humiliation.

Private life was no better. Mary's negligence led to a riding accident at Friday's Hill in which Karin suffered concussion, lost consciousness and went into convulsions. Frank was furious when told, and complained of always being made to appear a killjoy when opposing Mary's recklessnesss. Mary's account (to Berenson) was revealing: 'I couldn't help feeling thankful beyond words that it wasn't Ray. There is an unspeakable difference in my feelings to them. [....] Karin is awfully sweet, and I hate to see her suffer. But Ray – it is another world.'[35]

In early August, despite his ever more painful ear problems, Frank took the children away for a short holiday abroad. By the time they returned to England, disappointment and constant pain had reduced Costelloe, normally a self-confessed 'incurable optimist', to despair, with deep depression and worsening physical symptoms.[36] The letters of Grace Worthington to Hannah (at a cure in Aix-les-Bains with Mary) chart Frank's gradual decline throughout September: 'B.F.C.C. is quite meek & so weak that I score off him in our religious conversations. […] B.F.C.C. is still in agony' and, passed on by Hannah: 'Grace […] says Frank is very bad, and Fraülein has to syringe his ear every hour, and can hardly leave the house. She says he looks awfully ill. […] She says Frank is so weak that he can hardly do anything.'[37] Therese Fürholzer's role now went far beyond the normal remit of a governess.

In late September Costelloe underwent a series of operations on his ear. Hannah, assuming that the problem was an abscess, explained to Alys that Frank had had the bone in his ear scraped, a serious operation during which he was under chloroform for thirty minutes but apparently successful in relieving his pain. The children could only see him for a few minutes at a time as he had to stay perfectly quiet in bed for two weeks. The swelling recurred so more operations followed. When his children went to visit, 'they found him very weak so that he could scarcely speak to them. […] Fraülein thought he seemed very ill, but he himself said all was going on right'.[39]

Frank returned home, but his doctors had privately told him that they had found cancer in the ear and the temporal bone behind it and warned that this would ultimately prove terminal. With no indication of how long he had to live, Costelloe persuaded himself that it might be some years during which he might still perform useful work. He set himself the task of recovering so as to make the most of whatever life remained to him.

While the rest of the family pursued their normal activities, Frank found the inactivity of convalescence trying, 'the hardest work he ha[d] ever had in his life', and the company of his daughters was vital to his attempted recovery.[40] They played Halma with him, made wax seals together, and told him stories. For a while his energy and cheerfulness seemed to return and, to the astonishment of his doctors, he managed to attend a meeting of the Council. But the improvement was only temporary. On 22 October Hannah reported to Mary that Frank's difficulties in opening his mouth preceded his operation and if permanent would destroy his career 'for he can hardly talk, and could not make a public speech to save his life. He can only manage to eat by cutting everything up very small, and putting it into his mouth in tiny quantities.'[41] Two days later, after Frank had been to the School Board, 'Fraülein says he carried a point against considerable opposition, tho' how he managed to talk I cannot imagine, for he can only open his mouth a quarter of an inch. Fraülein says not one man in 100 would be willing to be seen looking as he does, but she supposes he has no vanity!'[42] Frank's depression returned, hardly surprisingly as 'his face is so dreadfully swollen and his mouth all twisted.'[43]

Frank's sense of duty did not allow him to abandon the cause he had championed. The report of a sub-committee Frank had chaired on underfed pupils, which concluded that compulsory education placed responsibilities for the care of children on official bodies as well as parents, and that even if it were 'better for the moral character of the parents to let the children starve', the sub-committee would not advise it, was to be discussed by the School Board on 16 November 1899.[44] The subcommittee sought an extended role, further investigations and the supervision of remedial action. The main attack came from a fellow Progressive, who

> saw in all this the demoralising of the people, and he at any rate, at whatever cost, would stem this alarming tide. He thought most people ate too much […] and a little lack of food was not so bad as the emasculation of the moral fibre. […] He was strongly opposed to this scheme, which was mischievous and dangerous in every way.[45]

Costelloe's attendance at the meeting, obviously gravely ill and struggling to speak, drew cheers of sympathy, but he made no concessions to his own suffering nor to the sensibilities of his opponents. Costelloe ridiculed the logic of his opponent's position and pressed for immediate action to prevent unnecessary suffering during the winter. 'He did not see how it was good for the moral fibre of parents to see their children starve'; moreover:

> it was humanly cruel and financially uneconomical to attempt to teach hungry children. The teachers of the poorer schools knew and felt this and nobly ministered themselves to the wants of their poor little charges. [...] He had done his duty. He had come from a sick room to plead the cause of the hungry, and the Board might throw out the Committee's scheme. But he had the profound consciousness of the rectitude and wisdom of the course he had taken.[46]

After further discussion, the Report was referred back to the General Purposes Committee.

This was Costelloe's final public effort. While the country's attention was focused on the war in South Africa, Frank retreated to the family circle in 40 Grosvenor Road. Friends later commented on his calm and uncomplaining acceptance of his fate during his last weeks in the winter gloom. His children's reaction to seeing the suffering of the parent who had been the main factor in their lives for the past eight years is not recorded.

By mid-December it was clear that Frank was dying. A telegram summoned his wife back from Italy. By the time she arrived he was only semi-conscious, with brief intervals of lucidity, apparently not in pain but 'a terrible wreck', according to Mary.[47] He managed to recognise Cardinal Vaughan, a visitor on 13 December, and the following day, during a brief return to full consciousness, saw his children and was reconciled to Mary, kissing her hand. Doctors carried out a further exploratory operation on 16 December, but it was a forlorn hope and confirmed that nothing more could be done. After taking his last nourishment on 19 December, Frank started to sink rapidly, and stopped breathing at 5 a.m. on Friday 22 December 1899. Within an hour Mary had taken their daughters to Hannah's house, from where only a court order could remove them.

Confined to bed in her new home at 44 Grosvenor Road by a bad cough, Ray did not attend her father's funeral service, a Requiem Mass held on 28 December in St Mary's Catholic Church, Horseferry Road, just round the corner from Grosvenor Road, with many of London's great and good among the mourners. Frank died, aged forty-five, with many of his ambitions unfulfilled. He had persistently failed to be elected to Parliament; his legal career had not fulfilled its early brilliant promise; and even within the LCC, where he had made the greatest impact, his early dominance had stalled. His financial position remained insecure, dependent largely on income from journalism, and the capital he had to leave was modest. He had been a loving father, and had provided his daughters with an outstanding example of selfless commitment to the public good, devotion to his Church, and courage in the face of acute physical and mental suffering, but in the aftermath of Frank's death, the Pearsall Smith family viciously condemned him because of the provisions of his will.

The will made by Frank Costelloe as he faced death was a well-intentioned if impracticable attempt to preserve the status quo as closely as could be achieved with the limited funds likely to be available after his death. It committed his daughters, aged twelve and ten, to the care of five guardians to ensure that they were raised in his Roman Catholic religion and protected from the spiritually damaging influence of Mary and the lover for whom she had abandoned them. Without their father's earnings it would be impossible for the girls to remain in 40 Grosvenor Road. The children, under the care of their governess Therese Fürholzer 'whose influence [...] in the formation of their moral & religious character has been most admirable', were to maintain a separate, but less expensive, establishment and were 'not to live with any of their relatives or connections', but reasonable access was to be granted to Mary and her family, 'similar in amount and conditions to that which I have allowed'.[48] In explanation Frank added:

> I give all these directions in no hostile spirit towards my wife who knows well that I have always treated her with more than justice &

consideration but for the protection of my children for whom I am
responsible before God & man against the influences to which they
wd infallibly be exposed if they lived with her.

Costelloe's assets were to be held in trust for his daughters, who
should continue at their present school and, before the age of twenty-
one, each 'be trained in some occupation by which in case of need she
could earn her livelihood'. Frank was certainly not alone as a father
in envisaging his daughters as working women; many fathers now
preferred to see their daughters trained to earn their own living rather
than struggle to survive on a barely adequate annuity.

Hannah and Mary, supported by Alys and Bertrand Russell,
had already had the girls made Wards of Court. Now they refused
to surrender them and challenged the will. Weeks of rows and tears,
legal negotiations and desperate contingency planning followed.
The leading guardian – the sisters' doctor – furiously threatened to
separate the girls entirely from their mother. The will proved legally
flawed, despite the testator's legal credentials as a barrister. The fierce
battle subsided into compromise: the guardians lost most of their
power, Hannah gained custody of the girls on condition she raised
them as Catholics and made financial provision for their future, and
Mary reluctantly accepted continued separation from her daughters
for much of the year. The permission of the Chancery Court had to be
sought each time the girls visited her in Florence.

This arrangement brought peace of a kind but no forgiveness
from the Pearsall Smiths towards Frank Costelloe, who remained
unmourned and reviled by his widow and her family, particularly
Hannah. Internationally renowned for her piety, she had during her
years as an Evangelical preacher (a temporary deviation from the
Quaker faith in which she was born and died), promised the readers
of her most famous work, *The Christian's Secret of a Happy Life*, that
'sweetness, gentleness, meekness, patience, long-suffering, charity,
kindness will all be natural to the Christian'.[49] She felt none of these
sentiments towards her recently deceased son-in-law. He had been,
she declared, 'an unnatural father [...] little short of a fiend' and an

'awful incubus of a man'; five months after his death she dreamed 'that Frank came back, and it was unspeakably awful. But he must be full of worms by now, thank goodness!'[50]

The provisions of the will may have been impracticable – Therese Fürholzer was almost certainly not mature enough to take on such responsibilities – but the fury of Hannah's response had far more to do with her fixed belief that children belonged wholly to their mothers than to any rational assessment. For the girls, the venomous conflict meant painfully divided loyalties and the forced suppression of whatever love they felt for the father who had raised them. In these circumstances their grief could hardly be expressed, except to each other. Given the girls' very different temperaments – Ray quiet and self-contained, Karin emotional and outgoing – even this may have been difficult

If Ray's childhood can be seen as a struggle for influence between her father and grandmother, Hannah appeared to have won. There is no doubt that Ray loved her deeply, followed much of her advice and derived considerable self-confidence from her unswerving support. In adulthood she published a book commemorating her 'Quaker Grandmother' while maintaining in her letters and diaries an almost complete silence about her late father. Nevertheless Ray's diaries make it clear that her most intense feelings were rarely committed to paper (except in the guise of fiction). It took that skilled interrogator, Virginia Stephen, to extract from Ray many years later the admission that her mother had treated her father 'very badly, as he really had great merits'.[51] The Pearsall Smith attempt to blacken Frank's name and write him out of his children's history had not convinced his elder daughter.

CHAPTER TWO

The New Girl: 1900 –1905

Perhaps shy but never humble.
Even your worst enemies never accuse you of that.[1]

As rebellions go, it hardly counted. The dispute over whether the letter or only the spirit of school law had been breached during the October 1903 election of the hockey captain at Kensington High School was not enough to persuade the teaching staff to risk their careers in support of two schoolgirls seeking the dismissal of their headmistress for backing a cheat. All the anger, indignation, mental torment, moral fervour and self-righteousness (occasionally qualified by a sense of her own unworthiness) which young Ray Costelloe poured out in her diary led only to humiliation and a forced apology to a fellow pupil she despised and to a headmistress who favoured 'outside manners & not inside uprightness'.[2] It was a painful lesson for Ray, struggling to assert her own values. She learned that, in any cause, seeing oneself as a heroine charging into battle was useless: what was needed was self-control.

Ray and Karin had been pupils at Kensington High School since 1900. The Pearsall Smith family regarded a good education as essential preparation for adult life, and the girls' mother (soon to become Mrs Berenson) and grandmother had taken early action to remove them from their previous, Catholic, school. Kensington High School, which occupied a large grey-brick building in St Alban's Grove, not far south of Kensington High Street, had (in its previous incarnation as Chelsea High School) been in 1873 the first of the schools set up by the Girls' Public Day School Company. By 1900 there were over thirty such establishments, products of the late Victorian movement to provide better schooling for middle-class girls, who were considered to be most in need, given that elementary schools now catered for the poorest children while wealthy families could afford to pay for private tuition.

Although its prospectus boasted that 'The High Schools of the Company are designed to supply education of the highest class, and to occupy for Girls the position taken in the education of Boys by the Great Public Schools', Kensington High School, like its sister-schools, differed in two major respects from the its male counterparts.[3] Firstly, it was a day school, with compulsory attendance between 9.15 a.m. and 1.15 p.m. from Monday to Friday, and optional activities during the afternoons; and secondly, academic ability was valued before social background – fees were kept as low as commercially possible to allow a wide social mix. The curriculum was wide and intellectually rigorous: girls were expected to have brains and use them. Many of the staff were themselves graduates and hence the progression of pupils to the new women's colleges at Oxford and Cambridge was encouraged.

The rapid spread of day schools for middle-class daughters led to a major change in the behaviour and ambitions considered suitable for girls. Whereas young girls had usually been allowed to romp with their brothers, a young lady had been forbidden such activities. Even as young children, Ray and Karin had been banned by Grandmother Costelloe from climbing trees and riding astride their hobbyhorse, as such behaviour was not ladylike. Now girls' schools (and women's colleges) started to adopt the boys' school ethos that participating in sport and using one's brain were an essential part of the formation of character.

(Figure 5) Sixth formers at Kensington High School c. 1900.

The decades immediately before and after the turn of the century were the age of the tomboy, when it was acceptable for a girl to have similar ambitions to a boy, to long for adventure and the chance to be a hero rather than a heroine.[4] Family responsibilities still mattered, but so too did the possibility of independence which a thorough education and increasing career opportunities for women could provide. Whereas the New Woman of the preceding generation was often torn between public and private roles, the New Girl saw no such conflict and assumed she could have both. While the New Woman often seemed obsessed with her own sexuality, the New Girl largely ignored it: marriage was simply one option among many (though intense relationships between girls were not uncommon, in literature and in life).

The New Woman literature of the 1890s had its parallel in the 'high school' novels written for the younger generation, particularly those by L.T. Meade.[5] Meade's school stories, many set in a high school context, promoted the values of courage (both physical and moral), loyalty to other girls, warm-heartedness and self-reliance. Obedience and tidiness, so much valued in earlier generations, were barely seen as virtues at all (though family responsibilities still had to be honoured). Slyness, vindictiveness, sneaking and cheating were abhorred and 'feminine' weaknesses, such as tears, despised.

By the end of the Edwardian era, this once revolutionary change in attitudes had been accepted as the norm. It was 'no longer enough – or appropriate – for girls to be docile, obedient, self-sacrificing, and kind'.[6] According to a 1913 advice manual, an appropriate ambition was 'to be an all-round girl, good at games and good at lessons, able to cook a dinner or make a speech if at any moment you should be called upon to do so'.[7] Moreover, 'the old silly idea of masculine superiority would hardly be tolerated by the modern schoolgirl'.[8] The peak of this New Girl culture coincided exactly with Ray Costelloe's schooldays in the opening years of the twentieth century and significantly influenced the approach to life of Ray and her contemporaries.

In principle, Hannah Whitall Smith was all in favour of a good education for girls. But her insistence that what children needed was fun, outdoor exercise and plenty of sleep made her blind to the idea that education demanded hard work. 'They are all studying too much, and it worries me' was a typical (unrealistic) comment.[9] Ray always enjoyed composition but was not otherwise given to over-work; despite numerous good resolutions to put in more effort, her usual practice was to do just enough to get by. Hannah was quite capable of launching a tirade against any school which she thought was overworking her precious granddaughters. Later Ray explained how alarming Hannah's attitude had been:

> I can remember most vividly the anxieties I used to suffer when I was at school, lest she should take steps, in her extreme partisan spirit, to upbraid the mistresses who thwarted our desires or failed to appreciate our talents; and I was not at peace until I had made her promise to take no action with regard to school affairs, without first consulting me.[10]

Hannah encouraged Ray and Karin to exploit opportunities in school for exercise and non-academic activities. Ray later recalled that, to start with, she had been unenthusiastic: 'I can remember the shyness that prevented me from wanting to join the various clubs at school, for games and debating, or the other affairs of school life: and I believe she came nearer to coercion over my resistance to this than at any other time.'[11] Hannah prevailed and, over time, the household became dominated by sporting commitments. In school Ray played hockey, cricket, basketball, tennis and swam for the school. Outside school Hannah organised as much physical activity as she could cram into the girls' lives, testing Ray's enjoyment of sport to the limit:

> She is awfully stirred up about exercise – thinks we don't get nearly enough [...]. She wants us to ride & swim & skate & goodness knows what [...]. Add to this the fact that she wants us to bicycle & ride to school on the bus & walk – actually go for walks! - & you see that she maps out for us a life which excludes work entirely.[12]

Although tall and slender at fourteen, Ray had inherited Mary's tendency to put on weight – her family nicknames were 'Fatty' and 'Monster'– and she gradually filled out. While Ray revelled in the competitive aspects of team sports like hockey, her physique was not always an asset. In the water she was completely at ease, but on land it was probably Ray's enthusiasm and organisational ability rather than outstanding sporting talent which propelled her to leadership in school games.

Ray's later reputation for equable cheerfulness was hard won. In 1896 Hannah compared the two sisters: 'It is curious to see how differently Ray & Karin take disappointments. Ray despairs at once and can see no brightness anywhere, while Karin is full of hope, and consoles herself with something else.'[13] A few years later she commented that 'if Ray [...] can learn to play games now without losing her temper, she will know how later to play the game of life ditto '.[14] Ray's temper continued to be a trial to her and everyone else for some time.

(Figure 6) A hockey team at Kensington High School. Ray is second from left on the middle row, Karin at the right of the front row.

During her mid-teens, Ray felt isolated. The security and self-belief which Hannah's constant praise instilled in her readily mutated into arrogance and a tendency to condemn other people. Even though Ray used her diary as a safety valve to express feelings she repressed in public, and her self-belief was leavened by an ability to laugh at herself, frustration and contempt for others were a regular theme: '[Terry] is an ass. So is Karin – so are most people'; 'I have to come to the conclusion I am the only sensible person in the house'; 'Why does Gram irritate me so?'; 'a more detestable false and abominable woman than Mrs Rollings cannot exist'; and 'Just imagine sending a nasty vulgar society affected self conceited idiot like that to represent Kensington!! Unfortunately I am afraid she is rather typical of Kensington girls at present.'[15] She had at this time few close friends, and although adored and admired by younger girls, was frequently considered bossy and opinionated by her peers ('school is full of different people, none of whom agree with me, & I have a great desire to make them all see things the way I do, & do things the way I want, & know I can't possibly succeed').[16]

The diary which Ray started in April 1902 defiantly proclaimed 'This is to be the diary of Ray Costelloe, which is to be strictly private', but privacy was something Ray could never rely on.[17] Making a virtue of necessity, she used her diary as a means of communicating with Mary: 'I am writing this journal for mother to read when she comes home, so that she can see exactly what goes on in my head without my having to try & express it all at once.'[18] Ray and Karin both suffered from the favouritism Hannah and Mary forced on Ray. When Karin showed signs of scarlet fever, Hannah's apparently uncaring reaction in not sending for the doctor lest Ray should be forced to miss games at school produced an outpouring of resentment from Ray:

> I wish she would not pet me so much. I can't do anything without it being published & admired & talked about till I am more than heartily sick of it. When I feel sick the house is turned upside down for my comfort – & it is not comfortable. If anything goes wrong Gram worries far more than I do. She seems to think I am a perfect being but I am afraid she is much mistaken. This morning at breakfast, for instance, she told me to move the flowers off the table so that she could watch me eating my breakfast!! And I was just rejoicing in eating no porridge without her making an outcry![19]

The unequal treatment benefited neither girl: 'She doesn't seem to care half as much about Karin – I wonder if Karin minds. She certainly would not if she knew how horrid it is not to have any privacy.'[20]

The family habit of broadcasting personal information to the world was an added burden:

> I wanted to read some poetry today, but I did not dare, because Gram would have written enthusiastic letters to Mother about how I was growing up & Mother would have answered that she was glad I was growing a taste for the beautiful at last, & Karin would have

heard all about it, & published it to the cousins, & they would all have said that "Fatty" has certainly grown up. So I read no poetry, & will not until I get some time to myself.[21]

Protest was useless ('if I told Gram I would like to be alone she would have made a great fuss about that, with much the same results'), especially as her grandmother was essentially well-meaning ('I guess I am an ass to make so much fuss over the fact that I am loved, & I have great doubts as to whether I shall let Mother see all my foolishness).[22] Mary did read the 'foolishness' and added an encouraging comment in the diary, but the problems remained unresolved. Unsurprisingly, Ray developed a love for isolation and silence as a defence against intrusive probing, for which her family dubbed her 'the Oyster'.

In early 1903, as she approached her sixteenth birthday Ray felt trapped in the uncomfortable no-man's-land of adolescence, neither child nor adult. She had no desire to lose the freedoms of childhood, but had lost interest in what appealed to the younger children in the family and could not stifle her own increasingly adult responses to the world around her. The inevitable comments of her family that she was 'growing up' provoked fury: Ray felt that she was seen as conforming to a pattern rather than reacting as an individual ('why can't I be allowed to grow up my own way?').[23] Fiercely aware of her own abilities, with strong moral views, often contemptuous of her schoolfellows and struggling with her own anger, Ray felt powerless at home and at school:

> I am horribly bored. I don't mean all the time, for I am never bored when I'm alone, but somehow everything seems so dull & uninterresting [sic]. You just get up, & go to school, & say your lessons in a dull kind of way, & if you begin to be interested you get snubbed – at least I do, & everyone says the same obvious dull things, & the mistresses dilate on the dull parts of the work, & skip over the others, & then you come home, & Terry bores you, & Karin bores you, & Gram bores you (I mean me) & then you go to bed & have dull dreams.[24]

She sought the clarity of absolutes: 'the only thing that is fun is the thing which has only one way of looking at it – either it is right or not – either you see it or not, & no nasty dullness about it'.[25]

Ray seems to have been in search of a cause, and a person to inspire her. Ironically, it was a future leader of the Anti-Suffrage Movement who showed her a way forward. The speech that Lady Jersey made at the Kensington High School prize-giving on 3 July 1903 may well have contained no more than the moral exhortations to do one's best which are common to such occasions. But for Ray it came at the right moment. Lady Jersey's emphasis on not giving up hope even when progress seemed impossible made a particular impression on her. At the end of her V Form year Ray recorded her increased understanding of how an organisation like a school works and should be run:

> It is the question of doing things as they should be done, & talking to people in the way which is most likely to make them see daylight – it is a question of tact & good humour & patience & cheerfulness & hope [...]. It is a question of expecting the good from people & getting it – of doing the right things in the right way, & helping the school along – Helping the mistresses & the girls, & most of all, I suppose yourself.[26]

She made good resolutions about fighting with her own temper to achieve the best for the school:

> The great thing is to cool down, & to try to understand other people – only they are so stupid! It makes me wild – & then of course I spoil everything. [...] I feel just now as if I should like to run it all myself – only of course I shall be only lower VI & a new prefect & if I'm not hockey captain there won't be much of all this fine authority etc that I am considering.[27]

The low moral standards of her classmates, among whom minor cheating ('a lack of uprightness in small things') was rife, had caused Ray a great deal of disquiet; her previous attempts to deal with it had met with very limited success but Lady Jersey's speech about 'hope – not being discouraged by failure, & not minding if no results appear at first – or ever – but just sticking on & on & on' was inspirational.[28]

A more significant problem was the Headmistress, Miss Ethel Home, 'a woman of intense determination and demanding energy', who had studied mathematics at Newnham College, Cambridge, and joined Kensington High School at the same time as Ray.[29] Miss Home praised Ray's mathematical skills to Mary ('the cleverest pupil at Maths she had ever had, & the idol of the lower school!!!!!') but Ray had a low opinion of her Headmistress, who, she believed, was destroying the school's moral ethos in favour of that very emphasis on producing refined young ladies which the High Schools were designed to replace.[30] Getting round her needed 'lots of tact & perseverance', a resolution which fell by the wayside during the battle over the election of the hockey captain.[31] Despite the attempt by the Head Prefect and Ray to unseat her, Miss Home remained at the school until her retirement in 1931, one of the few women in her profession to favour the Anti-Suffragist cause. Nevertheless, the short-lived campaign of defiance brought Ray one gain. The defeated candidate, Ellie Rendel, became her lifelong friend.

Frances Elinor ('Ellie') Rendel was the daughter of James Meadows Rendel, a barrister, and his wife Elinor, the oldest of the ten surviving children of General Sir Richard and Lady Strachey. Elinor was highly intelligent, like the rest of the Strachey family, but the only one of the five sisters to make a conventional marriage; the next, Dorothy, married a French artist, Simon Bussy, and became a translator and novelist herself, while the three youngest sisters – Philippa (known as Pippa), Pernel and Marjorie – remained unmarried, devoting themselves to their careers.

By the time Ray met the Rendel family, Ellie's grandfather Sir Richard Strachey, a man of considerable achievement in developing the infrastructure of India and in the scientific world, was in his late eighties, but her much younger grandmother, Lady Strachey (née Jane Maria Grant), remained a formidable figure and a powerful influence on the lives of her descendants. Ellie was the second of the Rendel

daughters and had three younger brothers. Two years older than
Ray, intelligent and sharp-tongued, she was a regular prize-winner at
Kensington High School. She and Ray soon formed a fast friendship
and by November Ray admitted to her diary 'I am getting awfully
fond of Ellie – I think she is the nicest girl – after Winnie [Buckley] –
who has ever been at Kensington.'[32]

Ellie became Head Prefect of Kensington High in January 1904.
As well as working together on school matters, the girls became
almost inseparable out of school and Ray frequently went for tea at
the Rendel house in Melbury Road, Kensington. Having a close friend
at school made the next two terms far more bearable. Ray's frequent
resolutions to put more effort into her academic work bore no greater
fruit than they had done in the past, but she flung herself into every
sport available and was soon running most of them. Ellie was due to
leave school for Newnham College, Cambridge, and Ray was chosen
to replace her as Head Prefect. The prospect of two more terms at
school had little appeal: 'There is no office I do not hold, no position
I can want, no one I care about & a beastly dismal prospect. It seems
funny that one small person should make such a difference, but so it
is.'[33]

Ray's organising ability and practical good sense had been obvious
since childhood: aged five, she had stopped a pony and cart from
going up a narrow hill with no room to turn round. As Head Prefect
she, like her grandmother and aunt before her, was serving on – and
chairing – committees, and gaining experience which would prove
invaluable in her later public life. The side of school life she found
less appealing was the prevalence of schoolgirl infatuations, so-called
'cracks'. Although Karin and her friends, strongly encouraged by
Hannah, happily indulged, Ray described the whole idea of 'cracks'
as 'silly unhealthy sentimentalism' and was embarrassed at becoming
the object of some thirty cracks herself.[34]

Hannah was becoming increasingly immobile, so in October 1904 the
household moved to a flat in Morpeth Mansions, next to Westminster
Cathedral. Ray did not regret the move and felt no sentimental

attachment to 44 Grosvenor Road, but the decision to give up Friday's Hill House, the scene of so much childhood enjoyment, left her ready to 'weep tears of sorrow'.[35] Two years later the family left London for Oxford, where they shared Court Place, Iffley, on the banks of the Thames, with Ray's Uncle Logan.

At the start of 1905, with only a term to go before she left school, both Ray and her mother were looking ahead, Ray to university and Mary to Ray's adult life. Ray seriously considered classics as a university subject before settling on maths, to Mary's disappointment. Although Ray's intelligence was essentially practical rather than theoretical – Karin was the abstract thinker – she preferred subjects with clear right or wrong answers, and 'the immensity' of maths gave her 'a queer feeling of insignificance' and awe at

> the great solid & infinite truth standing calmly still to be realized. It is not affected by my moods or powers, but continues sublimely on, self sufficient. I wonder no one has made a god of mathematics. Every day I am more happy in my choice, even though not a very brilliant success personally. It doesn't seem to matter so much, when it is an infinite & abstract god you are serving, whether you personally are good or bad, clever or stupid.[36]

Mary had agreed that she could apply to Newnham College, Cambridge, for entry that October if she passed the entrance examinations. Newnham had an excellent reputation for nurturing mathematicians.[37]

Working for the Cambridge entrance examination included weekly visits to Uncle Bertrand Russell, a 'terrifying, but elucidating' experience'.[38] The examination took place in Cambridge on 15 March, with an agonizing wait until 21 March when the news came that Ray had passed. Ray's last day at school, for which she had longed, was 13 April. Instead of joyful release, the day provoked misery ('I nearly became sentimental and wept'), acute embarrassment at the flattering send-off she was given ('I really hardly think I can blush again'), and the realisation of how different life after school would be:

It is not possible that I shall ever again have a position in any degree the same as the one I imagined I held at school – it is not possible that I can anywhere be as completely spoilt & flattered & made much of – & I have become so used to it, I have been so pleased by it that it almost seems to break my heart to go![39]

That new life began all too soon. Within days, Ray set off for an extended visit to Florence, to confront the sentimental and cultural education her mother planned for her.

CHAPTER THREE

'Hurrah for Ray!':
1905–1906

And I will work hard all day, and she must just play around,
and spend my money and be always charming.[1]

The Berensons' way of life in Florence had little in common with the world Ray had left in London. Its values were cultural and social: religion, philanthropy, academic success and sport counted for nothing. From being in a position of authority and influence, Ray now found herself treated as a beginner, subject to pressures to re-invent herself physically, mentally and emotionally. Her main challenge was Mary's delight in orchestrating the lives and loves of others.

Since moving to Florence, Mary and Bernhard Berenson had both established names for themselves in the art world. Berenson's four major works on the art and artists of the Italian Renaissance, which established him as a leading art historian, were written in collaboration with Mary, and although her contribution was not publicly acknowledged, she achieved independent recognition from her own writings on art under the name of Mary Logan. Berenson began the process of procuring neglected masterpieces for American art collectors which would eventually make him a wealthy man. At this stage, his main client was Isabella Stewart Gardner, the patron who had originally funded his trip to Europe. (Berenson's association with the art dealer Joseph Duveen did not commence until 1906.)

In 1900, just as Mary and Berenson (somewhat reluctantly on his part) had agreed to marry once she had been widowed for a year, the Villa I Tatti, between Fiesole and Settignano, became available to rent; they snapped it up. Built mainly in the sixteenth century, I Tatti was, in 1900, little more than a large farmhouse, and far from luxurious. Its main attraction was its site on a hillside with extensive views over the surrounding area. Much basic work had to be undertaken before its new tenants could move in, and even then there was no electricity, no telephone and very limited plumbing.

Ray's first visit to I Tatti (by permission of the Court of Chancery) was later that year, when Mary's family arrived en masse for her wedding to Berenson. After the civil ceremony on 27 December in the Palazzo Vecchio, Florence, a Roman Catholic ceremony followed on 29 December in the small chapel at I Tatti – for the sake of correctness and to avoid problems with the children's Catholic guardians. Even though Ray and Karin were practising Catholics, they did not take the wedding very seriously. As they considered Mary 'too middle-aged and fat to have a wreath of orange flowers', they planned a wreath of large oranges instead.[2] Mary had hired ex-Army horses so that the girls could explore the Tuscan countryside, but the horses had a liking for their training ground on the Campo di Marte, and the wedding reception at I Tatti was disturbed by the eruption into it of the bride's two windswept and excited daughters who had 'been carried by their steeds into the midst of real manoeuvres'.[3]

Ray had been back to I Tatti twice since then. On the first of these visits, at Christmas 1902 when she was accompanied by her school-friend Winnie Buckley, I Tatti had seemed to Ray 'like a fairy palace – so warm & comfortable & quiet' (despite Mary's constant lectures on Berenson's artistic theory of Tactile Values). Her visit at Easter 1904 with Karin and Winnie was less successful. Mary was often ill, and found fault with Ray and Winnie for being insufficiently

(Figure 7): I Tatti in 1909, two years after the Berensons became its owners.

communicative. Now Ray was to spend several months at I Tatti and Mary was 'planning *all sorts* of things' so that Ray should ' "see life" '.[5] Mary's aim was to mould her elder daughter into her own cultured, socially adept, flirtatious image.

One problem for Mary was Ray's appearance: she resolutely refused to make the best of herself. Hannah had slipped a back-straightener into the bottom of her trunk in the hope that this – if Mary could induce Ray to use it – might improve her habitual slouched posture. Hannah's Quaker background meant that fine clothes had been a rarity in Ray's teenage years. Although Ray considered that 'dresses are awful bores' and resented the occasions when she was forced to dress for dinner, even she felt that Hannah took plain dressing too far at times, pressing her to wear clothes which were uncomfortable and too small, as well as hideous to look at.[6]

Mary's very different approach, and her plans to transform Ray into a young lady of style and culture, had an initial but temporary attraction. The purchase of the 'most wonderful new garments […] evening dresses & silk things […] elegant & young ladyish' provoked mixed reactions in her daughter:

There is a certain kind of entertainment in it but it does not at all compensate me for my loss of principles & the shocking way in which I ignore my convictions. To go out shopping, merely to shop, to buy merely fine clothes at great & ruinous prices […] it is a great come-down. I never thought that I should sink so low.[7]

Mary lectured Ray about the importance of dressing well (and was amused soon afterwards to be on the receiving end of a similar ticking-off from Berenson). But it was all to no avail, as Mary lamented to Hannah: 'If the old monster only held herself decently she would be stunning.'[8] Instead 'I find she has a sort of dread and horror of looking nice and attractive – I fear it is the fruit of thy preaching about Man, for she distinctly wants *not* to be attractive.'[9]

The instrument selected by Mary for Ray's education about the world was an American second cousin from Pittsburgh, Willy Taylor. William Nicholson Taylor, the grandson of Hannah's sister Sarah, was five years older than Ray, had studied architecture at Harvard, and was now at the American Academy in Rome. Ray seems to have been looking forward to the prospect of some male company – and Mary had written enthusiastically about Willy's charms and intelligence – but Ray found the reality a disappointment, 'not half so nice as I half hoped, & not half so nasty as I expected.'[10]

The main problem was that Willy's views seemed to Ray 'selfish, brutally conceited, self assured impudence', despite Mary's insistence that 'to be with him ought to constitute a liberal education in itself'.[11] His opinion was that 'no woman was of more brain power or brain importance than a boy of 15'.[12] Mary could laugh at Willy's assumption of superiority and outdated views on how women should behave and be treated ('women's sphere was to be men's companion', he alleged), but Ray found them insufferable and started to understand Hannah's views on men.[13] Willy, 'accustomed to see girls yielding to his spell', was taken aback by Ray's resistance.[14] Mary lamented that 'she doesn't seem to have the faintest leaning towards a flirtation – wretched young "Miss Beale and Miss Buss" that she is – that of course would entertain and amuse her'.[15] Ray had her own ways of entertaining herself, and treated Willy and his pronouncements as a continuing source of comedy.

After falling out with Mary because of her attempts to dictate their every activity and direct their artistic appreciation, Willy first tried to shift the blame for his troubles onto Ray for refusing to play the role of the ingénue he had been led to expect, then started making advances to her (perhaps not as seriously as Ray assumed). Her conclusion was that 'his overweening vanity was much mortified because the lovely heroine found nothing in the noble hero but food for intense amusement'.[16] Nevertheless, Ray grasped that Willy was as much Mary's victim as she was. By trying to manipulate the two into a flirtation – if not a longer-term relationship – Mary had put Willy into a humiliating position when Ray responded with hilarity to his attempts at gallantry.

Neither Mary nor Willy seems to have grasped how knowledgeable about life in general Ray already was; even Hannah's description of Ray at this time as 'unconscious & natural' seems mistaken (although Hannah had been right in her earlier warning to Mary that Ray 'seems to be very high-principled, and we must be careful not to shock her with our adult, easy-going principles').[17] The habit of being a silent observer had given her a far more mature understanding than her family realised. She had read widely, had a lively imagination, and had 'for some years had her eyes open – for which reason she has tried to shut her mouth – for fear she should let out things she was not supposed to know'.[18]

Mary expounded the doctrine of not taking life too seriously. But her uncooperative daughter turned the tables by undertaking, for her own entertainment, a cool, detached and perceptive analysis of the goings-on at I Tatti and the motivations of her companions. Hannah, who came to suspect that Mary had planned to marry Ray off to Willy, rejoiced that Ray had the good sense and independence to outwit her mother's match-making schemes: 'Hurrah for Ray!'[19]

After Willy's departure the next few weeks were mostly unexciting but pleasant: 'Everything seems amusing – except when everything seems tragic. There are moments when the world appears the most sordid & horrible place – but I don't find that those moments are so frequent here as in London.'[20] Excitement arrived with Mary's next scheme – introducing Ray to the delights of motoring. Not yet owning a car of their own, the Berensons had relied on the goodwill of friends for the motoring tours about which they had recently become enthusiastic. The previous year their friend Edmund Houghton had taken them on a successful tour in the Siena region and Mary now sought his aid on Ray's behalf.

Edmund Houghton and his wife Mary were English expatriates who lived in a medieval tower in Florence, the much-envied owners of a de Dion car. Motoring had become a craze and car-ownership a widespread ambition. Even so, motoring remained the preserve of the well-to-do and mechanically adept – breakdowns were frequent and the owner had to be prepared to deal with much regular maintenance.

On the four-day motor trip in the Lucca area which the Houghtons, Mary and Ray undertook as soon as Ray turned eighteen, Edmund Houghton (a 'kind-faced cow' according to his pupil) taught Ray to drive. [21] She took to it instantly, with skill and delight, and was soon doing most of the driving. Women drivers were not unknown, but few were as young as Ray. On their return to I Tatti Ray admitted 'I am motor-mad. I can scarcely think of anything else'.[22] Mary bought her 'a real motor cap, with the 'Eyes' sewn in, and a false nose, and all the rest of it' and 'a large long pair of gloves', and weighted the front of her dress with 'some little bags of shot' to keep it in place: 'She looks very funny […] but she glories in it!'[23]

Soon the Berensons, Ray and various friends were off on another trip, this time to Venice, where Willy made an unwelcome reappearance. Relations between them were no easier. Ray had started to fictionalise their previous encounter in a novel, and his renewed presence encouraged further literary vilification. Edmund Houghton lent his car to the Berensons for a week, so Ray took them round the Veneto in it, discovering the difficulty – and the thrill – of driving on wet roads and the amount of hard work involved in keeping the vehicle clean and roadworthy.

Ray's driving had so far been relatively problem-free (crumpling a sidelight on a door-post could happen to anyone), but now disaster struck. Berenson, en route to accept an invitation from an aristocratic

lady friend, planned to inspect an altarpiece in a church at the small
town of Portogruaro before catching a train on from there. Ray drove,
with Willy, the Berensons, and one of their friends as her passengers.
Back-seat dissent about the correct route meant that Ray had to turn the
car round on a road banked up high above the level of the surrounding
fields. Reverse gear was a recent innovation in cars and turning round
not a simple process. When one rear wheel went over the edge of the
embankment, passengers and driver hurriedly disembarked. Ray
climbed back in to restart the car, but as the rear wheels had no traction,
she had to jump clear again as the starting motion sent the vehicle
slithering backwards down the embankment into the muddy ditch at the
bottom. Ray considered it 'the funniest sight I ever saw – the traditional
Punch motor accident' (and sketched the scene in her diary).[24]

(Figure 8) Ray's sketch of the accident.

Berenson, already enraged by earlier delays and nervous of missing his train, rushed off in search of oxen. These duly pulled the car back onto the road, but by then there remained less than half an hour before the departure of Berenson's train from Portogruaro, some twelve kilometres away. They set off again in a hurry (with a further stoppage to get the car back into proper running order). Nevertheless Ray's speedy driving got Berenson to his (fortunately slightly delayed) train in time.

Back in the suffocating heat of Venice, Willy's behaviour finally drove Mary to share Ray's dislike of him, his 'egoism and native boorishness' convincing her that he was 'the most disagreeable person to travel with'.[25] The party broke up with relief. From Venice, Ray and Mary escaped to the cooler climate of Lake Garda, Milan and Andermatt, and thence home via Paris. This may have been the occasion when Mary, in an unthinking moment she later regretted, sent her daughter to call on members of a Parisian circle of lesbians. As she later recalled:

> It seems that the tenets of this sect were enthusiastically imparted to Ray on their way to call on a very highly placed and talented priestess of this strange religion. When they arrived at her house they were ushered into a salon hung with oriental tapestries, where their hostess was reclining on a luxurious couch, clothed only in a panther skin. "Ray, I exclaimed, weren't you horrified"? "No, Mother", she said, "I was only amused. I certainly was not tempted to join the company, but I already knew all about it".[26]

Ray pressed ahead with her novel. It was a demanding and lengthy task, even given her old love of composition, and she felt such affinity with her heroine, Charlotte, that introducing other characters bored her. Nevertheless, writing fiction came naturally to her: 'once I have settled what a chapter is to bring about, I don't have to think of the incidents, for they come out of my pen of their own accord'.[27] On her return home Ray sought comments on the finished work from several literary practitioners, including her uncle, Logan Pearsall Smith. To her gratified astonishment, he pronounced that it was 'far above the average and had decided merit' and suggested publication.[28] When a publisher turned it down as too short for a novel and too long for a short story, Mary – without Ray's knowledge – paid £70 [£6,800] for its publication.

The World at Eighteen was eventually published in 1907, against opposition from Hannah and Alys; it produced acute embarrassment for Willy, anger among his family, and continuing dissension among Ray's closer relatives. The novel is a piece of juvenilia, but has narrative energy, clearly delineated characters (of whom the naive heroine, loosely based on Ray herself, is the least successful), fluent dialogue and vigorously expressed general ideas, particularly on the role of women. Clearly autobiographical, the novel describes the fears and fury of eighteen-year-old Charlotte, on a visit to her mother in Florence, when confronted by the conceit, male chauvinism and amatory advances of her American cousin, Mortimer. The events of the plot soon depart from Ray's own experience; how closely the heroine's emotions resemble the author's is less clear.

The general tone of the book is pessimistic. Charlotte complains of the complexity of life ('Why could not life be straightforward and simple? Why could she not always have clear Mathematics to do, and straightforward games to play when she had done them?'), comes to feel 'the insignificance of human life, and the pitiful triviality of her own concerns', characterises the World (largely but not entirely as represented by Mortimer) as 'brutality, selfishness, egotism, spite, envy, malice, diabolic cleverness, and blind self-absorption' and, more generally, concludes that 'the World is a terrible yet beautiful place, in which each separate being struggles alone, desperately alone, without comprehension or insight or thought or care for anything but itself'.[29]

The heroine's bewildered loneliness contrasts with Ray's amusement over her dealings with Willy as recorded in her diary; but, given Ray's hints that she felt isolated and had bouts of depression, Charlotte's despair may be an exaggerated version of Ray's own feelings. The impression Charlotte gains, from the conversation of adults, of a world 'full of complications and unknown dangers' surely springs from exchanges in the Pearsall Smith family: 'when she heard her mother or any "grown-up" person talking about other people, it was always in a tone of pity. Something, apparently, had gone wrong for everyone. And the most terrible thing was that they all seemed to take pleasure in recounting the misfortunes of these "other people" '.[30]

The novel displays an affectionate relationship between mother and daughter, even though the foolish machinations of Charlotte's mother ('a beautiful woman, tall and fair' looking younger than her forty years) are largely responsible for the problems the heroine faces.[31] But the name of Mrs Kingconstance which Ray attributes to the mother is not original. In Sarah Grand's *Babs the Impossible*, Mrs Kingconstance, mother of the heroine Babs, is an amiable, handsome, gullible, unimaginative, shallow, weak-willed, self-centred glutton, mainly preoccupied with her own comfort and the delights of her next meal.[32] Ray's use of the same name for the mother in a fictionalised version of her own experiences may imply a harsher verdict on Mary than is at first apparent – or perhaps just affectionate teasing.

Mary took her failure to transform Ray into her own image with equanimity, cheerfully concluding 'Wait till I get Karin in my claws!'[33] Her chance came when her daughters returned to I Tatti the following Easter. Ray was now a student at Newnham College, Cambridge; Mary noted with approval that she had 'come out tremendously since she went to college – she often takes part in the conversation and never says anything banal', on the contrary contributing 'a lot of very subtle interesting things'.[34] Karin, normally ebullient, was at first uncharacteristically subdued. In December 1905 she had undergone a serious ear operation, which revealed that a suspected mastoid was really 'a terrible abscess and the bone frightfully diseased'.[35] Although apparently successful at the time, it was to be the first in a long series of operations, which failed to prevent her increasing deafness.

As companions for the girls, Mary had invited two young Englishmen suggested by her sister Alys. Geoffrey Scott, an undergraduate in Literae Humaniores at New College, Oxford, was the nephew of C. P. Scott, editor of the *Manchester Guardian*; John Maynard Keynes had recently graduated in mathematics from King's College, Cambridge, but was still studying there, his interests moving towards philosophy and economics. Although at that time Scott and Keynes had similar homosexual interests, in other respects they were very different. Keynes, a year older than Scott and far more self-confident, was the more down-to-earth and cynical of the two. Scott, a convinced aesthete, was neurotically in thrall to his passion for the beautiful – both in art and men. The two young men clung fiercely to their differing university loyalties and discussions on general topics often turned into disputes between the Oxford and Cambridge ways of thought.

Mary converted the planned reading party into a motoring trip and hired a large chauffeur-driven car. Her memory of the whole week-long trip in late March was of her own discomfort during their cold, wet and muddy journeys and of the good humour among the four young travellers squashed into the back of the car: 'to them everything was fun – the scrappy lunches under trees in a drizzle, the arrival at cold carpetless and fireless inns, the horrible meals, the mud that one day simply covered poor Scott, [...] the enforced changes of route....everything was an occasion for laughter and merriment'.[36] The hazards of the journey only added to its excitement: they were sorry that they 'had only two punctures & only caught fire twice!'[37] In compensation, there was the excitement of going, at sunset, down a precipitous route from a little walled town on the summit of a ridge, and a race to reach Orvieto before night, running '20 miles or so in the dark with no lamps – it was awfully thrilling rushing along the valley with the great black hills on each side, & seeing it grow darker & darker'.[38]

Amid the sightseeing and adventures, there was, of course, a great deal of talk, much of it by Mary. Ray was full of admiration for the entertainment her mother provided:

> giving us, in a mild form, her views on life, youth & middle age, practical philosophy, art, love, duty of mothers & children, society, enthusiasm & standing up straight. This last she gave in no moderated form! All these subjects she talked of with a continual flow of conversation, all charming & often screamingly funny.[39]

Left (figure 9) Geoffrey
Scott , early 1910s. He
and Ray came to dislike
each other.

Right (figure 10) John Maynard Keynes, with whom
Ray struck up an enduring friendship, c. 1908

The presence of young men, particularly good-looking ones like
Scott, rejuvenated the 'fat, middle-aged, red-faced lady', as Mary
described herself.[40] (Keynes could not compete with Scott on looks
– he resembled 'an incarnation of Mephistopheles' according to
Karin.)[41] With money to spend, art and good food readily available,
a captive audience and the prospect of extending her influence over
new admirers, Mary was in her element. Keynes had never spent a
pleasanter week, and there were no dissenters from Ray's opinion that
the trip had been a perfect success.

After the week's tour, the group separated temporarily so that the
young men could catch up with their studies in a pension in Siena:
Scott was preparing for his final examinations at Oxford and Keynes
was about to undertake the extended examination process for entry
to the Civil Service. Then they all then met up again for a few days at
I Tatti. When Mary recounted to them Villiers de l'Isle-Adam's short
story Le chapeau chinois, in which an elderly musician is confronted
by a musical part for his noisy percussion instrument consisting
solely of significant silences, and, defeated by the interpretative
complexity, drops dead, Ray drew from it a 'working philosophy
of life'.[42] Silence would always be important to her, but her habitual

refusal to participate in social exchanges gained her a reputation for discourtesy: 'she ought to have been soundly whipped' was her cousin Pug Worthington's verdict on one such incident.[43]

Mary incited mildly outrageous behaviour whenever she could. She had already introduced Ray to the delights of smoking, to which she took 'with rapture' and adopted as a lifelong habit, far exceeding the two hundred cigarettes per month for which her mother continued to subsidise her.[44] Now Mary facilitated cross-dressing bathing parties in a local lake, for which the men wore ladies' knickers and competed for possession of a pink chemise; and on the last evening she provided a splendid dinner with top-quality champagne for the cross-dressed four (Scott in Mary's black lace dress with a gold coronet, Keynes in a chiffon gown with a pink ribbon head-dress), which led to general tipsiness, Ray being sick and having to be put to bed, and Karin sitting on Keynes's lap. When Hannah eventually heard about some of the activities in Italy, she held forth at length to Ray about 'how contrary to English ideas [Mary's] behaviour was'.[45]

To Ray's relief, the Englishmen were 'utterly unflirtatious' and talked as if she was 'a reasonable being', saying:

> what they really felt, quite as much as the great Willy; & yet in a way that made one, somehow, self respecting to hear them. I mean they did not volunteer information to a poor inferior creature, information about themselves, supreme beings, but they behaved rationally & naturally, just as if they had been clever well read girls! And this is a very high compliment.[46]

Ray initially liked both men equally ('it is hard to say which was the nicer'), but their reaction to her was very different.[47] From the start Scott found her silent and (unlike her mother) unresponsive to his charm; later encounters led to mutual dislike between them, in parallel with a growing closeness between Mary and Scott. When in August that year, after Scott had visited Friday's Hill, Mary claimed that Ray was discontented with her life, Scott admitted that he found Ray apathetic:

Her mind has come to seem to me a kind of Polar district, very fascinating to contemplate, but depopulated and frozen. [...] She has constructed a mental landscape which I think has a curious fascination of its own. But if it does not fascinate her, – if she is unhappy, it is all wrong.[48]

In contrast, Ray and Keynes got on well from the start and the exclusively male enthusiasms of the Apostles came under threat, as he admitted to Lytton Strachey:

I seem to have fallen in love with Ray a little bit, but as she isn't male I haven't [been] able to think of any suitable steps to take. Of course she practically is male – for she obviously practices sapphistries and its attendant train. But you would really be surprised how nice she is. [...] Oh Ray looks like a very charming boy in her pyjamas with her hair down.[49]

For Keynes and Strachey there could be no higher compliment than to consider someone worthy of election to the all-male Apostles, and Keynes did not withhold this: 'I would even be prepared to elect her at once – without a qualm of any kind.'[50]

Keynes was almost certainly wrong about Ray's sexual orientation. The desexualizing and empowering New Girl culture could make young women seem unusually masculine, but Ray admitted to Virginia Stephen a few years later that she had always been susceptible to men and had been seriously interested in several (none of whom had reciprocated the feeling). Keynes may well have been among the men who attracted her. When he and Scott came to visit Ray's family at Fernhurst in September 1906, Ray concluded:

I like Keynes a good deal better than Scott. I had many walks with him, & we got on very comfortably, with a sort of vague, woolly talk that was rather entertaining. He is extraordinarily different from Willy, & made no attempt to talk about himself, except in connection with the vague things we talked of – the tendency of the age – Cambridge – absolute reality etc. I really enjoyed it very much, & there is something very attractive about him.[51]

By then both Ray and Mary were well aware of the 'peculiar *culte*' to which he and Scott belonged, indeed Scott had expounded to Mary the wonders of adoring 'a handsome, talented, beautiful youth', despite the dangers that such a love affair might become sordid.[52] Mary doubted whether either man had gone much beyond the spiritual, but she was wrong about Keynes. His relationships with his male lovers had recently moved back from the spiritual to the (criminally) physical: always discreet, he did not admit this to Ray.

Ray had good reason to be nervous about male/female relationships which went further than friendship, since there was no happy marriage within her immediate family to encourage her. Her parents' marriage had broken up in acrimony after a short time; the longer-lasting marriage of her grandparents had given Hannah a loathing of men, especially husbands; the breakdown of the marriage of her aunt Alys and Bertrand Russell was not yet public knowledge, but her aunt's misery was hard to disguise; Grace Worthington's marriage had ended in a painful divorce; her mother's second marriage had its good moments but the constant friction between Mary and Berenson – and Mary's interest in young men – hardly made this a model relationship. Even Ellie Rendel's family did not present a harmonious picture of domestic life: 'They are in a continual state of fury with everyone & everything, & it is most exciting to be there.'[53] Exciting, but also alarming.

The pain that men and women can cause each other may explain Ray's admission to Keynes and Scott that 'she found the world such a dangerous and tragic place' and had thought about entering a convent.[54] Outside religion, mathematics alone offered certainty, 'a world governed by reason and law, in which there were no loose ends, and where every conclusion followed from the premises'.[55] Keynes encouraged her to press on with mathematics, but the discussions she had with him and Scott about religion were, in Mary's view, the beginnings of the end for Ray's religious faith, which gradually 'dropped away' over the next few years.[56]

Ray made many further visits to I Tatti, liking the lifestyle there less and less as it grew ever grander, but none were of greater importance to her own development than those in 1905 and 1906. Both Keynes and Scott kept up their association with Mary and her daughters. Maynard Keynes remained a family friend (and financial adviser), bound to Ray by their common links with the Strachey family. Geoffrey Scott's tortuous love life, and Mary's growing obsession with him, came close to destroying Mary's marriage – on one occasion even threatening her life – and succeeded in driving a wedge between Ray and her mother. For Ray the values she absorbed at home and at school proved ultimately far more significant than those espoused by the Berensons at I Tatti. Now university life offered Ray opportunities to express those values in practical action.

PART TWO

The Young Suffragist

CHAPTER FOUR

Embracing the Cause: 1905–1908

They began to look at themselves and their mission in the world in a new light, and poured into the suffrage societies all the enthusiasm which they had thought to devote to other ends.[1]

Ray's need for a cause to follow was easily met: the battle for women's suffrage was the obvious choice for intelligent, independent-minded young women. Ray's grandmother and aunt were active suffrage campaigners. Her father had been an enthusiastic supporter (as, before her defection to Italy, had her mother). Hannah Whitall Smith had impressed on Ray that women were not just equal to men but decidedly superior. Ray's involvement in political action for women began gradually, but by the time she wrote a history of the Women's Movement, she was happy to admit 'I am both open to and proud of the charge that I cannot take a wholly impartial view. [...] My assumptions are undoubtedly feminist, and my eyes perhaps blinded to the virtues of the past.'[2]

The need for reform in the role and rights of women had been discussed for over a century, and some progress had been made. During the nineteenth century some of the legal iniquities concerning a married woman's status, rights, property and guardianship over children had been removed. Education for women had been improved: good day schools for girls – like Kensington High School – were now available, as was the possibility of a university education (though not necessarily a degree). A wider range of employment had opened to women, from secretarial, clerical and retail positions up to highly-qualified posts as teachers and doctors. Some areas of employment still remained closed – the law stayed resolutely male – but the idea that a respectable woman could earn her own living was gaining ground. Nevertheless suffrage, which many women had come to see as the key to further progress for women, lagged behind: laws were still made solely by men, no matter how deeply women might be affected by them.

Societies to promote women's suffrage had existed since 1866 (leading to John Stuart Mill's unsuccessful attempt in 1867 to move an amendment to the Reform Bill to provide for female suffrage), organised since 1897 in a federation – the National Union of Women's Suffrage Societies (NUWSS). But persistent attempts by sympathetic MPs to secure a Parliamentary majority for female suffrage had been defeated. In 1907 women ratepayers gained the right to vote and stand in all local elections; they could already act as Poor Law Guardians and as members of School Boards. Nevertheless, gradual easing of the qualifications for male suffrage in national elections meant that from 1884 about 60% of men had a vote, but no women. A rising tide of resentment among women made the question of whether women should be given the vote one of the major preoccupations of British political life between the Boer War and the First World War.

In 1903 the female suffrage cause was revitalised by the founding, in Manchester, by Mrs Emmeline Pankhurst and her suffrage co-workers there, of the Women's Social and Political Union (WSPU). Made indignant when in 1904 the MP Henry Labouchere wrecked a Private Member's Bill introducing female suffrage, the group soon turned from talk to action: their motto was 'Deeds, not words'. The strategy adopted by Emmeline Pankhurst's eldest daughter, Christabel, a law student at Manchester University, was to seek publicity by way of a deliberate clash with the authorities. The disruption she and Annie Kenney caused to a Liberal election meeting in the Free Trade Hall in Manchester on 13 October 1905, and their subsequent arrest and imprisonment, marked a turning point. Constitutional suffragists were divided in their response. Many deplored the WSPU action, but Millicent Garrett Fawcett, the President of the NUWSS, refused to speak out against it, realising the boost which the publicity had given to the suffrage cause.

The Strachey family had been involved in the Women's Movement for many years, offering consistent and unwavering support to the moderate suffragist cause. In the 1860s the former Jane Maria Grant and her husband Richard Strachey (later Lieutenant-General Sir Richard Strachey) were both admirers of John Stuart Mill and in favour both of improved education for women and of female suffrage. Jane Strachey published an article in favour of women's suffrage in 1866, signed (and helped circulate) the petition for women's suffrage presented to Parliament by Mill in 1867, joined a suffrage organisation in Edinburgh soon afterwards, and made a substantial donation to the foundation of Girton College, Cambridge. Her husband's career in India, and the raising of a large family, delayed her further active involvement in the suffrage movement for some years, but after the family settled permanently in London in 1879 she gradually took on a more prominent public role.

In 1903 Lady Strachey became president of the Women's Local Government Society (for which Frank Costelloe had often acted as legal representative), whose purpose was to lobby for greater rights for women in local government, as electors, elected and employees. Closer involvement with the wider suffrage cause followed. Although valued for her title, social position and Conservative political allegiances (the Stracheys had abandoned the Liberal Party when Gladstone supported Irish Home Rule), Jane Strachey was far from a passive figurehead: she corresponded, lectured, lobbied, organised and marched, and brought her children along to do likewise. All of her daughters and most of her sons took part in suffrage activities, and her third daughter, Pippa, made it her life's work. Her eldest daughter, Elinor Rendel, shared her mother's deep commitment to the women's movement – even though her husband was unenthusiastic – and transmitted it to her own daughters. It was therefore not surprising that the younger daughter, Ellie, should attempt to interest her close friend Ray Costelloe in the activities preoccupying the women in her own family.

Some twenty years later – when the battle was all but won – Ray came to write the history of these momentous years. But it was not the details of protests and repression, advances and setbacks, which she dwelt on, rather the shift of the Women's Suffrage movement from the periphery to the centre of public consciousness.

> Day after day, as the militants provided fresh headlines for the newspapers, the breakfast tables of England resounded with the debate, and the comments flowed out from the domestic hearth to railway trains, smoking rooms, clubs, and public-houses, and wherever men gathered together.[3]

She described the 'almost religious fervour' which overcame many women supporters of the cause, and which had its earliest impact on girls at college who 'had believed in, but had not cared for suffrage'. Many of these girls rejected the divisive arguments of the militants and rapidly came to understand that the suffrage movement 'was not primarily a fight between men and women' but sought 'an extended power to do good in the world'.[4] Ray herself had been at the heart of the generation of girls so affected.

Ellie had already been at Newnham College for a year when Ray arrived there in October 1905. The girls re-established their close friendship and Ray came to enjoy college life more and more. She made several new friends at college and there is no sign in her sporadic diary entries of the sense of isolation she had often suffered at home. Ray and Ellie were, according to their friend Lynda Grier, responsible for much of the fun in college life, 'so ingenious were they in hatching innocent plans for gaiety'.[5] She remembered working in Ray's sitting room with Ellie while Ray

lay on her tummy & played patience or painted suffrage posters
[…]. Now & again we would stir her up with our toes & suggest that
she should do a little work, but she merely turned a beatific smile on
us, stretched out a lazy arm & fetched a tin of delicacies from under
her sofa & fed us on them.[6]

Ray was 'a noted beauty in the college', captaining the beauty hockey
team against the brains team captained by Ellie.[7] Ray's mathematical
work, though often a struggle, retained her interest if not her constant
attention, and she found it possible to continue with many of the
sporting activities she had enjoyed at school, supplemented by rowing
or canoeing on the river.

Ray's first active involvement in the suffrage movement did not, at
the time, signify any long-term commitment to the cause. The arrest
and imprisonment in October 1906 of a number of suffragettes for
a technical offence in the Houses of Parliament caused nationwide
uproar. Acting on her own initiative, Millicent Fawcett arranged a
banquet at the Savoy Hotel in early December for the prisoners so
far released, including her friend Anne Cobden-Sanderson, Richard
Cobden's daughter, and Adela, the youngest of the Pankhurst sisters.
Not all suffragists approved, but amongst those present were Ellie's
grandmother, Lady Strachey, and Ray's aunt, Alys Russell. Impressed
by the propaganda victory scored by the suffragettes, the NUWSS
determined to seek further public attention for the suffrage cause in a
less confrontational manner.

On 9 February 1907, a wet and cheerless Saturday, some three
thousand women, including Ray and Ellie, spent the afternoon
marching in a procession a mile long from Hyde Park Corner along
Piccadilly and Regent Street, with bands playing, to meetings in
Trafalgar Square and Exeter Hall on the Strand. They carried placards
('The cabinet is to blame for militancy' read one) and waved banners,
some in the NUWSS colours of green, white and red, some showing
the numerous individual organisations from all over the country
which were taking part.

For women to march was unconventional, to say the least – many regarded such an action as an affront to propriety, if not public decency. The weather made propriety even harder to maintain, for heavy rain reduced the route to a mud-bath and the women's long skirts soon became filthy. Nevertheless the event, whose planning had largely fallen on Ellie's aunt Pippa Strachey, was judged a great success. The presence of ladies of unimpeachable respectability like Mrs Fawcett and Lady Strachey, marching at the head of the procession, warded off much criticism and the number and variety of women taking part demonstrated the breadth and depth of support among women for their right to vote.

Lady Strachey's descendants were there in force, though Ellie's brothers lacked enthusiasm, as Ray reported:

> The [Rendel boys] were walking alongside trying to look as if they enjoyed it, and protesting that they didn't believe in Suffrage. I think they must have been rather sad at seeing a grandmother, mother, four aunts and two sisters walking in the mud for what they didn't see fit to approve of.[8]

The Mud March, as it became known, seems to have been for Ray an entertaining day out in congenial company rather than anything more serious.

Ray's long-term involvement with the suffrage cause began as little more than a piece of fun, an adventure to enliven the last days of the summer vacation before she and Ellie returned to Newnham in autumn 1907. While Ray was staying with Ellie's family at her Rendel grandparents' country home – Rickettswood, near Charlwood in Surrey – the girls arranged to hold a suffrage meeting in a nearby village. Ray described to her family how they

> stole away from the house at 6, & bicycled to Leigh, & there found a great many people standing about on the outskirts of the green, & sitting in the neighbouring gardens. So we went boldly up to the pump & waited for them to come. They didn't budge. We sent

small children round – still no movement. Then I went round – they looked sheepish & wouldn't come. [9]

At last Ray rounded up two women and a great many small children, and Ellie started speaking.

At once all the others came strolling up – & we had about 30 men there. We held forth in turn, & then they asked questions & we had a discussion with them. They were extraordinarily pig-headed, insisted that it was the entering wedge & that what we really wanted was for women to sit in Parliament, which was not woman's sphere. […] However we converted two incredibly ignorant women, & had a perfectly serious meeting. [10]

Bicycling back with a young man, they continued the discussion: 'he quoted Scripture about wives obeying their husbands – but he was more or less for us because he said unmarried women should vote, if they paid taxes'. [11]

Another night, a canvass of Charlwood produced an interested and friendly audience of 200, which Ellie and Ray both addressed 'standing on a chair & feeling squeamish but excited'. [12] It had been, Ray concluded, a wonderful occasion, but did not indicate a commitment to a political cause. Many young women were inspired to become suffragists by a speech or a book, but Ray admitted to more down-to-earth influences. Her motives, she assured her mother, were as much 'novelty, the excitement, the kudos, the joy of doing it secretly, the desire to do what Ellie does' as her belief in the need for female suffrage. [13]

The consequences were less pleasing, for word had got out into suffrage circles that two new speakers were now available, and within days three invitations for Ray to speak elsewhere arrived at Court Place. 'Furious, sulky & disgusted', she felt trapped into accepting:

If I only had the driving fire of enthusiasm to carry me through! Or could go on with a strong sense of duty behind me urging me along.

But neither comes my way, & I just do disagreeable things to get them over & because I can't help myself.[14]

As Ray confessed: 'it's horribly difficult to hang back – yet we have both had enough'.[15] This reaction continued for some time. After a visit to the Russell household in December she complained 'the talk at Bagley Wood is all politics & social reform & women's suffrage. How I hate it! And how they revel in it!'[16]

Newnham College, whose very existence represented a feminist success, was bound to offer fertile territory for suffragists. Despite Ray's misgivings, during the autumn term at Cambridge Ellie and Ray went 'suffrage mad', holding suffrage meetings and weekly 'At Homes' to discuss suffrage questions, and founding a suffrage society which rapidly acquired '110 members, & a lot of funds'.[17] Early in 1908 the suffrage society Ellie and Ray founded at Newnham – which by now included three-quarters of the college – merged with its counterpart at Girton to become the Cambridge University Women's Society for Women's Suffrage.[18] Ellie was Honorary Secretary and Ray the Treasurer, a role to which she was totally unsuited given her carelessness over money. Predictably, Ellie later had to take Ray to task over her casual account-keeping.

The pair went to several suffragette meetings in London, where Ray 'lost her heart' to the cheerful militant Mary Gawthorpe and very nearly joined the WSPU.[19] It was the first of several moments when the militant cause attracted her, and emotion battled with reason. Reason always won, even though some close friends threw in their lot with the Pankhursts and their followers. Ray was never one to get carried away and lose her capacity for detached observation, even of her own actions.[20]

One of the first meetings Ray spoke at drew from her a perceptive account of the psychological processes at work during a public meeting, starting with 'a dull feeling of what an endless fag it's all going to be' followed by the hard work 'composing the speech, canvassing the people, trudging about and utterly loathing the whole business':

when the day itself comes, you take comfort in thinking "in so many hours it will all be over". Then the thing begins – great anxiety as to how many people will be there, and a certain feeling of excitement. Then the speeches, and as they go on your own enthusiasm grows and grows, until you begin to think Votes the only important thing in an otherwise trivial universe. Then your own turn comes, with the usual sensations of speaking – half nervous, half excited. Then the end of the meeting, clappings and enthusiasm.[21]

After a peak of thinking suffrage meetings 'quite the most heavenly things in the world':

Ten minutes later you are criticising the speakers, and gradually gloom and sordidness come over you. If you are not careful you will, at this point, remember your own various faux pas – it's always possible to find plenty. After half an hour you begin to get bored with it, though you still discuss it of course. Within an hour you have registered a solemn vow never to do any such thing again. The next day you probably accept an invitation to speak somewhere else.[22]

The invitations to speak kept coming, and Ray continued to find it difficult to refuse them.

During the early months of 1908 Ray and Ellie took time away from preparations for their final examinations to address letters to former Newnham and Girton students and to stuff envelopes in the suffrage cause; the responses were generally favourable, with a great many cheques and postal orders and letters of sympathy which more than offset the few 'crushing replies'.[23] Suffrage activity had spread throughout Cambridge with 'meetings, debates, plays, petitions etc. all through the term'.[24] Even the male undergraduates formed a society for women's suffrage. At the national level hopes were raised when a Liberal MP introduced a Private Member's Bill granting suffrage to single and married women, which achieved a substantial majority on second reading. But within weeks came a major setback: Herbert Henry Asquith, implacable opponent of female suffrage, became Prime Minister. The Bill was blocked. Asquith's opposition to, and apparent contempt for, the suffrage movement soon led to an escalation in the WSPU's militancy. And those opposed to votes for women began to organise themselves, with the formation of separate anti-suffrage societies for men and women.

Ray sat for Part I of the Mathematical Tripos at Cambridge in May 1908. One of the examiners was Geoffrey Thomas Bennett, whose achievement as Senior Wrangler in that same examination in 1890 had been surpassed by Philippa Fawcett. There was no likelihood of Ray achieving a similar distinction and she knew it: 'I am remarkably bad', she confessed.[25] Suffrage activities – and a severe bout of influenza with unpleasant after-effects early in the year – had eaten into her academic work, and, as she acknowledged, 'it's extremely easy not to work here'.[26] It was not until she was in her final year that Ray realised that her speed of understanding had hindered wrestling with problems to produce original thoughts. Ray's persistent belief in the importance of education always left her uneasy about her own shortcomings: 'you can't be educated without knowledge & you can't get knowledge without work, even though [...] knowledge isn't the only point of education'.[27] Her main aim now was to achieve the equivalent of an Honours degree. She barely succeeded: last of the Newnham contingent, equal with the 80th placed man.

Their examinations over, Ray and Ellie threw themselves into suffrage activities. First, on 13 June 1908, came a grand NUWSS suffrage procession from the Victoria Embankment to the Albert Hall, for a meeting chaired by Mrs Fawcett. The girls had rounded up a Cambridge University presence of over 300 marchers ('I have been writing 20 letters a day for several weeks'), who proceeded – six abreast, some in cap and gown – under their colourful new banner stencilled with the Newnham daisies and Girton irises and bearing the motto 'Better is Wisdom Than Weapons of War'.[28] Ray brought up the rear carrying a Joan of Arc banner. Ray found it all great fun, but the organisational effort reduced Ellie to collapse. She retreated to bed with a severe headache, delaying by a day their departure for

Amsterdam for the Fourth Congress of the International Woman Suffrage Alliance, which was to start on 15 June.

As relatives of prominent suffragists (Ray's aunt Alys Russell and Ellie's grandmother Lady Strachey), the girls were accepted into the inner circle of suffrage leaders. In Amsterdam Millicent Fawcett took them under her wing, so they had access to the main congress in the Concert Hall and were invited to a multitude of peripheral events. Crowded receptions, inaudible entertainments and dull financial statements soon palled, but Ray was impressed by the Presidential address given by Carrie Chapman Catt, the American feminist. What struck Ray most at the Congress was the restrained good sense of the speakers ('none of the gas I expected') and the growing internationalism of the suffrage movement.[29]

When the congress ended on June 20, Ray and Ellie travelled back to London overnight for a suffrage demonstration organised by the WSPU. On Sunday 21 June – 'Women's Sunday' as it was dubbed – thirty thousand suffragettes and their sympathisers from all over the country marched in seven processions from different areas of London to Hyde Park, where speakers addressed them from twenty platforms. Curiosity, brilliant sunshine and genuine sympathy for the cause combined to swell the crowd, and Hyde Park was crammed with around a third of a million people. Ray and Ellie marched from the Embankment with Ellie's aunt, Edith Rendel (a suffragette who ran a pioneer working girls' club), and her contingent of factory girls. 'We were in a howling mob of hooligans, & it was great fun' was Ray's verdict.[30]

The NUWSS had taken up the idea of using horse-drawn caravans as a means of spreading its message to parts of the country remote from the main centres of suffrage activity. The Newnham College suffragists, organised by Ellie, were amongst the first to put the idea into practice. Five of them planned an ambitious trip (substantially funded by Hannah) lasting the whole of July and covering over 300 miles between their starting-point near Glasgow, through the Lake District, West Yorkshire and Derbyshire, to Oxford, their final destination. On 2 July Ray and Ellie took possession of 'Eva', their 'perfectly heavenly' caravan, in Beattock, met Charles the driver, a 'silent Scotchman', and the 'huge and rapid horse', Jock, and were eventually joined by their first complement of fellow-caravanners, Emilie Gardner, Gwen Williams and Peggy Colson.[31]

One newspaper report suggested that the trip was little more than a summer holiday for the girls, and certainly Ray enjoyed it immensely.[32] But it was 'horribly hard work' too.[33] The girls had to write and deliver speeches, find and publicise venues for meetings, liaise with local suffragists, shop, cook and wash up for themselves, find places to sleep, and cope with the rigours of life on the road in all weathers. They had two bicycles with them and took it in turns to ride ahead looking for campsites or other accommodation as well as identifying places for meetings and publicising them. In the Lake District they encountered persistent rain, wind and thunder-storms, in Scotland, Yorkshire and Derbyshire intense heat.

At their meetings, often two or three in a day, the girls always stressed their allegiance to the peaceful suffragist cause.

> We always began by saying what we wanted, and to what society we belonged. Four of us spoke, and the meeting lasted about an hour and a quarter. We said why we wanted to vote: talked of Justice, of Taxation without Representation: of the needs of working women, and the influence of the home on politics: of the actual political position of women, and their need for political power, and of all the other various reasons for advocating Women's Suffrage.[34]

They sold badges, distributed literature, passed round a hat to raise funds, and argued the suffrage case with persistence, eloquence, humour and charm; all the speakers, reported the *Lakes Herald*, 'were of prepossessing appearance and their powers of eloquence were such as would put to shame many a male speaker'.[35] Newspaper reports singled out Ray's speaking style for particular praise: she 'quite captivated her audience, and her remarks were punctuated with applause'.[36]

(Left: figure 11) The caravan 'Eva' with Jock the horse, Charles the driver, Ray,
Ellie Rendel, Emilie Gardner and Gwen Williams.
(Right: figure 12) Ray giving (or practising) a speech.

Crowds of several hundred people at meetings were frequent, mainly men. Most audiences were curious and respectful, committed supporters usually outnumbered by those willing to hear the arguments but not necessarily convinced. Only occasionally did they meet outright opposition, as in Kirkby Lonsdale where a meeting was 'very wet and rather unfriendly', with our only supporters Adult Suffragists, and our enemies unpleasant' (the small boys in Kendal 'who thought they were being very funny when they yelled "Votes for women!" ' hardly counted).[37]

Sometimes suffrage supporters offered food and accommodation (baths were particularly welcome) but many nights were spent in farmers' fields or the backyards of inns, three sleeping in the beautifully equipped caravan, the rest in the tent they carried with them. One night Ray slept in the hay under the caravan. They cooked many of their own meals on a portable stove. Only occasionally did they resort to staying in an inn, usually when heavy rain made the idea of pitching the tent on wet grass and sleeping in wet bedding unappealing or when a campsite could not be found.

At Keswick a newly-formed suffrage society was keen to make the most of the caravanners' visit. The society's energetic and efficient Honorary Secretary, Catherine Marshall, had written to local papers, publicising their route and meetings and seeking help with accommodation. In Keswick itself she had set up three meetings,

'one at 12 in the market, another at 4 on the lake (the audience to
be in boats) and a third at 8 in the market again'.[38] It was all rather
intimidating: 'we are terribly afraid of getting to Keswick, because of
all their preparations for us, but it's exciting too. We are now trying to
compose three different speeches each – a terrible task on a subject so
ludicrously simple'.[39]

When they reached Keswick, they were overwhelmed by offers
of hospitality and the strength of local support. The meeting on
Derwentwater had to be postponed until the following day because of
bad weather, but those in the market place went well. 'We are awfully
encouraged, and the local Society is very pleased with us I think!'[40]
They spent the night 'most luxuriously' at Hawse End, the home of
Catherine Marshall and her parents.[41] (Future relations between Ray
and Catherine Marshall would not always be so harmonious.)

The attraction of this gypsy lifestyle was its liberation, a return
to the unfettered outdoor life Ray had enjoyed at Friday's Hill as a
child, with an added spice of adventure. Between Kendal and Kirkby
Lonsdale, in pouring rain, those in the caravan worried that the
bicyclists had gone a different way:

> Charles, growing reckless, set the horse to running, and we sat,
> dripping, in the rocking, jolting caravan, staring out at strange
> roads and hustling through the night. We inside – Ellie, Betty and
> I – clutched each other and laughed for joy – it was such fun – but
> it was reckless wild joy. [...] The horse ran faster and faster, and the
> rain went on quite steadily while we grew more and more gay.[42]

Approaching Glossop, Ray and Ellie, on bicycles, were 'misled by
wicked passers-by as to the road'.[43] They found a camping-site at a
hilltop farm

> only to discover that the town below was not Glossop at all! It was
> dark by then and we had no lamps and not a penny between us! We
> could do nothing but go back and chase after the caravan. It was one
> of the most exciting things I have ever done – moving along dark

roads speculating on our chances of spending a night in a ditch. A thick fog came on. We had to cross a reservoir and then a railway and then on and on. Finally, & rather unexpectedly, we dropped into Glossop.[44]

Inevitably all physical resemblance to well-brought-up young ladies was soon lost. Ray's aunt Alys took part in the final meeting in St. Giles, Oxford, and reported back to Mary:

By this time the crowded life in the van had worked havoc with their clothes, but none of them equalled Ray, who, when her turn came to address the crowd, appeared from the caravan door in a butcher's apron which she had borrowed to hide her torn and filthy dress, with bare sunburnt arms and a battered straw hat on the back of her head. People were inclined to laugh, but she spoke so well, developing her theme with such clear logic, lightening her enthusiasm with so much humour, that she ended amidst hearty cheers from the crowd, and generous contributions were dropped into the hat that was passed round to help pay for the leaflets distributed to the listeners.[45]

The girls returned 'convinced that the average English working man is perfectly ready to approve of Votes for Women'.[46]

CHAPTER FIVE
Apprenticeship: 1908–1910

...there is a time when the individual appears, before the age of thirty, to be getting nowhere, accomplishing none of his aims, or altogether unclear as to what those aims might be. Such a person is, of course, actually preparing for the task that, all unrecognized, awaits.[1]

Mary Berenson had not abandoned her plans to turn her elder daughter into a clone of herself. Losing Ray to the pernicious influence of mathematics and the questionable environment of Newnham had been a setback – and Ray's growing interest in suffrage work and politics a major blow – but now Mary saw her chance to fight back. She proposed that after completing her time at Cambridge, Ray should spend a year at the American college of Bryn Mawr, near Philadelphia, whose President was Mary's cousin, the formidable M. Carey Thomas. Mary and Berenson were to spend some months in the United States furthering his career as an art adviser and could therefore oversee Ray's first experiences of American social life.

Karin would also attend Bryn Mawr. She had not settled happily at Newnham, in part because of her increasing deafness, and she had been allowed a year away; the Philadelphia area offered excellent tuition in lip-reading and her close friend Mary 'Pug' Worthington would also be at Bryn Mawr. Hannah suggested that Ellie Rendel should be invited to accompany them to provide an equivalent friend for Ray. Carey Thomas provided a scholarship for Ellie, and her family were persuaded to agree, but Mary was horrified. Ellie's presence would disrupt the process of separating Ray from what Mary saw as undesirable influences.

On 10 September 1908, an uncomfortable group of six set off for Mary's homeland: Mary (to be followed later by Berenson), Ray, Karin, Mary's cousin (and Carey Thomas's sister) Grace Worthington and her daughter Pug, and Ellie Rendel. The ten-day voyage, mainly rough and windy, was not an enjoyable experience. Ray never became a good sailor and sea-sickness was a constant feature of her sea journeys. On arrival they were caught up in a social round, meeting some of Mary's and Berenson's relatives, and Berenson's patron Mrs Isabella Stewart Gardner.

First impressions of America were favourable. Observing that 'people are so very amusingly equal' and encountering (almost to excess) the deliciously different American food ('oysters, cakes, melons, corn, icecream') gave Ray 'an exciting feeling of a really new country'.[2] Ellie, the outsider in the group, noticed that Mary's attempt to regain her long-lost youth led her to infantilise the younger women, to their inevitable annoyance:

> Mrs Berenson became more youthful in manner to her friends [...] & spoke of us as "the children" always. She told Mr Cannon who had given us a box of sweets that we were accustomed in England to have sixpence to spend on sweets & that she had forbidden us to eat any of his sweets before dinner.[3]

Mary also irritated Ray by fussing over her clothes: Ray 'had to change about three times a day quite needlessly & her temper suffered'.[4]

On 28 September the party eventually arrived at Bryn Mawr, a campus of beautiful buildings spread over a low hill some miles outside Philadelphia, where Ray and Ellie 'fell almost immediately into a state of overwhelming gloom'.[5] No-one seemed ready for them and the rooms Pug had carefully selected for them were a disappointment. More seriously, they felt out of place among the other students (400 undergraduates and 60 graduates), inwardly stiffening when Pug was greeted by a 'screaming and shrieking' crowd and being shocked that conversations about flirtations were regarded as normal and amusing.[6]

The following evening Ray had to settle her subjects of study with Carey Thomas. She had written to ask whether it would be possible to study electricity, but, as Mary reported to Berenson with satisfaction, that idea received short shrift:

> Carey was magnificent and started her just as I should wish, banishing from her fancy forever those silly dreams of 'electrical engineering' [...]. She said 'Ray, it's *ridiculous* to imagine you aren't going to lead a life of Culture. Of course you *are*, with all your advantages,' and went on to praise that life above all others (she is never in doubt about her own opinion) and Ray came right round.[7]

Few people were capable of standing up to Carey Thomas's energy and determination. She had had to struggle to achieve her impressive academic qualifications and become President of Bryn Mawr, and could be ruthless in pursuing high aims for her students and for women in general. Ray never did understand 'how the students remain so utterly impervious to her views of the importance of intellectual seriousness' and soon came to have a great regard for her: 'she is a very extraordinary person – & very charming. I half fear her, half disapprove of her & half adore her. Three halves which make a curious whole.'[8]

Ray and Ellie admitted to each other that they were both 'miserably home-sick' and that the 'prospect was black'.[9] Isabella Stewart Gardner's pronouncement that 'no one in cultured circles approved any more of education' seemed to be true.[10] A distant cousin spelled out the realities of college life in more detail:

> She says that every girl's business is to live a gay social life & have as many beaux as she can, & that if they find that they can't succeed in

that – either because their families are not "good families", or because the girls themselves are unattractive, then they go to college. And she says that none of them at all prefer to try to be "intellectual" or "educated" but that they do it as a pis aller![11]

Plainly the American equality that they had noticed on arrival was more complex than it appeared.

Part of the problem Ray and Ellie had in settling at Bryn Mawr was the American educational system, which made the girls from Cambridge 'shocked and indignant, and then greatly amazed'.[12] Scholarly concentration on one subject was deferred until the post-graduate stage in American universities. Undergraduates were prepared for 'LIFE' by courses of extraordinary breadth designed to turn each girl into a 'well informed person'.[13] It was all very different from Newnham.

Later in their trip Ray and Ellie saw several other American colleges and discovered that Bryn Mawr was not atypical. They remained disapproving, concluding that 'the aim and object of American colleges was to make students really fit to study later, but […] the net result was to send them out of college able to read magazine articles with intelligence, and to talk glibly and superficially on everything under the sun'.[14] Ray conceded that 'you cannot study any one thing properly until you have a background of many other facts'; but she queried 'if your attention is fixed on acquiring these facts, do you ever study anything at all?'[15] The American tradition of Liberal Arts seemed to require a great deal of work for little intellectual reward. The two girls were already hoping to cut their trip short and return to England after Christmas – and their fellow-students were longing to be rid of their constant complaints. The turning point came through women's suffrage.

The suffrage movements on both sides of the Atlantic had undergone periods of stagnation. In Britain the years of little progress at the end of the nineteenth century were ended by the vigour of the WSPU. But in America the doldrums which had lasted since 1896, when Idaho and Utah voted for female suffrage, still continued. No further states had followed their example and there seemed little prospect of Federal action on the matter. A widespread view in the American suffrage movement was that the lack of organisational skills of the Rev. Dr Anna Howard Shaw, the President of the National American Woman Suffrage Association (NAWSA), was partly responsible. Morale was low and new approaches were clearly required.

The 40th NAWSA Convention was to be held in Buffalo, New York State, 15–21 October, 1908. Carey Thomas was a fervent supporter of female suffrage and had already raised a substantial sum for the cause. At Buffalo she was to make an important speech to re-launch the National College Equal Suffrage League, an organisation under the aegis of NAWSA for promoting the suffrage cause among college women.

Carey swept her family along with her to Buffalo. Ray was due to speak at a meeting on 17 October to re-launch the College League and was determined to make a good impression: 'I had carefully prepared a speech, & rehearsed it in my bath for many mornings (it's the only time one is perfectly sure to have no interruptions) & I was not very nervous.'[16] She spoke well and, according to Ellie, 'made quite a sensation'; Mary attributed Ray's success to her grudging agreement to wear stays and a new green dress.[17] Already the girls were noticing a difference between suffrage activities in England and in America: English fighters for the cause were inspired by fervour and quasi-religious devotion, whereas in America (at least on the East Coast) suffrage was in general part of the social round.

Anna Shaw ('very ugly very squat and fat with a very humorous face and a bulldog nose with a black bonnet on the back of her head, and a large smiling mouth full of teeth') was about to travel west to observe women voting in Colorado – one of the few areas to have granted female suffrage already, in 1893 – and to preach the cause in the unenlightened states she would pass through on the journeys there and back.[18] Ray was immediately enthusiastic about a suggestion that she should go too. Mary saw the idea as an opportunity to separate Ray from Ellie, but Ray wanted Ellie to go as well.

Ellie was torn. She was horrified at the idea of being left at Bryn Mawr without Ray, but going on the trip would probably mean sacrificing her scholarship and infuriating her parents. Ellie's relative poverty was a constant source of friction: the Pearsall Smith family regarded as spongers many of Ray's friends, including Ellie, who benefited from her careless generosity and extravagance, and thin-skinned Ellie resented the implied criticism. Ray was caught in the middle, as Ellie admitted: 'I have felt rather slighted; and as if Miss Thomas and Mrs B. looked on me as a paid companion. This has made me feel injured and instead of treating it as a joke I have made the wretched innocent Ray bear all my abominable tempers'.[19] Ellie's hesitation was short-lived. When Carey Thomas obtained Anna Shaw's agreement to take the girls with her, she abandoned her scholarship to go with Ray.

It was with trepidation that on 24 October Ray and Ellie joined their travelling companion for the overnight train journey. Ray admitted to shyness: she knew little about Anna Shaw 'beyond the fact that she was a magnificent orator & had a very kind face' nor how she would treat them.[20] They had little time to find out. Tired, they went straight to bed and woke in Chicago. There Ray and Ellie spoke about suffrage in England to students at the University ('older and less rich and more serious and studious looking' than their equivalents at Bryn Mawr), and were delighted when their 'charming, very friendly and talkative' hostess Sophonisba Breckinridge confirmed that Bryn Mawr had its faults. [21]

From Chicago they headed west. Anna Shaw was an amiable travelling companion and to pass the long rail journeys recounted her remarkable life story. The tales Anna Shaw told the two girls about her early life not only entertained them, they provided Ray with an interest in the early days of American social reform which would occupy her for years. Of Scottish descent, Anna Howard Shaw had come to America as a young child, living in New England until her father took up a concession as a pioneer in northern Michigan. The life was physically demanding and young Anna played a major role in the family's survival. She grew up wild and rebellious but,

THE DENVER POST—DELIVERED A

SUFFRAGETTES FROM
ENGLAND HERE TO
SEE WOMEN VOTE

(Figure 13) Americans did
not recognise any difference
between suffragists and
suffragettes, but the visit
of Ray and Ellie attracted
considerable press attention in
the Mid-West.

to the disapproval of her family and the astonishment of the local community, resolved to become a preacher. Through her own determination Anna acquired an education, the beginnings of a career as an itinerant preacher and the chance to study theology at Boston University. At every stage she faced a battle with male prejudices and power, and was often on the verge of starvation. She spent seven years as Methodist pastor of two churches in Cape Cod, during which she also studied and qualified as a doctor. Needing a new challenge, she resigned from her parishes and became an itinerant lecturer on suffrage and temperance, a way of life whose adventures, dangers and physical demands equalled those of her early years as a pioneer. Suffrage soon dominated, and for many years Susan B. Anthony, who died in 1906, and Anna Shaw were the leaders of NAWSA, Miss Shaw becoming President in 1904.

From the moment Ray and Ellie emerged from the train in Boone (Iowa), they found themselves 'in a new world – surrounded with friendly energetic and intensely funny people who took us by the arm, joked us, kissed us, sprang speeches upon us and generally behaved in an incredibly unexpected way'.[22] They plunged into suffrage activity. At her best, Anna Shaw was a speaker of genius and her young companions now found themselves thrown in at the deep end and expected to make impromptu speeches: it was excellent learning experience. Mary had earlier criticised Ray's speaking style (perhaps for being over-prepared) and Ray now learnt to think on her feet.

'Soon', she exulted, 'we shall be quite good extempore speakers! [...] I simply love the West and these Westerners'.[23]

Their next destination was Denver, 'a very pretty place' with rather ugly politics.[24] At a Republican political meeting Ray and Ellie 'sat and gasped at the horrible corruption and bribery of which the other side were accused. Horrible, sordid, third-rate, meezely [sic] meeting, speaking atrocious, sentiments worse'; but the Democratic political women were no better, seeming 'for the most part unpleasant, & [...] stupid'.[25] Both girls were attracted by the independent lifestyle of the young professional women they met ('doctors & lawyers & dentists [...] Quite uneducated, wild & western, but intelligent & nice & very friendly') who took having a vote as a matter of course but, disappointingly, 'don't really want to vote for anyone as all the politicians are so corrupt'.[26]

Election day was 3 November, and the two local newspapers were in competition to show the English suffragists what an election with women voting looked like. Ray and Ellie agreed to be shown round by both papers and were pleased with what they saw: 'polling-places not in public-houses any more, orderliness, no drunkenness, and general good sense'.[27] It appeared that, with women involved, elections were no longer violent and corruption had been reduced. Women voters turned out in large numbers and had clearly thought hard about their voting decisions.

Ray set down her approval in an article for the Denver *Daily News*:

The thing that struck me most forcibly was the way the women took their privilege of franchise as a matter of course. To us women who are struggling so hard on the right of suffrage, and who are willing to go to prison for our convictions, it seems marvellous that the Colorado women can take their voting for granted as much as they accept their right to go on a shopping trip or attend a musicale [sic]. The matter of fact way in which your women vote seems to me to answer all objections to suffrage, their orderliness and ease in casting their ballots show that it has become a part of their life. And it is evident that the ballot, in thus becoming a part of their lives, has

worked no detrimental revolution in the character of the women of
Colorado, nor taken one iota from their charm and womanliness.[28]

To her family she was rather more critical of the whole American
election process: 'the difference between parties is so largely one
of personalities, especially for offices such as sheriff, policeman,
judge, undertaker etc. [...]. It seems a queer kind of election to leave
to people who can't know much about the men – but they say it's
DEMOCRACY'.[29]

The sequence of speeches and train journeys continued through
Nebraska and Minnesota. The girls' efforts had pleased Miss Shaw,
who requested permission from Carey Thomas to take them with
her on a further tour around Indiana, Tennessee and Kentucky.
Carey telegraphed agreement, so instead of stopping in Chicago,
the party travelled through it to Indianapolis, and from there to
Memphis, Louisville, Richmond and Union City before returning
to Bryn Mawr.

The girls were by now much more self-confident about speaking
– when Anna Shaw arrived fifteen minutes late for a meeting in
Indianapolis Ray spoke in her place – but increasingly despondent
about the state of the suffrage cause in America. Earlier in their
travels Ray had lamented to Hannah that 'they are not awake enough
here: all the meetings are drawing-room ones, and consist of the
converted'.[30] Now they moved into areas where the converted were
few on the ground. Ray admitted that she 'hadn't the vaguest idea of
the difficulties of reformers until this trip' and was overwhelmed by
admiration for Anna Shaw's stamina and commitment.[31]

On their return to Bryn Mawr the girls were almost penniless – the
trip had eaten up their money – and determined to secure more
congenial subjects of study. To her delight Ray was moved to a
graduate seminary on Elizabethan non-dramatic literature. Soon
she was reading 'Theocritus with complete fascination', as well as *The
Faerie Queene*, and other pastorals and epics in English and Italian,
supplemented by 19th century American fiction and works on the

history of women's suffrage, especially biographies of the pioneers, as background for the novel she planned to write about the pioneers of the suffrage movement in America.[32]

By Christmas the social season was in full swing and the Berensons were making the most of it, impressing millionaires and multi-millionaires with their artistic credentials. Ray's experiences of American socialising left her incredulous as to why anyone ever went to social functions when they might avoid them, and convinced that 'people who decide to be fashionable all their lives must be very wretched'.[33] But 'a glimpse now & then is rather entertaining', she conceded, as when she visited the Widener family:

> It was a palace, furnished in such a way that one expected railings round the carpets & requests not to touch or sit upon the chairs. [...] The floors were covered with enormous bear skins, over the stuffed heads of which one continually fell, & the walls were hung with tapestries. The food was served on silver dishes, & was incredibly rich & various. The butlers were bewildering in number, size & importance, & the whole place incredibly magnificent.[34]

Nevertheless 'the people who owned it were wholly inadequate. The younger ones were vulgar & ostentatious (not blatantly, but by nature)'.[35] At the grand dinner party Ray predictably 'talked Suffrage to everyone who came near': 'They none of them approved & I could have bitten them all!'[36] Sitting next to the editor of an evening paper, she emerged with a commission to write an editorial.

At meetings with non-suffragists Ray was constantly asked to explain her convictions, which she found hard, confessing that:

> The reasons I pour forth from the platform are not my reasons for believing it – I am not a democrat, nor do I think W[omen's] S[uffrage] will bring many material changes: one or two slightly better things perhaps. Nor do I think that I shall be any better off: in fact, all I can find to say is that I am angry at not being able to vote if

I want to: and that I think the vote is a sort of peg onto which a lot of useful morals can be hung – so that the agitation is better than the having of the vote.[37]

By the time she was interviewed by a sympathetic female reporter from the *Philadelphia Evening Telegraph* in February 1909, Ray had clarified her position. What mattered most was 'the effect of the vote on the woman rather than the woman on the vote, for a while at least'.[38] Dismissing as the last refuge of men who did not think for themselves the proposition that men and women belonged to separate spheres, Ray argued that a woman should have the same freedom as a man 'to work at that which she finds to her taste; and there is no reason why she should always remain within a certain specified four walls to do it'.[39] Furthermore

to vote right, she must know; to know, she must read, study, observe; and all of this tends to develop character and make her a better woman, whether single or wife or mother; and the greater number of better citizens we have the greater benefit to the country.[40]

Ray and Ellie had undertaken to speak at various of the women's and mixed colleges on behalf of the College Equal Suffrage League, of which Carey was president. The meetings were of varied success, but the experience gave Ray a broader view of education in America, confirming many of her doubts: the students seemed bent on acquiring facts rather than learning to think. The heartfelt speeches of Ray and Ellie were treated like just another lecture: 'here was another subject to be learnt, another field of information to explore, and another lecturer from whom to hope for a few jokes'.[41]

In Boston Mary forced the girls to act as volunteer clerical assistants to Isabella Stewart Gardner ('rather a fiend').[42] More congenial were the friends of Berenson's sister Rachel and her husband Ralph Barton Perry, a Harvard philosopher. At one gathering, which included the philosopher William James, talk inevitably turned to suffrage, and a lively discussion followed to which James contributed some more or less impartial & very wise remarks', […] then suddenly burst out […]: "How you must despise us all": he said "you two, who come all burning & snapping with your cause – with the whole thing rushing through you like electricity – & you find us everywhere – dull, uninterested, unenthusiastic, superficial, scoffing & frivolous about it – just a great lump of unenlightened & commonplace humanity who won't take this serious thing seriously: I am going home to sign that petition just for your sake. I believe in it for my own – but I will do something just to let you know that your enthusiasm does not meet with no response".[43]

Ray 'could have kissed him for it'.[44]

The main purpose of their visit to Boston was an annual hearing before the Massachusetts Legislature on the subject of suffrage. The procedure was for large numbers of people to make short speeches and for many more to turn out in support. Ray and Ellie had been invited to take part. On 19 February Ray and Ellie supported Anna Shaw in giving speeches in the historic Faneuil Hall. The following day came the hearing before the Legislature in the Massachusetts State House, an imposing building approached by many tiers of wide steps, the ideal place for an outdoor meeting. For Ray, who spoke six times on the steps, it was a memorable day, even though the thronging crowds prevented her (though not Ellie) from getting in to speak before the committee herself; eventually she got in to hear Miss Shaw 'finally demolish the opposition'.[45]

Ellie sailed for home on 13 March and Ray, with her mother and stepfather, left New York on the *Mauretania* on 17 March. To pass the voyage, Mary introduced Ray to Tolstoy's *War and Peace*, which she read 'day and night', 'so carried away by it that she almost forgot her usual sea-sickness'.[46] For the rest of her life, Ray regarded Tolstoy as the supreme novelist and as the inspiration for her own writing.

Ray's American trip had allowed her to observe a suffrage movement from the outside, to hone the speaking skills which a suffrage activist needed, and to refine her ideas of what she wanted to do with her life. America would continue to be of the greatest interest to her – but America's past held more attraction than America's present. The America of 1909, and its democratic ideals, had proved a disillusionment, and Ray concluded that 'the more I see & hear of the workings of things' in America, 'the less am I inclined to believe that most people, men or women, are ready to exercise the "natural right" to govern themselves to their own advantage at this stage of civilization'.[47]

The English suffragists had learned much from the suffragettes. Gone were the genteel drawing-room meetings of earlier days; in their place came processions, outdoor campaigns and a closer involvement in grass roots political activity, in addition to high-level lobbying. On her return home, even without the high-profile drama of suffragette activity, Ray could find an unending sequence of suffragist roles demanding her time, energy, speaking skills and organisational activity.

The NUWSS hoped to repeat the success of its 1908 caravan tours round rural areas. Mary Fielden, a NUWSS organiser, joined forces with the Leeds suffragist Isabella Ford, on a further caravan trip in Yorkshire. For two women on their own it was a demanding task, especially as Isabella Ford was in her fifties and unused to manual labour. Ray joined them for a week in mid-June, on the section from Malton via the Hambleton Hills to York then on to Ripon. She was able to put her experience from the previous year to good use: Isabella Ford found her 'invaluable, a very excellent collector [of donations] (and cook)'.[48] Ray described 'thrilling adventures with swindlers and horse merchants and policemen' and near conversion to Socialism by the kind and charming young man who rescued them, but the main problems seemed to be getting horses to cope with the hilly terrain (some anti-suffragist horse-owners refused to provide them) and Ray's conclusion that 'it is quite impossible to make Yorkshire people laugh'.[49]

On her return to England Ray had achieved a long-held ambition: Mary bought her a second-hand 9hp de Dion car, in 'thoroughly good condition' and seating five people, costing £140 [£13,390] (with another £12 [£1,150] for spare parts).[50] Ray revelled in the freedom her car gave her, within weeks declaring 'My motor is invaluable – how does one get on without one?'[51] But motoring was rarely problem-free; one early excursion included 'three different kinds of break-down' and 'two hours in a ditch'.[52]

On a hectic campaign around the Birmingham area, with Ray committed to a heavy speaking programme, the car allowed a new approach to suffrage work: three meetings each evening, with the mornings spent finding the meeting-sites, chalking the pavements with advance information, and sending round the town crier to alert the residents. Ray had a constantly changing cast of helpers, including Ellie, Emilie Gardner and various local suffragists. Their commitment to suffrage activity was put to the test, as the rain poured relentlessly (her car was open-top, and the waterproofs did not always live up to their name). The area was fiercely anti-suffrage. At Tewkesbury the police were unusually uncooperative and the audience hostile. The girls

> had to stand in the middle of the road, with a huge & rough crowd all round us. The noise was horrid – the people pushed & yelled, & it was quite excitingly rough. When the speaking was over they got much rougher, & pulled the sign board off our motor, & our hats off our heads. They threw things at us & booed & hooted.[53]

Ray and her companions fled in the car and were relieved to find the next meeting, in Upton-on-Severn, far more orderly.

While her primary allegiance was to the NUWSS, Ray had been quite happy to march in WSPU processions and, in September 1909, to join her aunt Alys Russell on the picket of the House of Commons organised by the Women's Freedom League, a breakaway group from the WSPU. But the suffragettes' increasing recourse to violence split the suffrage movement. The NUWSS had already, in November 1908, affirmed its commitment to action within the law and moved to distance itself from the WSPU disturbances within and around the Houses of Parliament. Now the divergence widened.

On 29 June 1909, Ray was present at a riot in London which marked a turning point in suffragette militancy. Emmeline Pankhurst repeated an attempt made a year earlier to lead a deputation to the Prime Minister. Once again, she was refused entry to the Houses of Parliament. To ensure her arrest, she hit a policeman; over one hundred further arrests followed. That evening several suffragettes took independent action not sanctioned by the WSPU leadership and broke windows in Downing Street. Damage to property was a new form of suffrage activity, and the subsequent imprisonments led to yet another – the hunger strike.

Ray enjoyed the day's action, meeting many old friends and keeping out of trouble herself; but her contemporary at Newnham, Kitty Margesson, who looked 'like a kind of Burne-Jones angel' and at whose home in Worcestershire Ray was staying at the time, was one of those arrested and imprisoned with Mrs Pankhurst.[54] At the time Ray was impressed by the courage of the suffragettes and wished that 'they got more return for their sacrifices – for they do go through a lot'.[55] Later, unimpressed by the efficacy of the militants' tactics and wary of their emotional self-indulgence, she came to view the suffragettes as 'so repulsive as well as so fine!'[56]

An even more ambitious motor tour soon followed. Setting off on 17 July, Ray and Ellie drove to Leeds to collect Isabella Ford on their way to a four-day speaking tour in Cumberland organised by Catherine Marshall. Their problems started on the way from Ingleton to Whitehaven, where a decision to follow the coast road proved a disastrous mistake. Deep inlets and impassable hills forced long detours in driving rain and they missed their first meeting, arriving several hours late 'wet through, blown to bits & as dirty as coal heavers'.[57] The demanding run had been too much for the car and the next day saw various breakdowns; nevertheless the car was a useful advertisement, decorated with red and white ribbons and with a blackboard indicating the time and place of the next meeting hanging at the back.

The eleven meetings in Maryport, Workington and various parts of Whitehaven were deemed a great success, with large, interested and mainly sympathetic audiences of working men and women, not deterred by the heavy rain. Ray took a great liking to Isabella Ford, but her letters home make little mention of Catherine Marshall; in her account of the campaign, Catherine Marshall paid tribute to 'Miss Ford and Miss Costelloe, who can always be relied upon to delight any audience' but this sounds routine compared with the personal feeling with which she describes the effect of the car's late arrival : 'I hired a lorry and walked through the town, carrying the Keswick banner, a forlorn little procession of one, accompanied by a rabble of small boys and a shower of banana skins and other unpleasant but harmless missiles'.[58] Perhaps this trip, with all its transport difficulties, produced some mutual irritation between Ray and Catherine Marshall which fed into the later acrimony between them.

From Cumberland Ray drove to Scotland for a holiday with Emilie Gardner, joining their Newnham friend Peggy Colson, who was teaching at a school in St Andrews. Here Ray recorded a surprising decision. Her suffrage colleagues argued that 'the next few years are going to be the critical ones here – that if the next Government doesn't bring it in, it will be indefinitely postponed. [...] now is the time to make sacrifices & now the moment when every helper is needed'.[59] Recent meetings had been so good that the possibility of success seemed real, but Carey Thomas was again trying to persuade Ray to devote herself to a life of culture and literature, and not let suffrage activities distract her. Ray had been 'thinking violently' about Carey's advice and eventually resolved, despite feeling 'a horrible traitor', that 'I won't do any more Suffrage work, in England anyway, for a year'. [60]

As a New Girl, Ray was never likely to settle down to a life as an unmarried daughter at home; and in any case the home she had was in itself a temporary one, bound to disappear when her grandmother died. Nor was she in immediate search of a husband, even though her long-term aims included a family of her own. Her own income of £500 [£44,000] gave her enough to exist on without necessarily earning her own living, but some form of independent life was vital to her: suffrage work, paid or unpaid, and writing were the most obvious outlets for

(Figure 14) Court Place, Iffley, Ray's home from 1906 to 1911.

her talents and energy, and each met different needs in Ray. Suffrage work offered action, drama, joint effort with like-minded people, and the satisfaction of making a real contribution towards a worthwhile objective; writing allowed Ray the solitude she craved between bursts of activity, contact with great minds through their works, intellectual satisfaction and an outlet for her own creative urges.

In practice, Ray only partially stuck to her decision to suspend her suffrage involvement. Her suffrage work did continue, at a less intensive pace; in between she stayed quietly at Court Place reading extensively and working on her latest literary project. This was a biography of Frances Willard (1839–98), an American social reformer with particular interests in education, temperance and women's suffrage, who had been a friend of both Hannah Pearsall Smith and Anna Shaw.

These months at home were for Ray a moratorium, in which she attempted to prepare herself for an as yet unidentified calling: 'I know that there is something I have got to do, though I'm not sure what it is. I know that I am by no means ready to do it now – and that the more I read and think the more ready I shall become.'[61] To the despair of Hannah and Alys she refused to extend her social circle in the Oxford area, took little exercise, started smoking a pipe and was even more than usually careless of her appearance. She recognised that only a small circle of people mattered to her as individuals – her interest was in people en masse.

Despite Ray's loss of religious faith, relationships between people seemed to her far less important than 'something else – their relations with God, perhaps'.[62] 'Deny it as we may', she concluded, 'we've got inside us a something that cares for abstract things – generally right & wrong, or justice, or charity or, more rarely, art'.[63] Her basic belief was that 'it would be awful […] to have personal ambition, or personal happiness, as the only reason for life' since 'nothing matters but the conviction that there are things in themselves worth doing, and that one will be free to do them'.[64] Despite Ray's outward self-confidence, she was damning about her own character ('On top I am quite nice with several pleasant virtues. But underneath what horrible cowardice, laziness & selfishness!').[65] Finding who she should become and what she should do with her life was the next challenge.

Ray's attempts to combine reading, writing and suffrage work were not entirely successful. Reading Carlyle's writings tempted her away from work on Frances Willard, and suffrage demands were difficult to resist: 'when things don't go quite right it is almost impossible to refrain from taking part in the general muddle' even though 'suffrage work is awful – it takes so much effort & organization for so little result'.[66] As suffragette violence widened the split between the NUWSS and the WSPU ('They will certainly try to murder Asquith. Poor man!'), Ray approved of the NUWSS condemnation of suffragette violence and had long discussions with her 'wildly militant' friend Winnie Buckley, during which neither convinced the other.[67] Ray by now viewed the WSPU as 'emotional, unscrupulous, unwise and dangerous' while Winnie saw them as 'devoted, brave, statesmanlike and self respecting'.[68]

Public reactions to suffragette violence made life more difficult for law-abiding suffragists too. In Bermondsey, where the London Society for Women's Suffrage (LSWS) undertook suffrage propaganda during campaigning for the by-election on 28 October, Ray and Ellie were followed by a mob who threw dirt at them. Ray 'was hit on the "derrière" while chalking, by a rough boy, who was promptly put into the gutter by a passing workman', while 'Ellie was cursed by a man who drove her away from in front of his shop "Damn you & your Suffrage" he said – so she hastened away!'.[69]

The general election in January 1910 saw Ray back in the world of suffrage and politics, racing round all thirty-eight Town Halls in London in search of registration information and returning to the role of stump speaker 'from Hornsey Rise to the Docks'.[70] Ray managed to combine disapproval of political activity ('the pretences and lies are enormous. The more I see of politics the less do I believe in "principles"') with total commitment to ensuring that women had the right to take part in it ('whatever system we have, good or bad, women ought to have their fair share').[71] Her time soon became completely taken up with helping the LSWS collect signatures for a suffrage petition, for which each polling station was to have people 'with forms & pencils & expressive eyes'.[72] Inevitably there were not enough volunteers to go round, and the incompetence of many of those who were available aroused Ray's contempt. But she came to rely on the great abilities and commitment of the Secretary of the London Society, Pippa Strachey (Ellie's aunt), endorsing the universal opinion that she was 'a delightful person'.[73]

A typical day was hectic.

I get up at 9, dress and breakfast and read my letters and then go round to the office at 10. There I find a howling mob of people clamouring for speakers and wagonettes and leaflets and information., etc, etc. Out of this mob I have to sort workers for N. and S. Paddington, literature, posters and information, and trundle them all into my motor and go with them to the two committee rooms. There I have to listen patiently to the complaints of the local people about what happened the day before, pat everyone on the back, tell a lot of lies and bluff a lot and pretend I know everything, give minute instructions to the workers – to say, for example, that they must sharpen pencils before they ask people to sign petitions with them; and then I have to come flying back to the office. There from 12–1 I have to plan and arrange who is to go where, or rather to execute the orders of those who plan and arrange, and telephone to people to make plans for open-air meetings, etc.[74]

After lunch

I have to dash off to open a committee room in, say, Poplar. I have to see house agents, sign agreements, keep a watch on rates and taxes and extras, engage window-cleaners and charwomen and get the place in order.[75]

The shop they leased in Poplar was 'so filthy that it took 3 men 8 hours to get it clean. [...] The final result is delightful, and Poplar is a charming place, for the men are so friendly, but it was hard work getting settled.'[76] Ray had to

instal a worker who is to take charge, tell her all the things she has to do, supply her with posters and literature and local information about candidates and printers and bill posters and so on, and get some special leaflets printed, and a sign writer to make us a sign, etc, etc, etc'.[77]

After another meeting on a street corner Ray would rush back to the office.

By then it is generally 7.30, and I have dinner. Then I settle down and write letters, trying to get helpers for polling day. We have 500 polling places and want to get workers at each. There are also endless circulars to concoct, lists and plans to draw up, and accounts to do. All this goes on from 7.30 to 10. Then I rush off to some big meeting and get in for the tail of it in time to get signatures to the petition at the door and distribute hand bills. Then I come home and am in a hot bath by 11. It's hard work, but it's fun.[78]

As the election approached, working hours of 6 a.m. to midnight became normal. The January 1910 election produced a short-lived hung Parliament. Ray's efforts were rewarded when in March she and Ellie were elected onto the Executive of the NUWSS.

Having decided to make a further visit to the United States, Ray fitted in five weeks of relaxation in Florence first. The Berensons' purchase of I Tatti in 1907 had led to ambitious plans for expansion, but when Mary returned from America in the spring of 1909 she found that the work which should have been done in their absence had made little progress. She immediately replaced her Italian architect by Cecil Pinsent, who was to be assisted by her protégé Geoffrey Scott. Pinsent was a qualified, if inexperienced, architect and, although Scott had briefly been an architectural student, his illnesses and attempts to find other work initially meant that Pinsent worked effectively alone.

During the alterations, disaster followed disaster and Berenson, suffering from temporary eviction from his home, disquiet over Mary's obvious feelings for Geoffrey Scott, and his own obsession with a woman he had met in the US, Belle da Costa Greene, became more and more prone to rages, piling blame onto Mary for all that went wrong. Accounts of Mary's woes arrived at Iffley by every post but were not greeted with due seriousness by anyone, least of all Ray:

> Do send us a list of what is actually unfinished now. Our imaginations vary from I Tatti a heap of ruins to I Tatti spick & span with one little wave in one little zoccoli in front of which you & Uncle B. sit all day & weep, while Cecil & 40 workmen paint & repaint it.[79]

Now Ray could inspect for herself the remodelled I Tatti which was slowly emerging from the chaos.

Property ownership appeared to have had a serious impact on the Berensons' priorities, as Ray told Alys:

> Never have people fallen so fast and so far as Ma and Uncle B. from their high intellectual lives. The questions of whether the chairs

are to have castors and the curtains valances now take the places
of whether humanity can be sensitive to art or whether poetry and
music are definable.[80]

The Berensons were not yet rich, as they had taken on a major burden
of debt to buy I Tatti even before the expensive alterations, but Ray's
comment foreshadows the distaste she later felt for the worship of
luxury at I Tatti, where she felt increasingly ill at ease. She spent this
visit reading American history and literature, learning Italian, and
writing an article about the Women's Temperance Crusade, but more
importantly the trip gave her a chance to recoup her energies and
gather her strength for the challenges of a solo visit to America.

On 23 March Ray sailed for America once more, this time alone.
Her aim was to acquire material for her next novel and for her
biography of Frances Willard, but further visits to her American
relatives were unavoidable. Ray's first foray into research took her to
Chicago to see Forest Home, near Janesville, where Frances Willard
spent part of her childhood, and Rest Cottage in Evanston, her home
in later life. There Ray met Anna Adams Gordon, Frances Willard's
long-term secretary and close friend, and acquired important reading
material.

The National American Woman Suffrage Association (NAWSA)
was to hold its Annual Convention in Washington 14-19 April, with
Anna Shaw, its President, facing rebellion. Rather than fighting for
Federal action on female suffrage, NAWSA had opted to campaign in
individual states. In 1908 President Theodore Roosevelt had advised
the suffragists to 'get another State', but this desirable event was still
awaited.[81] Criticism of Anna Shaw's leadership was growing and
younger women, aware of the methods of British suffragettes, pressed
for more forceful – and better organised – campaigns. Ray enjoyed
her 'lively time' at the Convention, and succeeded in persuading her
American counterparts of the value of outdoor meetings, but Anna
Shaw's struggles there left the older woman 'terribly melancholy &
ill' for the exhausting tour on which the two of them were about to
embark.[82]

This time the speaking tour was through the Deep South, but there was none of the fun and entertainment which had marked Ray's earlier experiences, just heat, dirt, her companion's life-threatening exhaustion, and her own sense of failure at not being able to offer the emotional support Miss Shaw wanted. One of the worst days came in Birmingham, Alabama, where, having to wait four hours in the middle of a blazing hot day, Anna Shaw

> was siezed [sic] with an overwhelming sick headache & could hardly stagger up the street & had to lie in the fly ridden waiting room with ice on her forehead & her head in my lap: & she could hardly get into the train when at last it came – & then lay there half asleep & half in agony for 5 hours while the beastly jogging jolting smelling affair bumped along over the very dreariest imagineable [sic] hot plain. The carriage was full of dirty spitting chewing smelling farmers who shouted & tilted their hats & their heels [...]. The train stopped at every back door, & ran over 4 cows on the way.[83]

They reached their destination at 11 p.m. and had to leave at 6 a.m. the next morning for another, even longer, journey. Despite her suffering, Anna Shaw retained her eloquence as a speaker, so the gruelling travel continued, with Ray in constant fear that her companion would not survive.

Ray was glad to accept a more cheerful invitation to spend a week in Warm Springs, Virginia, at the home of a new acquaintance, Mary Johnston. Swimming each day in the naturally warm pools of bubbling mineral water which gave the spa its name, reading, exploring the beauties of the Virginia countryside, and indulging in hours of talk with her kindly hostess provided a restful contrast to the rigours of the weeks with Anna Shaw. Mary Johnston was a leading suffragist in Virginia, but her main fame was as a novelist. Her second novel, the historical romance *To Have and To Hold* (1900), had been a best-seller and allowed its author thereafter to support herself and her younger sisters by her writing, despite her frail health. Memories of the Confederate struggle against the North, in which her family had been deeply involved, had dominated her childhood, and in 1910 she was busy working on novels with a Civil War setting, *The Long Roll* (1911) and *Cease Firing* (1912). Meeting her gave Ray a valuable opportunity to talk to a practitioner of just that type of historical fiction she was hoping to produce herself and to explore the Southern point of view. Her previous sources of information had all been Northern, which gave her 'ideas [...] as lop-sided as a one-legged elephant'.[84]

A final round of visits and information-collecting followed before Ray sailed for home on 11 June. This was one crossing where she avoided sea-sickness because of the entertaining company. Carey Thomas and her companion Mary Garrett were on the same boat, and Ray was accompanied by Anna Shaw: a motor tour round England and Scotland in Ray's little car was to provide the complete rest she clearly needed.

Ray later wrote to Mary Johnston that she had had 'such a wonderful time with Miss Shaw', but her diary tells a different story.[85] Anna Shaw demanded loyalty above all and was becoming over-reliant on, and possessive of, Ray. Ray was anxious to catch up with suffrage developments in England, then at a critical stage, but 'the Rev. Anna wanted nothing but to get away from everyone & to hear no news & see no one & get no letters';[86] Ray wanted to see her family and friends, especially Ellie, but Anna Shaw had developed a hatred of Ellie. As Ray admitted, 'it was all very difficult & parts of it were very distressing'.[87]

Miss Shaw asked Ray to live, work and travel with her in the United States and became miserable and angry when she declined. Ray was never tempted to accept, being quite clear that: 'I can't do it. I hate the country & the people & the civilization too much. And I don't want to leave this country & these people & this civilization & all my interests here'.[88] Although the motor tour, during which they pottered slowly up the east coast, across Scotland, down the west coast through the Lake District and into Wales, was just the restful change Anna Shaw needed, the fear of an emotional confrontation preyed on Ray's mind. She retained great admiration and affection for the Rev. Anna, and felt guilty that, while intending to help her, she had unwittingly made her unhappy.

Once Anna Shaw sailed for America on 30 July, Ray was free to resume her normal life. The two years since she left Newnham had been so full of travel that she promised herself several months of tranquillity. She resigned from the Executive of the NUWSS to which she had so recently been elected and resolved to spend the winter at Court Place working on her biography of Frances Willard. At first this went well and, despite the difficulty Ray found in grasping Miss Willard's religious convictions, the first chapters were written. But Ray always found it hard to stick to one task to the exclusion of all others ('I do wish I didn't want to do so many things at once!').[89]

Ray had 'long cherished a desire to be an electrical engineer' and decided not to wait until her hoped-for move to London before tackling engineering.[90] She obtained the permission of Professor Charles Frewen Jenkin, Oxford's first Professor of Engineering Science, to attend lectures and laboratory sessions, and in October 1910 started driving into Oxford each morning to do so. Unconcerned at being the only female in a class of men, Ray remained fascinated by the work and derived great satisfaction from it, even though she acknowledged that she did not expect to do it well; it was her own pleasure rather than any non-existent 'Purposes & Ambitions' which kept her engrossed.[91] Miss Willard was relegated to the afternoons.

The general election in December 1910 provided a further diversion, as Herbert Jacobs, who had founded the Men's League for Women's Suffrage in 1907, was standing as a Woman's Suffrage Liberal candidate in the constituency of East St Pancras, where Frank Costelloe had twice been a candidate. Ray responded to the appeal for helpers. It was 'Hell', she reported to her family, 'every meeting was howled down or sung down' and 'the poor candidate [was] nearly frightened out of his wits', but all to no avail: Mr Jacobs polled only 22 votes.[92]

Although Ray relished the hours of solitude in her room at Court Place and admitted that 'seeing people makes me want to be alone more than ever', her social contacts enlarged significantly during these months.[93] Her growing friendship with Virginia Stephen (a 'literary friend' such as Carey Thomas had recommended to her) brought Ray into contact with the whole Bloomsbury circle, 'a queer self absorbed fantastic set of people' in Ray's view.[94] A visit to a Friday Club meeting left Ray with little admiration for its intellectual content, but she derived her usual enjoyment from detached observation, concluding that 'they don't seem to do very much, these people, but they talk with surprising frankness. One of their greatest joys seems to be to tear their friends limb from limb'.[95] Ray, too, was quite capable of savage dissection of people she met, but she never came to share the Bloomsbury elevation of personal relationships above all else. Her rejection of 'affection & interest for other people' as 'the real meaning of living' set her apart from the Bloomsbury Group, and she remained immune to some of its most cherished values.[96]

By the end of 1910 Ray had settled contently into a pattern of life in which her various needs and activities appeared to be in balance. Her diary reflects 'a delightfully settled quiet feeling, as if there was plenty of time before me'.[97] There was no indication that the next year would turn her life upside down.

PART THREE

Wife, Mother, Feminist

CHAPTER SIX

Ending and Beginning 1911

It would be so exciting to be in love![1]

In November 1909 Ray Costelloe dreamt of 'a perfectly charming young man with whom I fell in love at first sight. He was an explorer just returned from India. I woke up to think to myself "what an odd dream", and fell asleep to be proposed to by him and accept him'.[2] The dream is easily explained. When Ray first met members of the Strachey family, three of the five sons were married, while the two youngest, Lytton and James, 'ran away with all their legs the moment they espied a female'.[3] The third son, Oliver, was in India, working for the East India Railway. In October 1908 he announced that he was to divorce his unfaithful wife. The divorce, in March 1909, made Oliver a free man again.

Ray had met various members of the Strachey family before her first trip to America. In spring 1909, a visit to the Strachey household in Belsize Park Gardens, Hampstead, where she observed their idiosyncratic lifestyle for the first time, rendered her 'so full of enthusiasm for the Strachey way of living' that her mother accused her of preferring it to her own family's ways.[4] Ray acknowledged this:

there's no polite pretence about it. When I arrived Lady Strachey was sitting by the fire warming her stockinged feet and reading the latest novel by Stevenson. She hardly looked up from her book to greet me, though I had been away such a long time. She just said 'Well Ray, there you are', and went back to her reading. It was the same when the boys, Lytton and James Strachey, came in to dinner. They scarcely noticed me, but went on talking of their own affairs, while Ellie and I talked of ours and Lady Strachey propped her book against a tumbler and went on reading.[5]

For people to do exactly as they wanted put Ray at her ease, whereas her own family were 'so polite [she] couldn't be sure they really meant it'.[6] 'With the Stracheys you know they want to listen to you if they encourage you to talk'.[7] Within a year Ray, sharing the Stracheys' literary and political interests, was clear that she wanted to marry into this family.

Ray's suffrage work brought her into frequent contact with Pippa and she became fond of Lady Strachey. In the spring of 1911 the Strachey family rented Bagley Wood, Bertrand and Alys Russell's house near Oxford. There was frequent contact between Court Place and Bagley Wood, and it was probably in one of these houses that, in late February or early March 1911, Ray first encountered the elusive – and newly eligible – Oliver.

Oliver was the sixth of the ten surviving children of Sir Richard and Lady Strachey. When Oliver was born in November 1874, his father, Sir Richard Strachey, was close to retirement from his career in the Indian Army and the family had settled in Clapham. Sir Richard went back to India in 1877, and the next year his wife and older children joined him; until their parents returned in 1880, the younger Strachey children lived with their much-loved maternal aunt, Elinor Colville. In 1884 the family moved to 69 Lancaster Gate, which was to remain their home for over twenty years until reduced income required a move to a smaller house in Belsize Park Gardens, Hampstead.

Oliver was educated at Summerfield preparatory school in Oxford, then at Eton, which he loathed.[8] A music-mad intellectual snob who hated games might well find himself a misfit in any public school, but it appears to have been an incident when Oliver complained about a sexual approach from another boy, who was expelled as a result, which resulted in Oliver being 'hated, despised and ill-treated as a sneak'.[9] His university career at Balliol College, Oxford, lasted only for Hilary Term 1893, apparently because a love-letter from another undergraduate was found in the pocket of his dressing-gown. His family – and Oliver himself – later derived great amusement from the idea that strongly heterosexual Oliver had ever been thought to be involved with another man. Oliver was good-looking, charming and highly intelligent, but lazy, and his disinclination to apply himself to work was an increasing worry to his parents. The problem was deferred by sending him round the world on a tramp steamer for nine months. Oliver later claimed that it had worked wonders for him, but for his parents it introduced a further problem: Oliver's susceptibility to women.

Oliver announced that he wanted to go to Vienna to study music in hope of a career performing on and teaching the piano. His parents eventually bowed to the inevitable, and sent him to Vienna, where he spent 1897. But although Oliver seems to have enjoyed his time there – almost at once falling for an Australian girl – he was forced to accept that his musical abilities were not sufficient to support a professional career. So May 1898 saw Oliver arrive in India to take up a lowly post in the East India Railway, arranged for him by his father, the Railway's Chairman.

Oliver spent most of the next thirteen years in the service of the East India Railway, in various locations. Even though his position had been obtained by nepotism, it was no sinecure. Oliver's responsibilities for traffic management required frequent journeys throughout his area of responsibility. He had to deal with timetables, rates of carriage, recalcitrant workers (who staged a major strike), technical problems, natural disasters (including an elephant sitting on the line), demands for special treatment by self-appointed VIPs (among them his sister Pippa) and a host of miscellaneous tasks. On one occasion he had to conduct the burial service for a man who had died of cholera, his dislike of religion reinforced by the local clergyman's refusal to visit the dying man because he was a Roman Catholic.

Socially, Oliver was a fish out of water in India. Although he gradually came to admire those without literary or musical sensibilities who had skills he lacked ('I now class your big engineer with your big artist'), he always missed European culture and intellectual conversation, and had no time for the social niceties of Anglo-Indian life ('kowtowing to nobodies').[10] Although a social success, he was almost certainly lonely: whisky offered a respite.

Oliver's first marriage may well have been prompted as much by the appeal of joining a large, affectionate family outside the narrow Anglo-Indian community as by the evident charms of the girl herself. Slim, blue-eyed Ruby Mayer was the daughter of an English mother and a Swiss-German father, a leading builder in Allahabad, Oliver's first posting. The Anglo-Indian community disapproved of Oliver's growing acquaintance with Ruby and her family and he was posted elsewhere in an attempt to break the relationship. After over a year of separation during which they met only three times, Oliver and Ruby nevertheless became engaged in March 1900. Within weeks she left to spend the summer in Europe, apparently meeting the Strachey family while she was there. Ruby returned to India in November and was already pregnant when she and Oliver married on 21 January 1901. Their daughter, Julia, was born on 14 August 1901 in Allahabad.

Although Julia later described an idyllic childhood as the adored object of her parents' constant attention, the reality was considerably more complex. Oliver was frustrated by the lack of progress in his career and there were constant money worries. The family was often separated. Oliver had to spend days at a time travelling the lines; Ruby habitually took Julia up into the hills for several months to escape the intense heat of summer, and paid long visits to her mother and married sisters. In the autumn of 1903 Oliver returned to England, hoping to transfer his skills to an English railway company; Ruby and Julia spent the summers of 1904 and 1905 with him, living in York and visiting relatives. But career prospects in England were even more dispiriting than in India, so the whole family returned there in late 1905.

Both Oliver and Ruby demanded constant attention and in its absence diverted their attention elsewhere. Oliver, who displayed a lifelong need for adoring female company, was probably the first to stray, perhaps during Ruby's summer absence in 1902. Ruby's affair during the summer of 1906 had more serious consequences, as it left her pregnant. Julia had reached school age and, like most children of Anglo-Indian families, was sent home to absorb English culture and education. Ruby travelled with her, her pregnancy concealed from Oliver, intending to give birth secretly in Rome. While there, she encountered a member of the Strachey family and was persuaded to confess to Oliver. Never a jealous man, Oliver agreed to accept the new baby as his own: the rest of the Strachey family were not to know. Julia was sent ahead to England soon after the birth in January 1907, while Ruby and her son followed later.

Oliver hoped that his wife would stay in England and provide a home for Julia. Ruby's letters suggest that her daughter was of less interest to her now that she had the son she had always wanted. She accepted an offer from Oliver's oldest sister, Elinor Rendel, to provide a home for Julia, and in October 1907, claiming she disliked England, she and her son joined her mother and sister on their return to India. Oliver sought reassurance from his mother about the arrangements being made for Julia, adding 'it is terrible to think of her being left behind there, but a great comfort that you will be looking after her. How awful for the poor wretches who have to leave their children with strangers'.[11]

On Ruby's arrival back in India in late 1907, there followed a painful few months during which she and Oliver lived as virtual strangers in the same house. He was willing to give their marriage another try but was possibly involved with another woman and probably drinking too much. Ruby moved out in early 1908, went up into the Lahore hills and found a new lover, James de Graaff Hunter, by whom she soon became pregnant. He agreed to take on Ruby's son. In the autumn of 1908 Ruby wrote to Oliver asking for a divorce so that she could marry Hunter. Her second son was born in January 1909, and Oliver was granted a divorce in March.[12]

Oliver was granted legal custody of Julia but the divorce decree makes no mention of access, or lack of it, by Ruby. Before the divorce, Ruby had promised the Strachey family to cut off all contact with Julia, though Lady Strachey among others continued to give her regular news of Julia's progress. The reason for this arrangement is not clear, but the tone of the correspondence suggests agreement that a clean break would be in Julia's best interests. By then Julia had been living with the Rendel family for several years, and it may have been argued that cessation of contact with her mother would help her to adjust to life in London. Oliver was clearly fond of his daughter. On her departure from India he had complained 'That particular Julia is gone for ever – Depressing'.[13] His letters display concern for Julia's plight and a surprising amount of consideration for Ruby and her sons, while Ruby's letters dwell mainly on her own sense of loss and rarely on Julia's well-being. As he could not obtain leave sooner, it was not until 1911 that Oliver was able to return to England to be reunited with his daughter.

Julia later wrote a powerful and moving account of the culture shock and sense of abandonment she suffered in her exile from India and her parents, making it clear that she blamed the mother she had adored, not the Stracheys, for her abandonment.[14] She 'always thought of my Strachey Uncles and Aunts as very nice people', while her close friend Frances Marshall (later Frances Partridge), whose sister married Elinor Rendel's eldest son, confirmed that 'the whole family were touched and charmed by their pretty little cousin, whose desolation and harrowing nightly sobs they tried impotently to assuage'.[15] Julia 'referred to her own rejection by Ruby as a shattering blow from which she never recovered', Frances recalled.[16] Ruby later made various lurid accusations against Oliver, which Julia was reluctant to accept wholesale: her mother's accounts of events were 'always graphic and fabulous'.[17] Frances Marshall confirmed that Oliver, whom she later came to know well, though probably unfaithful, was unlikely to have behaved cruelly towards his wife.[18]

In the early weeks of 1911, while Oliver was making his way back to England for his long-awaited leave, Ray was busy with her usual mixture of engineering classes, suffrage work, visits to and from friends, the writing of a biography and a novel, and plans for continuing her engineering studies in London the following winter. On a shopping trip to London with Mary in February, Ray yielded to an impulse to have her hair cut short, at that time a radical decision. She was also full of plans for the future. Determined to pursue her engineering studies further, Ray had been advised to continue them at the Central Technical College in London in the autumn; the Professor was enthusiastic about taking on a female student, so all Ray needed to do was to pass the entrance examinations. The family plan was that she should share a flat in London with Karin, who was soon to leave Cambridge, although Ray had doubts about whether her resolve to study was compatible with Karin's taste for an active social life. Before then, she intended to go to Stockholm in June for the congress of the International Woman Suffrage Alliance and had promised afterwards to take Anna Shaw on a motor tour round Cornwall and Devon.

Ray and Karin spent some of their Easter vacation with the Russells at Vann Bridge Cottage in Fernhurst, arriving on 25 March. Bertrand Russell was tutoring Karin in philosophy in preparation for her final examinations that summer, and Ray intended to work on her biography of Frances Willard. Her writing was not helped by the philosophical discussion group with which their visit started; Russell and Karin were joined by the Cambridge philosopher G. E. Moore and by the Costelloe girls' new acquaintance Oliver Strachey, who took a keen interest in philosophy and had already corresponded with Moore.

The effective ending of the Russells' marriage in 1902, which had reduced Alys to years of misery, had been kept secret. But on 19 March 1911 Bertrand Russell and Ottoline Morrell recognised their mutual passion; now Russell wanted a separation from Alys. He broke the news to her on 27 March, while the cottage was full of visitors. Russell found the house-party 'horrible': Alys got on his nerves before his announcement and, he unsympathetically remarked, displayed 'the pain of a wounded animal' after it.[19] Karin he admired for her excellent brain and liked (despite her lack of 'gracefulness').[20] But Russell had little enthusiasm for Ray, regarding her as 'exactly like Alys – kind, hardworking, insincere and treacherous.'[21] Ray certainly resembled Alys in her organisational efficiency and care for others, and, like Alys, tried to conceal any emotional suffering; but 'treacherous' is an extraordinary word to apply to two women notable for their loyalty. Perhaps Russell was aware of being watched and judged by his observant niece.

Ray let the philosophical talk swirl about her while she worked at her biography, listening with one ear to 'Moore & Strachey [...] discussing consciousness' while Karin and Russell were 'pounding away at Hegel or Leibnitz'.[22] The evening before the party broke up, Oliver, Karin and Ray had a cheerful midnight feast of scrambled eggs, tea and toast. Karin's description of the 'perfect trio' she and Ray had formed with Oliver and the gloom his departure plunged them into shows that both sisters had taken a great liking to him.[23] The girls remained with the Russells over the following weekend before Ray left to join her new friend Virginia Stephen at her cottage near Lewes.

Ray spent three days with Virginia, and that expert dissector of inner lives provided her sister Vanessa Bell with the clearest picture we have of Ray's emotional state then: 'Ray told me that she is really very susceptible to men, though no man has been in love with her. She always stakes out the ground, as she calls it, with a new man; and considers the possibilities.'[24] As for Oliver 'she said "I can quite imagine falling in love with him". I said "I suppose you mean you *are* in love with him". She said "No: I only see that I might be – but don't want to be."'[25] (A few days later, Ray wrote that 'she'd felt much the same for 4 or 5 other men'.)[26] Virginia continued questioning her: 'I said "Is he in love with you?" She said "Oh no – not a bit. But he was very friendly." This morning however, she had a letter from him asking her to go over some railway works. This evidently pleased her very much.'[27] Virginia's verdict on Ray was 'a good satisfactory creature, as downright as a poker, and very queer in the tremors of imagined love. But perhaps one would find her a little heavy?'[28]

Oliver, 'in a very susceptible state of mind', had shown interest in both Virginia and Vanessa.[29] Virginia now suspected that Ray had caught his attention.

Ray and Ellie Rendel spent Easter in lodgings at Corfe Castle, Dorset, where Ray planned to revise her biography of Frances Willard. Barely had they arrived when Ellie developed problems with her eyes and was advised to rest them completely until new glasses could be obtained. For a few days she stayed in bed during the morning while Ray worked, then, with her eyes closed, was led around by Ray in the afternoon. When Ellie's eyesight improved, she and a newly-arrived friend explored the countryside on bicycles while Ray stayed behind to write. The glorious weather tempted her to work in the hill-top ruins of Corfe Castle itself, a splendid vantage point for observing that Lytton Strachey and Henry Lamb had arrived.

The following day James Strachey called on the girls in search of a thermometer, as Lytton had a temperature. By 14 April (Good Friday) Ellie, with new spectacles, was back to normal, but Lytton remained ill. On Easter Saturday James came to announce (wrongly) that Lytton did not have mumps. He was followed by the 'disagreeable' Henry Lamb, to whom Ray had taken a great dislike on previous meetings.[30] Finally, 'a delightful change': the quite unexpected appearance of Oliver, who had just arrived to replace James as Lytton's nurse.[31]

Oliver stayed in Corfe Castle with Lytton for several weeks, so it is likely that he and Ray met frequently before her departure on Thursday 20 April. (Two decades later, Oliver recalled that Easter in Corfe as one of the great times of his life.)[32] By 24 April they were clearly on close terms and at work setting out the ground rules for correspondence. The five 'Articles' put forward by Oliver included 'complete liberty of subject matter' and 'dwelling on what happens to interest at the moment', to which Ray added 'Spelling not to be noticed (for that's one of the very few things I can't do)' and 'Inconsistencies to be freely displayed'.[33] The correspondence was a deliberate step towards mutual understanding. Ray's first letter concluded: 'I agree with you – I think we should very easily get intimate. We might say shall instead of should, I think.'[34]

Writing to Oliver was one of the few excitements of life back home at Court Place, where Ray's former habit of gazing into the fire instead of applying herself to work threatened to overwhelm her again. The revision of her book proved demanding and she immersed herself in the Bible in an attempt to capture her subject's mode of thought. Lunch and sailing on the river with her engineering lecturer David Pye 'didn't constitute an excitement', despite the hopes of Ray's family that her acquaintance with the young academic might develop into a romance.[35]

The peaceful life at Court Place came to an end on 26 April, when Hannah suffered an attack of illness, probably a slight stroke. She could hardly move, slept most of the day and agreed to have a night nurse. Ray spelled out her fears about the suspected stroke to Oliver: 'She herself is longing to die, & would be only too glad if it were a severe one. But we can't any of us be unselfish enough to want her to. She has been so completely the centre of the universe.'[36] Despite a reassuring medical diagnosis, Ray was deeply worried: 'It will be awful when she is dead: & of course she can't live much longer. I don't know what will become of us all.'[37] To add to the general depression, Alys Russell, who was staying there, was having a breakdown caused by Russell's behaviour, crying when alone but not revealing the cause.

Hannah's condition deteriorated and she died on 1 May aged seventy-nine. Mary Berenson, summoned from Italy by telegram, arrived too late. On 5 May, after the cremation, Ray wrote to Oliver about how much her grandmother had meant to her:

There is nothing to be unhappy over for her sake, for it could not have been more exactly what she had always wanted. But for me it is dreadful. You see, I have lived with her since I was 12, and had a letter from her every day I've been away. She was always in the same place, always interested and always approving. She was always on my side, no matter how foolish a side it might be, and everything that happened to me had its understanding echo with her. She never made a claim of any sort, either for attention or affection, – & we all knew that what she really wanted was for each of us to please ourselves in every way. And all this was quite unfailing – never once, even in the smallest thing was she unlike all this.[38]

Her grandmother's death was 'like losing the one safe sure thing – far worse than coming to an end of a belief in God'.[39] She would miss Hannah's comments on events – 'always so entertaining, as well as wise & sympathetic' – and her 'tremendously good company'.[40] Hannah's death appears to have been decisive in accelerating Ray's growing intimacy with Oliver.

The family gathering at Court Place was bleak. Mary and Alys were both struggling with their own marital problems as well as mourning their mother. Mary nevertheless came to recognise that Ray had developed 'a very strong and sweet and reasonable character' and that the whole family relied on her and had 'a sense of restfulness and trust and wisdom from her'.[41] To Oliver, now sharing rooms with Lytton in Cambridge, Ray complained of 'long endless afternoons of talk when there is nothing to be said'.[42] But one thing was said: by 8 May Ray had confided to her mother that marriage to Oliver was a possibility.

The new term of engineering classes ('absolutely thrilling') offered some respite from family pressures, but Ray's suggestion of a weekend in Cambridge, ostensibly for Mary to meet Oliver, may well have emerged in part from an urge to escape the gloom at Court Place and to rouse her mother out of her depression.[43] Ray had earlier forecast that they would be a 'lost & scattered family' when Hannah died, but at this time they were oppressively close.[44] Cambridge would be a cheerful contrast. Oliver was clearly enjoying himself there (and indulging in a mild flirtation with Karin, who had returned there for her imminent Tripos examinations and whose verdict on Oliver was that he fully understood 'the fine art of not being very serious').[45]

Ray drove Mary to Cambridge on Friday 12 May. The next day Oliver joined them for lunch at the Blue Boar, followed by boating on the river. At Mary's invitation he returned to Iffley with them on the Sunday, prompting in Mary speculation as to his exact intentions.

Neither she nor Karin was certain of Oliver's feelings: he might be too
bemused to choose from among the abundance of nice English girls.
But 'probably Ray, with her direct methods, may bring him down with
her little arrow. Her behaviour is "simple as snow-flakes" […] just a
calm assumption that he cares'.[46] To Mary's despair, Ray continued to
refuse to pay attention to her personal appearance: not only was she
reluctant to dress well, 'her face is spotted like the pard and she *won't*
brush her hair'.[47] If Oliver could stand her appearance now, he was
well and truly hooked, Mary surmised. But although Ray and Oliver
were much together over the next two days, taking walks and boating
on the Thames, he took no action.

Ray took matters into her own hands. Mary's recollection of the
events of 16 May was romantic:

> I had gone to bed one evening before they got in from their
> moonlight walk, and I was peacefully going to sleep when Ray
> cautiously opened my door and looked in, a candle lighting her face,
> which looked particularly lovely when I became awake enough to
> see it. "What is it, Ray?" I asked. "Mother, I have done the deed", she
> replied. "What deed?" I stupidly asked. "Oh, Mother," she said, "I
> proposed to Oliver and he has accepted me."
>
> Having decided that Oliver wanted to propose but was put off by
> practical considerations – his lack of money or career prospects, his
> divorce and daughter – she had raised the subject with him. ' "What
> had I better do, mother?" Ray asked, "I really love him;" "Well,
> Ray, then marry him," I said, "and trust to luck for making enough
> between you to live on." '[48]

Ray's version of the event typically debunked unrealistic romanticism
and downplayed her real emotional involvement: 'We were happily
situated between the sewage station & the lunatic asylum at Littlemore,
& the place was so romantic that it couldn't be avoided.'[49]

The Strachey family were taken aback at the speed of events but
approved of Oliver's choice of bride. 'We love and admire Ray already',
Pippa wrote to Alys.[50] (Lady Strachey assured friends that Costelloe

was an Irish, not a Jewish, name.) Karin was delighted at the prospect of having Oliver as a brother-in-law, thinking him 'almost perfect'.[51] Alys soon succumbed to his charms: 'I like Oliver more and more; he is extraordinarily unprejudiced and young in his outlook, and very, very, tender and kind. I am sure he will make a good husband. Ray seems more and more in love.'[52]

Mary's response seems to have been more uncertain. Before her return to Italy, Mary had been, according to Oliver, 'too sweet for words – in fact she has behaved most improperly over it!'[53] More mature reflection, perhaps influenced by the difficulties she was suffering with her own husband, seems to have provoked a less favourable reaction. By 30 May Oliver found himself writing to allay her fears:

> I am afraid you have been seized with misgivings; [...] I must admit that in a way I have the same terrors. I know perfectly well that I am not up to Ray's mark really; she's too good for the likes of me [...]. She is so grandly simple and big, and yet so subtle and fine as anything. [...] I'm afraid of her finding me out – and not being able to stand it. But then again I really think she sees through me pretty well now [...]. She won't I hope expect impossibilities. Your fear seems to be that I shall get bored with her; I can only say I don't believe I ever could.[54]

They were, he explained, trying to be completely honest with each other. Affection had preceded the lust they now felt, giving their relationship a far securer foundation than his first marriage:

> Ray is so made that she goes quite straight and true to the right thing; and I have learnt by experience a lesson in the same direction. I have known, you see, a marriage on wrong foundations, known it from the inside; and I'm not for another dose of it.[55]

Their circle of friends and acquaintances largely agreed with the 'sedate' David Pye in considering the rapid engagement 'astonishingly

head over heels behaviour'.[56] Ray herself was intensely happy,
though her usual calmness and self-control never deserted her. It
all felt so completely right and natural to her that the conventional
expectations of others that she should behave differently – even
abandon her beloved engineering – seemed ridiculous. Fortunately
Oliver agreed. Ray returned to her engineering classes, her thoughts
elsewhere:

> Every now and then [the world] turns bright rose coloured, & then
> it stands on its head & shines, & turns right over & glows and then
> comes back with a rush to its quietest state of absolute contentment.
> All this rather seriously interferes with the valency & specific heat
> of elements.[57]

Her own liberating desire to tell Oliver everything, in total contrast to
the emotional reticence she maintained within her family, was a key
part of this happiness.

To Grace Worthington in New York Ray freely acknowledged
both the drawbacks of her choice and her total commitment:

> he is most ineligible, thirty-six years old, with no money, a daughter
> of nine, and work in India; but he is so absolutely charming that if
> he were one-hundred-and thirty-six, with a daughter of ninety and
> work in Mars, it would make no difference. He has the right views –
> not only views, but feelings that are right, and we are going to make
> a success of our marriage.[58]

'We are both in love right up to our noses', she explained, 'plunged
in almost out of our depths.'[59] Ray might seem calm but those who
knew her well could see how swept away she was. Karin reported
to their mother that Ray was 'sweeter than ever now that she is in
love: not very shy – silent with large happy eyes. […] She did not
tell me much, except that she could not believe anyone had ever felt
that way before. I think she is in very deep'.[60] She was. Her letters to
Oliver radiate adoration of him and her unswerving conviction of

their future happiness together ('we've started off for heaven by way of a lunatic asylum, and it seems to be a very short road').[61] Elizabeth Barrett Browning's sonnet 'How do I love thee?', which she quoted in full in one letter, spoke for Ray too.

The main fly in the ointment was the reaction of Ellie Rendel. An undated letter (probably from 1909) makes clear the intensity of her devotion to Ray: 'It does make all the difference to me between Heaven and Hell to be with you. [...] I am quite sure that unless you marry, I love you too much ever to marry.'[62] The announcement of Ray's engagement led to emotional arguments and painful letters from Ellie which Ray found deeply worrying. Oliver was briskly dismissive ('I'm afraid if you decided to marry Ellie and live with her instead of me, I should feel a good deal upset').[63] Within days Ray, with the support of Pippa and a sympathetic doctor, had bullied a reluctant Ellie into a rest cure in the country.

Neither letters from Mary describing her own marital disharmony nor Ray's discovery of the cause of Alys Russell's misery seem to have dented Ray's confident predictions of a happy marriage. Alys's position was 'incredibly bad', Ray admitted, and marriage 'a terribly risky affair to embark upon'; she could not imagine how her aunt had lived for the previous nine years.[64] But Ray's sympathy for Alys did not prevent her from pulling the wool firmly over her eyes. The complicated sequence of official meetings dragging her and Oliver to London and then Cambridge which Ray described to Alys concealed other arrangements, set in place soon after her engagement. At 1 p.m. on 31 May 1911, Ray Costelloe married Oliver Strachey in Cambridge Register Office, with Lytton and Karin as witnesses.

Ellie Rendel and James Strachey had known about the wedding too, but apparently no-one else. And so it remained for some days. Ray and Oliver returned to Court Place in the guise of an engaged couple, and Ray wrote obfuscatory letters to her mother in the hope that the revelation could be deferred until she and Oliver had departed on a trip to Scotland in July. However a snooping servant discovered her wedding ring hidden in a drawer, so on 9 June Ray broke the news to her mother, without any apparent remorse.

No doubt a chaste engagement lasting months would not have been to Oliver's taste nor perhaps Ray's either. Ray would certainly have abhorred all the fuss which a conventional wedding would have involved, particularly her mother's attempts to turn her into a well-dressed bride. But there may have been other forces at work too. Ray was dreading having to fulfil her commitment to take Anna Shaw on a motor tour of Devon and Cornwall, and facing the all too likely repeat of Ellie's reaction. Marriage gave her an excuse to back out. 'I believe it was wrong of me not to take another motor trip with her', Ray later admitted to Carey Thomas, 'but the truth was that I simply could not face it'.[65] In the event, Anna Shaw was indeed angry, greatly disappointed and 'full of the gloomiest anticipations', refusing to believe 'that it was anything but the deepest tragedy that had befallen [Ray]'.[66] They continued to keep in touch but their friendship was never the same again.

Both families were horrified by the haste and secrecy of the wedding. There were tart comments about *égoïsme à deux*. But no serious harm seems to have been done and everyone's attention was in any case pleasantly distracted by the news of Karin's brilliant achievement in her Cambridge Tripos (a First Class result and the first Distinction in Philosophy ever awarded by the University to a woman). So Ray was able to concentrate on her new roles as wife and stepmother.

CHAPTER SEVEN
Mrs Strachey: 1911–1914

It's all quite incredible for I don't feel at all "grown-up".[1]

'I find it very astonishing to travel with a man', the new Mrs Strachey, on a belated honeymoon in Copenhagen, admitted to her family, 'we have been behaving most childishly'.[2] The rapid transition from chaperoned young lady to wife, stepmother and (soon) expectant mother was challenging, and growing into new roles not an easy process.

Oliver needed to return to India to resign his job and wind up his affairs there. En route the couple stayed at I Tatti, living in the nearby villino, an idyllic refuge from the luxury of the main house and the ailments afflicting its owners. While Ray was at I Tatti, or very soon after, she became pregnant. On 18 October Ray, Oliver and Karin set sail from Marseilles on the *SS Polynesia* for the calm, uneventful and increasingly hot two week voyage to Bombay. To Ray its main merit was the opportunity to work on her novel. Karin pursued her usual hectic social life and Oliver played bridge, but Ray found her fellow passengers unappealing and kept away from them as far as possible. From Bombay they travelled by train to Oliver's new posting in Dinapore, a garrison town where the East India Railway had a workshop, some 150 miles north-west of Calcutta. There the immediate problem was finding accommodation, engaging servants and retrieving Oliver's stored belongings. Karin followed her own schedule, spending much of the visit in Calcutta and Burma.

Ray did not take to India. She was ill for most of the two months they spent in Dinapore, physically wretched from morning sickness, and suffering from bouts of despair then an exhausting liver attack. Pregnancy heightened her sense of smell, a particular problem in India. After a brief respite, during which she and Oliver went to Calcutta to visit his brother Ralph, and Ray observed Oliver's work at first hand, she succumbed to a chill in early December. The nurse who was called in restricted her to little more than hot milk and rusks for ten days, a frustrated invalid who remained alarmingly weak for some time.

In India Ray came to know no-one as an individual. She regarded the English community as 'first class bores & horrors', and made no attempt to overcome her instinctive (and at the time not unusual) racism: the 'hordes of natives' were 'not in the least like humans'.[3] India was a 'detestable country [...] fully as bad as anyone describes it'; she was, she conceded, glad to have seen 'this plague stricken stinky filthy section of the globe', but she longed for 'English rain & food'.[4] Once Ray had recovered and their departure from India was arranged, she and Oliver set off to see its more appealing parts; Agra, Simla and Delhi gave Ray an appreciation of some of India's architectural glories to set beside her dislike of the dirt and squalor. Nevertheless as the trio set sail from Bombay on the SS *Rubattino* in mid-January 1912, Ray and Oliver were determined never to return.

Ray once again disliked her fellow passengers, so she concentrated on re-reading and sorting her grandmother's letters, which she hoped to prepare for publication. It was a delightful task which brought Hannah's personality vividly back to her and reminded Ray of Hannah's 'steady central position' in her own memories. Back in Europe the couple spent a few weeks as paying guests of Oliver's sister Dorothy and her husband the French painter Simon Bussy at La Souco, in Roquebrune, during which Simon painted Ray's portrait. Oliver went back to England for a job interview on 13 March and Ray braced herself for ten days at I Tatti. On 21 March she was back in England.

Life in India had been affordable within Oliver's salary, but life in England would be a different matter, especially with a baby adding to their expenses. Mary, increasingly doubtful about her daughter's choice of husband, had been horrified by the poverty-stricken state in which Ray and Oliver left for India, and both families agreed that a new job for Oliver was essential. The couple themselves were confident, though unenthusiastic, that Oliver would be offered the post he had applied for, helping to run the systems of unemployment and sickness pay established by the 1911 National Insurance Act. But low pay (£250 [roughly £22,700] with only two weeks holiday a year) for hard but uninteresting work, based in Southampton, offered at best 'a somewhat dreary prospect'; and in Southampton Ray would not be able to continue studying engineering.[6] So there was relief as well as shock at the news that Oliver had not been offered the job.

The couple briefly examined and dismissed alternative sources of employment: their decision caused a storm in both families. Ray, Oliver and their family would live on Ray's income of £500 [£45,430] per year (of which £200 was an allowance from Berenson) while they researched and wrote a history of British India, since 'working together is so much more fun than anything else'.[7] Perhaps Ray's mother and stepfather would help them out with the rent of this delightful house they had found in Cambridge? They would not. While Lady Strachey adopted a policy of silent disapproval, Berenson made his views known. Karin, recently returned from I Tatti, reported that 'what "is thought" is that Indian history is simply a grand name for idleness on Oliver's part'.[8] Ray put up a spirited defence of her husband ('he is 38, & has slaved away for 13 years in an office & that's rather a hard reason for saying that his character is incapable of working in the way that Uncle Logan & Bertie & B.B. do').[9] She made no claim to the moral high ground:

I have always looked upon money as a thing of which I had plenty, & [...] I've always believed that even if I did things of which my family disapproved I should still be backed up just as readily as if I didn't [...] You see I have no pride whatever about taking money – the whole property system is so absurd – but I have a belief that it's unwise to take unwilling money because of the hateful consequences, & Oliver has this belief about twice as strongly as I have.[10]

She asked for the chance to give their idea a try without family disapproval: if it didn't work, they would have to think again.

You may think it's easy enough to talk like this, but that in reality we shall come on you for vast unexpected sums – education of children, illnesses & so on, & that we shall mean to live cheaply & not succeed, & mean to work & not succeed. But at least we can try – & if we don't succeed, & do turn into exacting weights on your necks, then we can always set to & try to earn money again. But the chance of working together, & of living the kind of life we both think congenial seems too tempting to be lost.[11]

The criticisms she envisaged were only too justified. For Ray the painful path to financial realism would be a long one.

Mary Berenson smoothed matters over. She would pay Ray's confinement expenses; and Ray and Oliver found a cheaper house, this time in Hampstead, at a rent of £65 [£5,900] per year. 96 South Hill Park backed onto the ponds on Hampstead Heath so had a rural feel at the rear, offered generous accommodation, and would not require many servants. For a young couple on a low income it was an attractive – even self-indulgent – first home. Mindful of possible suffrage implications, they took the house as joint householders.

It is difficult to avoid the impression that the early years of Ray's marriage represented a return to childhood. Liberated from the worst of her family's intrusions, though still financially dependent, she and Oliver formed a close bond, based on shared values, resistance to conventional (and familial) expectations, constant critical teasing of each other and considerable independence of action. They did not always give the impression of being mature adults. Julia commented to her close friend Frances Marshall that she considered her father and stepmother 'more like irresponsible, grown-up cousins' than parents.[12] Ray admitted that she did not feel grown-up enough to be a mother, and in the constant battle between her strong moral principles, bolstered by her lively conscience, and her childish assumption that she could have whatever she wanted in life, the latter was firmly in the ascendant.

While Ray's letters detail the external events of her first year of marriage, her diary focuses on impending motherhood. It is a detached, almost dispassionate, account which combines hopes for the moral character, good sense and happy disposition of her child with intense curiosity about its personality. Astonishment at the idea of becoming a mother is a constant theme, as is Ray's total ignorance of the care of babies, and her revulsion both from their physical messiness and from adult sentimentalising about them. The sex of the child was of no importance to her, as she hoped for a large family of boys and girls.

Family pressure overruled Ray's preference for a fuss-free delivery in a London nursing home. In mid-June Ray and Oliver moved to Ford Place, Arundel, where Alys Russell and Logan Pearsall Smith now lived, to await the birth, surrounded by Ray's relatives. By then the prospect of settling into their own home had become Ray's main preoccupation; as time passed, the expected infant seemed increasingly unreal. It proved a long wait, but eventually, in the early hours of 17 July 1912, Ray gave birth to a daughter.

Motherhood came as a shock to Ray. The birth itself she remembered only as 'a great wriggling', the pain made endurable by deep draughts of chloroform administered by Mary on a gauze cone.[13] Far more worrying was the low psychological state ('a very curious bleak sort of feeling') and physical weakness which followed.[14] Breast feeding proved difficult and painful (and was soon supplemented by bottles), and Ray later remembered feeling no immediate bond with her new-born daughter, who was 'a horrid bore – ugly, senseless, troublesome, noisy & incomprehensible, messy smelly fidgety & a constant anxiety'.[15]

As a new mother, Ray had lost control over her life (and may have been suffering from mild post-natal depression). Medical wisdom dictated that she must stay in bed for several weeks after the birth; the servants at Ford Place resented the extra work the Strachey family caused; and Ray's nursery nurse had far more experience of babies than she did and disapproved of departures from her normal practice. Ray was not even allowed to choose her daughter's name: she favoured Olivia, but a family gathering in early September backed Oliver's preference for Barbara. By then the baby had been formally registered as 'Female Strachey', and not until the baby was almost six months old did Ray start to refer to her as Barbara: before then – and sometimes afterwards – she was dubbed 'the creature'.

Ray's unrealistic assumptions about child-rearing – and resentment at the disruption a baby could cause – soon became a running theme in her letters. Barbara 'has been horribly spoilt by all the people she has been with – & when we are settled some painful noisy disciplining will have to take place!', Ray complained, concluding that 'the creature is very naughty' because 'she screams & yells till someone comes in sight, & then laughs like anything!'[16] When Barbara was less than three months old, Ray 'had a great tussle with the creature [...] & left her to have her cry out:

> It took an hour – & the worst of it is that the nurse simply will not keep it up. Unless I sit there day & night forever, she takes the creature up whenever it cries. It is very annoying, & I am going on struggling with her.[17]

An understanding of babies' needs came gradually to Ray (helped by the ideas of Maria Montessori), as did enjoyment of her daughter's robust personality and physical vigour, but even as late as October 1913, when Barbara was about fifteen months old, Ray needed the guidance of her wise mother-in-law: 'Lady S. scolded me well for not picking her up & cuddling her when she fell down. She said B wd never learn to sympathise with other people if no one sympathised with her!'.[18] Ray was never a tactile person and found Barbara far easier to cope with once she could talk.

The family moved into their new home in Hampstead at the beginning of September and Ray devoted herself to the expensive decorating and furnishing. The planning and planting of the garden absorbed and delighted her, though it drained her purse. After the initial excitement had subsided, 96 South Hill Park proved less satisfactory than it had at first seemed ('It rattles & shakes itself like a dog when the wind blows […]. Things fall out of the walls & I shouldn't be at all surprised if it all sank down in a heap one day').[19] Ray's forebodings proved correct. In September 1913 the plumbing seized up and the nursery ceiling fell down, so, after arguments with the landlady, disruptive major work was undertaken to make the house safe.

Ray's expectations of a normal lifestyle had been formed in a well-funded childhood in well-staffed homes, so trying to live off her modest income proved difficult. She had no interest in elegance or smart clothes, she assured her mother, but dreamed of having 'a motor & to be able to buy books when I want them. […] I should like to be able to take a cab when it's raining & to set up an electrical lab. in the loft'.[20] However in less than a year her account was 'perilously low' and Ray concluded 'we are evidently living about £60 [£5,400] a year above our income'.[21] After a full year she would analyse their spending and look for savings, but until then could Mary help out?

It would have been an unusual family of Ray's background which did not rely on servants in the years when they were readily available at low wages. Financial constraints meant that they had to make do with the minimum: one cook/general servant, Lily; the unnamed nursery nurse, competent with babies but disliked and distrusted by Ray; and a part-time charwoman. Ray never felt comfortable dealing with servants. She recognised how hard a servant's life could be and dreaded having to discipline or dismiss an unsatisfactory one, but the option of doing without domestic help was unthinkable ('It's awful to feel we are overworking Lily, & equally awful to have to clean our own grates & lay our own fires which is the other alternative').[22]

(Figures 15 and 16) 96 South Hill Park, Hampstead, Ray's first home as Mrs Oliver Strachey, appears to have changed little during the past century. The path beside the house gives ready access to the Heath; the garden wall descends into one of the ponds.

Oliver and Ray unconventionally agreed to share domestic responsibilities: Ray would deal with 'rent, chimney sweepings, washing curtains, wages, repairs etc.' while Oliver's realm was to be 'all food & food bills & everything appertaining to meals'.[23] Oliver began by 'reading cookery books & anxiously discussing with Lily how to use up scraps', so Ray was initially confident of the scheme's success, but as he had little culinary imagination and refused to eat vegetables, his meal plans rarely ventured beyond mutton followed by rice pudding.[24] Ray eventually took sole charge of running the household, while Oliver found more congenial occupations. 'Oliver is busy all day long composing things, & he refuses to go anywhere or see anyone. [...] He only changes over from piano to clarionet with intervals of Indian books'.[25] A little later he started learning Persian. Oliver gave little impression of a family man of nearly forty, on one occasion – having taken part in 'a great romping fight' at Belsize Park Gardens with Karin and his brother James and cousin Duncan Grant – being soundly ticked off by his mother 'for disgracing her house on Sunday by their wild yelling & scampering'.[26]

As a frequent visitor to the Rendel home before her marriage, Ray already knew Oliver's daughter Julia, who liked and admired her.

Once married, Ray successfully dipped her toe in the unknown waters of childcare during Julia's weekends away from her preparatory school in Hindhead, but by the end of Julia's school term Ray's travels to Scotland and Scandinavia had begun. Alys Russell offered to take temporary care of Julia, and, in default of alternatives, was accepted. Despite Ray's misgivings, Julia immediately took to Alys and Mary (on her usual summer visit) and enjoyed her 'happiest summer for several years' at Court Place, to which Ray and Oliver returned before leaving for India.[27]

While Ray was in India, Alys Russell suggested that Julia was unhappy at her small boarding school, so Oliver gave the necessary notice. Alys's perceptive and kindly analysis of Julia's character led her to suggest that 'a loving home atmosphere' and a day school might suit her better.[28] Julia, she argued, had 'intensely strong feelings, but is afraid of giving herself away, & is afraid to trust people'; if Ray could gain her 'love & confidence' then her 'proud dignified reserve would gradually melt away'.[29] But Julia's 'fearfully careless & heedless ways' did 'make her difficult to live with'.[30] Both Pippa Strachey and Mary Berenson seem to have argued that Ray could not be expected to cope with the full-time demands of Julia as well as a new baby and a husband who 'requires a great deal of attention, & doesn't want to give much'.[31] Such an arrangement would in any case be impossible if Ray and Oliver decided to live permanently in Fernhurst as Ray hoped.

Ray suggested that Bedales School, known for its secular, liberal ethos, might suit Julia and eradicate the 'germs of foolishness' she was developing.[32] For the time being, she and Oliver accepted Alys's next suggestion, and arranged that from Easter 1912 Julia should spend school terms at Durbins, Roger Fry's home in Guildford, where his sister Joan kept house for him and cared for his children after his wife was committed to a mental institution.[33] Joan Fry undertook to offer Julia a Quaker upbringing and education with the Fry children. Rather to Ray's surprise, Julia seemed to settle happily there.

Day to day arrangements for Julia normally fell to Ray. Oliver was enthusiastic about encouraging Julia's artistic talent and fostering her musical sensitivity, and happy to join in pillow fights or riotous games of Animal Grab, but made himself scarce when practical decisions were under consideration. It was Ray who made sure that Julia was included in family events, helped her buy the ragtime music she loved (to which her strictly classical father objected), and noticed how short-sighted she was. It was a blow when after two terms Joan Fry declined to keep Julia at Durbins beyond Christmas 1912 (perhaps because of Julia's delight in walking round the guttering beneath the house's high mansard roofs, accompanied by Roger Fry's terrified daughter Pamela). The two terms remaining before Ray and Oliver planned to send her to Bedales would present problems if she were to live full-time at home in Hampstead and attend a day school. Ray was about to start research in the India Office and was not satisfied that her current nurse could take charge of Julia as well as Barbara; worried that Julia needed company of her own age, she freely admitted 'I dread having Julia living at home from every possible point of view'.[34]

As usual, Alys Russell offered to help out. She would take in Julia and another child at Ford Place for two terms and, with the help of a governess, see to their education.[35] Although Ray accepted the proposal with relief, and on many later occasions left her own children in Alys's care, she may have had misgivings. Ray recognised Alys's kindness but was exasperated by the sentimentality in which she and Mary indulged ('When Aunty Loo says down the telephone, as she does every day she's in town "Tell me some little anecdote about Barbara to send to thy Mother" I feel inclined to go straight away & throttle the child').[36]

Alys's well-meant attempts to improve Ray's childhood behaviour had infuriated her, and Alys now intended to take a far more interventionist approach to Julia's shortcomings than came naturally to Ray. Ray's relaxed approach to child-rearing differed from Alys Russell's erratic but more intense practices. When Ray cancelled an intended visit to Ford in favour of the Russian ballet, and then briefly proposed to go abroad with Oliver but without Julia for part of her school holidays, Alys wrote to Mary 'I hope R. & O. will get off, tho' I honestly think they are neglecting Julia. However, that they evidently mean to do always, & I shall cease thinking about it & look on myself as her mother', explaining that 'I have now arranged our holidays with visiting children, etc. I want Julia to feel this is a settled home for her till she goes to school, as it is her one chance of getting into regular home habits'.[37] The difference of opinion between Alys and Ray over parenting styles reflected the two families' broader patterns of behaviour, Pearsall Smith interference against Strachey laissez-faire. (Even so, Alys Russell remained one of Ray's most devoted admirers.)

Beneath the superficial good relations between Ray's family and her in-laws, tensions lurked, social and intellectual values in opposition. Alys and Mary both resented the Stracheys' influence on Ray, and the 'Strachey tomb' of unsociability, as Karin dubbed it, in which Ray chose to bury herself (though Mary admitted that Ray had 'always been queer. […] She isn't a bit like us').[38] Alys aimed to rescue Julia, of whom she was genuinely fond, from her Strachey relations ('eccentric and *weird*' according to Alys), even the universally popular Pippa, whom Alys condemned for 'sheer rudeness' in not notifying travel details.[39] Pearsall Smiths and Stracheys remained in a (normally well-disguised) state of mutual disdain, with Ray as the chief conciliator.

There were tensions within the Strachey clan too. While Oliver's brother Ralph was in India, his wife Margaret often remained with him, leaving their two sons, Dick and John, at preparatory school in England, under the oversight of Pippa and Ray. Margaret Strachey was mentally fragile and inclined to become obsessive over health risks, perhaps not surprisingly since, as a young woman newly arrived in India, she had seen her mother die in agony from a burst bladder. Conventional and unintellectual Margaret's attitudes often appalled Ray. When Margaret decreed that the boys should stay at school for the Easter holidays instead of visiting Hampstead and Ford Place, it was 'the nastiest trick I ever heard of, to try & cut off those poor devils' holidays' and Margaret was a 'brutal woman';[40] Margaret's decision, on arrival from India, to await the arrival of her trunks of clothes before going to see her sons was announced by Ray with two exclamation marks;[41] and Ray was reduced to speechless horror at the prospect facing Ralph's baby daughter when Margaret admitted 'how afraid she was that Ursula would be clever, & how she was determined not to educate her at all "as a woman's life is only made unhappy if she is clever"!'.[42]

Ray became a favourite with the Strachey boys, thereby incurring their mother's wrath. Dick later recalled Ray's 'sensible matter of factness' and that 'she was direct and spontaneous in her approach to us, and seemed to know the language of boys and what would appeal to them better than any other woman I had met with up to that time'.[43] Chats about sport and hidden treasure, building wigwams and dressing the boys up as Indians all came naturally to Ray: she had only to recall the childhood activities she had enjoyed with Karin and her Worthington cousins in the Fernhurst woods.

Julia started at Bedales in September 1913, after Berenson had generously offered to pay the fees. Ray wrote her a solemn letter of good wishes and advice about fitting in with the rest of the class, then left her in peace to settle in, as long as her letters sounded happy. Alys, on the other hand, made frequent visits to Bedales. 'Don't you think you'll unsettle Julia, Aunty Loo, by going to see her so often?' Ray queried, 'Or do you think she's so settled that it doesn't matter?'[44] Alys's tart response 'I had a very nice visit to Julia & found her very unhappy! So it is not unsettling' suggests that an element of competition had developed between Julia's surrogate mothers.[45] Julia was indeed unhappy at Bedales. Too much of an individualist to conform to the school ethos, she was continually in trouble, particularly at first; but greater parental intervention might not have helped.

Ray enrolled in evening classes on electricity at the Northern Polytechnic Institute in nearby Holloway but later admitted that she had not learnt much there. She was anxious to start working with Oliver. In early 1913 they began intensive research into Indian history, mainly in the Library of the India Office. Working with Oliver was 'great fun', and they made occasional exciting discoveries.[46] Nevertheless she was soon bored by the substance of their research, perhaps because the East India Company was so male-dominated. But unless she kept working at it, Oliver did little; Alys noticed the skill Ray developed in steering her idle husband towards his work and away from his piano.[47]

Another drawback to working together was the incompatibility between their writing styles. Ray soon admitted, 'Oliver's style is great long sentences with great long words, & mine is much more colloquial', an analysis which does not quite identify the difference in their approaches.[48] As a narrator, Ray normally made herself transparent, whereas there is an archness to Oliver's writing style which makes the reader continuously aware of the author's presence. Ray certainly had a far greater capacity for scene-setting and narrative drive. So their collaboration was restricted to contents and sequence, with Oliver left to write their account of a minor episode in the early history of the East India Company, published as *Keigwin's Rebellion*.[49]

Gradually the plan of working together on Indian history as a way of life withered, and Ray returned, somewhat regretfully, to her earlier interests: her own writing and women's suffrage. Ray's biography of the American suffrage campaigner Frances Willard was published in 1913, 'compromised', as she admitted, by her one-sided enthusiasm for her subject.[50] Now she was anxious to follow her affectionate reminiscences of Hannah as *A Quaker Grandmother* (written mainly during her return from India and eventually published in 1914) by editing and commenting on some of the documents which Hannah had left dealing with strange religious sects, and started working on these.

The world of suffrage activism gradually reabsorbed Ray. It proved a short step from producing tapestry work for Pippa's Great Oriental Bazaar to making suffrage speeches, and by May 1913 Ray had virtually taken over the local Hampstead society for women's suffrage, finding herself 'laden with volunteers to organize, with meetings & entertainments & all kinds of things on my hands. I hate it, yet I want to do it because of my beastly conscience'.[51] Doubtless her conviction that she could get things done better than other people played a part too; by July she reported having 'attended a long committee meeting at which I was in the chair, & the people were so vague & silly that I had to propose, second & carry all by myself all the business that was done'.[52]

1913 was a year of high drama in the women's suffrage movement. Three versions of a Conciliation Bill offering limited female suffrage based on a measure of cross-party agreement had been introduced since 1910, each time unsuccessfully. The NUWSS had greater hopes of the government's Reform Bill, introduced in June 1912, which Herbert Asquith had promised would be open to modification by amendment to include women's suffrage. When the Speaker ruled at the Bill's Third Reading in January 1913 that such an amendment would not after all be allowable, the Bill was withdrawn, and the NUWSS lost the final vestiges of its faith in the Liberal Government. Ray's personal view was rather different: 'my belief is that although it's all a monstrous disgrace, it's really a very lucky thing for us, as the amendment would have been defeated'.[53]

The WSPU had returned to militancy after truces in 1910 and 1911, and the British public paid little attention to the distinctions between suffragists and suffragettes. In October 1912 Emmeline Pankhurst had exhorted her followers to add attacks on private property to their existing repertoire of civil disobedience and attacks on public property. A violent campaign including bombing and arson in empty houses, churches and post boxes followed, producing a major public backlash against the suffragettes and the passing of the Prisoners [Temporary Discharge for Ill-Health] Act in April 1913, colloquially known as the Cat and Mouse Act.

Earlier sympathy for the campaign was rapidly eroded by suffragette violence and, despite being 'so horribly respectable', the law-abiding suffragists often faced hostility.[54] On 23 June (two weeks after Emily Wilding Davison's disruption of the Derby and her subsequent death had divided the nation) Ray 'was mobbed at a meeting at Greenwich, & pelted with mud & things, clothes completely ruined, dirty to the skin, & finally had to take refuge in a shop, & hide for an hour till the police said it was safe to escape!'[55] Her balanced conclusion that 'it was very exciting, but nasty & dirty, & all due to mismanagement' was characteristic of Ray in uniting a taste for drama, a dislike for emotional outbursts and a belief that good organisation could resolve most problems.[56]

Ray's role in the suffragists' Great Pilgrimage of June–July 1913 does not emerge from her own letters as, with her mother on her annual visit to England and the rest of her family close at hand, letter-writing took a back seat. It seems that she helped to plan the Great North Road route but did not walk it. Mary reported that she, Ray, Alys and Grace Worthington all walked for a few hours along the Southern route, less hostile than some of the other routes, even though the hurling of rotten eggs and cabbages occasionally replaced offerings of flowers and refreshment. Ray was among the many speakers at the Pilgrimage's culmination in Hyde Park on 26 July.

Within the suffrage world, Ray's main loyalty was now to the London Society for Women's Suffrage (LSWS), whose Secretary was her sister-in-law Pippa. Within the largely democratic structure of the NUWSS, the London Society occupied a somewhat anomalous position, partly for historical reasons and partly because London's position was genuinely different from the rest of the country. Millicent Fawcett had close links to the London Society, having been a leading member of its Committee until 1912, but despite this, tensions were growing between the LSWS and the NUWSS. London had been allowed to remain an exception to the system of regional federations introduced by the NUWSS in 1910 in the interests of greater democracy. Federations were designed to boost the role of the provinces within the National Union, and to ensure all strands of opinion were taken into account in each area. London already played a major role in the workings of the NUWSS (too much, according to many of the NU officers); and the LSWS had made no moves to democratise its internal constitution. Now the question of whether the LSWS should conform to the national pattern was raised again, with Ray in the thick of the argument.

On the agenda of the LSWS annual meeting on 24 November 1913 was a revised LSWS constitution devised by Ray and proposed by her Hampstead society, seconded by Maude Royden (who later withdrew her support), and backed by most LSWS Executive Committee members. The revision covered financial arrangements and the system for electing the Executive Committee, taking the

LSWS nearer the national model without incorporating all aspects of it. The justification for this half-way position was that, because of the multiplicity of other suffrage and political organisations operating in London, schemes intended to offer democracy were only too likely to provoke take-overs by other vested interests (the WSPU had made a determined attempt to take over the LSWS in 1909), and hence eventual disintegration.

Always preferring effective practice to unworkable theory, Ray openly rejected any idea of allocating specified seats on the executive committee to each area of London, and opted to retain the existing system of open election which made it 'possible to choose the 20 most competent people, no matter where they live.'[57] Some loosening of the centralised purse strings was proposed – but not so much as to weaken the Society's often precarious finances. Elected to the LSWS Executive Committee at this meeting, Ray made a 'great speech' in defence of her scheme and in retrospect remembered with some nostalgia the 'great turmoil of buz, intrigue, gossip & excitement' which surrounded it.[58]

The new constitution was opposed by Helena Swanwick of the Richmond branch (a close friend of Millicent Fawcett) with the support of a significant group of NUWSS officials and staff, acting in their private capacities as members of the LSWS. They argued that the LSWS should adopt a fully federated constitution as all the other NUWSS societies had done. The meeting had to be adjourned until 15 December, when the vote backed a slightly modified version of Ray's scheme. Nevertheless ratification by the NUWSS looked unlikely in the middle of the major row which developed between the LSWS and the NUWSS about the private actions of NUWSS personnel. After a great deal of behind-the-scenes activity within the two organisations, a compromise was reached and a revised scheme accepted at the NUWSS annual meeting in February 1914. But the friction on this issue between the LSWS and the NUWSS was a sign of trouble ahead.

Ray's suffrage activities did not oust Oliver from the central position in her life. In January 1914, when Oliver, laid low as usual by the English winter, went round the Mediterranean on a cargo boat for the sake of his health (encouraged by Ray), her letters to him are undoubtedly love-letters, despite their concentration on suffrage matters. She admitted how dependent she had become on Oliver's presence, explaining 'I haven't said I miss you because I want you to stay away. But I'll say instead that I love you. My dear – there's nothing in the world so important as you & your concerns'.[59] Two days later she confessed 'I used to be so very cocksure that I was really independent & self sufficient, & now I'm not. [...] I love you rather too much, & I hope you're happy'.[60] Her love for Oliver, she concluded, had eroded earlier certainties:

> the whole subject of whether people do or don't get swallowed up by being in love is rather obscure to me now. It used to be quite clear. But I'm not so sure these last few days, because I do miss you so horribly.[61]

On Oliver's return in early February, Ray made another attempt to engineer a shared working life by involving him in her suffrage activities. Unlike the WSPU, the NUWSS welcomed male members; Bertrand Russell had even been a member of its Executive Committee. By May Oliver was making speeches, on the committee of the Hampstead Society and attending the classes for suffrage workers Ray gave twice a week at the LSWS office. The couple's lives were firmly entwined professionally as well as personally.

CHAPTER EIGHT
Wars and Peace: 1914–1916

...the world is crashing to pieces just out of sight.[1]

1914 was, Ray later claimed, the year in which she suddenly grew up. She still longed for a large family, and most of 1913 was spent in monthly hope that she might be pregnant. Not until February 1914 was Ray able to announce to Mary that she was expecting a baby in the autumn. Ray was 'more delighted than I can say'.[2] She felt well – with hardly any sickness – and later recalled thinking that 'no one in the world had ever been so happy before'.[3]

The two events, private and public, which were to destroy that happiness both took place in June 1914. During a weekend with Leonard and Virginia Woolf at their cottage at Asheham, Ray, Oliver and other guests were sitting in front of the cottage when a steam traction engine and coal truck, with three people on board, ran slowly out of control down the hill towards the cottage and overturned directly in front of them. No-one was killed; the driver suffered a broken leg. Some of the women screamed or had hysterics, but Ray exerted her usual self-control and remained calm.

They returned home and for the next few days Ray, five months pregnant, looked and felt ill. A visit to the amusement park at Earls Court to celebrate her twenty-seventh birthday on 4 June was a wretched experience: 'I shall never forget, & can't bear to describe, the horrors of that – for I realized after I'd gone down the chute that I'd probably done for my baby.'[4] That night she began to miscarry. For several hours, after an injection of opium, she lay in a 'stupor of horror & misery' before the foetus (a boy) slipped out 'like an egg into the bedpan'.[5] The only comfort Ray found was in the medical verdict that the baby had been dead for several days: she was told that the suppressed shock at Asheham, not going down the water-chute at Earls Court, had killed it. (A modern diagnosis might dismiss both these events as likely causes of miscarriage.)

Ray's letter to Mary made the best of things ('considering that it happened, it couldn't have turned out better'), but her diary entry (written nearly two years later) is more honest: 'I've never been so blankly miserable before & I hope I never shall be again. […] I can't bear to remember that time even now.'[6] For the next three months she wept 'night after night', her nerves in pieces, while trying to preserve a composed façade for the outside world.[7]

Ray and Oliver had already arranged to rent a cottage near Pangbourne for six weeks from the beginning of July. Without running water (though with a piano hired for Oliver's benefit), and infrequently served by tradesmen, Clack's End was not an ideal venue for entertaining; nevertheless Karin, Ellie, Lytton, James, Bertrand Russell, Keynes, G.E. Moore and Vanessa Bell were among their visitors. Despite her lowered state, Ray could not escape a mixed bag of responsibilities as their hostess. When a horse broke out of a neighbouring field and got among the potatoes:

> Nothing could have been tamer than the horse: but the well known physical courage of the brothers Strachey almost made me believe it was a dangerous feat to put a halter on him & lead him back to his field. However I did the deed of rescue, & was called a heroine.[8]

Ray continued writing her novel, while, largely unnoticed by most of the British population, the sequence of events which followed the assassination of the Archduke Franz Ferdinand in Sarajevo on 28 June unfolded. As late as 29 July, just as her mother arrived in England, Ray felt that 'a real European war is incredible'.[9] A few days later Britain joined that war.

As pressure grew for Britain to remain neutral, a meeting of women's organisations was arranged for the evening of 4 August in the Kingsway Hall, London. The NUWSS executive put forward a powerful resolution: 'this meeting of women…deplore[s]…the outbreak of war in Europe as an unparalleled disaster. […] The women here assembled call upon the Governments of their several countries to support every effort made to restore peace'.[10] By the time the meeting was held, Britain's entry into the war was certain. Most of the 2,000 strong audience had come to support a peace campaign, but Millicent Fawcett, in the Chair, had moved past this (though this did not spare her the angry reproach of Lord Robert Cecil, a staunch Conservative supporter of women's suffrage, that the NUWSS involvement in a peace rally 'seems so unreasonable under the circumstances as to shake my belief in the fitness of Women to deal with great Imperial questions').[11] The NUWSS suspended political propaganda and committed itself to relieving the hardship caused by 'the economic and industrial dislocation' of wartime.[12] 'Let us show ourselves worthy of citizenship,' Mrs Fawcett soon appealed, 'whether our claim to it be recognised or not'.[13]

Within days Ray could report that 'the suffrage societies are hard at it organizing classes for first aid, cooking, sewing & district visiting, farm-work & all kinds of things'.[14] In Hampstead she tried to ensure that the newly formed Citizens' Committee included 'useful women with experience' and later worked successfully for the establishment of recreational facilities for soldiers on Hampstead Heath; but relief work was 'too horrible for words to describe' as 'everyone is muddling, including myself, & the confusion & general rage is horrid'. [15]

Both the NUWSS and the LSWS helped to manage the flood of women seeking to contribute to the war effort, the London Society 'setting up as a clearing house, giving the applicants advice how to train & who to go to, & trying to put the incompetent off nursing. Everyone rushes to nurse, & what will be needed will be people to distribute the relief funds'.[16] The general frenzy deflected Ray's attention from her personal misery for a time, but her feelings of frustration and futility are unmistakeable.

As his contribution to the war effort, Oliver volunteered his services as an unpaid assistant to his oldest brother Dick, a career soldier in the War Office, working from 9 a.m. to 8 p.m. doing 'endless amounts' of clerical work.[17] Soon Oliver heard a rumour that 'the War Office was looking out for someone with an ingenious head for puzzles & acrostics to decipher unknown codes & piece together the scraps of wireless messages picked up from the enemy'.[18] A friend suggested Oliver, who was then 'taken by Dick to see Gen. Anderson, who took him on at once at £400 [£35,230] a year! […] He's trying to find the code from undeciphered messages, & says it's most entertaining work'.[19]

Working initially on German field communications, Oliver felt that 'there is practically no hope of ever reading any of the code messages', but he was kept busy and interested.[20] All night sessions soon followed and for the first few months he had scarcely any free time and no pay – the Treasury made a fuss over his salary. The War Office was unimpressive ('Oliver says he's only met one officer who knows German so far, & one other who pretends to! And that is the Intelligence Dept!') and reduced Ray to despair by its firm resistance to Oliver's suggestion of using womanpower to meet the manpower shortage: 'They made use of the ancient old notion that no woman could keep the official secrets! It makes me sad to think that the destinies of Europe are in such antediluvian hands.'[21]

By December the pressure had eased slightly, as trench warfare used landlines rather than wireless for communication. Oliver would not get Christmas Day off, but his evenings were now usually his own. As the flow of military messages diminished, the War Office cryptanalysts turned their attention to diplomatic messages transmitted by cable, which the censorship undertaken by a parallel section now made accessible. Knowledge of the stance of important neutral countries like the United States became vital (it was an intercepted telegram which eventually brought the United States into the war) and in the analysis of diplomatic codes Oliver at last found a career which exactly matched his talents and interests.[22]

The war fever of August 1914 was transmuted into 'a heavy anxiety we don't like to look at too often'.[23] The sight of soldiers became commonplace – 'hot dripping Territorials [...] marching & countermarching on the heath' in August, their successors drilling in intense cold in November, clearly visible from Ray's window ('Barbara is as military as a Prussian baby with imitating them!').[24] Dark streets and the sound of Zeppelins passing over the Heath became familiar, as did 'the dreadful daily casualty lists'.[25] There was a spurious appearance of normality but priorities and motives were transformed: 'Christmas shopping for instance is now done almost entirely to keep people in work & to keep up the show of being happy'.[26]

Ray reassured her overwrought mother that 'most people have enjoyed the excitement of it all more than anything in their lives – not only the ones at the front but people in England. If you have no money & no brains ordinary life must be very dull'.[27] But she felt none of this herself. Disbelief and horror dominated her letters: 'This beastly war is going to last for years & years'; 'it still seems incredible that England is at war'; and 'it would be nice to be like Barbara & have not even the faintest notion that the world has come to an end'.[28] With access to inside information in the War Office, Oliver 'varie[d] from hope to gloom daily', though gloom dominated: rumours of impending invasion were rife.[29] Oliver's time was taken up by his work, and relief activities offered little satisfaction to Ray. She pinned all her hopes on her determination to have another baby as soon as her doctor allowed.

In September 1914 Ray believed herself to be pregnant again and, feeling unwell, retreated to bed for some days. When she did eventually venture on an outing with Oliver, his sister Marjorie and Julia, a jolt brought on the symptoms she remembered from her last miscarriage. She returned to bed again but on 6 October believed that she had had another miscarriage; her doctor advised further bed-rest.

This cycle of suspected pregnancy, a retreat to bed to minimise the risk of miscarriage, apparently in vain, then further rest for recovery happened twice more, in November–December 1914 and February 1915. By installing a bed next to the phone Ray was able to keep in touch with the relief activities in Hampstead, and with developments in the wider suffrage world; but there was too much time for thought, and brooding on the babies she thought she had lost made matters worse. After the third episode, a medical examination suggested that all three assumed pregnancies over the winter of 1914–15 had been hysterical, the result of her own intense wishes. A specialist confirmed that she had a 'mania' but offered the comforting verdict that future pregnancies were perfectly possible and that hard work was likely to help more than going to bed.[30] Ray's miscarriage (and perhaps some associated feeling of guilt) appears to have had a devastating and long-lasting psychological impact on her. She had a fibroid which might at some point merit surgical removal – but not urgently. The priority was to cure her mind.

In mid-March 1915 Ray went to I Tatti 'to clear the cobwebs out of my brain'.[31] The mobilisation of Italy had little effect (Italy did not abandon its neutrality and join the Allies until 23 May), Florence itself was pleasantly empty, a small car was at Ray's disposal and the occupants of I Tatti were unusually bearable. Ray persuaded Pippa, convalescing with her sister Dorothy at Roquebrune in the South of France, to join her at I Tatti to inspect 'this place with all its stage splendours & all the odd people in it – gold spoons & Chinese heads & a collection of all the rats & bores in Europe' before both women returned to Dorothy's house, La Souco, in mid-April.[32]

La Souco, a three-storey house clinging to a cliff below Roquebrune with 'the best view in Europe' towards Monte Carlo, lacked the scale and luxury of I Tatti, but charmed visitors; George Mallory and Rudyard Kipling both enthused about their stays there.[33] As Dorothy and her French husband Simon Bussy, a painter, were always short of money, taking in paying guests supplemented their income: a succession of Stracheys would regularly turn up to be restored to health or to find peace in which to write. To Ray it offered an abundance of wild flowers in the surrounding countryside and 'heavenly days, filled with idleness & laughter' in congenial company.[34] Ray worked on her novel and time slipped away, interrupted by complaints from Alys about Ray's inconvenient prolonged absence and news about suffrage battles from Oliver ('Things are whirling about in England & he seems to be in the thick of it').[35] By early May, Ray's holiday had had the desired effect: 'I'm perfectly restored to health, & it's time I was back.'[36]

The war had brought previously suppressed tensions in the NUWSS to the surface. Millicent Fawcett had always insisted that the NUWSS should remain non-party, hence its supporters embraced a multiplicity of political opinions. A group of dynamic and capable women sharing similar political views had come to occupy some of the key positions on the NUWSS Executive Committee.[37] Their sympathies were in general democratic, even socialist, and in 1912 they had been influential in steering the NUWSS into an alliance with the Labour Party, the only party to be officially committed to women's suffrage.

Many NUWSS members, including Ray, were uneasy with this alliance – Eleanor Rathbone had staged an unsuccessful rebellion against it – and in particular with the Executive and its organisers, who wanted 'to become a genuine labour society, instead of just an ally on one point'.[38] 'Our organizers now talk pure socialism instead of suffrage,' Ray complained, '& the Ex[ecutive], in the effort to keep on good terms with the Labour Party, seems to be prepared to go to almost any length'.[39] Ray felt that the Executive Committee was pursuing a political agenda alien to most of the NUWSS membership and that 'they need a few elementary lessons in democratic government'.[40]

During autumn 1914 pressure built up for the NUWSS to state a position on the war, for the guidance of its members. Its leaders were split. Despite her longing for peace, Millicent Fawcett was fiercely patriotic and could not countenance anything less than full support for her country in its war effort; an obituarist later claimed that 'she could endure only by energetically willing to believe nothing but the best of her own "side" '.[41] Other leading members of the NUWSS agreed with her; and the increasingly anti-German mood of the country as a whole meant that any peace moves by the NUWSS risked damaging public perceptions of the female suffrage cause.

Some members of the Executive Committee (mainly those with socialist sympathies) felt differently. Their feminism was inherently internationalist and pacifist; support for the war struck at their deepest beliefs as to the meaning of feminism, since for them feminism and militarism were radically opposed. They believed that arbitration rather than violence was the way to resolve conflict and hoped that the links built up with woman suffragists in other countries, including Germany, could be used to end the war by mediation; and they saw that if the anti-German fever sweeping the country were translated into a punitive peace settlement, further conflict was inevitable.

Discussions between what came to be referred to, rather simplistically, as the 'patriots' and the 'pacifists' failed to produce an agreed NUWSS line on the war and on whether it should undertake any peace-related activities. The 'patriots' and 'pacifists' held many views in common. Neither side wanted a German victory nor the spread of Prussian glorification of war. Most 'patriots' loathed war and longed for peace. Most 'pacifists' accepted that peace work should be directed at the final settlement and the years following the war rather than at attempts to influence its course. What divided them was their different hopes and fears. The 'pacifists' shared a view of human perfectibility in which the nurturing role of the mother could overcome male aggression and put an end to war, and were motivated by fear of the damage done by war in general. The 'patriots' feared defeat in this particular war.

At first Ray kept out of these dissensions, since her efforts to have a baby had to come first ('The Suffrage world is heaving & tossing – & may heave & toss for all I shall do').[42] But her views were already clear. In mid-December, she set them out in a letter to Mary Johnston, the novelist who had been her hostess in Virginia four years previously. This overlooked and revealing document indicates that Ray's objection to the 'pacifists' was the timing of their actions rather than the content of their beliefs:

I thoroughly agree with you that we are all in the wrong, & yet it does seem, as you say, that the Allies are less responsable than Germany. Now we are in for it of course the only thing to do is to go for it for all we are worth; & yet what a miserable thing to be striving for! The only consolation is that it will have to be the last war. We can't go through a thing like this again.

I can't help feeling that it is a sort of judgment on the world for being such an unjust world to its people – man trampling on woman & class on class – & yet of course when one gets away from vague theories into actions the things get muddled again & seem to follow an inevitable sequence.

There is a sort of peace party springing up here with which I have no patience. I agree with almost every word they say, & yet I don't want them to say it! It seems to me it only does harm now when we really have our existence to fight for, to be theorizing about armaments & democracies: it sets all the slow thinking people into opposition. The thing to do is help in every way we can so as to have a right to help in some rational settlement at the end. But of course being a woman I can't help as much as I'd like, because our Governments are so stupid. I don't want to fight, but I'd be a very good paymaster's assistant![43]

Key decisions would be taken at the NUWSS Annual Conference in February 1915. As Ray's energy temporarily returned at the end of 1914 after her months of lethargy, she joined Oliver in the battle to protect the suffrage movement from moves likely to prove as damaging to its reputation as suffragette violence had been.

On 31 December 1914 a questionnaire with a covering letter from Ray was sent to at least some of the candidates for the NUWSS Executive Committee election in February. Designed to elicit 'yes' or 'no' answers, the questionnaire's sub-text was that the NUWSS could only take up educational campaigns 'concerning the general questions of war, peace, diplomacy, arbitration, or armaments' at the expense of 'the cause of Women's Suffrage for which alone it was created'.[44] It is not clear who drew up this document, although it was probably what Ray had already offered to the LSWS (who opted to use an alternative, less bluntly phrased version). Oliver was himself a candidate (apparently more for the sake of having a platform to express his views than from any desire to be elected) and the final question 'would you wish [the NUWSS's] attitude to be at one with the nation or otherwise' echoes the wording of his election address ('In this time of National Crisis, it is both the duty and the interest of the NU to be at one with the nation').[45]

There is no reason to suppose that Ray disagreed with the thinking behind the questionnaire, but the wording and impetus behind it may well have come from Oliver, whose position in the War Office would have sharpened his views of what was realistic in wartime. His election address crisply summarised his position:

> Women's Suffrage is essential to Progress, and I place it before all other political considerations. [...] there is no need to build up public opinion either
>
>   (a) to the view that Peace in the future is desirable, or
>   (b) that it is our immediate duty to win.
>
> The nation already knows both these facts. [...] it is neither the duty nor the interest of the N.U. to embark on a campaign of propaganda or education on a subject on which it is not itself qualified to be a teacher. [...] the N.U. platforms are neither for the recruiting sergeant nor for the Union of Democratic Control.[46]

Realism, not imperialism, motivated both Ray and Oliver in this debate.

The balance of their marriage had been threatened by Ray's months of misery, since her normal role was the carer, not the sufferer, and working together in support of his views would have had domestic as well as political advantages. By early February, as Ray once more retired to bed, feeling ill and believing herself pregnant, Oliver appears to have been the driving force in the campaign to keep the NUWSS silent about the war: 'He is as keen as I am, if not more so' Ray reported on 1 February, and, a few days later, 'Oliver is deeply in it, & reports by telephone how things are going – towards a compromise of course'.[47]

At the NUWSS Annual Council held 4–6 February 1915 Oliver was elected to the NUWSS Executive Committee – 'greatly to [Ray's] joy & his horror' – but as far as the war was concerned, the Council did indeed produce a muddled compromise.[48] Its ambiguous resolutions left members confused, and were no help when a further crisis broke. An unofficial International Women's Congress was being planned for April 1915 in The Hague, with the NUWSS 'pacifists' deeply involved and a considerable amount of public support aroused. Of the 180 women from Britain who applied to attend, many were prominent in public life.

At a meeting of the NUWSS Executive Council on 18 March, an acrimonious discussion of a resolution (moved, successfully in the end, by Millicent Fawcett) that the NUWSS should play no official role in the congress reflected widespread bitterness over the recent resignations of Kathleen Courtney and Catherine Marshall from their posts as Honorary Secretary and Honorary Parliamentary Secretary to devote themselves to peace work. Harsh words had been spoken on both sides which would never be forgiven or forgotten. The ensuing NUWSS letter to its constituent societies banned them from sending delegates to The Hague, though individuals were left free to go. The resignation of eleven further members of the NUWSS Executive Committee, all supporters of the Hague Congress, followed; of the total of four officers and twenty-one members of the newly elected Executive Committee, over half had now resigned.

Ray had briefly considered standing as Honorary Secretary ('egged on by Oliver & my own folly') but soon advocated a compromise candidate as the best means of averting a split in the NUWSS (which happened anyhow a few days later, when Ray was abroad).[49] Once the Executive Committee had broken apart, Ray expressed delight to Mary (whose husband was fiercely anti-pacifist):

It is a marvellous triumph that it was they who had to go out & not us & shows that there's some advantage in internal democracy, for we only did it by having the bulk of the stodgy members behind us. Oliver has been frightfully active over it, & is full of excitement & triumph.[51]

Spending time in France brought the reality of war into closer focus for Ray:

> The Riviera is the most melancholy sight, all the country empty, all the villas & shops closed, & every hotel & hospital swarming with wounded soldiers. The reported gaiety & cocottes make no show at all, & every peasant you meet talks hatred to the Bosches.[51]

France had been the country most strongly opposed to the Hague Congress ('The local rag had a leader today full of indignation against the Hague congress, & praise for the French women who refused to take part') and being in France hardened Ray's own feelings against the 'lunatics' attending it.[52] She admitted 'I grow less pacifist every day – not less theoretically pacifist, but less practically. What is the good of passing resolutions at congresses, & splitting hairs about words & interpretations! […] if I were a man I should enlist, Quaker or no!'[53] There was no doubt about Ray's national loyalties, for all her pacifist sympathies. Having rejected her American heritage and showing no obvious interest in Ireland, Ray, though not really English herself, had since childhood been a devoted admirer of 'Englishness […] so real & so reliable […] & so reasonable', 'one of the solidly good things in the world'.[54]

Returning to London in early May, Ray faced further battles, as those who had resigned sought reinstatement at a Special Council Meeting to be held in June. In Ray's view their aim was 'to capture the name & funds & the whole organization, & use them "to promote a just settlement after the war" ', which to her meant 'vague & visionary propaganda, & […] the ruin of suffrage'.[55] But the resignations had decisively altered the balance of power: the 'pacifists' had lost their influence and quit the field. The LSWS nominated Ray as Honorary Parliamentary Secretary of the NUWSS and she was elected unopposed.

Ray did not at first expect her new role to be onerous. She was, she assured Mary, 'just filling a breach & keeping out some poisonous pacifists' (the adjective apparently aimed at specific people rather than at pacifists in general).[56] To start with, the NUWSS work had to take a back seat. Ray's main priority remained the work being done by the LSWS of 'placing women in "war works", & trying to see that they don't ruin the whole labour market by taking low wages'.[57] The work was difficult and slow, but the LSWS, despite chronic shortage of funds, proved remarkably effective, although 'every authority that has to deal with anything is at loggerheads with every other'.[58]

When in December 1915 Ray described her contribution, the list was formidable: interviewing employers about new openings for women and attempting to extend their scope; clarifying women's wages; interviewing candidates for the most important posts; negotiating with often hostile Labour Exchanges; keeping an eye on the LSWS training classes for women engineers to ensure adequate standards were maintained and sensible placements found; contributing to efforts to have women members on Government Committees; herself sitting on numerous committees to further women's interests; and, perhaps most significantly, overseeing the supply of women munitions workers. In October the Arsenal at Park Royal had sought the help of the LSWS to supply at short notice several thousand women to become munitions workers and (as also for Woolwich Arsenal) a far smaller number of educated women for supervisory posts. Ray became particularly involved with delicate negotiations over industrial problems at the Woolwich Arsenal ('Both sides were palpably in the wrong, so that it wasn't hard to sympathise with both!') and over wage rates with the Ministry of Munitions.[59]

Ray was particularly proud of the LSWS workshops to train women in oxyacetylene welding for aircraft manufacture and other semi-skilled engineering jobs. In March 1916 the workshops received an unexpected visit from Queen Mary. Ray – 'clad in my limited best (new brown coat & skirt) & white gloves' – received her for what started as an embarrassingly stiff tour of the welding workshop, and was surprised when her last-minute suggestion of a look at the filling and filing workshop as well was accepted.[60]

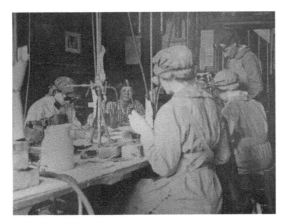

(Figures 17 and 18) The school for women welders run by the Women's Service Bureau of the LSWS, in 1915.

There had been no preparation at all there, & the atmosphere was much more agreeable, & suddenly she thawed, & laughed, & joked & listened to stories & poked into everything. Then she agreed to have tea, & sat down on our only chair (which had no seat) & drank out of our broken cups & eat [*sic*] cakes off a tin lid, & evidently thought she was seeing life. She seemed really to be enjoying it – & stayed ¾ hour.[61]

The visit's success and subsequent newspaper coverage was a great help in badly needed fund-raising.

Ray's NUWSS work involved assessing the likely impact on women of proposed legislation and where necessary lobbying against it ('rushing to & fro trying to catch illusory MPs […] not very attractive people'), writing regularly for the NUWSS newspaper, the *Common Cause*, and – inevitably – attending numerous committees.[62] Her main preoccupation was the Election Fighting Fund (EFF), introduced in 1912, at the instigation of the now departed socialist-pacifist group on the Executive Committee, which provided organisational and financial support for Labour election candidates. Even though Labour remained the only political party formally committed to female suffrage, Ray's view was that the war, and the move in May 1915 to coalition government, had so changed the political situation that a 'clean slate' was needed.[63] Her opponents, notably Catherine Marshall, who remained a member of the EFF Committee, held that undertakings already given could not honourably be abandoned.

The two main questions were the general policy, and the situation in certain specific constituencies where, despite the general suspension of political work by the NUWSS at the start of the war, their organisers had continued to work closely with Labour candidates. Meetings between the NUWSS and Labour leaders produced vague agreement that EFF work would be largely held in abeyance during the war: what would happen thereafter was less clear. The position in constituencies where active NUWSS support was being given to a Labour candidate needed resolution, given that an election might well take place during the war. Attempts within the EFF committee to resolve this led to a blanket suspension by the Executive Council of further EFF activity and a consequent howl of protest from the constituencies worst affected. Ray undertook a detailed investigation of the circumstances in each and concluded that active EFF political work was in progress in three constituencies. In the end only one, East Bristol, posed a major challenge to the change of policy. The EFF organizer, Annie Townley, an active ILP supporter, was involved in voter registration work for the Labour candidate, Walter Ayles, for whom the promise of financial support from the EFF was crucial.

(Figure 19) Catherine Marshall, influential Parliamentary Secretary of the NUWSS 1912–15, supporter of closer ties with the Labour Party and leading pacifist, in 1916.

By the time the Executive Council reluctantly agreed in December 1915 to make a limited exception for work in East Bristol, bitterness had been caused all round, with much talk of broken pledges and dishonourable conduct. The bond between the NUWSS and the Labour Party had been weakened, both in general and in the constituencies most affected, and personal relations between the supporters and opponents of the EFF policy within the NUWSS had deteriorated still further, with Catherine Marshall in particular demonstrating 'considerable ill will' towards Ray.[64] As Alys Russell reported to Mary Berenson:

> The Labour-Pacifist people on the Election Fighting Fund Com[mit]tee want to put the National Union in the wrong by saying we have broken our pledges, & that they were justified in breaking up our Union to form a Suff[rage] Labour Society. Ray's gigantic efforts are to put them in the wrong [...]. How they hate her! They write her awfully insulting letters, but she keeps calm. Her good temper is a great asset.[65]

The episode caused Ray 'more trouble & work [...] than it is easy to express'.[66]

In April 1916 Ray withdrew from NUWSS work for the time being. She had arranged to have some time off for the removal of her fibroid. But a week before the operation was to take place she discovered that she was, eventually, pregnant. Ray was determined to run no risks with this baby; her work for the LSWS could continue for a few weeks longer but two jobs were too much. After almost a year of intensive public activity it was time to focus on private life again.

CHAPTER NINE
Triumph! 1916–1918

In the past we have opposed the claim....We were wrong.[1]

During the summer of 1916, Ray's longstanding devotion to the cause of women's suffrage barely mattered to her. While the country followed, with hope and grief, the fighting on the Somme, Ray focused on her domestic life. Her desperately wanted and much delayed pregnancy was her greatest concern, but the practical problems from renting Durbins, Roger Fry's house near Guildford, for the summer claimed her attention: hordes of expensive visitors and the consequent need for extra servants, and rapidly diminishing financial resources. Wartime inflation was alarming – '£1 buys what 12/6 bought before the war' – and continued to increase.[2] Although the family's financial position had been rescued by Oliver's salary, that margin of comfort had been eroded and now 'even with O's £400 things are a close fit'.[3]

Durbins, the imposing (and aesthetically controversial) house, designed by Fry himself, where Julia had spent two terms, was not a comfortable residence. Fry's insistence on as much light as possible, and hence a high proportion of windows, led to poor insulation. Ray found the intensely hot summer unbearable in late pregnancy, took refuge in the only cool place (a north-facing bathroom), and slept as much as possible. The house's austere interior, with a two-storey

(Figure 20) Durbins, the house Roger Fry designed for maximum light, where Ray spent an uncomfortable late pregnancy in 1916.

galleried living area and a profusion of hard surfaces, was no better for sound insulation: Barbara became 'a perfect whirlwind in the house, through which her voice rings like a foghorn'.[4]

Ray's attempts to rest during May and June had come to nothing. Despite her determination not to risk another miscarriage, Ray found herself 'working just up to my limit of strength' to deal with an absorbing and highly important crisis in her LSWS work.[5] The oxyacetylene welders trained by the LSWS sought equal pay for equal work, rather than the lower rates usually offered to women; Ray recognised that 'if we can establish one skilled trade as a woman's trade among the engineering ones, & establish the correct skilled rates of wages for it, we shall have given a great lever to all the thousands of semi-skilled women in engineering, & broken down lots of barriers'.[6] They formed a Trade Union, the Society of Women Welders, with Ray as its first president, and eventually won at arbitration in two test cases.

It had not been an easy year for many of Ray's visitors. Draft legislation, introduced in January 1916, provided for compulsory military service to fill gaps left by the mounting casualties among volunteers. Ray expressed the feelings of many of her circle of friends and family when she described the scheme as 'the most stupid affair altogether, compounded of lies & ambitions & misunderstandings & the ravings of Northcliffe – but which will evidently go through & produce one of those stage effects that people read of in history books' and concluded 'our politicians are a set of idiots'.[7] Oliver, 'deep in protests against Conscription', appears to have had links with the National Council Against Conscription (NCAC) for which Lytton and James were working, though presumably his War Office post precluded public allegiance to protest bodies.[8]

Once conscription became law, Lytton failed in claiming conscientious objection but was eventually passed as medically unfit. James, sacked from his post on the *Spectator* because of his views, was classified as a conscientious objector and agreed to perform work of national importance. Oliver's important war work gave him exemption from call up, though he was in any case unlikely to have taken as strong a stand as his brothers. But his sympathies remained with the protesters and he was 'driven to rage by the raiding of the NCAC office'.[9] Ray shared his views: 'Whatever may be said against the poor foolish UDC, the anticonscription people are perfectly loyal & legal, & indeed thoroughly "English", & it's positively monstrous to try & make martyrs of them.'[10]

Ray's sister Karin had married Adrian Stephen, brother of Vanessa Bell and Virginia Woolf, in October 1914. When conscription was extended to married men, Adrian, who the previous year had become – at Karin's instigation and to Ray's horror – press secretary of the Union of Democratic Control (UDC), resisted call up as a conscientious objector. Directed by a tribunal to undertake work of national importance, he and Karin took up dairy farming. Ray (with justification) expected Adrian to be 'perfectly useless' as a dairy farmer and her initial incomprehension ('It's all so strange to me that I can't enter into their point of view in the least, but I suppose it's founded on genuine belief') gradually evolved into disapproval:

it all seems too thoroughly silly & rather despicable to me. It isn't as if either of them had really got convictions for which they would be prepared to work or suffer – they are just trying selfishly to escape their share of discomfort – a natural but not very exalted effort, about which it's tiresome of them to fix a halo of righteousness.[11]

The reaction at I Tatti was more violent; Berenson, furious, threatened to cut off Karin's allowance.

In late September 1916 Oliver was sent to Cairo to pass on his codebreaking skills, sailing on the *Megantic* to Alexandria via Salonika, the destination of the troops on board. His journey out was 'a most interesting trip', as he laconically remarked on a postcard to Ray from Salonika.[12] Once settled in Egypt, he explained that the danger from submarines had been constant: lifebelts were worn the whole time and placed under the wearer's chair during dinner, and detours had to be undertaken when the presence of a U-boat was suspected. When Oliver returned home just before Christmas, Ray gave her mother, in convincing detail, an even more alarming account of the journey out. Oliver's ship, she claimed, had been torpedoed off Crete and only the skill of the captain in finding the one safe place to beach it – and great good fortune – saved most of those on board and, eventually, most of Oliver's belongings. The two accounts do not tally.

Ray's story of lucky survival is repeated in many authoritative accounts of Oliver's life, but it is almost certainly fictional. Oliver's account is consistent with external evidence of where his ship was on given dates, whereas Ray's insertion of a frightening and uncomfortable further fortnight on a cattle boat after the alleged shipwreck is disproved by the dates of Oliver's postcards from Salonika and letters from Egypt. An attack on so large and well-known a ship as the *Megantic* would have been reported in newspapers, as the sinking of the *Franconia* at around the same time and place was. There is no record of any troop ship apart from the *Franconia* being sunk or damaged by a U-boat around the date or place of the alleged attack, and indeed the further career of the *Megantic* is well documented. The most likely explanation is that, as a joke, Ray and Oliver decided to provide Mary with some of the drama she craved, and Ray enjoyed exploiting her skills as a novelist. Perhaps during Mary's recent visit to England she had been as obsessed by the risk from torpedoes as she was by fear of the common cold; or perhaps a story of serious danger was meant to put her overblown health worries into perspective.

After a gap during the early part of 1916, Zeppelin raids on London had resumed, causing much damage. Ray's baby was due in November, and she contemplated staying away from London to avoid the risk of being bombarded and confined at the same time. But she longed for her own home and doctor – and anyhow 'I never can believe in future dangers' – so returned to Hampstead at the beginning of November.[13] Oliver would still be away for the birth, and for some time it was unclear whether Mary would come. Berenson's bitter complaints that she put her own family before him initially persuaded her to remain with him, but she eventually changed her mind, and was staying with Ray when the baby was born.

Christopher arrived late, but although Ray was physically uncomfortable she was spared the depression and tears she remembered from Barbara's birth. Ray bonded at once with her new son ('a little red lump of ugliness'), admitting 'I like the young creature most irrationally' and speculating that her reaction was because he was 'the result of so much wishing & such a long drawn out effort of determination'.[14] To Oliver she wrote ecstatically of 'the contentment that fills up all my mind – it's as if all the work in the world were now done, since I have produced that ridiculous ugly baby'.[15]

The reawakening of suffrage activity took Ray by surprise. At the outbreak of war, suffragists had assumed that their cause was stalled for its duration (and the suffragettes had given up suffrage action in favour of supporting the war effort). An unexpected technicality brought suffrage back into the public eye. The general election due in 1915 was deferred until 1916, by which time continuing difficulties over the now out-of-date registration system caused a wave of support for legislation to award the franchise to fighting men. Since extending male suffrage was likely to damage the chances of female suffrage even after the war, the NUWSS and other women's organisations pressed for female suffrage to be included in any adjustment of the franchise. Public opinion had swung round to support the suffragists. In politics and the press many previous opponents announced their conversion to the women's suffrage cause; and even Asquith, the major stumbling block before the war, now admitted that the case for a measure of female suffrage was 'unanswerable'.[16]

Ray was glad to be out of the fray (though Oliver remained deeply involved). Sceptical about the usefulness of political pressure, she at first believed the suffragists to be powerless and dependent on 'a wave of sentimental public opinion', which would only materialise if the Government introduced a service qualification – which they would not.[17] Asquith's speech in August 1916 astonished and delighted her. Congratulating Millicent Fawcett now that women's suffrage now seemed certain to be granted very soon, Ray had mixed feelings about their former foe:

> There is one thing I have always thought about Asquith – & admired him for. Wicked as he is, he does travel along the safe middle of public opinion, & his attitude towards things reflects the average opinion, I believe, more or less like a barometer. This seems more than ever proved since he has allowed himself to be moved by the (irrational & sentimental) shifting of public opinion about women since the war began.[18]

The 'old rogue', she admitted, was 'an ideal democratic leader!'[19]

Political consensus proving elusive, the whole franchise question was referred to a Speaker's Conference of both Houses of Parliament, chaired by the Speaker of the House of Commons, which sat in private between October 1916 and January 1917. In December, Asquith's Coalition government was replaced by one led by David Lloyd George, with substantial Conservative support. Ray was horrified ('Every decent person will leave the Govt [...] not that there are many to do so!!') and feared the impact of Lloyd George's policies such as industrial conscription.[20]

Ray's rapid recovery from Christopher's birth, and renewed energy, allowed an early return to political activity. She attempted – but failed – to choose between her work on women's employment with the LSWS and her role as Parliamentary Secretary of the NUWSS, and hence returned to a complicated balancing act between the two, exacerbated by a series of domestic problems over servants, food rationing, the Government's introduction of a 25% rate of income tax at the same time that a bitterly cold winter increased her heating bills, and her sister Karin's thoughtlessness in depositing on Ray her baby daughter Ann, with her nursemaid – and the Stephens' even less welcome large dog.

The early months of 1917 saw Lloyd George's government make strenuous, if not always well conceived, efforts to release more men for active service. Ray observed with pity and pessimism Neville Chamberlain's doomed attempt to set up a voluntary scheme of civilian National Service ('all moonshine'), deploring his decision to treat the potential of women workers as less valuable than that of elderly and unfit men.[21] Dictating a leading article for *The Times* (in conjunction with her sister-in-law Pippa and Athena Clough, both stalwarts of the LSWS) was an effective way of promulgating the opposing view.[22] Pippa and Ray worked through one night to meet a deadline for presenting a Womanpower scheme to Violet Markham (deputy director of the women's section of the National Service Department) and Ray pushed her 'old kettle' of a car to its limits to hand it in at the St. Ermin's Hotel in time.[23]

(Figure 21) Ray in one of her first cars, a Rover.

The War Office consulted the LSWS about using women to free men from non-combat roles within the armed services, but was predictably reluctant to take the offered advice. Ray and her colleagues had to rush

> to & fro like mad all the week concocting a great scheme to raise a sort of "Kitchener's Army" of women – which is easy enough as far as finding the women goes, but appalling when you come to details of discipline, selection, housing, pay, uniform, rates, drill, training, transport, illness, pay allowances, etc etc etc.[24]

The War Office's first scheme for what was to become the Women's Army Auxiliary Corps was, Ray thought, 'as rotten as possible' because the War Office placed the new organisation under 'a Colonel & three ladies with swaying earrings whose qualifications are that they have never had anything to do with the business before'.[25] Ray agreed with all the other women's organisations that women at work in large numbers needed to have women in authority over them: 'women must be selected, appointed, disciplined & dismissed by women, must have women inspectors to complain to, & women matrons to look after them, otherwise [...] the manners & looks of the girls go much further than their efficiency'.[26] But token females did not impress Ray: women in authority had to know their job.

Changing the official mind took a great deal of 'intrigue & wire-pulling', including a serious letter to the Prime Minister and various government departments signed by Mrs Fawcett and the leading anti-suffragist Mrs Humphry Ward.[27] The LSWS trio dashed about 'like the three black ladies in the Magic Flute, setting everyone to work', and Ray threatened press denunciation if the scheme went wrong (although 'the press is no engine to turn on lightly'). [28] The result was a gratifying change of heart in the War Office. Even Ray was surprised at the amount of influence she and her colleagues had been able to exert.

The Report of the Speaker's Conference, issued at the end of January 1917, stopped short of giving women the vote 'on the same terms as it is, or may be, granted to men', long the demand of the NUWSS.

Fear that women voters might outnumber men voters was still potent. Instead the Report proposed (by a majority vote) that the franchise should be given to women householders or wives of householders, aged over thirty or thirty-five, age limits which would exclude many of the women who had done most for the country during the war. Ray later characterised the age limit as 'absurd', but nevertheless it looked like a workable compromise, and 'if so much were once secured the rest was bound to follow'.[29]

Later descriptions of the year before Royal Assent to the Representation of the People Act produce a greater impression of inevitability than emerges from Ray's contemporary letters. The first stage was for women to speak with one voice on the proposals. On behalf of the NUWSS Executive Committee Ray had to 'interview everyone under the sun', some of whom, like Kathleen Courtney of the adult suffragists, were 'exceedingly unreasonable'.[30] The proposed age limit was a major concern, but suffrage supporters in Parliament strongly advised accepting what was on offer: fighting for more would be risky. Within days the suffrage movement had united in support of 'any Suffrage Bill, no matter how undemocratic'.[31] Ray's aunt Alys Russell, a member of the NUWSS Executive Committee, provided a not entirely impartial view of Ray's contribution: 'Ray, as usual, was very prominent and very capable, being asked to draft all the resolutions. [...] she is one of the most capable and useful women I have ever known, it is beautiful to see how Mrs Fawcett leans on her'.[32] Ray herself showed a rare lack of self-confidence; to Oliver, she admitted 'at any moment I fear I may make a fool of myself'.[33]

In February and March the demands on Ray were non-stop, as she accompanied Millicent Fawcett to lobby every member of the Government: 'I am packed so tight with interviews I can hardly breathe, & find myself parting from one Cabinet Minister at dinner time only to breakfast with another the next day'.[34] Enough people agreed with her that compromise was the only route to success that it was 'worth while to try hard to reconcile the irreconcilable', even though some of those she had to deal with were 'extraordinarily trying'.[35] Her morale rose and fell. Alys Russell's view was that 'if we get the vote now it will be entirely due to her, because even Mrs Fawcett can't do much without Ray's driving energy'.[36] When the NUWSS office was swept by illness, Ray had to shoulder even more of the responsibility. 'When you take on a job you can't let it down utterly, & they are all ill but me.'[37]

Since the conclusion of the Speaker's Conference, Ray had also been busy arranging 'a very picturesque deputation to wait on the P.M. in fancy dress (i.e. bus conductors, nurses, army cooks, munitions workers etc etc etc)', nearly a hundred representatives from all the trades and occupations now followed by women, all asking for the vote.[38] The final go-ahead for the deputation was given at short notice and with some unexpected conditions:

> no 10 Downing St. rang up to say Ll[oyd] G[eorge] wd. see our deputation on Thursday – just 42 hours ahead, & that we must combine in one dept. all the societies wanting to be received, & also Mrs Pankhurst. The next 22 hours were slightly feverish – I've never known time go so fast – for it's no joke to combine 24 suffrage soc[ietie]s & 10 other big women's societies into one basket together, & to make them all know what line is to be taken & to agree to it. It's like trying to harness a pack of wild elephants – & wild elephants with years of private conflict behind them. Moreover one & all objected to Mrs Pankhurst, & I had to go & see her & make an arrangement by which she came on, but was not part of, the deputation.[39]

It was Ray's idea to include a Welsh-speaking woman with whom Lloyd George could talk in his own first language, to his evident pleasure. The Prime Minister received the deputation, 'a huge success in every way', on 29 March, but by then the battle had been won.[40] After a weekend of apparently hopeless scurrying around to lobby Cabinet ministers against leaving women's suffrage out of the Bill, only cheered by a strongly supportive article in the *Observer*, Ray heard that the Cabinet had after all decided to include the necessary clause. When the House of Commons was told on 28 March, legislation to allow partial female suffrage was already being drafted.

With only brief breaks at Easter and Whitsun, Ray remained intensely busy, acting as secretary to 'a joint Co[mmittee] of MPs & wildcat suffragists' convened to plan tactics, and lobbying MPs ('I have to sit placidly listening to MPs while they dodder on, & I am simply fuming to get off to the next one. But the least sign of impatience upsets the whole affair, & you might as well not have come').[41] Distractions such as Alys Russell's operation for breast cancer, the removal of Barbara's adenoids and the need to find new servants received limited attention.

Not all the votes through which the Representation of the People Bill had to pass were of equal significance to the woman suffragists. The Second Reading passed by 329 votes to 40 on 23 May, but the Committee stage debate on the key Clause IV remained crucial. Ray was hopeful – but it had been impressed on her that the size of the Commons majority would be the decisive factor in getting the Bill through the Lords. A large newspaper advertisement appeared in The Times on 19 June, signed by Millicent Fawcett and Ray among others, stressing the amount of support now committed to the cause of female suffrage.[42] The vote later that day (385 votes to 55) exceeded their wildest hopes.

Ray had spent many days in the Ladies' Gallery of the House of Commons behind an iron grille which uncomfortably impeded sight and hearing of debates, and now joined with the Commissioner of Works and a Liberal MP in a 'frivolous little plot' to remove it.[43] On the day when a motion for the grille's removal was to be debated, MPs were confronted by a petition in support of the motion signed by their wives but secretly organised and undoubtedly drafted by Ray: 'we are assured that the interest of these Debates which we cannot hear, far surpasses that of any other legislative assembly in the civilised world'.[44] The motion was passed and the grille removed. It was a minor victory, but satisfying.

Taking advantage of the summer lull in Parliamentary proceedings, Ray underwent the delayed operation for removal of her fibroid in July. It went well, but her energy took several months to return. Oliver too was suffering from overwork, 'dreaming of cryptograms', and decided to take September and October as unpaid leave, despite the financial pressures which dominate Ray's letters to her mother during 1917.[45] Most of their holiday was spent at Chilling, on the Solent, the new home of Logan Pearsall Smith and Alys Russell, where Julia, Barbara and Christopher had been frequent visitors while their parents were working. In late 1917 increasingly threatening air raids, now mainly by Gotha planes, made London a hazardous place, and Chilling became a refuge for many children of friends, notably the family of Desmond and Molly MacCarthy. Night raids started in September but Ray's first experience of one was on her return to London at the end of October, when her normally taciturn housekeeper disgraced herself by going 'off on the shake & twitter' with fear.[46]

A further raid disrupted the House of Lords Second Reading debate on the Representation of the People Bill on 18 December. Ray found the whole evening theatrical. First came the antiquated arguments ('hardly any of them advanced up to 1884' and even fewer to 1917) from 'the fossilized old things, with their stupid & incredibly ancient faces' in a setting of 'red benches & gilt ornaments'.[47] When the guns started, the House adjourned. Ray and Athena Clough joined the throngs in the cellars, then engineered a dinner invitation from a friendly MP to spend a sociable evening in the dining room picking up Parliamentary gossip. The debate's conclusion the next day included an excellent speech from Lord Buckmaster and a good one from Lord Lytton, followed by 'an amazingly skilful & flowery effort of Lord Curzon whose total effect is astonishingly finished & cynical'.[48]

The final major hurdle for the suffragists was Committee stage on Clause IV in the House of Lords, whose Leader was that diehard anti-suffragist, Lord Curzon, President of the National League for Opposing Woman Suffrage. Many peers were known to share his views, and the attitude of many more was unknown. On 10 January 1918 Lord Curzon wound up the debate. Despite his continued opposition to the measure, he could not advise the House to oppose a measure which the Commons had passed by such a large majority. He was one of 13 abstentions; 71 peers opposed the Clause; 134 supported it.

A decade later, when Ray came to write her history of the women's movement and her biography of Millicent Fawcett, she made this the moment of supreme victory. But Ray's letters show this to be a novelist's moulding of events. Not only did Ray and her colleagues have to endure further days of mild unease, stuffy atmosphere and 'white gloves (4/6 a pair)' in the 'small pewlike enclosure' allocated to ladies, as the Lords debated and rejected a motion to submit female suffrage to a Referendum, but a totally unrelated matter threatened the passage of the entire Bill.[49] The Lords had inserted an amendment providing for a measure of proportional representation, which the Commons resisted. As the end of the Parliamentary Session approached, with time running out, the Bill was batted to and fro between the two Houses. 'The whole place', Ray observed, 'had the feel about it of a school on the last day of term.'[50] As Chamberlain, Asquith and Balfour indulged in personal slanging matches, their 'outburst of childishness' worried both the ministers in charge of the Bill and the watching suffragists.[51] In the end heavy Government whipping restored order, a compromise was found and the Bill passed. The elaborate ceremonies of Royal Assent in the Lords followed immediately and at last the suffragists could indulge in 'a great handshaking' and 'a mild celebration' over dinner.[52]

In Ray's haste to talk to Millicent Fawcett, who had left earlier, she drove into an officer (fortunately without injury) and performed 'a grand double skid' in St Martin's Lane.[53] Neither she nor Mrs Fawcett could quite believe that what they had so long been working for had been achieved. There was still work to do on the franchise, with its ridiculous age limit of thirty, and much more on the economic position of women, already dominating Ray's thoughts; but this first instalment of female suffrage was a turning point. For both women it was a moment of public triumph, when their efforts and achievements were recognised and honoured. Yet in Ray's private life all was far from well.

PART FOUR

Building a Better World

CHAPTER TEN
Aftermath:1918–1920

One has to swallow one's troubles...[1]

The prospect of an end to the war left Ray relatively unmoved: 'we had all settled down to the war as a permanent condition & so don't believe in it. And perhaps also we are a little afraid of peace.'[2] She had good reason to be wary of excessive optimism. Although the war had brought gains for women, it was already clear that some of these might be ephemeral; the task of restructuring a post-war world to prevent another such cataclysm was daunting; and during the months since her great suffrage triumph Ray's happy (if somewhat neglected) domestic life had been torn apart.

As the suffrage battle neared success, Ray was unwillingly dragged into her mother's problems. Mary and Bernard Berenson had a stormy marriage.[3] The sequence of young men who attracted Mary's attention, and her delight in emotional drama, infuriated the naturally irascible Berenson; and as his wealth and social standing grew, he became dissatisfied with his corpulent wife's appearance. Berenson's years of anguished love for Belle da Costa Greene did not improve his temper; nor did all the problems over the renovation of I Tatti. Mary's close friendship with Geoffrey Scott – far more than friendship on her side – had led to Scott's architectural partnership with Cecil Pinsent and his constant presence at I Tatti, giving Berenson a continuing cause of resentment.

While Cecil Pinsent developed a successful career as architect and garden designer to the Anglo-American community in Florence, Scott returned to scholarship. His major work *The Architecture of Humanism*, published just before the war, brought him international fame. But his private life, now heterosexual, was less successful. After falling in love with – and being rebuffed by – Karin in 1913, Scott was in search of a wife. In 1914 he met and fell in love with Nicky Mariano, a beautiful, cultured young woman of mixed Italian and Baltic ancestry. Mary encouraged the relationship, which she thought would keep Scott within her influence, but at the outbreak of war Nicky was in Estonia and did not return to Italy until 1919. Scott spent most of 1915 and 1916 working as Berenson's secretary, to Mary's delight, and pursuing unsatisfactory relationships with other women. In October 1916 he moved to Rome to work in the British Embassy. A year later Berenson also left Florence for Paris, where in the guise of an interpreter he worked for the US Army Intelligence Section; this move effectively ended his relationship with their neighbour Lady Sybil Cutting, who had replaced Belle Greene in his affections in 1914.

The war initially had little effect on life in Florence, even after Italy joined the Allies in May 1915, but the Italian defeat at Caporetto in October 1917 made I Tatti liable to requisition for refugees. Mary therefore returned to Florence after a visit to England, instead of remaining in Paris with Berenson. A few days after her arrival, Geoffrey Scott became engaged to Berenson's ex-mistress Lady Sybil Cutting. Mary succumbed to bitterness towards both the men in her life and hatred towards her rival. She retreated to bed, and wrote vituperative letters to Scott about his intended. Mary turned to Berenson for sympathy and received none. In February she rejoined her husband in Paris, but he was deep in a new affair with a French Baroness, and his tactlessness about the sexual ecstasy he was enjoying further twisted the knife. What remained of Mary's mental stability disintegrated: Berenson stopped her from throwing herself out of the window of their fifth floor flat on the Avenue du Trocadéro, but she then succumbed to a major nervous breakdown and various painful physical ailments (some probably psychosomatic).

During the early weeks of 1918 Ray had more on her mind than her mother's emotional state, but a rescue mission eventually seemed essential. Obtaining a passport (valid only for a month) and a visa took some string-pulling and it was not until 10 April that Ray reached Paris, a city many of whose residents had already fled because of the recent German Spring Offensive. Air attacks and bombardment from Big Bertha, the giant German gun sited forty miles away, were less threatening than the possibility of a German breakthrough. Ray later recalled that the largely female, drably dressed, population who remained were 'anxious and weary'; food, coal and clothing were expensive and in short supply. 'The newspapers, which sold like wildfire, were bought in silence and read in silence by people standing anxiously still in the streets. […] everywhere there were women and children in heavy mourning, black with the overwhelming crêpe of French widowhood, and with sad, pale faces.'[4] In this setting the life of luxury in the Berensons' flat seemed obscene: 'huge endless 8 course meals, with every conceivable extravagance of food & wine' served up by 'rows & ranks of menservants' for 'Polish poets, Bohemian patriots, American novelists, French ministers, ambassadors, Italian journalists, Russian princes, Danish inventors, cosmopolitan adventurers of every sort & kind, mixed up with smart ladies & their attendant cavaliers.'[5] Their endless talk was 'the greatest nonsense I have ever had the misfortune to hear.'[6] When she could, Ray escaped to find out the state of the campaign for female suffrage and women's employment in France.

The doctors could find nothing physically wrong, but Mary, suffering from 'a gloom that is almost impenetrable', wanted to be 'ill & weak & floppy'; she needed to be removed from their demanding social life and the main irritant, her husband.[7] To Ray's surprise, she found herself sympathising with Berenson ('a man of no sense & stores of information who is interesting to listen to when one has patience').[8] Mary later recalled how comforting Ray's 'calm, steady companionship' had been, but at the time both Ray and Berenson were

reduced to despair.[9] Eventually Mary recovered enough to be capable
of travelling. On 1 May mother and daughter reached England, where
Ray had arranged for Mary to go into a nursing home. Her physical
and mental condition became worse before it improved, and she
threatened suicide. Much of Ray's summer was devoted to her care,
while she faced her own marital crisis.

Oliver Strachey liked women. He respected their abilities ('I hold that
Women at present have their fair share neither of opportunities nor
of responsibilities').[10] He enjoyed their company and the admiring
attention his charm could attract. He fell in love easily. And he found
the process of seduction irresistible ('it's neither the copulation nor
the desire to copulate that is the great thing for me, but the being on
copulating terms and the arrival at that point').[11] He was not naturally
monogamous: new conquests could happily co-exist with continuing
devotion to an existing attachment.

   For several years Ray and Oliver were almost always together,
on their travels and their shared foray into Indian history, before
Oliver's job divided them. Their involvement with the NUWSS gave
them another shared interest, but was often pursued separately. Ray's
difficulties in conceiving, and the eventual birth of her adored son,
meant that Oliver had competition for her attention. Her year of
frantic activity before the vote was won had allowed them little time
together. In the spring of 1918 Oliver conceded that 'we hardly ever
meet when you are here' – but her absence made life 'dismally dull' as
Ray was 'really so much the only person in the world'.[12]

   Their attitudes to social life had diverged from the start. Oliver
liked parties and relished the Bloomsbury milieu to which his brother
Lytton belonged. Ray did not, even though some of the individuals
concerned, such as Virginia Woolf, were her friends. In January
1915 she acknowledged that despite – or perhaps because of – all
the Bloomsbury parties and dinners the couple were attending 'I
am not of a sociable disposition, & I cannot disguise that'.[13] By April
1917 Oliver had become 'a regular old club fogey', frequenting the
Oriental Club for bridge and 'that ridiculous club-talk' as 'a reaction

from Bloomsbury, where the rest of his social life is carried on!'[14] In contrast, and to Ray's 'great relief', 'my social life remains nil'.[15]

At the end of 1917 a new feature in Oliver's life separated them further. Several of Lytton's friends agreed to subsidise a country retreat to allow him to escape from Belsize Park Gardens and have somewhere congenial in which to write. In return for £20 [£1,000] a year each, the external shareholders could use the property on an occasional basis while Lytton acted as caretaker and Dora Carrington as housekeeper.[16] Lytton and Carrington moved into The Mill House in Tidmarsh, near Pangbourne, just before Christmas 1917, and from then on Oliver had a bolthole of his own.

It is not clear how soon or how seriously Oliver's attention began to stray from his wife. He later claimed to have been in love with Vanessa Bell on his return from India in the few weeks before his engagement to Ray, and their separate social lives certainly allowed scope for brief encounters during the war. But Oliver's first serious extra-marital involvement arose from his role in the NUWSS. Inez Ferguson was born in Aberdeen in 1895, but after her advocate father went bankrupt and fled abroad to escape charges of fraud and embezzlement in 1901, his abandoned wife, daughter and son moved to Berkhamsted, where Inez was educated. She then read Classics at St Hilda's College, Oxford, before taking a Diploma in Economics. In June 1917 she joined the NUWSS office and by 1918 was its salaried Secretary, a role which would have brought her into frequent contact with both Ray and Oliver.

Ray's letters in the early months of 1918 are full of public activities, barely mentioning Oliver but brimming with energy and excitement with no hint of marital trouble. The likelihood is that Oliver turned to Inez for attention while Ray was in Paris in April 1918. Inez was clearly a feature in Oliver's life by May, when Oliver made arrangements for a weekend at Tidmarsh 'avec ma dame'.[17] Three months later, in an anguished and guilty letter to Ray, Oliver mentioned an intended holiday with Inez and admitted 'My goings on may be scandalous, they may even be grossly selfish inconsiderate & immoral, of bad taste & doubtful decency'.[18] Nevertheless, he proclaimed that 'I will

(Figure 22) Inez Ferguson

not have it suggested that it means in any way that I love you less than before' and, because of their 'big common [...] stock of intimacy', 'you're far the most important person to me in the world'.[19] (The letter – from Tidmarsh – ended rather more prosaically 'Butter and washing recd. with thanks'.)[20]

Ray herself left no record of her reaction to Oliver's affair. She apparently kept no diary from 1916 to 1924, but in any case she always shrank from committing her most intimate feelings to paper. Her grounds for objection may have seemed limited. She was well aware of the unconventional marital arrangements in Bloomsbury and subscribed – at least in theory – to the need for personal freedom of action; the marriage had been largely her doing in the first place; and her grandmother had drummed into her the inappropriateness of jealousy ('people are always going to give you just as much love as they can: and if they don't give you more it's *your* fault, not theirs, and it's no use blaming *them*!').[21]

Nevertheless Ray seems to have been hit hard by the combined strain of coping with Mary, making practical arrangements for Julia and her own children, and coming to terms with Oliver's affair. Oliver described one letter from her as 'a shriek of agony' at being deserted by everyone, including him.[22] To Millicent Fawcett Ray admitted that 'things are very difficult both publicly & privately just now, & I suppose the only thing to do is plough through them'; she fully expected to break down herself with the strain of dealing with Mary and admitted that she needed to 'get away into solitude for at least a fortnight to recapture a little peace'.[23] In the end her working life provided an escape route.

An invitation from Dame Edith Lyttelton for Ray to join the British delegation to 'a huge gathering of American and English war workers, convened by the YWCA with the object of "drawing together the women of England and America so that their efforts at reconstruction may proceed along similar lines'" took Ray back in late August to a rather more cheerful Paris, along with Dame Katharine Furse, the Duchess of Atholl and Dame Edith herself.[24] The Women War Workers Conference, where Ray spoke, was 'outwardly very successful, but remarkably hollow within'.[25] The British were an oddly assorted group, she continued: 'Mrs Furse piles on the official correctness till I feel inclined to explode, the Duchess piles on her coronet, & Mrs Lyttelton flutters off into psychic regions at a touch.'[26] Nevertheless the change of scene felt like 'a long & refreshing holiday', particularly as Ray had the opportunity to visit the Scottish Nurses' Hospital at Royaumont, the VAD Headquarters at Boulogne and various Base Camps and WAAC units.[27]

Some months later Mary remained as a house-guest who showed no signs of moving on. Oliver reported to Lytton that 'Ray begins to show signs of such irritation & disgust that I fear I shall have to take some steps […] I'd rather quarrel with my bread and butter than put up with unpleasantness'.[28] He escaped for weekends at Tidmarsh with Inez. Mary returned to Italy in the spring but by then relations between Ray and Oliver had deteriorated. Virginia Woolf observed that 'the situation between them is now considerably strained' and 'Ray is becoming tart under the perpetual presence of Inez'; 'the case of husband and wife who have no love for each other, but still live together is an embittering spectacle', she concluded.[29] Although Virginia had earlier felt rather in awe of Ray (she 'makes me feel like a faint autumnal mist, she's so effective & thinks me such a goose'), now Ray did not escape Virginia's caustic assessment.[30] 'More and more the public woman', she had become 'floppy, fat, untidy, clumsy, and making fewer concessions than ever to brilliancy, charm, politeness, wit, art, manners, literature and so forth', and her talk of 'women's future' did not thrill Virginia: 'my God, if *thats* the future whats the point in it?'[31]

As so often in Ray's life, public activities offered a distraction from private sorrows. To the suffragists' surprise, women would be allowed to stand in the December 1918 election. As the enabling legislation made its way through Parliament, the political parties looked for female candidates, and prospective candidates (including Ray) hurriedly looked for constituencies. Ray found it difficult to choose a party: the Conservative talk of economic warfare to come and Lloyd George's dishonesty were equally unappealing. She was offered the unrewarding prospect of contesting the solidly Conservative seat of South Kensington as a Liberal ('But then I'm not a Liberal!') but the Conservative central office was 'violently opposed to women M.P.s' and refused to see her.[32]

Eventually an opportunity arose at the traditionally Conservative but socially mixed suburban constituency of Brentford and Chiswick. The local Coalition supporters were split over the choice of Colonel Walter Grant Morden as the official Coalition-Unionist candidate. Grant Morden, a wealthy Canadian financier, had recently been accused of profiteering from a wartime contract for the supply of 'dope', cellulose used in the manufacture of aeroplanes. A breakaway group looked for a rival candidate. Ray could offer excellent references, both Conservative and Liberal. H.A.L. Fisher praised her 'rare capacity for conducting business with the minimum of friction and the maximum of despatch' and her 'steady, substantial judgment';[33] Millicent Fawcett claimed that Ray's 'transparent straightforwardness and power of speaking would quickly win a popular audience';[34] Jack Hills, Lord Robert Cecil and Lady Rhondda gave her enthusiastic support; and F. D. Acland endorsed her 'knowledge and work', adding that, in discussions with fellow MPs of the women best fitted to become MPs, Ray was the universal first choice. [35]

The selection committee eventually opted for Ray as an Independent Coalition candidate, forcing her to confront the financial demands of standing. '£700 [£31,300] will cover all I am legally allowed to spend, & I ought to do it for less.'[36] She looked to the NUWSS, who supported various women candidates of differing political allegiances, for financial help, supplemented by a contribution from Mary and some borrowing.

It was a last-minute campaign, with Ray still recovering from a bad attack of flu. By the time she had found an agent and committee rooms, Grant Morden, 'a regular Tory', was 'splashing his money about'.[37] The Labour candidate did not have 'a ghost of a chance' – but could split the progressive vote.[38] Ray's election address followed the standard Coalition line, ending on a personal note:

> I make no apology for asking you to vote for a woman. [...] I hold that the interests of men and women are so closely bound up together that they cannot be divided, and that what is for the good of one sex must certainly be for the good of the other.[39]

One of her flyers promised 'Real Reconstruction without Revolution'; another committed Ray to 'Honesty and Independence in Parliamentary Government'.[40] The electors never saw less serious publicity material drawn up by Oliver, which described Ray as 'well provided with adipose tissue'.[41]

The early days of December were filled by election meetings, some with prominent supporters such as Mrs Fawcett and the Countess of Selborne (Lord Robert Cecil's sister). There was strong local feeling for revenge against Germany: Ray's arguments that punitive measures would be counter-productive and that placing the entire cost of the war on Germany would be unworkable usually produced 'hisses and catcalls', sometimes breaking up the meeting.[42] Mary compared Ray to her father in the skill with which she dealt with hecklers, the *Daily Mail* confirming that she spoke 'rapidly and eloquently with a telling gift of repartee'.[43] The favourable press comment Ray's candidature received may well in part have reflected widespread suspicion of Grant Morden, as well as dislike of his patronising comments that 'the Lady Candidate ought to stay at home and look after her kiddies' and 'doesn't know anything about business'.[44] By election day on 14 December, *The Times* was unrealistically referring to Ray as the favourite.

Despite some strong support for her in the constituency the final results (a fortnight later) were decisive: Grant Morden received 9,077 votes, William Haywood, the Labour candidate, 2,620 and Ray 1,263. Of the sixteen other women candidates, all were defeated except the Sinn Feiner Countess Constance Markievicz, (who never took her seat); of the remainder, Christabel Pankhurst, a coupon candidate, came closest. Ray lost her deposit – but so too did two ex-cabinet ministers, and only ten of Ray's forty-five friends in the House were returned. She took defeat calmly: 'Why should I grumble? I don't.'[45]

Ray's election campaign left her with debts and Oliver's future income was uncertain. By April 1919 the proposed fusion of the military and naval codebreaking sections to form the Government Code and Cypher School (GC&CS) meant that Oliver would still have a job, 'a financial comfort, but an awful bore for poor O'.[46] The war over, Oliver hankered for a life of leisure, as Virginia Woolf noted disapprovingly: 'Oliver was very testy because the Berenson's [sic] won't endow him so that he needn't work.'[47]

Berenson had for some time been meeting any shortfall below £2000 [roughly £84,500] per annum in their income (excluding Ray's journalistic earnings). Ray had to produce a financial statement every six months, and a scrupulously detailed list of any gifts from Mary. Ray never seems to have felt any guilt about taking their money. Much of the spending she incurred was the result of her busy public life. If she had been earning a salary, all would have been well. As she believed her work was a contribution to public well-being, it seems likely that she considered that financial support from her mother and stepfather was only appropriate: their life of luxury benefited no-one but themselves.

Ray turned to journalism to boost her finances. Already a prolific contributor to the *Common Cause*, she now courted the main national newspapers. The increasingly influential popular press devoted considerable space to 'modern woman' as a topic, and women who could write for and about women, especially in relation to their new political roles, were in demand. In the first quarter of 1919 Ray earned £32 [£1,350] from articles, but openings were sporadic and over-exposure counter-productive. During 1919 Ray wrote irregularly for the *Daily Mail*, the *Daily Express*, and the *Daily Chronicle*, despising the ease with which she could produce 'all these ridiculous articles, which drip like inkblots off my pen'.[48] Later she added the *Observer* and the *Daily News*. A weekly 2000-word piece in the *Queen* had to be 'topical, political, & specially meant for women', written ten days in advance without touching on 'anything controversial in politics!'[49] When, 'sick to death of writing platitudes of a highly innocuous character', she ventured into political controversy, she was nearly sacked.[50] It was, Ray came to feel, 'a grisly job, writing slush' with 'no intrinsic value & a good deal of degenerating effect on me', but it kept the household financially afloat.[51]

Ray edited (or co-edited with Ida O'Malley) the *Common Cause* and its successor the *Woman's Leader* for most if not all the period from July 1919 to May 1923. Although theoretically paid, Ray seems to have mainly worked on a voluntary basis because of the paper's financial problems. Crisis followed crisis, with Ray deeply involved in the paper's finances and its written content, producing much of it herself. Ray was never comfortable fund-raising and these were difficult times.[52]

Ray's voluntary work remained time-consuming. The Women's Emancipation Bill, introduced by the Labour Party in April 1919, would have swept away barriers against women in public life, equalised the franchise and allowed peeresses to sit in the House of Lords. During the Second Reading debate, Ray noted, 'there was not a rag of the old prejudice left, not an echo or a squeak, & the only fault anyone could find with the bill was that it did not go far enough'.[53] This concord was short-lived. Despite intensive lobbying by Ray and her LSWS colleagues, Labour's Bill was defeated in the Lords in July after the Government introduced its own Sex Disqualification (Removal) Bill. The resulting Act was less far-reaching but paved the way for easier access by women to University degrees and employment in the Civil Service, also allowing them to qualify as solicitors and to serve on juries and as magistrates. These gains only benefited a small minority of women. As Ray pointed out in June 1919: 'On the one hand the learned and scientific professions are opening to women [...]: and on the other, the trades and industries are closing against them with a determination only equalled by the success that their brief entry has been'.[54]

The previous year Ray had been more hopeful. She was convinced that women workers should join the men's Trade Unions: 'good or bad the women must be in with the men or die'.[55] In January 1918 the Society of Women Welders, with a membership of 500 and a 'meagre little record of two arbitrations & one strike', took their problems to the mighty Amalgamated Society of Engineers (ASE), 'the most important body of men in the country at present [..] tiresome & refractory to the last degree, exclusive to the verge of folly, [...] hundreds of thousands strong' and 'madly antifeminist'.[56] Ray's interview with their Executive Committee was 'very odd':

> They are of course engineers themselves, quite uneducated, very slow, but very very intelligent. And I got the feeling that they knew what they were after – which you don't always get from interviews! They were more solid than many of the La[bour] Men I have seen – their heads less turning & turned, & their power less obviously pleasant to them. [...] I liked them very much. [57]

To Ray's delight the Committee offered 'all the practical technical help in their power – which is unlimited' and seemed interested in the idea of admitting women members, 'quite the most important thing that could happen for women in England now that the vote is won'.[58] Negotiations with the Ministry of Munitions about welders' wages and with the ASE about admitting women dragged on for months. In July 1919 Ray was heartened by an invitation to the delegate meeting of the ASE in Manchester which was to discuss the admission of women, particularly welders. The outcome was 'a great disappointment': women were not admitted to the ASE or its successors until 1943.[59]

Women's wholescale entry into industry during the war had been bought at a price, as the Government had undertaken that the men who had been replaced could return to their previous occupations and terms of employment afterwards. The Restoration of Pre-War Practices Bill, introduced with little warning and on an accelerated timetable in June 1919, was the legislative means of effecting this.

Although Ray was well aware that widespread dismissals of women from their wartime jobs were inevitable, the Bill went far beyond this, returning industry to inefficient pre-war practices and banning women completely from many jobs, apparently as a result of secret negotiations between male Trade Unionists, male employers and a male Government. Ray and her assistant sprang into action:

> before 4.o'clock in the afternoon I had primed up five different members to speak on the subject and had circularised the whole of the Labour Party and all the other M.P.s interested in the matter. I got up into the Ladies' Gallery just in time to hear first Major Wood and then Mr Acland making the speeches that I had just put into their mouths, and I am bound to say that they did it very creditably.[60]

Ray was, inevitably, 'simply gasping with rage at not being able to make the speeches myself'.[61] The Bill was referred to Committee for possible amendment, driving the Labour Party into 'a perfect fury', while Ray and the LSWS continued lobbying press and Parliament.[62]

In a circular to MPs, Ray claimed that the Bill's terms were unwise, unjust and unstatesmanlike in the limitations they placed on women's role in industry: amendment was essential.[63] In the *Common Cause*, she was more outspoken. Her article is a masterly blend of amazed indignation at the proposals, shrewd conjecture at the reasons for them, fair-minded understanding of the Trade Unions' position, acknowledgement that their ranks included many 'far-seeing and enlightened men', and gratitude 'that the House of Commons still remains to protect the interests of unrepresented sections of the community'.[64] This fusion of indignant passion with reasoned argument, moderation and generosity towards others (for tactical purposes), all produced at speed and under pressure, was typical of Ray's working approach. But by 1919 public attitudes to female employment had changed, with resentment replacing the former gratitude towards the women munitions workers. The Bill was enacted almost unaltered.

Even before the first tranche of female suffrage was achieved, the NUWSS was considering its future. At the Council meeting in March 1918 a divergence between those (including Ray) who wanted the Union to concentrate on equality of franchise and opportunity and those in favour of working for broader social changes led to a compromise resolution. The goals of the NUWSS would include equal suffrage and 'all other such reforms, economic, legislati[ve] and social, as are necessary to secure a real equality of liberties, status and opportunities between men and women'.[65] Widows' pensions, equal guardianship rights over children, and admitting women to Parliament and the legal profession were adopted as immediate aims while 'the endowment of motherhood' (family allowances), pressed for by Eleanor Rathbone, was to be studied for possible future adoption.

The divergence between two types of feminism could not be drafted away. Egalitarians, such as Ray, whose priority was the removal of political, legal and financial inequalities between men and women, minimised differences between the sexes. Protectionists stressed the peculiar problems facing women and argued for special measures, such as the endowment of motherhood and the promotion of birth control, to assist them. Ray had no objections to these measures in themselves, arguing against Millicent Fawcett's firm opposition to the former: 'I do really believe that the next few years may see a complete shifting of values, and, when they have shifted, Mothers' Pensions might be an unmixed blessing'.[66] Nevertheless allowing women greater self-determination by enlarging their employment opportunities – at the same rates of pay as men – was difficult to achieve at the same time as campaigning for legislation which assumed women's weakness. Equality had to come first.

In February 1919 three possible schemes came to the NUWSS Council for discussion. Ray proposed reducing the NUWSS to a single 'Fawcett Trust' for the provision of information; an amendment by Eleanor Rathbone would have widened the objectives of such a body; Oliver suggested expansion rather than contraction. Under his scheme the NUWSS would continue 'to work for a real equality of status, liberties and opportunities between men and women' but would now accept affiliation from any society promoting sex equality.[67] Oliver's scheme was adopted with slight modifications. Millicent Fawcett retired as President, being replaced by Eleanor Rathbone, and the National Union of Women's Suffrage Societies renamed itself the National Union of Societies for Equal Citizenship (NUSEC). Ray's verdict was that the Union was 'left with […] an unworkable & paper scheme'.[68]

Oliver's major role in determining the future of NUSEC presumably reflects his relationship with its current Secretary, Inez Ferguson, and her wishes for the organisation employing her (although Inez only remained with NUSEC for a few more months, then became General Secretary of the National Federation of Women's Institutes). For Ray, freeing herself from any responsibility for putting Oliver's scheme into practice made her feel 'as if a ton weight had been removed from my back', but it must have been painful to accept that her attempt to engineer a close working partnership between herself and Oliver by drawing him into her sphere of activity had, by introducing him to Inez, resulted not only in personal estrangement between them but a public defeat by him in her area of expertise.[69]

Ray's two children had spent the last months of the war with Alys Russell at Chilling on the Solent to escape the air-raids on London. When Miss Prynne, the governess who had taught Barbara there, was poached by the family of Sir Douglas Freshfield, a distant relation of the Stracheys and Stephens, the families reached a friendly agreement that Barbara should board at the small informal school taught by Miss Prynne at Wych Cross, the Freshfield home in the Ashdown Forest. Barbara spent several happy and productive years there, interrupted by a term at I Tatti, with her cousin Ursula, in the autumn of 1919. Ray had been resisting Mary's demands for a visit from Barbara for years and, with the war over, eventually gave way.

In Barbara's absence from home, Oliver's brother Ralph and his children moved in; so did Julia, and her friend Frances Marshall came to stay. Ray, not at her most tolerant, found the presence of two young women with interests so different from hers to be uncongenial:

Their room is like a rag bag, their habits worse than Oliver's & their conversation appalling. The same sickening old tunes go on incessantly, & the same numbers telephoning. But I suppose it is their way of living, & as much of a way as anyone's.[70]

A few weeks later, things were no better: 'Julia & Frances are quite impossible from any point of view known to me, but no doubt there are other points of view.'[71] When Julia started a course at the Slade School of Art, her non-existent time-keeping made it 'a terrible struggle to get her out of the house by 9.30AM. She & Oliver have a 6d bet on who is down first each morning, so far he is well ahead.'[72] Ray suffered 'a good deal from dressmaking in the drawing-room, & hairpins on the stairs' but recognized that her own reaction was unreasonable (which made matters worse).[73] Lady Strachey was moving house from Belsize Park Gardens to Gordon Square, so during the removal process Ray's overflowing house had 'a nightly incursion of two Stracheys or so to dinner to add to my already immense collection.'[74]

(Figure 23) A crumpled press cutting announcing Ray's appointment as Nancy Astor's Parliamentary Secretary shows Ray looking strained in an unflattering hat.

The world of politics offered a respite from stresses at home. In early November Ray went to Plymouth to speak on behalf of Lady Astor, who was standing as a candidate in the by-election in her husband's constituency after he inherited his father's title. Ray did not consider her 'a good specimen for the first woman MP' but 'she is quite sound really, & Christabel would be far worse.'[75] On 15 November 1919 Nancy Astor, born in the State of Virginia and married, after an early divorce, to Waldorf Astor (now Viscount Astor), became the second woman to be elected to the House of Commons (and the first to take up her role there).

Even before the result was officially

announced on 28 November, Ray offered to assist Lady Astor with her Parliamentary work while she found her feet in the Commons: 'It is so very important that the first women MP should act sensibly, & she, though full of good sense of a kind, is lamentably ignorant of everything she ought to know'.[76] The Astors were 'sufficiently advanced conservatives to exactly coincide' with Ray's wishes.[77] Her plan was to 'run her work for a time, & write her memoranda & speeches, watch events for her, prepare her Parliamentary questions, see her deputations, select [what] invitations she must accept & so on'.[78] Ray would receive no salary, merely some help with expenses such as her own invaluable private secretary, Miss George.

Ray arranged to spend her afternoons in the new Lady Members' room at the House of Commons and when Lady Astor took her seat on 1 December was already convinced that 'it is all going to be not only useful but very great fun'.[79] Soon she had 'never been so busy before'.[80] The Christmas recess allowed Ray to collect Barbara and Ursula from I Tatti, but then her main task was to prepare Lady Astor for her maiden speech. This was to take place on 24 February, opposing a Bill to remove wartime restrictions on alcohol.

Nancy Astor had seen the evils of drink in her own family and among her constituents in Plymouth, and longed for her adopted country to introduce Prohibition, as the United States had just done. The speech had to convey Nancy's passion while recognising that Prohibition was unpopular in Britain and that the House of Commons did not respond well to being hectored. Ray did not share Nancy's commitment to temperance, but she had been brought up in a pro-temperance household, knew all the arguments and understood what would work in the debate. The half-hour speech was no doubt a communal effort, with Ray as a major contributor; it was, she admitted, hard work to prepare someone whose natural approach was so unparliamentary. In the end Lady Astor 'did much better than we any of us hoped, & it made a very good impression in the House'.[81]

'Ly. A. being what she is, & I being what I am, I think we'd make a good combination' Ray had predicted.[82] She was right. Ray's mastery of facts and figures complemented Nancy's existing interest in causes affecting women and children, and helped her to respond to the demands placed on her by the many women outside her constituency who expected the sole woman MP to speak for them.

Writing later about Lady Astor for an American audience, Ray stressed her courage, kindness, humour, energy, outspokenness, unexpected talent for mastering complex material and strong moral convictions.[83] These qualities all appealed to Ray. Well aware of the drawbacks of Nancy's disregard for Parliamentary etiquette and her shortcomings as a public speaker, she nevertheless developed a strong and lasting respect and affection for her. Ray's self-confidence protected her from the cruelty Nancy Astor could turn on people who did not stand up to her. Lady Astor had a large and competent staff, including the 'perfectly splendid' Hilda Matheson as political secretary, but it must have been reassuring to have in her camp someone with as much Parliamentary experience, wide knowledge of the problems facing women, organisational ability, good humour and calm good sense as Ray, particularly at a time when Nancy was facing hostility from many MPs and persecution from Horatio Bottomley.[84] In return, Nancy's ebullient vitality cheered Ray. The 'filthy International Suffrage Alliance congress' in Geneva that they attended together in June was made bearable for Ray by Nancy being 'great fun'.[85]

Ray appears to have given up her formal role with Lady Astor at the end of the Parliamentary session, but they kept in close touch, and Nancy often sought advice and information from Ray. By mid-1920 Ray was disengaging herself from public activities. Her attention was fixed on developments in her private life.

CHAPTER ELEVEN

'A Reckless Woman':
1920–1923

I am simply longing for a house of my own
& a garden to potter about in.[1]

Ray had never lost her attachment to the hills and woods above Fernhurst. Over New Year 1915 she and Karin had spent a brief writing break in Friday's Hill Cottage, the Costelloe family's former holiday home, indulging in nostalgic memories of childhood. The idea of buying land behind the cottage to build her own country retreat first occurred to Ray then, but its realisation had to wait until after the war, when a succession of strikes fuelled fear of a working-class uprising similar to the Russian Revolution and prompted Lloyd George's Government to pour money into a campaign for improved housing, 'Homes Fit for Heroes', to appease demobilised soldiers. Under the Housing (Additional Powers) Act, 1919, grants were offered for a limited period to private house-builders erecting small dwellings, the aim being to boost the housing stock for the working classes (not to provide holiday homes for the middle classes). New building land became available (over a million acres sold in 1920 alone), including the very plot that Ray had longed for in 1915. Now that family life in Hampstead had been soured by Oliver's affair and the demands of

Julia, the temptation to build a new nest for herself, and to recreate her own childhood for her children, was irresistible.

During the spring of 1920 Ray was preoccupied by the financial challenge of buying the land and building on it. She convinced herself that a house would be 'a safe investment [...], because there is such a demand for houses near London' but caution did not play a major part in her calculations: 'I want the land so much that I'm going to do it and d_d the consequences'; 'I don't see how I can resist it. [...] Well well, I'm a reckless woman.'[2] By the end of April the land was hers. After selling off 2 acres she was left with just over 5 acres at a net cost of £750 [£27,000], funded mainly by a favourable exchange rate when she sold her American steel stocks and re-invested in England. To qualify for a grant, a cottage had to be built quickly.

Oliver's cousin, John St Loe Strachey, editor of the *Spectator*, had long been a proponent of affordable rural housing, particularly advocating the use of *pisé de terre* (rammed earth), which was allegedly a cheaper and quicker process than building in brick, minimising reliance on scarce skills and raw materials. Official trials were started, and for a while rammed earth was hailed as a major advance in cheap housing. The technique involves using heavy mallets to compact soil within shuttering erected on a low masonry base to form an eighteen-inch-wide solid wall, blocked out as needed for windows and doors. St Loe's son-in-law, the architect Clough Williams-Ellis, became an acknowledged expert in the technique. Relying on his advice, Ray opted for *pisé de terre*.

The original building plans were ambitious, with, as the first phase, 'a small trial garage, dressed up as a cottage, so as to earn the Govt. grant of £260'; the upstairs rooms would eventually be for servants and would be a useful 'camping ground' while a larger house was built.[3] In late May Ray was in Fernhurst arranging for stump-clearing, an access road and an expensive water main.

Building (with advice and almost certainly personnel from Exervis, a company set up to provide employment in the building industry for ex-servicemen) started soon afterwards; although men were used for bricklaying and carpentry, Miss Clarke, an ex-agricultural labourer, and Miss Brown, formerly an aircraft worker, rammed the earth.[4] Brickwork was used for the chimneys, and for the internal walls. Originally called Copse Cottage from the chestnut copse surrounding it, the two-storey house had four bedrooms, a bathroom, a kitchen and a large area with garage doors, used as a living room; slivers of wood left over when chestnut saplings were cut into triangular fencing stakes formed the traditional local thatch.

The walls were completed by September and the rest by the end of the year, just making the deadline for the grant. After her first night there Ray proclaimed it 'absolutely heavenly' and that she had had 'several thousand pounds' worth of satisfaction already!'[5] The following summer extra rooms were added to cater for visiting family and friends. Mary provided $1000 (nearly £250 [£9,200]), (later supplemented by a loan of £50 [£2,000]), to fulfil Ray's dream of a vast swimming pool, which became a playground for visiting crowds of children as well as a place of exercise and relaxation for Ray. Building the cottage was an extravagance Ray never regretted: it became a crucial part of her life, a refuge from all the stresses of London and a place for family and friends to gather. But it led Ray into one of the biggest mistakes of her life.

(Figure 24) The Mud House (originally known as Copse Cottage) in 1923.

Ray convinced herself that she could cover her own costs and make her fortune by setting up as a building contractor to build similar *pisé de terre* houses. Her brother-in-law Ralph Strachey, a civil engineer, was enthusiastic and joined her as a partner; each was to put £1000 [£36,860] into the venture. By September 1920 the contracting business was 'getting very real. Ralph now works all day in the office getting out plans & estimates, & we are quite solidly undertaking 3 houses in Devonshire, & have many others half nibbled'. Ray's 'visionary fortune increase[d] every moment'.[7] Premature press coverage led to a rush of interest, almost too much to handle, and by October their company (Rammed Earth Houses Limited) had '5 firm contracts & many others pending'.[8]

The first signs of problems came in December. Although Copse Cottage became known as 'the Mud House' (or even 'Mud'), this was a misnomer: the technique requires dry soil, and winter building in Britain is fraught with problems. Paying workmen for weeks when no work could be done rapidly exhausted capital. Ray's house had by chance been built on land ideal for the purpose, and the earth used had been that dug out for the foundations; not all the sites for which the firm had contracted were equally suitable, and importing soil drastically increased costs. Skilled workmen resented seeing their role usurped by unskilled labour: bricklayers were uncooperative. Over the period during which Ray was building in *pisé de terre*, experience on other sites demonstrated that the expected cost savings were illusory and dramatically reduced official enthusiasm for it as a building material.

Even so, the company's main problem was financial: it was under-capitalised, especially for unproven technology. Delay in receiving the Government grant on her own house left Ray's personal finances in an even worse state than usual (the gas in Hampstead was cut off because of an unpaid bill). Ralph put in £1000, Ray only £300 of the £1000 she had planned but 'we shan't get any appreciable returns till May, & meanwhile have to pay out week wages to nine people & get together the plant & materials'.[9] She tried to interest Berenson in investing £1000 in the company, but her approach had more of desperation than confidence in it:

I can't of course absolutely guarantee that the concern is safe – I am so inexperienced in business, & so optimistic, that I don't trust myself much. But at any rate it's a sporting attempt to provide a thing that's very badly wanted, so it has the forces of supply & demand in its favour.[10]

Berenson declined.

As Ray tasted the joys of being a home-owner, she also experienced the terror of living on the edge of financial disaster. She was forced to borrow heavily from friends. By the summer of 1921 Ray and Ralph accepted that the venture had been a mistake. They scaled down operations, found other jobs for their workmen and bore the losses. She admitted to Berenson that the building enterprise had been 'foolishness' and that he had been right not to invest in it since 'although there certainly is money to be had out of it, I am not the person to get it out. I've learnt a lot about "business" in this year, & now know what it involves'.[11] Ray's dream of making her fortune (and even of relieving Oliver of the onerous task of working for his living) had ended in heavy debts.

She took drastic action. Being able to spend weekends and holidays in Fernhurst meant that the cost of running the Hampstead house became unjustifiable. Ray began to lodge in Gordon Square with Lady Strachey at Number 51 or Karin at Number 50 during the week and cut down on outgoings in Hampstead; Oliver also lodged in Gordon Square, with the conductor Ernest Ansermet. Although Oliver sometimes visited Mud, his 'delightful & refreshing fortnight' in Vienna in May was with Inez: he and Ray were leading semi-detached lives.[12]

Having a base in Bloomsbury suited them both for convenience, cost and social reasons. When Oliver's office moved to South Kensington and a recent increase of his salary by £200 [£8,150] was withdrawn as a result of the Anti-Waste campaign, they decided to make the move permanent. By October 1921 Ray's household was living in the top and bottom flats in 41 Gordon Square, James Strachey's house, on a semi-boarding basis. Ray's long-standing housekeeper lost her job, and 96 South Hill Park was returned to the landlord for the remaining months of the lease.

These measures were enough for the household to be able to live off Oliver's salary and Ray's journalism, and for her (rapidly declining) six-monthly income from investments and her allowance from Berenson to be put towards paying off the £500 [£25,000] she owed friends and then her bank overdraft. She was, she assured Berenson, practising 'violent economy'.[13] When Mary, somewhat hypocritically, accused Ray of extravagance, she protested 'it's true that the motor & Miss George are both costly, but nothing else is. We eat nasty food, & as for clothes-- !'[14] 41 Gordon Square remained Ray's base for a year until, with help from Mary, the family returned to independent living by leasing 42 Gordon Square.

Hero worship was characteristic of Ray. The objects of her admiration were typically older, committed leaders of a cause, notable for their moral integrity; the two most influential were Millicent Fawcett and Lord Robert Cecil. To both, Ray became a trusted and valued lieutenant and friend. Writing to Mrs Fawcett in the wake of the 1918 suffrage victory, Ray expressed her profound gratitude for the opportunity and the example which the young women of her generation had been given: 'You have not only done the thing, but shown how such things should be done: & the way has been as important as the end.'[15] Those who had caused Mrs Fawcett pain by the manner of their resignation from the National Executive in 1915 'missed the whole essence of the thing when they didn't learn to be honest & straightforward'.[16] Political and moral leadership belonged together for Ray. She found both in Lord Robert Cecil.

As Parliamentary Secretary of the NUWSS during the later stages of the suffrage campaign, Ray had been in frequent contact with Cecil, one of its most trusted supporters, a reliable adviser on political strategy and a never-failing Parliamentary voice on their behalf. Despite his roles within the Coalition government, Cecil was hardly a typical Conservative. A member of an aristocratic family with High Anglican religious convictions and centuries of political involvement in its bloodline (his father had been Prime Minister), Cecil was an independent-minded man whose sympathies often seemed more Liberal than Conservative and who was regarded as a maverick by his own party. A conviction politician whose energetic commitment to the causes he favoured was not always popular, a devout Christian, and a devoted husband to his deaf wife, Cecil had much in common with Ray's father, Frank Costelloe; he was very different from Oliver Strachey.

The political world which Ray had joined held many echoes of her childhood and many of the political figures she encountered would have known, or known of, her father. Ray's colleagues in the Women's Movement would recall with gratitude his efforts on behalf of those women who attempted to become members of the LCC. Millicent Fawcett and Frank Costelloe had both been active in the Vigilance Association. And when Ray represented the LSWS on a deputation led by Lady Astor in June 1922 to persuade the Minister of Labour, T. J. Macnamara, of the importance of providing training for unemployed women, both Ray and Macnamara may have recalled his close association with Frank Costelloe on the London School Board. Macnamara had been Costelloe's close ally in the battle over underfed schoolchildren and, as editor of *The Schoolmaster*, almost certainly the author of the long tribute to Costelloe, praising his 'sublime debating power and rare force of character' and 'kindly and considerate feelings', which appeared in that paper after his death.[17] The ideals with which Ray had been raised remained a potent factor in her life, reinforced by her association with Lord Robert Cecil.

During the post-war period, Ray became deeply involved with two of Cecil's main preoccupations, the attempt to set up a Centre Party and his championing of the League of Nations. Ray had come to believe that 'the time had come for women's politics & real politics to amalgamate – & the only way to do that is through the parties.'[18] But along with many other politically active women of the time, she could not bring herself to work through the party system. Like Cecil, she despised Lloyd George for his dishonesty; the Labour Party had never attracted her, particularly because Trade Union influence was

often detrimental to women's interests; and although progressive
Tories held views not that far from her own, the party as a whole was
depressingly reactionary.

The post-war political situation was complicated. Instead of
straightforward opposition, coalition government and the fractured
Liberal Party produced factions and shifting loyalties. Those who found
Lloyd George despicable sought new Liberal leadership to restore the
high moral standards of pre-war Liberalism to party politics. Cecil
and, within the Liberal Party, Gilbert Murray and the Gladstone
brothers, Herbert and Henry, saw the former Foreign Secretary,
Viscount Grey of Fallodon, as the ideal leader, either instead of, or in
conjunction with, Asquith. Cecil's aim was 'Liberalism – constitutional
democracy – peace, retrenchment, co-operation' and he argued that
Grey was the living embodiment of 'the spirit which should direct
our policy' and could offer 'a super-party rallying point' for 'the great
mass of non-political voters', and 'the non-reactionary Conservatives
who passionately desire clean Govt'.[19] Grey was untainted by recent
political manoeuvring, but his health and eyesight had deteriorated
and he had little desire to return to politics. Pressure on him to do so,
and negotiations between an increasingly wide circle of disaffected
Liberals and Conservatives over the nature and policies of a possible
new Centre Party, continued for over eighteen months.

Throughout 1921 and early 1922 Ray was 'in the thick of a group
of discontented Conservatives of whom Lord Robert Cecil is the
chief'.[20] She found them 'almost indistinguishable from Liberals', and
expected 'some kind of fusion in the end'.[21] While never sanguine
about the prospects for a Centre Party, Ray relished being back in the
buzz of politics ('I am thoroughly enjoying myself behind the scenes,
& have immense secret confabulations, all about nothing, as is the
way with political intriguers').[22] Lord Robert was 'a delightful person
to work with, because he is so outspoken & candid'.[23] The impetus
towards a Centre Party gradually faded, and Lloyd George's departure
from office in October 1922 finally ended it.[24]

The war had made Cecil a committed internationalist and the
League of Nations became the great cause of his life. Ray came to

share his enthusiasm. The need for an international peace-keeping body had been widely recognised during the war. The 1919 Paris Peace Conference accordingly established the League of Nations as a forum for the resolution of international disputes, designed to provide mechanisms to defend member states' territorial integrity, protect minorities, allow arbitration and preserve peace through sanctions both economic and military. Although US President Woodrow Wilson had been one of its main champions, the US never became a member, and Germany was not allowed to join until 1926. Lord Robert Cecil was involved with the League from its inception.

In February 1919 Ray had, with Millicent Fawcett, attended the Inter-Allied Suffrage Congress in Paris, whose purpose was to ensure that the Peace Conference paid proper attention to the interests of women. Their method was personal interviews with leading participants, including Cecil, who headed the section of the British delegation dealing with the formation of the League of Nations. It was Cecil's efforts which Ray later credited with securing that 'the eligibility of women as delegates to, or officers in, all the positions under the League of Nations was written into the Covenant from the beginning'.[25]

On his return from the Peace Conference Cecil became Chairman of the League of Nations Union (LNU). His commitment to the League, the Covenant of which had now been embodied in the Treaty of Versailles, had received inconstant support from Lloyd George and President Woodrow Wilson. Working through the LNU to build up public support for the League and its aims offered an alternative means of preventing a slide back into the patterns of diplomacy which had failed to prevent the war. Recruitment and publicity for the Union were tools to ensure future peace.

By 1921 Ray was immersed in LNU work alongside her other activities. When the Union held a mass recruiting rally in Hyde Park ('ten platforms, six processions, 10 bands, all the bishops & archbishops, & crowds of bigwigs') on a scorchingly hot day, Ray was hard at work: 'Lord Robert made nine speeches in succession – running from platform to platform, & hounded on by me, & the afternoon grew hotter & hotter'.[26] In December their shared commitment to the League of Nations Union had made her 'as thick as thieves with Ld. Robert whom I see daily'.[27]

Ray's working life was thus extending far beyond the demands of feminism. Personal relationships strongly influenced the causes she took up. As well as responding to inspirational leadership, she cemented personal ties by working with close friends and family – with Ellie when they first joined the suffrage campaign, with Oliver on Indian history and in the NUWSS, with Pippa on women's employment, and with Ralph on the house-building scheme. She and Cecil had much in common (moderate centrist political views, powerful work ethic, strong moral sense, lack of interest in personal appearance) and her personal respect and affection for him were crucial. She later admitted that the realisation that she was achieving little was only one reason for eventually giving up most Union work: 'If Lord R had stayed in the LNU I should have hung on for the love of seeing him.'[28]

The League's acceptance of the role of women was a minor part of its importance to Ray. She became convinced of the need for 'a wholesale turnover of opinion towards absolute & all-round disarmament' and despaired of the apparent lack of any such movement.[29] The League was necessary for humanity not just for women. For Ray, feminism was part of a wider project to make the world a better place. Clearly the world would be more efficiently organised, as well as juster, if all women were allowed to express their wishes through the ballot box and use their energies and abilities for the public good. The experience that women gained while campaigning for the vote and the wider opportunities open to them once it had been won should prove valuable for the whole of society, men as well as women. But there was nothing magic about the vote itself, nor any need for Ray to confine herself to women's issues in her public work.

By the end of 1921 the political world was contemplating a further election. Ray still wanted to enter Parliament and was approached by several unpromising constituencies, which she declined. Another attempt at Brentford and Chiswick appeared the most hopeful, but 'I can't afford to fight without a chance of success'.[30] Lord Robert Cecil's offer to help fund her expenses if she stood as an Independent made up her mind. By July 1922, when she was formally adopted, she had an agent in place and considered that an early organisational start gave her 'a sporting chance'.[31]

The straight fight between Ray and her previous opponent Grant Morden produced a lively campaign. An early meeting raised her expectations, with the emergence of the outspoken side of Ray's personality, seen more often in public than in private and nicknamed Sally in her family:

> I made a long & lugubrious speech (all against France & America). [...] When I had finished they began asking questions, on everything under the sun, & by the mercy of Providence Sally came forward with appropriate & even witty answers. Then they flowed with compliments & several important ones actually agreed to come onto my committee, & the whole sense of the place was overwhelmingly favourable. It was more than my most sanguine hopes.[32]

Ray's election address committed her to supporting the League of Nations, Free Trade, domestic social reform, the Anglo-Irish Treaty which had established the Irish Free State, and 'any sound proposals for Temperance Reform' short of prohibition. Damning the Coalition's record and those of any party whose policies fostered a 'serious danger of class bitterness', Ray proclaimed herself 'a sincere believer in Democracy, Free Speech and Constitutional Government', seeing 'no reason to be in the least afraid of the judgment of the British people'.[34] 'I do not approve of extremes in politics. I distrust Revolution on the one hand and Reaction on the other, and I believe we ought to pursue a middle course.'[35] With perhaps rare honesty, Ray admitted that 'I am not a rich woman, and if you elect me I cannot spend money lavishly in the constituency, for I have not got it'.[36] But she would 'endeavour to represent the men as well as the women', and 'to stand out for honesty and openness in public life'.[37]

(Left: figure 25) This was Ray's response to her opponent's scurrilous accusations in 1922. (Right: figure 26) The allegations of child neglect required a public display of the plainly well-cared-for children. This specially-taken photograph appeared in Ray's 1922 campaign literature.

Grant Morden appears to have been rattled, judging by his accusations that Ray was neglecting her children. To refute them, Ray, much against her will, had to display Barbara and Christopher (plainly not neglected). Her campaign literature portrayed her as a 'New Broom' and she canvassed dressed as a female chimney sweep. Ray's confidence grew ('there is undoubtedly a serious chance of getting in' she told Mary), but although the election on 15 November showed a substantial increase in her vote (from 1,263 to 7,804) it was not enough: Grant Morden polled 10,150. Of the thirty-two women candidates, only the two existing women MPs, Lady Astor (Conservative) and Mrs Wintringham (Liberal), were successful. Ray had spoken on behalf of both when they were originally elected. Standing as an Independent, like Eleanor Rathbone, Ray had little chance against a sitting member, but, as commentators pointed out, most women candidates had been standing in virtually unwinnable seats. Ray took a rapid decision: if she was not to be an MP, she would see what she could achieve in the United States.

Ray's main motive for going to the United States in early 1923 was financial: she hoped to find an American publisher for her novel and make lucrative journalistic contacts. She was also investigating whether US suspicion of the League of Nations could be modified by a visit from Lord Robert Cecil. She succeeded on all fronts. Harcourt Brace accepted the novel subject to cutting its length by a third, a task which Ray quickly achieved. G. Arnold Shaw, the agent she took on, put her in touch with the prestigious *Ladies Home Journal* which commissioned two articles, and the *New York Evening Post* took 'a series of semi political articles'.[39] American journals paid substantially higher rates than their British equivalent, 'as much as $500 [approximately £125(£6,500)] for a thousand words – and though I can't get that much to start with, I am fairly well contented with $300! My English price is £3 [£157]'.[40]

A certain amount of social life was essential for Ray's League of Nations work and to get background for the articles she planned to write – and visits to relatives could not be entirely avoided. Grace Worthington, Ray's hostess in New York, noted how focused she remained: 'Her Novel, Money and the League of Nations, are her objects, and nothing else matters. She is an expert at eliminating non-essentials.'[41] The contacts she did make were influential. Helen Flexner (sister of Grace Worthington and Carey Thomas) wrote admiringly to Mary Berenson that Ray 'impressed Raymond Fosdick and Walter Lippmann with her knowledge and intelligence'.[42] She talked – or rather listened – to Colonel House, President Wilson's personal assistant during the setting up of the League of Nations, 'for an hour & a half. He went over the whole Wilson tragedy – it was thrilling, & rather touching to hear him talk of it'.[43] In Washington in search of political material for articles Ray 'dropped straight in among the very people who could show me what I wanted. I spend my days talking to Senators, to wirepullers, to "organizers" – with a modicum of social flip flap thrown which I am unable to avoid'.[44] Soon she had fallen into 'the bad old habit of packing my engagements as close together as sardines in a tin'.[45]

A further lure was the remunerative American lecture circuit. Ray had hoped to avoid lecturing but offers of payment were difficult to refuse. Her work for the League of Nations put her 'on intimate terms with all the bigwigs in politics', raising her public profile and the fees her agent could demand.[46] His promotional material attributed to her 'Knowledge, Magnetism, Humour – the essential qualities of a first rate speaker!'[47] She spoke in Philadelphia, at Bryn Mawr, at the Women's National Republican Club in New York, then (for $100 each) at a series of girls' schools near New York, on topics such as 'English Women in Public Life', 'The Position of Women in World Politics', 'Party Politics versus Non Partisan Organisations' and 'The Difference between American and English Education. 'I hate it a good deal, but the cash will be useful.'[48]

The first element of Ray's work for the League of Nations went 'as easily as melted butter on a hot plate' and by 21 February the Foreign Policy Association had agreed to host a tour by Lord Robert Cecil 'rather explaining than advocating the League of Nations'.[49] Ray was soon 'up to the eyes in arranging Ld. R.C's tour [...] The rush of hostesses eager to entertain the lion is frightful – they push & push & push. But I am good at keeping them off & we are getting a very useful plan worked out'.[50] She hoped to be able to delay her return to accompany the tour – if childcare arrangements could be found for the Easter holidays – and in that case the Foreign Policy Association would pay all her expenses after Lord Robert's arrival and her passage home, 'not in joy at getting rid of me I trust'.[51] As usual Alys Russell offered to help out, spending the Easter holidays with the children in the primitive accommodation of Ray's cottage at Fernhurst. So, equipped with a new summer hat, Ray joined Lord Robert Cecil and his private secretary Philip Noel Baker when they arrived in New York on 27 March for a five-week tour.

From the start Lord Robert made 'an astonishingly good impression [...] disarming criticism by his excessive sincerity' in his personal contacts, speeches and radio broadcasts.[52] Ray had 'never seen him in such an impressive frame of mind'.[53] Philip Noel Baker dealt with the tour's political content, 'preparing memoranda & heavy material for the serious people', while Ray's role was answering letters, day-to-day organisation and, most importantly, seeing 'important visitors who come hundreds of miles to try & arrange secret interviews between such men as Ford, or Borah and Ld. R.[54] In New York they kept up to five typists busy (one installed in Grace Worthington's flat) and Ray was rushed off her feet.

Ray's admiration for Lord Robert grew during their weeks touring America together. His 'deadly serious' absorption in his ideas was even more marked than his charm: 'He has no fringes of attention, & you can see his flame steadily burning. The closer I see him the more I admire the man. I think he has really got a quality of greatness'.[55] The tour had in Ray's view 'taken away one or two of the idiotic misconceptions, & has furnished ammunition to the League' and been 'an almost overpowering success. [...] it was undoubtedly the psychological moment'.[56] Cecil was less convinced, with 'a lingering suspicion that the great mass of this warm-hearted people would have entirely forgotten all about the speeches and the arguments in them in twenty-four hours'.[57] He later thought it probable that 'my visit produced little, if any, effect'.[58] Lord Robert was particularly taken aback by the prevalent hypocrisy – the Prohibition laws were disregarded even by judges – and by the broader 'tendency to try to enforce on people opinions or conduct which was antipathetic to them'.[59] Ray would certainly have agreed: to 'coerce or compel another person to act contrary to their own judgment' was one of the few things she considered really wrong.[60]

Ray's letters home mainly concentrated on the positive aspects of her visit: excitement, friendliness, political achievement, financial advantage. Her assessments of the American political scene were, at first, moderate: 'On the whole it seems rather elementary & crude, with an upper surface of super subtle & all round suspicion & an undercurrent of sheer ignorance. But there is a lot of force & some quite sturdy ideas too, and it's all in a state of evident change.'[61] But Ray was repressing far stronger feelings. Suffering from increasing homesickness and dreading the possibility of needing to return the following year for financial reasons, she exclaimed:

oh, what a country![...] there is nothing which seems quite real somehow and the strain of never feeling free to tell your mind is

horrid: & yet the results of doing so are worse. If it were not for the
cash, I'd certainly not go back there again. But it's easy money, there's
no doubt about that.[62]

In the diary entry she wrote over two years later she was less inhibited:

politically America is disgusting. [...]. I saw the "reformers" in plenty,
& the "idealists", & the real people, the machine politicians. I saw their
women (& their even more complete severance from reality was a
shock) & I saw the Senators. [...] I was utterly disgusted. Ignorance
& stupidity & above all bad faith were the outstanding things about
the people who had real power – & ignorance & futility those of the
people who were "reformers". It looked quite hopeless, & the apathy
& indifference of ordinary people gave my democratic faith a nasty
shock. It all seemed like England exaggerated, with all the tolerable &
serious elements left out. Not one of the people I met equalled a 5th-rate
MP. They had of course certain qualities – quick, agile, untrammelled,
energetic: but they had no knowledge, no background, no continuity,
no faith, I think, and dishonesty was taken for granted.[63]

She returned to England dispirited and 'profoundly discouraged
about the future' to face personal sadness.[64] Oliver's brother Ralph,
Ray's former business partner, had been diagnosed with terminal
cancer the previous year and was now dying. Ray had come to know
him well and was deeply fond of him: 'Christ-like [...] too good, &
so very lovable' she later described him.[65] 'Just to be in the room with
him was good,' Ray recalled, 'though he was often dreadfully dull, &
always inexpressive, & sometimes fearfully unhappy.'[66] Much of early
June she passed at his hospital bedside, with Oliver and Pippa, until
on 18 June Ralph died 'after a few days of quiet under morphia [...]
of course it was very trying.'[67] The under-statement was typical of Ray
when she felt strongly. Mary, normally incapable of seeing beyond
Ray's façade of permanent cheerfulness, remembered Ralph's death
as being 'the profoundest sorrow that ever entered [Ray's] heart': 'she
never willingly spoke of it afterwards.'[68]

More cheerful was the publication of Ray's second novel, *Marching On*, that autumn.[69] Written over ten years (and drastically cut in a matter of days), the book falls into two distinct sections. The first, tracing the childhood experiences of the heroine, Susan Bright, in mid-nineteenth-century Michigan, her escape from her disapproving family to a women's college, then her years working for the Abolitionist movement alongside the Quaker Angelina Severance, is based on the life-story of the Reverend Anna Shaw. The excessive devotion which Angelina develops for Susan, eventually driving her away and into a rash marriage, is closely based on Ray's own experiences with Anna Shaw; she recognised that the work could not be published during Miss Shaw's lifetime.[70] The Underground Railway by which freed slaves were helped to escape to Canada is the background to some of the most successful passages in this section.

The second section, recounting the experiences of Susan and her new husband Burt as some of the first settlers in Kansas, amidst violent conflict over whether Kansas should enter the Union as a free or slave-owning state, is more confidently written and demonstrates the amount of historical research which Ray undertook during its composition. The autobiographical elements relate to Susan's difficult first pregnancy and her greater devotion to her second child than to the first. But these are less gripping than the chain of events, mainly bloody, leading apparently inexorably to the outbreak of the American Civil War. In general the characterisation is sufficient to carry the story but no more. However the vivid but balanced portrayal of the fearsome patriarch John Brown, hanged for murder but treated as a saint by many Unionists, produces a genuinely complex and compelling figure who dominates the final chapters of the book.

Reviews were generally polite, with particular praise being given to Ray's detailed research, her handling of the historical background and her skill in telling a story. One example may suffice:

> She has accomplished a staggering task in masterly fashion. It is, on the whole, magnificent, but I doubt if it is, strictly speaking, a novel. [...] Mrs Strachey has not the graphic touch. But she has a notable

power of narrative and synthesis. As a novelist, she is a first-rate historian.[71]

It is a fair assessment.

In September 1923 Ray combined a trip to deliver Barbara to her new school in Switzerland with attendance at the Fourth Assembly of the League of Nations in Geneva, at a time when the League faced its first major challenge, over Corfu. Italy had bombarded and occupied Corfu in retaliation for Greek failure to safeguard Italian members of a boundary commission murdered in Greece. Although Greece had appealed to the League, the dispute was, at the insistence of Italy and France, dealt with by the Conference of Ambassadors, so discussions in the Assembly were little more than expressions of disapproval. Although the episode has often been cited as a major blow to the League's credibility, Ray remained optimistic. 'For all his bluster, Mussolini is afraid of the League' she assured Mary.[72] On disarmament she was equally hopeful that 'a new era in armaments' was on the way, with Cecil 'displaying the most marvellous gifts in driving the team along'.[73] Even though she noted the paucity of 'genuine politicians', and, with amusement, 'the wriggles & general aghastness of some of the nations as they realize the various implications of genuine support for the League', this period marked the high-point of Ray's political idealism.[74] The League offered an example of how politics should be conducted, in contrast to the realities of political life in Britain and America.

Ray's revulsion from the American political scene fuelled existing doubts about whether it was worthwhile to continue with a political career. There seemed little future in British politics for anyone outside the political parties. She questioned her own usefulness. In the suffrage movement, during her work for women's employment during the war, and in her work for the League of Nations Union, she felt she had achieved something; but the urgent need for non-Governmental effort in these areas was over, and her broader hope that politics could 'make human life a really better thing all round' looked increasingly unrealistic.[75] There were plenty of people to take her place.

She decided not to contest Brentford and Chiswick in the general election to take place on 6 December, but came under such pressure to stand again as an Independent – and was offered such generous financial support – that she gave way. The campaign was well organised and less demanding than the previous two. The excitement of campaigning, and Ray's natural optimism, took over and she scented – or rather feared – victory, despite the last minute re-entry of her Labour opponent from 1918; but she soon became 'so sick of repeating the same things over & over again'.[76] The results of the election, with a lower turnout than the previous year, did not follow the national trend towards Labour: Grant Morden 9,648, Mrs Oliver Strachey 4,828, W. Haywood 216. Despite her lonely status as the only woman Independent candidate, Ray seems to have established herself, in what she had come to feel was a 'detestable constituency', as Grant Morden's main rival.[77] Ray's reaction to her defeat was an amalgam of surprise, disappointment and relief. She did not stand for Parliament again.

Above: (Plate 1) Ray as a baby. Influenced by Dr Jaeger's pamphlets, Mary Costelloe put her 'defenceless little child entirely into woollen clothes and woollen sheets'.
(Plate 2) Devoted daughter, genial father, dour grandmother: Ray with her father and his mother c. 1895.

Below: (Plate 3) Bernhard Berenson c. 1900; (Plate 4) Hannah Whitall Smith c. 1892.

Above: (Plate 5) Bryn Mawr's redoubtable President, M. Carey Thomas, in 1910.
(Plate 6) Ellie Rendel c. 1908.

Below: (Plate 7) Alys and Bertrand Russell in 1907, five years after Bertie told Alys he no longer loved her. This was Bertie's election photograph for his campaign as a suffragist candidate in Wimbledon.
(Plate 8) Adrian Stephen and Karin Costelloe in September 1914, just before they married.

Above: (Plate 9) An uncharacteristically solemn Oliver Strachey in 1911 (without his habitual pipe).
(Plate 10) Pippa Strachey c. 1920.

Below: (Plate 11) Julia Strachey c. 1913.
(Plate 12) Oliver's older brother Ralph in 1910, later Ray's partner in her ill-fated building venture.

The changing faces of Ray

Above: (Plates 13–15) As a toddler in 1889; with her younger sister Karin c. 1896; and at the end of her years at Newnham in 1908.

Below: (Plates 16-18) As a new bride, uncharacteristically well-dressed, in 1911; an expectant mother on her way back from India in 1912; and a parliamentary candidate in 1922.

Above: (Plate 19) In exile at the Mud House in the late 1920s, writing her major works.

Below: (Plates 20 and 21) The professional woman at the height of her powers, in 1936 and c. 1939, one of the last pictures of Ray before her death.

Above: (Plates 22 and 23) Lord Robert Cecil and Lady Astor, both in 1920. Always smartly dressed, Nancy Astor confined herself to black and white outfits for her appearances in the Commons.

Below: (Plate 24) Mary Agnes ("Molly") Hamilton in 1932, Ray's close friend during the 1930s, a Labour politician who may have influenced her political views. (Plate 25) Oliver in the 1930s.

Above: (Plate 26) Four generations at I Tatti: Barbara (close to a breakdown), Roger, Ray, Mary.

Below: (Plate 27) Olav Hultin in 1932.
(Plate 28) Wolf Halpern with his stepson (and adopted son) Roger.

From the mid-1920s one of Ray's main leisure pursuits was dashing off portraits of family and friends, often caricatures. Painting portraits became more than just another way of diverting her thoughts and energies from professional tracks: rapidly executed caricatures of friends and acquaintances offered an outlet for suppressed emotions. Many have been lost – particularly the most unkind – but enough survive to indicate Ray's powers of observation and emerging talent.

Above (plates 29–38): assorted Stracheys (Oliver, Barbara, Julia and Lytton); Roger Fry; Barbara's second husband Wolf Halpern; Karin Stephen; Adrian Stephen in portrait and at considerable length; Virginia Woolf at Mud (May 1938).

Above (plates 39–43): Bernard Berenson; Grace Worthington: and the Bussy family, Dorothy, Simon and Janie.

When, as often, Ray was her own subject, the savagery of the portrayal could diffuse her anger or frustration without causing offence. Plate 44 (left above) is perhaps the most realistic. Later ones, like the unflattering plate 45 (centre above), clearly provided an emotional outlet. Plate 46 (right above) may have been the one Ray described to Christopher in November 1932: 'Yesterday, as I was feeling rather low, I took out my paints & indulged in another self portrait. You may think this an odd way of raising the spirits – but it had the desired effect. I produced a horror, & greatly enjoyed myself. I look like a kind of Gorgon, & the colour scheme is brick red & grey green. Most effective.'

PART FIVE

Progeny

CHAPTER TWELVE
A Mother's Place? 1924–1930

Modern young women know amazingly little of what life was like before the war, and show a strange hostility to the word "feminism," and all which they imagine it to connote.[1]

Ray turned to her private life as a more fruitful sphere of influence than politics:

> I begin to think all we can hope to do is to squeeze out a little corner of decency & bring into it a few individuals, & make what we can of that, & that the only thing to be done for politics is to hold decent opinions, express them & spread them privately, & keep a watch on public affairs to try to prevent war.[2]

She still cherished the hope that she might have 'something real & worthwhile to say' in her writing, and meanwhile resolved to 'enjoy life, & bring up my children well, & give a help here & there where I see the chance'.[3]

For the next few years Ray abandoned most public activities, retaining only her involvement with the LSWS, and concentrated on her children and her writing. It was not an easy transition. The young women coming to adulthood after the war seemed a different species from Ray's generation, rejecting the struggle to play a role in public life in favour of dance, romantic novels, fashion and sex. Within her family Ray had to deal with two of these incomprehensible creatures.

After training at the Slade School of Art, Julia shared furnished rooms with another girl, living on allowances from Alys Russell and Oliver, but failed to find much work as a commercial artist. The family had already paid her increasingly large debts on several occasions. In February 1924 she sought refuge with Oliver in Gordon Square. He adopted an uncharacteristically stern parental approach:

> She is not allowed to accept invitations without his express permission, & he has confiscated her allowance, & doles out small sums for specific purposes. It's an awful bore for him; but J says she has never been so happy before, & that it is like heaven to have the responsibility of life taken off her![4]

After Ray's experience of living with Julia in Hampstead, she had serious misgivings about trying again, but eventually 'decided to give it a really fair, & not a grunching, try', 'partly in justice to Julia, & partly because we can't afford to board her out comfortably'.[5] Ray reorganised their living accommodation to separate herself as far as possible from Julia; but the cheerful letters to her mother over the next few weeks about how well the arrangement was working concealed Ray's slide into what she later described as 'a morbid patch'.[6]

Ray started keeping a diary again, but cut out and burnt the most revealing passages a year later. It seems, from the hints that remain, that she felt an unvalued and unwanted intruder in her own home: 'Everyone I live with is quite unscrupulous about reading letters & private papers, & however little interest they really take in me, both Julia & Oliver would certainly enjoy reading such a document as this.'[7] A little later, 'Oliver is away, I don't know where & Julia stayed in bed all morning'.[8] Father and daughter were both fully at home in the Bloomsbury social circuit so uncongenial to Ray, so 'I often go out to dinner when they give a party, to the satisfaction of all concerned'.[9]

Preoccupied by her social life, absorbed by fashions in dress and design, Julia appeared to Virginia Woolf as a 'gifted wastrel'.[10] Julia's life-long friend, Frances Partridge (née Marshall), later admitted that 'to make an effort that was in itself boring, even to gain what she earnestly wanted, was impossible to Julia'.[11] Intelligent but resolutely uneducated, Julia had

> a vision of herself as intangled in a web of intransigent practical circumstances created by what she liked to think of as a hostile Cosmos. Getting up in the morning, shopping, being on time – disagreeable molehills to most people – were almost unscalable mountains to her, nor do I believe she fully realised their ubiquity.[12]

According to Barbara Strachey, this made her half-sister 'about the most incompetent and impractical person one could imagine':

> She lost job after unsatisfactory job as a model or shop assistant by being hours late every morning; she would leave the front door open time after time so that a fur coat of Ray's and several other clothes were stolen; she insisted on having baths at three o'clock in the morning; occupied the telephone for hours at a time; would arrive for a weekend on a Monday and would invite several young men, each to a tête-a-tête lunch at home, unknown to each other, fail to turn up and leave Ray to cope with the result. [...] and there was an endless succession of cooks and maids [...] – all leaving after a week's experience of her.[13]

Unsurprisingly, Ray found living with Julia unbearable.

Ray worked through her depression, but the problems – and expense – caused by Julia remained. It was 'a most heavenly relief' when Julia decided to move out again in October, despite the cost implications. 'I shall allow her £2 [£105] a week, & Aunt Loo £1 & Oliver 10/- pocket money & all her dress bills.'[14] The new arrangement lasted for a year before Julia fell into 'an aimless breakdown' ('digestion upset, sleep upset, more depressed & listless than usual') and wanted 'an occupation, home life, care, sympathy & good food'.[15] Julia's illness, Ray surmised, was 'probably just thoroughly disordered nerves, & the penalty for a foolish illspent life'; she needed 'fresh air, exercise & no racketting about' so was packed off to recuperate with the Bussy family at La Souco.[16] In the long term no solution occurred to Ray but the possibility that Julia might marry, for which Ray developed a most unfeminist enthusiasm ('we must get Julia married off'), even though 'that would no doubt be as temporary as anything else'.[17]

When Julia returned to London in early 1926, Ray took a drastic decision:

> It is so disagreeable to me to live in the house with her that I have decided never to try it again. I get exasperated, & spend too much of my life raging against her careless & shiftless ways – & why should I do it? It does no good to her, only harm, & it poisons me.[18]

She arranged that Oliver and Julia should occupy two floors of 42 Gordon Square with one servant to look after them and a fixed housekeeping allowance administered by Julia. Ray would live mainly at Fernhurst but retain a room in the house as a pied-à-terre for her visits to London; the rest of the house would be left empty, saving on servants' wages and keep, as well as on Julia's allowance. It meant the effective separation of Ray and Oliver. Once again, the arrangement began well but deteriorated; Oliver started spending his weekends with Ray at Fernhurst and most evenings at his club.

Ray found visiting the London house positively distasteful:

> I don't like going there, however, for the horrors of the general upkeep worry me, & the servant will come & pour out bushels of complaints against Julia. And then there are beginning to be scenes between O & J, which I had much rather not be present at.[19]

The plan would clearly not last much longer: 'O. is too uncomfortable, & is beginning to grow as irritated as I did before I ran away. And I shall have to step in & rescue him.'[20]

By the autumn Oliver had come to share Ray's view that Julia was 'unbearable to live with'.[21] The situation, Ray decided, could be resolved by giving up the lease of 42 Gordon Square, finding a much smaller place for Oliver and herself, and telling Julia that 'she must shift for herself':

> O will allow her £3 a week, & with the £2 Aunt Loo has endowed her with and the £3 she is capable of earning she will be able to be perfectly comfortable if she chooses.[...] She is now 25, & had really had as fair a chance as our circumstances permit.[22]

Ray found, and took on a seven year lease, part of a house in Westminster (53 Marsham Street) into which she and Oliver moved with relief.

To general surprise (and possibly out of desperation) Julia agreed to go to Paris with her sculptor suitor Stephen Tomlin ('Tommy') as a possible preliminary to marriage. Julia was 'not in the least in love, so far as anyone can see', Ray correctly noted.[23] Nevertheless, the couple married the following July, to the delight of Julia's family. Tommy was a universal favourite ('perfectly steady & reliable' and 'full of sense and kindness' as Ray then thought), who became a close friend of Oliver and whose letters to Julia record his warm appreciation of Ray.[24] Tommy's conventional family background – his father was a judge – led to a conventional marriage settlement, under which Oliver and Ray had to continue paying Julia's allowance of £150 [£8,200] a year. Nevertheless Ray considered the marriage 'an untold relief', and hoped 'that under the influence of happiness, & of someone who believes in her, she may come out in a new light'.[25]

At Fernhurst Ray abandoned all pretence at smart dressing, usually wearing 'cotton or corduroy breeches, a smock blouse, an impossible straw hat and long boots'. Although she favoured contact with local villagers (and allowed them to use her pool once a week), socialising with local gentry was to be avoided at all costs: she was prone to lock herself in the bathroom if such callers arrived. When free from the demands of children, Ray devoted herself to writing her new novel (inspired by the papers Hannah had left about religious sects in the

(Figure 27) Barbara and her cousin John Strachey (Ralph's son) in the pool at the Mud House c.1924.

United States), together with a small amount of journalism, and a new project proposed by a publisher: 'a history of the women's movement, 100,000 words' which, she thought, would be an easy source of money though 'a tedious job'.[27]

Keen though she was to get down to writing, it was hard to resist the attractions of planning and planting the garden, dealing with her hives of bees, foraging for mushrooms and berries in the surrounding countryside, and bricklaying for a further building in her field. The practical side of life was dealt with by Mrs Glazier, her (intermittently resident) housekeeper, though Ray gradually took on more of the cooking herself. The main problem was finding enough time for writing. Visitors came in vast numbers – sometimes with the cottage so full that children had to camp outside – and the seclusion Ray cherished was threatened by the tendency of certain relatives to use the Mud House as a place to house temporarily unwanted children. Her own children already took much time and attention.

The developing personalities of Barbara and Christopher, and the striking contrast between them, intrigued her. In early childhood, during morning visits to Ray in bed, Barbara would pretend to be a tiger and 'dive down under the bedclothes to the bottom of the bed and then hurl [her]self from that vantage point on to Ray's stomach, uttering loud and muffled roars'.[28] Christopher would

> lie still and calm beside her but insisted that they should play game after game of imaginary noughts and crosses – "Now I put a nought in the top right hand corner…" As he got older the game became imaginary three dimensional noughts and crosses.[29]

Barbara remained physical and active, Christopher an abstract thinker.

Intelligent and quick-witted but lazy, impatient, energetic, headstrong, self-willed, vehement and bossy, Barbara was a born leader (no matter how much her intended followers tried to protest), but she could not control her violent emotions, indeed tended to revel in emotional extremes. When Ray sent her to the prestigious co-educational international École Nouvelle at Bex, Switzerland, for a year from September 1923 to learn French, they agreed on a private code ('PS Many happy returns') for Barbara to put in a letter should she need help.[30] On receiving the code while she was at La Souco in February 1924, Ray went immediately to Bex to find Barbara afflicted by the conviction that she was adopted – another girl had started a wave of mass hysteria. Once convinced of her true parentage, 'instead of weeping in my lap all the afternoon, B was full of pranks and laughter' and physically effusive ('as bad, & worse, than Christopher in the kissing stage').[31] 'But what a perverse fate', Ray lamented, 'to give me such kissing children!'[32] Ray refused to intervene in Barbara's problems in getting on with other children: 'she will have to learn to find her way through it unaided, for grownup help – or even notice – would be worse than useless.'[33] The incident typifies Ray's parenting style: total reliability in times of trouble, practical help and wise advice, calmly and often humorously offered, all within a context of maximum freedom from parental intervention (except for the crucial question of education, which Ray took very seriously).

Ray had high hopes that Barbara's brains and underlying good sense would bring her success in life, but realised that getting there would be a stormy process. Barbara was difficult to fit into the Fernhurst routine during school holidays, having 'no liking for occupations such as house-painting, gardening or path-cutting, or any such, […] only reading, cards, piano & conversation – a regular young Strachey'.[34] At fourteen, Barbara remained 'a perfect tornado of emotions' and 'so set on her own way that she is not easy to live with':

Every encounter with her is like a battle, & takes out one's energy disproportionately even though she is fundamentally very good & perfectly reasonable. She is also in a very painful stage of mountainous caresses – & she is so big & rough, & has so little observation of times & moods & seasons that it is really a great trial to me. I could scream with irritation at times.[35]

Ray, so self-controlled, rational and non-tactile, had produced a highly physical daughter who inherited Hannah's vehemence, Mary's emotional self-indulgence and, it emerged, Oliver's weakness for the opposite sex.

Barbara had been a determined pursuer of boys and men from the age of three, when she proposed marriage to Desmond MacCarthy's son Dermod, who later sagely concluded that 'Barbara might be rather hard to manage as a wife'.[36] Contact with her grandmother Mary, which Ray minimised but could not eliminate, brought out the worst in Barbara. Material over-indulgence and too much excitement were followed, as she grew up, by Mary's encouragement of precocious flirting, which horrified Ray.

Christopher was seven when Ray retired from political life, a nervous, excitable chatterbox, maddeningly slow in some ways but already showing a passionate love of music and an interest in science. (Aged six, he complained to Ray about his seven-year-old cousin: 'I can't get Ann to talk about electricity for more than a minute.')[37] Ray resolved to teach him herself over the summer of 1924, to conquer his 'straggling attention' by means of 'a little old fashioned discipline' instead of the "Modern Methods" in which her sister-in-law Marjorie was training her: 'All these new things seem designed for stupid children who have to be cajoled into taking an interest in using their brains', and were hence quite inappropriate for Christopher.[38] That summer Ray divided her week between London and Fernhurst, starting a gentle routine of lessons with Christopher, interspersed with outdoor activities. The satisfaction from being with him ('funny clever fragile creature') was intense: 'It's sheer happiness to see him about.'[39]

Ray selected Fernden, a small preparatory school near Fernhurst, for Christopher to attend as a weekly boarder from September 1926. By then the unevenness of his abilities was apparent. Ray was repeatedly amazed by his intelligence and general knowledge:

C [...] gave me a long lecture on Free Trade yesterday, which he had worked out after hearing Aunt Loo's account of having to pay duty on a silk dress. He had arrived at most of the usual Free Trade arguments for himself, including the idea that universal Free Trade might reduce the risk of war. He is at times an alarmingly grown up companion. However he still finds acute difficulty in spelling such words as "sky", so I trust there is still a little period of education in front of him.[40]

At school he struggled to express himself on paper, 'having nothing much to understand but a great deal to put in practice – writing, spelling, neatness & so forth'.[41]

Christopher soon made rapid progress through his school and continued to astonish Ray by his interests and achievements at home, asking her for extra algebra lessons and making from Meccano a working ice-cream machine and 'a very ingenious model [...] for measuring distances'; he 'surprised me by his real understanding of gear wheels, worm wheels, & ratios. He doesn't seem to find such matters any effort at all, & did the most abstruse calculations without turning a hair.'[42] Although Ray made sure he had practical activities too – learning the violin, carpentry lessons in Fernhurst village, bricklaying, and running a printing press at the cottage – Christopher's intellectual skills raced ahead despite his emotional immaturity. He was fortunate to have a mother who could respond to his needs. On one occasion, when an upset stomach made him feel too ill and sick to eat, Christopher insisted on Ray's 'teaching him how to solve simultaneous equations graphically, & quadratics by algebra. We broke off only for him to rush away to vomit – & resumed after!'[43] His precocious intellectual self-confidence ('nothing is really difficult to understand in itself, if you can find the right way to get at it. The difficulty is in me'), which dropped 'out of his infantile mouth amidst his torrent of nonsensical chatter', staggered Ray even more.[44]

Ray's own children were not her only concern; she often took on responsibility for several others, including Ralph Strachey's youngest children, John and Ursula, and her own nieces, Ann and Judith Stephen, who were frequent guests at both of Ray's houses. Her sister Karin, under strain from qualifying first as a doctor then as a psychoanalyst while suffering from fluctuating but increasing deafness, temporarily separated from her husband Adrian Stephen in late 1923. Karin rediscovered her enjoyment of social life, and her children suffered. Mary Berenson had long been aware of the damage Karin's brilliant intelligence could do ('She does things in her thoughts, and then they are finished, and her practical life goes to the devil') and although Karin considered herself 'the most careful & devoted mother', her approach remained abstract, as Ray discovered: 'the children simply don't enter into her scheme of life at all. Karin was quite aware of Ann's needs, but only as one is aware of starving Armenians.'[45] Karin looked to psychoanalysis (for which Ray had little sympathy) to resolve her elder daughter's all too obvious misery, while Ray realised that 'what the child wants is to feel wanted by & necessary to someone'.[46]

Both Stephen girls had bouts of serious illness during 1924, leaving Ray angered by Karin's neglectful behaviour. Practical care of Ann and Judy was often left to the Stephens' overworked servants and to Ray, with medical assistance from Ellie Rendel, now a doctor. James Strachey observed one episode when Ann was recovering from a serious ear operation and Judy had typhoid:

On Saturday morning, she was slightly better, and Karin decided to go away for the week-end leaving one nursemaid in charge. Adrian also announced his departure. Ray however intervened, & forbad. But in spite of it all, he slipped away on Sunday morning. [...] When Karin returned & Ray attacked her, saying the nurse had been up day & night for five days without leaving the house, Karin said quite innocently: 'Oh, but she went out on Thursday. She went with me to the nursing-home to bring Ann back.'[48]

Difficult though Ray found the non-stop company, conversation and amusements of young children, she fully accepted that Barbara and Christopher should be her first priority while they were at home.

Ray's trip to Athens with Carey Thomas in late 1924 should have provided a respite from looking after other people. Retired from the Presidency of Bryn Mawr, Carey Thomas had inherited her close friend Mary Garrett's great wealth, and now spent her time travelling the world in luxury (with vast amounts of luggage), indulging her passions for the theatre and fine living and continuing to pursue feminist interests. In Athens she was involved in establishing a hostel for women students. Ray knew that, as Carey's maid was not to accompany them, packing the seventeen trunks would be her task. A visit to Delphi brought weightier responsibilities.

On the return journey they were eight hours' drive from medical help when a mule sent Carey rolling down a steep rocky embankment. At first Ray thought her dead. Carey remained cheerful despite cuts all over her head and face – causing extensive swelling and bruising – a sprained left arm and damaged left thumb and (it later emerged) a broken right arm. A doctor eventually sewed up the cut in her head 'big enough to put a finger in lengthwise', bandaged her arm, and decreed that she might as well lie helpless on the Orient Express to Paris as anywhere else.[49]

It fell to Ray to bribe the train guard for the use of his sleeping compartment, procure food and drink for the journey (and cook it on a spirit lamp), administer drugs to Carey, re-bandage her wounds, see to her personal care – and do the packing. Problems continued right up until Carey's departure for the United States: 'the anti-tetanus injection took, the last night in Paris, & poor C swelled up so you wouldn't recognise her, came out with a rash as itching as small pox, & actually foamed at the mouth.'[50] 'Never have I been through such an experience before, & I trust I shall never go through it again', Ray concluded.[51]

When, in June 1925, Ray claimed that 'I am as healthy as a stone monument', she was exaggerating.[52] An operation to remove a polyp from her nose during her 1923 trip to the United States had drastically lessened her susceptibility to colds; and disappointment at her failure to have a third child appears to have waned. But Ellie Rendel had been treating her for 'various leakages' for over a year, and Ray's life, like that of her grandmother Hannah in old age, was now dominated by her bladder.[53] The repair operation performed in November 1925 revealed a more serious problem than expected and the 'very abnormal condition' discovered by the female surgeon would probably have led eventually to cystitis (the bane of Mary's life).[54] The recovery period was painful but the subsequent sense of liberation made Ray feel 'a human being again, & restored to normal life'.[55] The operation cost £77 [£4,000], paid by Mary.

Never fully recovered from her breakdown in 1918, Mary passed the 1920s in fluctuating health and steadily increasing acrimony with her husband, though the addition of Nicky Mariano to the household, first as librarian then as a universally loved third in a *ménage à trois*, improved the atmosphere. Ray found Mary's annual visits to what she still referred to as 'home' a trial. Her preoccupation with her own state of health, her expectation of high standards of living, and the entourage of servants she travelled with, were incompatible with the primitive arrangements at the Fernhurst cottage, and even after a further extension was added in 1926, Mary's presence was disruptive.

Mary often reproached Ray for her extravagance – but she almost always covered any financial need. Mary's grandchildren were encouraged to whisper any wants to her Magic Ear: the desired item would then be found under Mary's pillow (even the eight-foot-long ladder once requested by Christopher). Ray was quite prepared to take money from Mary herself but she recognised the dangers of, and vainly tried to stop, this constant indulgence of her children. Mary overstimulated and overindulged her grandchildren; their consequent bad behaviour, though predictable, provoked her harsh comments. (Berenson usually absented himself during their visits to I Tatti.) Ray tried repeatedly to defuse the tension and to restrain her mother's love of excitement and genius for causing trouble but recognised the underlying problem: 'Having not a grain of self restraint herself, how can she impose it on others!'[56]

As Ray's children grew older, they each developed a closer relationship with their father. Barbara later admitted that Oliver was 'not perhaps a sternly admirable man', and that his habit of assuming 'that anyone he met, of whatever age or background, was his equal intellectually and in every other way' made it difficult for him to relate to young children; but she nevertheless recalled him with affection:

> Oliver never got sulky or grumpy, though he was capable of complaining bitterly about anything. He was always bubbling, always ready to play idiotic games of a verbal or musical nature, to talk wittily and entertainingly to anyone about anything. This did not prevent him, like all Stracheys, from being hypercritical about matters which he considered important, such as writing or music, nor from thinking seriously, mostly about aesthetics or ethics, on which he was always intending to write a book.[57]

A family sailing holiday on the Norfolk Broads in 1925 brought Oliver and Christopher closer together; they became, Ray reported, 'very congenial companions – what with codes & puzzles & [musical] tricks of all sorts'.[58] When Barbara was fifteen, Oliver started to get to know her better too.

Ray's relationship with her husband had been badly hit by his affair with Inez and then by differences over Julia. In 1924 her patch of depression coincided with a period of particular lively socialising by Oliver who was 'so gay I can't keep up with it' and was 'always skipping off to parties'.[59] In contrast, Ray, whose preference was for 'a quiet evening at home, & only one person at a time', compared herself to 'an old fat spider' who preferred to 'sit in [her] parlour and spin'.[60] The move to Marsham Street in November 1926 seems to have marked a turning point. Ray may have had little respect left for her husband, but she retained an almost maternal sense of responsibility for him. Oliver appears to have been delighted to return to a well-run household, and the move from the heart of Bloomsbury helped the couple rediscover the mutual affection which Julia had put at risk.

Oliver had maintained his longstanding relationship with Inez, even after she married Frederick Jenkins in 1923 (possibly a marriage of convenience), and had even become friendly with her husband, but now his marriage to Ray achieved a new equilibrium. Even though they continued to pursue separate social lives, when they were together a midnight game of chess became part of their routine. By 1928 Ray had decided to abandon her avoidance of Inez at public events. The following year James Strachey was astonished to find Oliver uneasily sandwiched between his wife and mistress at Lord's.[61] Later Inez and her husband came to stay at the cottage, with Inez even helping to distemper the walls.

Ray developed a great affection for the 'sordid but enchanting slums of Westminster', but in January 1928 much of the housing in the area was dealt a death blow when the Thames burst its banks.[62] Several people sleeping in basement bedrooms were drowned and Ray's childhood homes in Grosvenor Road were badly affected. She was in Fernhurst finishing her book on the women's movement when Oliver, in Marsham Street, received a warning from the police three minutes before the water burst in. He rescued Barbara's trunk and Ray's clothes before the lowest rooms – the kitchen and Ray's bedroom – were flooded two feet deep: Ray assumed that he had been 'sadly incompetent', but the combined demands of Christopher, Karin's children and her book kept her away.[63] (The following winter the Fernhurst cottage was also flooded ankle deep when frozen pipes burst.)

Although insurance covered some of the damage, the house never fully recovered. Ray swapped her bedroom with the dining room, which made the damp less of a problem and saved the servant's legs. Redevelopment of the area soon followed and 53 was scheduled for demolition at the end of their lease in 1933. Noisy building work on the surrounding properties started well before then, making Marsham Street a far less desirable place to live.

Choosing the right school for the age and needs of each child always mattered more to Ray than continuity. Ray moved Barbara to St Felix School at Southwold in Suffolk in September 1924. Barbara took and passed her Matriculation exam just before her fifteenth birthday in 1927, at which point Ray decided to move her rebellious, rule-breaking daughter elsewhere. By then Barbara had outgrown boarding schools. But a day school in London would inevitably allow her to come into contact with the Bloomsbury circle which, in Ray's opinion, had had a disastrous influence on Julia. To Mary, Ray complained that 'Bloomsbury people have almost no sense of decency' and in her diary she was yet more outspoken:

> I feel disgusted with the super-civilized intelligenzia tonight, though for no reason of cause. But they suddenly seem to me a rotten lot of selfish parasites, who contribute next to nothing to the world – A most unjust & uncalled for criticism of all my circle of acquaintances.[64]

She never spelled out her concept of decency, but it seems to have comprised a mixture of integrity, private kindness and loyalty, and a sense of public responsibility, embodied in the people she admired most (her grandmother Hannah, Millicent Fawcett, Lord Robert Cecil, Ralph and Pippa Strachey). These were the people she wanted Barbara to take as role models, not the inhabitants of Ham Spray and Charleston.

Ray therefore arranged for Barbara to lodge in Oxford from autumn 1927 while attending classes at Oxford High School and being tutored by Lucy Silcox, her inspirational head teacher from St Felix School, now retired. This would, she hoped, provide Barbara with 'steady & wholesome influences' and reduce the risk that she might 'get cynical at 15'.[65] Problems soon emerged.

Ray's practice of eschewing strict parental control and allowing her children to discover what worked best in life for themselves had left Barbara, as she recalled, 'frustrated by the very freedom Ray gave me, which provided no excuse for rebellious opposition'.[66] The one subject on which Ray was prepared to lay down the law was the importance of education and intellectual activity. 'I want to be sure you don't miss the joys of using your brains to their fullest extent. There's nothing else so satisfying.'[67] This was the area on which, for over three years, Ray and her daughter conducted an affectionate, tortured, exhausting battle, which drained Ray's energies and purse but during which she remained unshakeable.

Barbara was already talking of 'taking no interest in anything but young men, & not wanting to go on with her education, or to go to college'.[68] Her letters were plaintive:

> I do want you so! I don't like it here. That doesn't mean I don't like the Browne ménage 'cos I do – as much as I could like anything here. But I just hate the whole thing – school and work. I can't work Mother. Must I go to College? I know I shall hate it even if I like people there cos I hate this & this is free enough. It's not deeds here it's just atmosphere – Oxford – work. I suppose I shall always be a failure – turn out like Julia cos I really can't bring myself to work even if I get awful rows for not doing it. Do help. I do want you so.[69]

Realising that 'direct preachment is worse than useless', Ray allowed Barbara to spend the summer mainly at Fernhurst, resting, eating well, reading popular novels, and recovering her physical health, which always reflected her emotional ups and downs.[70]

By the autumn a new plan had been devised. Oliver would take Barbara out to Vienna and instal her and a young woman companion, Irene Hancock, in a suitable family for the winter so that Barbara could learn further languages, especially German, and improve her music. For a term this worked well: Barbara enjoyed learning German, though Miss Hancock reported her continuing devotion to non-intellectual topics such as women's magazines. (However reading Ray's recently published book on the women's movement made Barbara 'a raging feminist'.)[71]

Ray, Christopher (who had just spent several terms at the school in Bex and was about to start at Gresham's School in Holt, Norfolk),

Mary and eventually Alys joined Barbara at a hotel in Vienna that Christmas. Mary later remembered it as 'a wonderful time', filled with concerts and operas, despite her own poor health (which Ray suspected to be imaginary); Barbara relished the social life Mary's presence opened up to her, took every opportunity to go clothes shopping, adored the Wagner operas they attended, and fell in love with man after man (when not playing with her brother's extensive train set); Christopher became 'very fractious with hotel life'; Ray, though trying to 'keep an impassive front', had 'never felt so much on edge' with 'every moment [...] complete torment', and was 'busy counting the hours to the moment of escape'.[72] At the time she had her own emotional stresses to deal with (and Ray never developed a taste for Wagner, no matter how much she came to enjoy other music). Ray returned home to '10 foul days' of furious temper.[73]

In Vienna, Barbara then succumbed to flu which left her physically drained and depressed. Ray was forced to arrange her return home. With the Oxford entrance exams coming up in November, time to get Barbara capable of passing them – and wanting to – was running short. Ray's reluctance to have Barbara living in London proved ill-founded, as her interests, such as acrobatic dancing, hardly coincided with those of Bloomsbury. While Ray arranged coaching for her in academic subjects, Barbara enrolled in other classes so that she was soon 'taking 6 dancing lessons 2 cookery 2 dressmaking 2 French literature & one History a week'.[74] To Ray's continuing disappointment 'she simply hates using her mind, & it is like a surgical operation every time she has to do it. Her talk is still absurdly young, & all about herself'.[75] Having Barbara in the house disrupted Ray's own work and Barbara's 'constant storms' of opposition to using her brain were exhausting.[76] Ray never backed down on the importance of a university education for her daughter, and Barbara reluctantly agreed to apply to Lady Margaret Hall, Oxford, where Ray's Newnham friend Lynda Grier was now the Principal.

Barbara chose to return to Vienna for the winter of 1929–30, this time without a companion, taking the Oxford entrance exams there in late November. She 'just slithered through – some of her papers

brilliant & others very poor, but none of them mediocre'.[77] But by then
Barbara was giving little attention to anything beyond her emotional
life, falling repeatedly in love and inundating her startled mother with
long letters on the subject. 'Do men really desire & demand virginity
in the girl they marry – not that I wish to test it – & do they throw over
a girl if they hear she isn't […]?' Barbara demanded, and drew equally
alarming conclusions: 'I am not only a flirt – that I knew, but also
entirely immoral, degraded & a low woman', with 'a morbid mania for
married men', and 'my life at the minute is composed of little outside
the opposite sex. […] I find them absolutely enthralling'.[78]

Barbara's outspokenness on matters of the heart was the antithesis
of her mother's reticence, but Ray took her daughter's outpourings
seriously. Her carefully considered, lengthy responses, tempered with
humour and tolerance, provide the clearest statement we have of her
own moral values:

> The tendency to be jealous […] is a beastly vice, as well as a most
> disagreeable & disturbing one. Especially as it so often leads to self
> righteousness towards oneself, & cruelty towards others.[79]

> About young men & virginity, I really don't know. […] I think it is
> entirely natural for people in love to wish to be, [or] to have been, the
> only object. […] But women always accept the fact that they aren't, if
> they aren't, & I daresay men do too. My own idea is that the sort of
> young man who wouldn't, nowadays, is the sort of young man who'd be
> intolerable on other grounds – stupid, unsympathetic & conventional,
> with a tendency to the "master in my own house" business.[80]

> love affairs carried to extremes are not unimportant matters to be
> lightly indulged in. I don't believe it wrecks chances of happiness in
> marriage (unless there are too many previous affairs!) but I do think
> it has a strong tendency to wreck oneself.[81]

> your tendency to revel in your own emotions is the only thing which
> causes me any anxiety about you. I don't want you to develop into

a scene maker either in solitude or in company with your friends. [...] I believe such people, for all their apparent feeling, lose the true secret flavour of the real thing. [...] emotional expression [...] is rather like onions in a salad. A little, sparingly produced, makes all the salad good. A lot, chopped in regardless, brings tears to the eyes.[82]

I firmly believe in free will. We can make or ruin ourselves from within, & it's not all a matter of temperament & one's make up. We've got to put our teeth into ourselves, so to speak, as well as into subjects.[83]

Fending off a stream of criticism from Mary about Barbara's attitudes and behaviour ('her inside mind is getting along quite steadily, & I don't feel the faintest ultimate anxiety, & never have'), Ray pursued the debate with her daughter over the relative values of thought and feelings. 'Do look into your mind (not your feelings)', she advised, 'Take a cerebral bite on something. It's a sure remedy for boredom.'[84] Barbara still resisted, and on a reconnaissance trip to Lady Margaret Hall 'made a grand pronouncement of not meaning to do any work!'.[85] As the start of the Oxford term approached, Barbara, 'protesting to the last that she would hate it like poison',

threatened to run away. But Ray was adamant. She said that if Barbara left Oxford, she would be sent to Cambridge, and that if she quitted Cambridge, she would be sent to one provincial university after another, and that if she wouldn't accept any college education, her allowance would be stopped.[86]

Within a fortnight of starting her university career in October 1930, studying history, Barbara was 'so madly happy that she couldn't express her joy'.[87] It was progress, but not a real solution.

Barbara's new-found enthusiasm for life in Oxford sprang mainly from her social life; she made new friends in her college and revelled in meeting numerous young men. Although her Principal and tutors

expressed satisfaction, her old demon, a 'hysteria about work', had not
been defeated, and she needed to pass examinations in the spring to
continue at Oxford.[88] Ray obtained 'a real slave driver to oversee her
actual working hours', with Barbara's 'enthusiastic cooperation', but to
no avail.[89] Barbara failed her exam. 'I can't help feeling that it may be
frightfully good for her because it will show from outside that things
can't be done without effort', Ray wrote to Mary; after all, 'learning
to work is the chief thing she is sent to Oxford for at all'.[90] For once
Ray's attempt to find a source of comfort in bad news proved correct.
Barbara's terror at the idea of being sent away from the life she enjoyed
so much drove her to work as never before, to discover that she could
force herself to work when not in the mood, and in the process to
find out for herself the satisfaction of work and the fascination of her
subject. When Barbara passed her exam in summer 1931, one of her
problems had gone for good.

'There's no doubt about it that one's own secret inner life is the
important thing in one's personal existence', Ray wrote to Barbara, but
no-one reading Ray's wise letters to her daughter about controlling
her emotions would guess that Ray had over the same period been
undergoing an emotional crisis of her own.[91] The 1920s were lonely
years for her. She enjoyed being alone and the chance to work
unimpeded but with so many domestic responsibilities and so many
people dependent on her this sort of solitude was rare. More often she
was coping with other people and their problems but feeling alone as
she did so. 'If I were to die tomorrow it wouldn't matter much to me or
to anyone, except perhaps the children' she wrote in September 1926,
and a few months later, depressed after flu, 'there is a nasty sinking,
due to the disease which makes me suspect that no one likes me &
that, tho obviously of some practical use, I have none of that intrinsic
glamour which carries one's [vanity] along so happily at most times'.[92]
     Her leisure pastimes were either solitary (reading detective
stories, playing patience, and learning the piano) or the sort of activity
compatible with keeping an eye on children (making a cross-stitch
carpet, gardening, foraging, swimming). Bricklaying could be done

in company – though there were few volunteers – and the portrait painting which Ray took up in 1925 provided some human contact, but after Inez and the Bloomsbury circle claimed Oliver there was a lack of a soulmate in her life. The Airedale terrier she acquired in 1926 to keep down the rabbits in her Fernhurst garden proved unexpectedly companionable and Ray, previously not a dog lover, found it a 'sad loss' when he disappeared two years later, assumed shot by a gamekeeper; she immediately bought his puppy son, naming him Rumple after his father, and valued his companionship.[93] But she needed more.

Ray's family reputation as an oyster (and her own self-perception as 'exceedingly reserved') masked a suppressed need for intimate communication, which was initially met in her marriage to Oliver.[94] Ray's relentlessly upbeat letters to her mother usually disguised her feelings, but the mask sometimes slipped in a final paragraph, as if the effort of suppression had become too great to continue. Her public utterances – especially rapidly tossed off journalism and book reviews – were often surprisingly, and savagely, forthright. Writing a diary was another outlet for 'that strong impulse to confide in someone else. There is no response from the book (but there isn't much from other people either), but to let it out is a relief'.[95] After Ray's death a friend commented on the strange paradox of someone who was habitually caustic in her comments but unfailingly kind in her actions; seeing the caustic comments as a necessary safety valve helps to explain the paradox.

The two people Ray confided in most were her sisters-in-law Dorothy and Pippa. Dorothy, warm and emotional, provided a refuge at La Souco where Ray regularly found freedom to write and to escape the everyday demands of her life. Pippa, whose interest in people drove even complete strangers to tell her their life-history, had been an important part of Ray's life since 1907. Fifteen years older than Ray, diminutive and bird-like in appearance, elusive in character, Pippa had worked with Ray on women's suffrage, the wartime employment of women, the post-war activities of the London Society and a range of political questions affecting women. Professionally, Ray, whose strength was as a tactician, admired Pippa's acute strategic thinking and seems to have felt some of the hero worship she often bestowed on those older and wiser. Personally, she valued Pippa as the 'one person in the world I feel free to talk openly with about my own feelings'.[96] At a time of emotional crisis over her estrangement from Oliver, it was a comfort to have his sister as a friend she could communicate with in companionable silence: 'Half a word does duty for a sentence & a whole string of associations besides. And there is no difficulty about following each other's train of thought.'[97] Such a 'little straggling disconnected talk' could produce an intimacy, otherwise lacking in her life, which 'was like an hour of sunlight in the day'.[98]

Ray's emotional attachment to Pippa provided a significant motivation in her life. Just as she would have stayed active in the LNU if she could have continued to work with Lord Robert Cecil, so 'I now hang on to Women's Service because of P'.[99] Pippa was the person in whose company Ray was happiest and, during her times in London, contact with Pippa was important: Ray's accommodation plans had to take this into account. Although Pippa was not demanding like so many others in Ray's life, the burdens she took upon herself and her own fragile health made Ray protective and willing to put herself out on Pippa's behalf.

In early 1928, while Barbara was in Oxford and Christopher at Bex, Ray reluctantly kept Mary company in Berne while she underwent a cure. Pippa became ill while she was away and Ray was impatient to get back to London ('I could have done a lot to ease her mind if I'd been there').[100] As she arrived home, Pippa set off to convalesce on the Riviera. Ray was left to run the LNSWS office just at the time her plans for Barbara were falling apart. She managed it by making occasional visits from Fernhurst and not provoking any additional office activity. The temptation to join Pippa in France proved overwhelming. Ray deposited Barbara in the care of the newly married (and astonishingly transformed) Julia, now a model of domestic virtue, and spent several weeks with Pippa at a small hotel in Cavalière.

Ray worked many hours a day on her introduction to her grandmother's papers on Fanaticism while Pippa rested, and swam for miles along the coast in perfect weather. She was able to clear her mind of 'complexities & turmoils & bothers [...] along with bills, & housekeeping problems, & children's arrangements & so on'.[101] But 'the chief joy of being at Cavalière was being with P. day after day', since 'I am always perfectly happy when P. is about'.[102] Ray succeeded in making long-term 'rifts' in Pippa's elusiveness which needed 'a great deal of time to break through – & it comes over her again very fast'.[103] The visit had been 'one of the most heavenly months I've ever spent', Ray later reflected.[104]

Ray was at the time pleased with her introduction to the Fanaticism papers: 'I've never had such a satisfied feeling about writing as over that, & I got the whole thing done in 4 weeks – read, sorted & written'.[105] But the danger of writing '30,000 words in 20 days' was 'that I have done it too fast for it to be good'.[106] Whereas books over which Ray laboured for years could be infused with freshness and apparent spontaneity, this rapidly tossed off piece was laboured and dull, especially in contrast with Hannah's writings which it introduces. When the book was published that autumn, an uncomfortably short time after her book on the women's movement, it was a complete failure and barely sold at all.[107]

Pippa's health was slow to recover; when she returned to London, she took up once more the burden of being the main carer for her eighty-eight year old mother, now blind. Lady Strachey's last years were painful for her and exhausting for her family:

> she spent all the time she could doing crossword puzzles & word games. It was wearing & rather difficult for those who had to do them, partly because she was so deaf, & partly because she was so unexpected – and after about half an hour of it one got very tired.[108]

For several years Pippa had spent most evenings so occupied; to help her out, Ray virtually moved into 51 Gordon Square for some two months, only going back to Marsham Street at weekends. To her mother Ray made light of this commitment: 'she has two nurses & dozens of children in attendance'.[109] In her diary Ray makes clear that the burden fell almost entirely on Pippa, and blamed the rest of the family for their neglect. The discrepancy between the two accounts may reflect Pearsall Smith antagonism towards Pippa, or it may indicate that Ray was trying to disguise the strength of her own feelings. There is no evidence that the relationship between Ray and Pippa was in any way physical (Barbara was sure that it was not) nor that Ray would have wanted this.[110] Her needs were emotional, not physical.

That autumn of 1928, despite her precarious financial position, Ray took on the lease of the rest of 53 Marsham Street so as to enlarge the family's own accommodation and have a top-floor flat to rent out. The damage the lower part of the house suffered in the Westminster floods may partly explain this, but several years previously Ray had identified the death of Lady Strachey, now clearly imminent, as being likely to lead to the break-up of the Gordon Square household. The prospect of then having accommodation to offer Pippa is likely have influenced her decision.

Lady Strachey died on 14 December 1928, but Pippa decided against Ray's suggestion of moving into her top-floor flat and remained in Gordon Square. At the beginning of 1929 Ray also faced the unwelcome necessity of scaling down her own writing because Pippa's continuing illness meant that she was needed at the LNSWS office to deal with 'Equal Pay, Protective Legislation, Election campaigns, Local Authorities, & such like subjects'.[111] The impact of these two disappointments was severe:

> I had somehow fancied she might come, & was cast down. What with one thing and another – but chiefly one! – I got into a bad way – not shopping, bursting into tears, & finding everything unbearably hard to do. I did not succeed in concealing this state of nerves very well.[112]

None of her previous morbid patches had 'felt so nearly a physical breakdown', but it passed fairly quickly and by Easter she had completely recovered, perhaps helped by her return to an active public life.[113]

CHAPTER THIRTEEN

Fame without Fortune:
1927–1931

*I do feel, however, as if I ought to be doing something in the
world, & I turn to my writing for that.*[1]

The portrait of Ray which Simon Bussy painted in the spring of 1912
(Plate 17) shows a young woman with short curly mid-brown hair, a
tendency to fullness round the chin, a lopsided smile revealing tombstone
teeth with a central gap, and a direct gaze from bright blue eyes. In a
photo taken over twenty-five years later (Plate 21), the hair is white, the
teeth no longer her own, the face heavier, but the clarity of the gaze,
now surrounded by laughter lines, remains the same. Ray's bright eyes
were what people remembered: 'living eyes' one colleague called them.[2]
Together with her fine, fair complexion, and her appealing speaking voice
– rapid and slightly breathy – they were considerable assets in her public
roles. A photograph taken in the late 1920s at Mud (Plate 19) shows a
very different Ray, grossly overweight with sad, lustreless eyes. Her self-
imposed exile in Fernhurst had harmed her. But the publication of her
third novel coincided with a revitalising change in lifestyle.

Ray's decision to embody in a novel her grandparents' experiences
of American religious sects meant that she had to enter into entirely

alien ways of thinking and believing. Oliver's determined atheism dominated the religious tone of their household. As a young boy, Christopher enquired innocently what the 'Holly Bibble' was and whether it was worth reading.[3] Barbara had been inspired by her High Anglican governess Miss Prynne to be baptised at Wych Cross; consulted about the baptism by telegram, Ray had shunned involvement by replying 'Your soul, not mine'.[4] Now she was forced to explore the religious urge in greater depth.

Ray could not feel – though she could grasp intellectually – 'the fear of death impulse, the sense of sin, the longing for actual contact with God, the joy of self abasement, & the creeping megalomania of self righteousness'.[5] Nor could she understand how people could pray (an extraordinary admission from a former practising Catholic). She read the New Testament straight through 'and was rather bowled over by it', recognising that it held up for admiration 'the essence of what is unrealizable in mankind – all the impulses & ideas which make a man unsuccessful & adorable if they are part of his make-up'.[6]

Despite the illogicality of venerating 'a system of conduct which runs counter to every human institution', Ray felt the pull of unworldliness: 'there is something quite irresistible about Christ-like people' such as Ralph Strachey and Lord Robert Cecil.[7] Ray's first hope was to embody this 'saintlike simplicity' in one of her characters, but, admitting 'there isn't much of that sort of thing in myself I fear', she moved on to the idea of exploring the subjective motivation of religious zealots: 'When people grow mad over saving their own souls is it like the fever to achieve some material success, to get a post or avoid an illness? Or is it really a secret prompting of the heart, trying to change themselves into an ideal?'[8]

Ray struggled with these concepts over the summer of 1924 and by the following spring was ready to look for a publisher. Her first choice, Harcourt Brace, rejected her book emphatically ('it does not seem to us to be publishable […] it runs pretty close to the border line of our censorship […] it would certainly be offensive to a great many people'), a verdict echoed by other publishers.[9] It was not until two years later that Faber & Gwyer agreed to take the novel: the religious sensibilities of their reader, T. S. Eliot, were clearly not easily shocked.[10] Ray's last completed novel was published in November 1927, to some critical acclaim: 'Serene, detached, economical, sensitive, her insight never fails, her humour never obtrudes, her tenderness never falters' wrote L. P. Hartley.[11] To everyone's surprise, *Shaken by the Wind* became an instant popular success.[12]

The novel tells the story of a religiously-minded woman in pre-Civil War America whose life is influenced and in the end almost destroyed by contact with various religious sects. Sarah Sonning is based on Ray's grandmother Hannah, and Sarah's husband Thomas, whose religious involvement is ended by a sexual scandal, on Ray's grandfather Robert Pearsall Smith. The verisimilitude of the novel's background derives from the papers left by Hannah detailing the remarkable beliefs and behaviour of the various sects she had encountered.

Although the novel's main theme is the deception and self-deception to which religious enthusiasts are prone, and the ease with which lust can be taken for divine guidance, Ray never ridicules the religious urge: 'In their strange and ludicrous way these people felt the love of holiness in their hearts, and in the humility which abandoned reason and common sense they sought salvation.'[13] Sarah is as earnest in her religious quest as anyone else, with an added leaven of common sense, and her search for religious peace of mind after tragedy has struck is both moving and convincing.

There is balance in the presentation of the relative strengths of men and women. Sarah and her son Edmund are strong characters, her husband Thomas and Edmund's doomed love, Lottie, are weak. The false prophet Rufus Hollins is a terrifying creation, but several of the female characters are far from admirable. Although Ray's sympathy for her heroine is clear, Sarah is shown falling into error too. Sarah's youthful enthusiasm for celibacy in marriage balances the later religious inspiration attributed to sexual feelings by Thomas and the false prophet who influences him: both approaches, the reader concludes, are the result of using religion as a justification for following our own desires.

Sarah may be based on Hannah, but there is much of Ray in her too, notably the longing for children and intense devotion to her son. Sarah's gradual disillusionment with her husband is convincingly and at times humorously portrayed ('She knew his groans by heart, and could interpret them accurately') and on occasion Ray's own feelings emerge explicitly: 'And Thomas talked his fill and felt better, and Sarah kept her temper and felt worse; it is a common human experience.'[14] Despite the serious subject-matter and semi-tragic ending, there are moments of quiet humour, as in the puzzled attempts by the false prophet's adherents to follow his complex arithmetical calculations of the date of the Second Coming. What makes the novel unfailingly readable is Ray's skill in weaving arcane questions of belief into her story without long exposition, together with her increasingly mature characterisation – these are real people, not just symbols – and in particular the liveliness and credibility which she imparts to her scenes of family life. As a novelist, Ray was inspired by Tolstoy; but the influence of Charlotte M. Yonge cannot be dismissed.

In Greece with Carey Thomas during the October 1924 election Ray was 'extremely anxious for news'.[15] A year later she felt 'more & more weaned from politics' and by September 1926 could reflect that 'politics seems now incredibly remote. It isn't very long in years since I was all wrapped up in them, but now I have entirely withdrawn, & feel not the slightest impulse to go back'.[16] Her links with the women's movement followed the same pattern. For the NUSEC she felt 'detachment & dislike of the way they do things now' and cared little who ran it or what happened to it, even though her longstanding 'habit of caring' occasionally drove her to express an opinion.[17] She remained active in the London Society, mainly because of Pippa's involvement, wrote a well-received short history of it, and at times found herself with a 'wild day of Co[mmittee]s. of the old style – 4 in one afternoon, & myself in the chair for all 4'; but she was thankful 'not to be doing such absurdities daily'.[18]

In 1927 Ray returned to political activity. The League of Nations Union was urging the government to agree to 'really drastic' naval disarmament.[19] Ray 'foolishly' promised Lord Robert Cecil to become involved in the campaign, so for several weeks found herself 'absurdly busy shooting off letters & pamphlets'; it was 'a nasty job, owing to the complexities of the organizations we have to work through', 'very slow & discouraging', 'thoroughly unprofitable & enraging, mismanaged & stupid' and she extricated herself as soon as possible.[20] The campaign had little effect; Cecil became increasingly disillusioned with the policies of his Cabinet colleagues and resigned from the government later that summer.

Ray remained on the side-lines of the battle between old and new feminists within the NUSEC which led to the resignations of nearly half of the Executive Committee, her sympathies remaining with the beleaguered minority of egalitarians (though she thought their resignations rash and unhelpful). Far more significant was the prospect of finally achieving equal suffrage. Since Stanley Baldwin's Conservative government took office in 1924, pressure from feminist organisations – in Parliament and through letters, public meetings and demonstrations – had been mounting for an extension of the franchise for women.

In March 1927 Nancy Astor introduced a deputation to Baldwin from fifty-six women's societies. Ray sneaked in after Eva Hubback, NUSEC's Parliamentary Secretary, had undertaken a 'violent struggle' to have NUSEC included, but she remained unimpressed by the deputation ('a pitiful show') and its social welfare bias: 'All the rag, tag & bobtail societies were in the forefront [...] there were a number of people with bonnets full of bees, & a great crowd of featherweights.'[21] Nevertheless Ray was confident that equal suffrage would soon be granted. Baldwin would not have seen the deputation, she assumed, if he had not meant to take action.

Baldwin was indeed broadly sympathetic, but opposition within the Conservative Party to enfranchising the 'frivolous and flighty' Flapper generation was stronger than expected.[22] Feminist agitation continued while different members of the government seemed to give out different messages. Baldwin eventually honoured the commitment he had given. The Representation of the People (Equal Franchise) Bill

DAME MILLICENT FAWCETT, MISS FAWCETT, MISS GARRETT AND
MRS STRACHEY AFTER ROYAL ASSENT TO EQUAL FRANCHISE
ACT JULY 2ND 1928

(Figure 28) 2 July 1928. Ray drives Dame Millicent Fawcett, her daughter Philippa, and sister Agnes Garrett, away in triumph after Royal Assent is given to the Equal Franchise Act.

was introduced in March 1928 and enacted that July. There was just time for Ray to add the final chapter of the suffrage story to the proofs of her book about the women's movement.

Ray's initial lack of enthusiasm for writing a book on the emancipation of women did not last long (particularly after the publisher offered acceptable financial terms). Within weeks she became interested in the project, which should be 'very easy to do, & ought to be highly entertaining'.[23] No argument would be needed, just the portrayal of 'the funny old people battling against those ridiculous taboos'.[24] She spent the next four years discovering how simplistic this verdict was.

The original plan was to cover a far wider sweep of history than eventually emerged, and Ray appears initially to have tried to help her friend and colleague Ida O'Malley by bringing her in as a collaborator. For some time Ray's other projects and commitments took precedence. In early 1926 she started to concentrate on the female emancipation book and felt she was making good progress. That autumn the publisher decided to split the book into two volumes: '1. The Pioneers & 2. The Movt. itself'.[25] Ray would tackle the second part, 'though we shall each help with each'.[26] Ray was relieved to be freed from a tight collaboration, but by January 1927, during a bout of influenza-induced depression, felt that her work was 'slipshod & useless & very much too scanty to be real work. However it's all I've got at the moment to cling to, so I cling'.[27] Ida O'Malley would have endorsed Ray's self-criticism; she 'spent a great deal of the time telling me how slipshod & unhistorical were my methods, how loose my writing, & how shallow my views. And though this was naturally rather trying, it was certainly true & salutary!'[28]

When, a few months later, the publisher abandoned the idea of a first volume and insisted that Ray work alone on the second, Ida O'Malley took it badly. Even though she was left with the earlier material (including much that Ray had written), and Ray insisted that the publisher make her some reimbursement for time and effort expended, Ray's continuing involvement with the project distressed and angered her, and caused a breach in their friendship. Ray was perplexed:

> She ought to be able to make a book of it [...]: but she is not very capable of working against her feelings. And her feelings tell her [...] she has wasted 3 years' work, & that I have run off with the plums. I can't combat this – though it isn't at all true – because I don't know how to deal with feelings. They make me terribly impatient.[29]

Although these events were 'exceedingly painful & difficult', the final ending of the collaboration felt like deliverance from 'a huge incubus'.[30] This was, Ray ruefully admitted, 'feelings' on her part, and unjustified, as the collaboration had been valuable.[31]

Even though Ray had to undertake a drastic revision of what she had written, her sense of liberation and greater enjoyment spurred progress. Ray's self-confessedly 'incurably hasty & inaccurate ways' caused problems with detail, but by the end of the year, after 'a lot of really hard work [...] arranging & clarifying all that material', with some parts re-written '6 or 7 times before it went smoothly enough', the book was nearly complete.[32] There was a final 'pit of despondency' in January 1928, when she lamented 'I can't get any free time except at night – & even though I sleep in the afternoon I can't go on working much after 1 – & the thing crawls'.[33] But that night she worked until 3 a.m., dug herself out of the hole she was in and felt cheerful about finishing. In March, Ray delivered the manuscript of *The Cause* to her publisher, 'thankful to be rid of it'.[34]

The book for which Ray Strachey is mainly remembered was published in October 1928, costing 15 shillings [£41.50]. Reactions were enthusiastic from the start. Ray considered the early reviews 'really first rate' despite a 'very spiteful' one from Lady Rhondda, and she basked in the praise.[35] A threatened libel action by 'that wildcat Sylvia Pankhurst' over Ray's claim that that the WSPU did not keep proper accounts ('They didn't, but they did publish some sort of audited statement, & I was misled into saying they didn't by Mrs Pankhurst herself!') was averted by the issue of an erratum slip.[36]

The Cause is broad in its scope (suffrage is only a part of Ray's story), impassioned, often ironically amusing, full of first-hand information and revealing anecdotes, swept along by its narrative drive, and 'immensely readable'; above all, it is generous.[37] In the best NUWSS tradition, the battle is not between men and women but between the enlightened of both sexes and 'the selfish and self-interested among men and the sheltered and lazy among women'.[38] Ray paid full tribute to those men ('honest and kindly, as most men are') who helped the cause of female emancipation.[39] Men who at various times opposed the employment of women were, she recognized, often motivated by genuine fear of economic hardship. Anti-suffragists spoke 'from their consciences and their hearts' out of honest error.[40]

In her Preface Ray acknowledged that she was 'an actor in the later stages of the Suffrage drama', and admitted that although she 'conscientiously tried to write history and not propaganda' her assumptions were feminist and her 'eyes perhaps blinded to the virtues of the past'.[41] Her personal links were invaluable: obtaining the memories and opinions of those she had worked with (and against) and consulting the records of the suffrage societies supplemented her hours in the British Museum reading biographies, autobiographies and histories of the period since the French Revolution. In the text itself she is totally self-effacing. There is no indication whatsoever of her own role, or of her presence at or contribution to the events she describes; she appears to class herself with the largely unnamed foot soldiers, rather than named leaders like Millicent Fawcett and the Pankhursts.

Nevertheless Ray's own involvement in the Cause gives her book two main advantages: inside knowledge of key events and a profound understanding of the movement's appeal to women. Her own vivid memories inform descriptions of 'missionary meetings, filled with the fervour of a gospel', the 'almost religious fervour', and 'the longing to do a reformer's work in the world' which 'sent young ladies to street corners to demand the vote'; the fun and excitement of her own experiences bubble through when she recounts that 'in their holidays they toured in caravans, setting up stalls in market-places and speaking on village greens, finding on the whole great friendliness, with just that spice of opposition which makes such deeds exciting'.[42] She projects her own generation's enthusiasm back in time to bring to life earlier fighters in the same cause, such as the Langham Place girls:

> How angry they all grew when the watchmakers' and the gilders' Trade Unions refused to allow girls to be apprenticed, and how they enjoyed it when *Punch* poked fun at crinolines! They were free and confident and happy, and many of them were young; and they had got hold of a living idea, and the world was moving in the right direction.[43]

And when Ray identified the appeal of philanthropy as 'the sense of being worth while' with its aim 'something good and concrete [...]

impersonal to themselves', she stated her book's dominating theme: 'to have the power of working for a cause was a new and thrilling and satisfying experience for the female mind'.[44]

The vigorous readability of *The Cause* owes much to Ray's earlier experiences as novelist and journalist. The reader is swept through the drama of defeats and successes and the energy of her writing style captures the zest of the participants:

> Why should not women do law engrossing? An office was opened at once and filled with women workers. Why should not women be hairdressers, hotel managers, wood engravers, dispensers, house decorators, watchmakers, telegraphists? Out! Out! Let us see if we can make them do it! Why does the school of design threaten to exclude them? We must have a petition at once; and the Royal Academy, why does it not admit women students? We must knock politely on its doors. And then there were the swimming baths in Marylebone, why were they not open to women?[45]

Ray had always favoured simplicity (despite her stepfather's criticism), shunning affectation as 'the worst of vices', and there are many instances in *The Cause* where her verdict is forthright, such as: 'the indirect or backstairs method [of the exercise of feminine influence in politics] was uninformed, capricious and dangerous'; the ladylike 'ideal of life' set out in 'poisonous little books of moral maxims' 'was none the less strong for being absolutely absurd'; and 'the action of Mr Gladstone and his followers in 1884 was but the first of a long series of similar betrayals, and made a rent in the prestige of the Party system from which, in the eyes of those who cared for the suffrage, it never entirely recovered'.[46] But she was anxious to avoid overt propaganda (and aware that her publisher needed a lively account to boost sales). The solution she adopted was irony.

Irony allowed Ray to introduce alternative points of view without disguising her own opinion, and often to add humour to her story. At an Anti-Slavery Convention to which an American delegation had been invited, '[William Lloyd] Garrison was delayed on the way, and of the seven members who did turn up, four were women! It was a most horrible disappointment [...] the abolition of slavery in British territory in 1833 had been gained without any such indecorous proceeding'; the honour awarded to Angela Burdett Coutts was 'one of the very few examples of a peerage bestowed on a woman for any other service than that of being a mistress to a king'; and women employed by the Post Office but sacked in response to male outrage were 'forty dangerous females'.[47] Irony even allowed Ray to poke gentle fun at her own sex: when rival suffrage societies reunited, 'vested interests (of the most innocent nature), and personal animosities (of the most ladylike kind) had grown up. Honorary secretaries were unwilling to give up the arduous tasks of writing letters and keeping minutes; honorary treasurers clung to the privilege of making up deficits out of their own private purses'.[48] And on the outbreak of war, women 'were willing to do "everything," but they did not know how to do anything, and a consciousness of a power of organisation (which so many of them felt) was not of much practical service in a carpenter's workshop'.[49]

Ray's main condemnation was reserved for the Liberal government headed by Asquith, which so often broke its undertakings to the suffragists. Her attitude to the suffragettes was mixed. While revising the book, she aimed to bring out 'not the vice but the narrow unwisdom' of the WSPU, 'their terribly limited understanding both of the world & of the meaning of enfranchisement. That is what struck me most in meeting Mrs P[ankhurst]. Provincial, ignorant, & one-sided, & her followers thought this single mindedness'.[50] Following Millicent Fawcett, she acknowledged the boost the WSPU gave to the whole suffrage campaign; she admired the courage of the hunger strikers, particularly Lady Constance Lytton ('a true martyr to the Cause', about whose treatment 'a great many people were furiously and justly indignant'); and admitted that 'the militant movement, which undoubtedly had its drawbacks at close quarters, and which was regarded with very mixed feelings by the majority of feminists in England, did nothing but good in other parts of the world'.[51] Ray's objections to the militants included their lack of democracy, their 'defiance, antagonism and suspicion' towards outsiders, the unreality of their world-view ('an artificial world of their own creating, where danger followed quick upon danger, and excitement always ran high') and the false position they adopted by using violence while claiming to be 'victims of aggression'.[52] Behind all these – implied but not explicit – lay her own mistrust of out of control, whipped-up emotions. The WSPU increasingly appealed to 'those whose natural inclination led them towards drama, hero-worship, and self-surrender', she stated; she might have been describing herself.[53] Ray's private verdict confirmed that only her rational head had kept her from joining their number: 'I have been a good deal impressed with the militant side of it, in looking at it in detail. I still think there were very unwise aspects of it, but it was a heroic affair.'[54]

Despite Ray's attempt to keep herself out of her story, *The Cause* is inevitably self-revealing. Her preference for non-confrontation, gradualism, the use of humour and the ability to see the other person's point of view (and if possible, make use of it) emerges in praise of 'that useful instrument, the thin end of the wedge' and in comments like 'the Hallelujah lassies were not consciously preaching feminism [...] but as they went about their business they taught the other lesson too, in that quiet and practical fashion which best carries conviction' and 'they learnt that to keep their own tempers, to make jokes, and to go on steadily with their business was the sure way to get the goodwill of the crowd'.[55] Perhaps the most surprising aspect of Ray's choice of heroes and heroines is the admiration she shows for those driven by religious conviction. Catherine Booth was one of the 'flaming spirits' whose religious beliefs led them to change the world; so too were Florence Nightingale, F. D. Maurice, and Josephine Butler.[56] Ray's admiration surely reflects values absorbed from her Catholic father and Quaker grandmother, too deeply embedded to be removed by her later 'a-religious' rationalism.[57]

There was pride and some optimism in Ray's account but no complacency. In 1928 'the Cause stands midway to success', the 'economic, the domestic, and the moral equality of men and women' were still unachieved, and only the first steps had been taken along the path towards 'the morality of justice'.[58] 'People remained, and still remain, as unmoral, as thoughtless, and as prone to evil as before' was Ray's verdict, and there was much to fear in the future.[59] Whereas the women of her generation and earlier sought 'an extended power to do good in the world', the generation containing her stepdaughter and daughter:

> seemed to be mistaking the meaning of their freedom, and to be using it only for excess of excitement. They spent the morning hours upon the make-up of their faces, idled through the afternoons, and danced all night. They discarded the semblance of manners and morals, and replaced them by licence and dissipation.[60]

Ray's forward-looking final pages dismissed this phase as 'ephemeral and unimportant', but it is possible that she was trying to convince herself as much as her readers.[61]

The book was regarded from the start as 'a really exhaustive and authoritative history of the movement' and soon achieved classic status. Even criticisms by later generations of feminists that Ray concentrated on educated middle-class women at the expense of the working classes, and that women continued to be oppressed by the very structure of family life, have not stopped later writers from turning to *The Cause* for information, interpretation and lively quotations. While accepting that 'feminist circles' would be her main audience, Ray had from the start hoped 'to succeed in making the thing of enough general value to take its place among the real histories of the 19th century in the long run'.[62] She did.

Ray's links with Cambridge had been strengthened by the appointment of her sister-in-law Pernel Strachey as Principal of Newnham College in 1923. In 1930 Ray helped to set up a Women's Appointments Board for Cambridge graduates, of which she became the first Chairman. (The women were graduates only in a limited sense, as Cambridge University did not grant full degrees to women until 1948.)

Another claim on her time was Ray's continuing role in the LNSWS. In 1927 a wealthy benefactor emerged to put a temporary end to its constant funding problems. A move to better accommodation (in Marsham Street, conveniently for Ray) followed in 1929, and for a while the Society flourished, but the benefactor's unexpected and intestate death in December 1930 before all the promised donations had been delivered plunged it back into financial chaos. The Society's much-needed work towards equality between the sexes, largely abandoned by NUSEC, continued in parallel with these fluctuating fortunes.

Ray had previously been involved in the campaign which secured women's admittance to the upper ranks of the Civil Service in equal competition with men. But the battle to bring equality of opportunity and pay to women in the Civil Service was far from over. For many years after the war ended, ex-serviceman were recruited in preference to women, women were often confined to mechanical tasks and, even where they were allowed to do the same work as men, they were paid less. The battle between the women's organisations and a recalcitrant Treasury (supported by the all male senior Civil Service) continued, with the LNSWS playing a leading role. In early 1929 Ray was 'engaged in a violent wrangle with Winston Churchill over the question of equal pay for men & women in the Civil Service'; the women now entered by open competition, and undertook interchangeable work with the men, so 'the present system is indefensible'.[64] Ray was hopeful: 'we beat the Treasury 9 years ago over equal entry, & we shall beat them now over equal pay if we stick to it; & so I am sticking'.[65] The Chancellor of the Exchequer resisted on economic grounds, and the question of the role of women in the Civil Service became just one part of the remit of a Royal Commission on the Civil Service, set up in October 1929.

Drawing up material for the Commission was demanding and giving evidence to it on 15 October 1930 was 'rather an ordeal', even for Ray.[66] The Chairman, Lord Tomlin (Julia's father-in-law, 'a crusted old anti who thinks women are a joke'), was 'exceedingly polite' during Ray's two and half hours of cross-questioning in the House of Lords, but afterwards 'one only remembers what might have been put better'.[67] Ray had to devote many days to listening to the other evidence, and had earlier spent a 'whole afternoon from 3 to 8 with one of the Commissioners & a group of Civil Servants, trying to hammer out a workable scheme. It is interesting, but so complex, & so tantalizing'.[68] Characteristically, she wished she were a Commissioner herself.

In the end little progress was made. The report largely favoured the status quo, but on the question of equal pay the five female Commissioners put female solidarity before party loyalty.[69] The Commission was almost equally split, with both camps setting out their conclusions about equal pay in the Report. Only after another war was the principle of equal pay for men and women accepted in the Civil Service.

Ray's broadcasting career started on 20 December 1927, when, after an audition, she gave a talk on 'The Flapper of 1827'; her annoyance at being introduced as 'Strakey' was offset by pleasure at earning £5 [£274].[70] A further talk and an appearance chairing a debate led in November 1928 to an invitation to give weekly talks summarising 'the events of the week from the woman's point of view' ('but of course there is no woman's point of view, and there are very few events in any week').[71] Five guineas a week was easy money for 'padding'.[72] Hilda Matheson, her former colleague in Lady Astor's office, now a pioneering Director of Talks at the BBC, sat threateningly in front of Ray to make faces if she spoke too fast. No such disaster occurred: aided by her pleasant voice and her facility at public speaking, Ray proved a natural broadcaster and soon became a popular favourite. Within a month, the talks were made 'more or less permanent'.[73]

The BBC's reluctance to court controversy was frustrating to both women – 'every time my feelings run away with me the blue pencil comes down', Ray complained – but she had more freedom from autumn 1930 in the talks she gave about books.[74] Designed for the non-literary with little experience of book-reading, these talks conveyed without condescension her passion for reading. The recommendations in 'Reading for Fun' were unsurprising:

specific novels by R. L. Stevenson and Anthony Hope for romance, Defoe and Rider Haggard for adventure, Conan Doyle and Erskine Childers for crime, Mrs Gaskell and Tolstoy for everyday life. Ray's second series on 'Books about People' dealt with biographies, most of which 'pay too little attention to these normal human aspects of their subjects; they say too much about their exceptional gifts, and too little about their ordinary lives'.[75] The recommendations here were less predictable. As well as Mrs Gaskell on Charlotte Brontë, Ray praised Emily Lawless's life of Maria Edgeworth, Washington Irving on Christopher Columbus and Richard Cobbold's *History of Margaret Catchpole* ('a book like this which gives us vivid detail of ordinary life, mixed up with wild adventure, and with the presentation of strong and individual character, seems to me one of the best relaxations to be had').[76]

Although Ray claimed that 'living character' was the most important thing in a biography, moral complexity had little attraction for her.[77] There is a clear distinction between saints and sinners in her recommendations, and in marked contrast to her brother-in-law Lytton, Ray enjoyed finding characters worthy of admiration. Her recommendations included *The Little Flowers* of St Francis of Assisi and the *Confessions of St Augustine* (which offered 'intimate knowledge of a great and acute intellect striving in complete sincerity to reach an understanding of truth') and she admitted that 'there is a quality of goodness in certain people which is quite unmistakeable and which even the wickedest of us are forced to admire when we meet it'.[78] 'The lives of people, struggling to some known end or ideal, seem to have a great attraction for you', one lady perceptively wrote.[79] Ray achieved a bond of intimacy with her enthusiastic but unknown listeners often missing from the rest of her life.

The risk-taking influence of Hilda Matheson waned within the BBC, leading to her resignation in late 1931, and her successor, Margery Wace, was less enthusiastic about Ray as a broadcaster. Invitations for Ray to broadcast became erratic and the conditions less appealing. Reviews of novels were banned and talking about politics became increasingly difficult: forced to broadcast about the

October 1931 election while saying 'nothing controversial', Ray found she 'could only talk drivel'.[80] A few weeks later she gave 'a horribly platitudinous New Year broadcast to the kitchens of England'.[81] 'It gets harder & harder to do these well,' she commented, 'owing to the timid new policy of the BBC. But anything for money.'[82]

When Janet Quigley replaced Margery Wace in the Talks Department in 1937, Ray's broadcasting invitations increased again. Defending women's right to work, in a debate in the *Men Talking* series in November 1938, Ray received rare praise from the chairman, the author John Gloag; in general he strongly opposed women participants in the series, but Ray was an exception, an excellent contributor who 'illuminated the discussion without dominating it'.[83] Ray collaborated on and eventually took part in a series of six broadcasts in early 1939 on 'Careers for Girls', by then a topic of central importance to her. Her final broadcast in 1940 commemorated the passage of twenty-one years since the suffrage triumph of 1918. She was due to broadcast again the day after her death.

On 5 August 1929 Millicent Garrett Fawcett died at the age of eighty-two. To Ray it was 'a great loss', causing her much short-term effort over obituary notices, funeral arrangements and the memorial service held on 19 November in Westminster Abbey, before she took up the major project of writing Mrs Fawcett's biography.[84] In 1926 Ray had obtained Mrs Fawcett's blessing as her eventual biographer, so access to the papers she had left was no problem. Through the correspondence column of *The Times*, Ray asked to see any of her letters, and was soon overwhelmed by the response: reminiscences as well as letters flooded in. By December she had a contract with the publisher John Murray (an advance of £200 [£11,200] and 15% royalties) and early in 1930 was ready to start writing. As usual the day-to-day demands of the LNSWS office broke into her writing hours, so she retreated to the Bussy home, La Souco, to write in peace.

Writing the biography proved both more interesting and more challenging than Ray expected. At first she worried that 'nothing sensational remained so in her atmosphere. It was all level & quiet &

eminently reasonable'.[85] By the time she had written two chapters – in between bouts of teaching André Gide to play Demon Patience – she had decided that 'there is more in it, when I come to actual writing, than I at first supposed, & I don't think it will be at all dull'.[86] Back in England daily life – the Royal Commission on the Civil Service, her BBC talks and having Barbara living in London – slowed progress and the summer holidays with the children at Fernhurst brought it to a complete halt.

Just as Ray got going again in earnest that autumn, her health interfered. Neuritis in her arm had once before been a sign of dental problems and now proved so again. She found that eleven front teeth needed to be extracted, 'a great practical bore as well as a great expense'.[87] The timescale for removing them had to take into account various speeches at Oxford and Cambridge as well as her appearance before the Royal Commission on the Civil Service. The first session to remove four teeth on 29 October left her with 'perpetual face ache' and much reduced energy for three weeks; the remaining three sessions were less painful.[88]

To cope with ten days of toothlessness, Ray sent the family to I Tatti for Christmas and incarcerated herself alone in Marsham Street to work on her book. Semi-nocturnal, and in almost complete isolation, she did 'nothing but crawl about the house from desk to armchair to dining room to bed, with an occasional delightful interlude at the piano', and reached the last chapter, 'the most difficult of all'.[89] Ray remained unsure whether she had captured the character of Mrs Fawcett ('an interesting person & very well worth knowing, at the time: retrospectively too') or whether the book would be 'worthy of her'.[90] Although she had expected that 'an orgy of rewriting' would follow the first draft, she appears to have rewritten only one chapter.[91] On 12 January 1931, the day she took possession of her 'most elegant' new set of false teeth, Ray delivered her manuscript to the publisher, feeling 'as if I had just sent a child to a new school!'[92]

Millicent Garrett Fawcett was published on 16 June 1931. Given the economic crisis, sales were unsurprisingly modest: as Ray acknowledged, 'everyone is bored with the women's movement nowadays'.[93] But reviews were in general kind and Ray was satisfied that it 'pleased the people I wanted to satisfy' and that 'I think she herself would pass it'.[94] The book is a celebration of a life rather than a forensic dissection of it. Ray appears to have considered it inappropriate for a biographer authorised by her subject, a trusted friend and colleague, to undertake an impartial historical assessment dragging faults and errors into the public gaze. The biography as a whole displays constant empathy, a useful means of evading critical judgement. But the book is far less one-sided and hagiographic than has been alleged. Ray describes many instances where Mrs Fawcett faced opposition and criticism. In some of these instances she adds her own defence of her subject's views and actions; in others she leaves the reader to make her own judgement.

David Rubinstein, a later biographer of Millicent Fawcett, described Ray as 'a competent though cloying biographer' and, while paying tribute to the usefulness of her work (and drawing on it extensively himself), regarded her book as 'marked by a reticence remarkable even at that date and by the implicit assumption that everything Mrs Fawcett did was right'.[95] There are certainly omissions. Some were perhaps inadvertent, as Ray appears to have undertaken little if any work in libraries or archives, some undoubtedly deliberate ('so far as it goes it's truthful' Ray characterised her portrayal).[96] Often an understated hint provides a marker for an unexplored area. Nevertheless, despite her admiration for her subject, Ray did not always agree with her, and any interpretation which assumes otherwise merely indicates her success in effacing herself from her account. Ray felt none of Mrs Fawcett's admiration for Lloyd George; her views on sexual morality were less rigid; and her letters often displayed an enthusiasm for state-sponsored social reform going far beyond what Mrs Fawcett would have tolerated.

Where the two women did agree, it is difficult to disentangle coincidence of views from the influence of the older woman on her younger colleague. Similarity of character was crucial: both were 'almost passionately reticent', mistrusted overt displays of emotion and disliked displaying their own.[97] Both were capable of 'caustic remarks', but hid considerable kindness behind a façade of self-control.[98] The ideal of 'Goodness–industry–self-control' which Ray attributes to Mrs Fawcett was – or became – Ray's ideal too.[99] Ray may well have been steered towards qualified admiration for the suffragettes and a dislike of political parties by Mrs Fawcett. She would certainly have learnt the advantages of a light touch and humour in public situations, hallmarks of her own way of doing business. Nevertheless, Ray was not someone to resign her own independence of thought.

Financially the mid- to late 1920s were years of frustration rather than disaster. Ray's attempts to pay off the debts from her building ventures were partially successful, but her substantial overdraft remained. The economies she did make were balanced by the drain of supporting Julia, the costs of growing children, hospitality at Fernhurst for friends and family, tax demands and Ray's habit of relaxing spending constraints as soon as the worst was over, instead of building up a contingency reserve. Moving to Marsham Street helped, but Barbara's stays in Oxford and Vienna proved unexpectedly expensive just as Ray's shares in Marconi – her main source of income apart from Oliver's salary and the allowance from her stepfather – were providing less. She tried with some success to cut expenses but admitted 'I do so hate economising – & am so bad at it. Earning is a better alternative for me I feel sure'.[100]

In these circumstances the decision in late 1928 to take on the lease of the whole house was rash, even though tenants were soon installed on the top floor. Not surprisingly Ray was soon on a financial knife edge again, rescued only by her substantial earnings from broadcasting. Oliver was soon to inherit various shares from his mother, but these were to be invested to provide for his rapidly approaching and woefully under-funded retirement. Earnings from Ray's books were never high but her growing reputation did at least attract better terms for future books, and she took on work as a publisher's reader for historical novels at two guineas [£117] a time. On the other hand, increasing paper-work led her to employ a part-time secretary again.

The real worry was that funding from I Tatti might dry up. For years a financial battle between the Berensons had threatened the continuation of Ray's allowance. Bernard Berenson was determined to leave I Tatti and its library – and the necessary financial endowment – to Harvard University, as a study centre for Renaissance art. Mary was bitterly opposed to this plan. Her endeavours – particularly the negotiations with the art dealer Joseph Duveen which she often undertook – had made a major contribution to their wealth, she claimed, and some of it should come to her. In particular she longed to have money of her own to bequeath to her descendants, and to be able to continue showering money on them whenever they indicated a need or she thought she perceived one. For the time being Berenson's generous support of Ray and Karin continued (though his relations with Karin and her family were cooler than with Ray) but Mary's uncontrollable, and often devious, spending on her family and her claims for a share of their capital led to constant rages on his part, exacerbated by the worsening financial position of their clients in the United States.

A crisis arose in 1930. Berenson wrongly attributed the Bloomsbury circle's dislike and suspicion of him to Ray, who protested to Mary her 'continual gratitude' for his 'pure kindness': 'You may think that in his shoes you would find it natural & inevitable to give it, but it actually isn't, & it is really your way of looking at money which is odd, not his!'[101] Ray could, she claimed, 'neither act nor write affectionately if I didn't feel it, for I am a hopelessly bad dissembler in such matters'; her 'absolutely true & heartfelt' letter to Berenson expressing profound gratitude for his gift of 'liberty of spirit' to her, 'the biggest gift any one person can give to another' had the desired effect and the storm passed.[102] But a few months later the offer Ray made to accept a small cut in her allowance, as she was earning and Christopher had been awarded a scholarship by his school, sent Berenson into another rage (a visit by Barbara and her friends may have been a contributory factor). At the same time Mary became less and less capable of fulfilling various promises of financial aid to Ray.

It was not a good time for Ray to have electricity installed in the cottage, much though this increased its usefulness, nor to give up

the rental on her top-floor rooms in Westminster to offer a home to
Ralph's daughter, Ursula. Ursula's home life was pitiable; her mother
Margaret, subject to regular bouts of mental illness, fiercely opposed
Ursula's wish to become an actress, and never offered her children any
warmth of affection.[103] Rescuing Ursula demanded 'considerable self
sacrifice' from Ray – time, money, worry, loss of freedom and some
thoroughly unpleasant dealings with Margaret.[104] Oliver was Ralph's
executor and Pippa had been close to her brother, so Ray had some
grounds for intervening, but her main motivation was concern for
Ursula herself: 'I really could not stand by & see her left to the care of
a lunatic in a third rate boarding house.'[105] Ursula, often ill and 'too
lazy & docile [...] almost like a ghost', was the complete opposite in
temperament to Barbara, but the cousins got on well and were happy
to move into their own accommodation in 53 Marsham Street in
April 1930.[106] When Barbara went up to Oxford that autumn, Ursula
started at a drama school.

The general economic position had worsened during 1930. 'The
industrial depression is really the worst we have had since the war',
Ray reported in December, 'The unemployment among professional
women is as bad as it was in 1919 – & that's saying a lot.'[107] It was clear
that Ray's income might collapse. In 1931 she cut as much spending
as possible, but Barbara needed coaching for exams, and at Fernhurst
the boiler needing replacing, the pool wall rebuilding and the drive
relaying. It was clear that 'if calamity is ahead' Ray would have to
make major changes in her life.[108]

The first blow came in August: her allowance from Berenson was
drastically cut, at a time when Oliver's job was under threat. Reducing
accommodation costs became a necessity, but no-one would 'take
the tail end of a lease in a house surrounded [...] by noisy building
operations!'[109] Ray sold her 'poor old tin kettle' of a car, dispensed with
her secretary, agreed to sell an acre of the Fernhurst land to her sister-
in-law Marjorie, and looked for a tenant for her top floor.[110] In late
September the remainder of her allowance disappeared; their income
had halved in a matter of weeks. Ray cut the allowances of Julia, Barbara

and Christopher by a third, and tried to reassure her panic-stricken mother: 'if need be I must use up my capital to finish the children's education'.[111] To Christopher she was more outspoken: 'I daresay we shall wriggle along till the whole country crashes to ruin: & then nothing financial will matter'.[112] His scholarship and an educational insurance Mary had paid would keep him at school and 'we have Fernhurst in which to retreat & live on rabbits & potatoes!'[113] In her diary Ray dismissed the practical challenges of her reduced income ('it can be done if it must') but admitted that she was 'hovering up & down on the edge of morbid depression' and that 'one's inside troubles or happiness seem so much more important than these outside things'; what emotional problems were troubling her she did not reveal.[114]

Although Oliver's post survived the axe, Ray clearly needed a job. She soon found one. Ray's support for Nancy Astor in Plymouth during her successful 1929 re-election campaign had led to Ray's undertaking various tasks for her, some of which paid handsomely. Working for 'that wild woman Lady Astor' still carried 'plenty of fun with it, though she's not at all easy to manage' and was easier now that Ray had learnt to delegate.[115] Lady Astor offered her the post of political secretary (occupied by Hilda Matheson when Ray first worked for her) at a salary of £400 [£22,300], 'with latitude about hours & holidays & all that' and 'the advantage of not interfering with BBC work, or of positively stimulating journalism'.[116] Although the job would be 'exactly right' for her, Ray briefly hesitated, apparently unsure whether Lady Astor would continue being 'most awfully nice' about these flexible arrangements.[117] She soon accepted, but her start date depended on Lady Astor's re-election in the forthcoming general election and her own fitness for work. At this critical moment Ray faced a major operation.

Ray's old problem of fibroids had reappeared. Drugs had at first controlled the consequent floodings and pains but Ray's periods had recently become irregular and almost continuous. Her doctor advised that fibroids might be a sign – or a future cause – of cancer, and that curetting and radium treatment 'would make it 100% safe, besides putting a stop to all the immediate troubles she expected during the change period'.[118] Ray burnt any papers 'which still feel desperately private' and made an informal 'note of wishes in regard to my will', requesting presents be given to her main domestic employees and LNSWS colleagues, making provision for Ursula, and setting out her strong wish to be cremated and 'the ashes disposed of with as little trouble to anyone as possible. The easiest plan is to leave the tiresome things at the crematorium, I think'.[119] She hoped that no one would go to the funeral at all: 'but of course the thing I want done is what is least troublesome'.[120]

In early October Ray went into the Marie Curie hospital, 'the very best & most modern hospital in the world, & [...] certainly inexpensive'.[121] The operation, which caused a premature menopause, involved the insertion of radium needles into her uterus and their removal 24 hours later, during which time Ray had to lie immobile and without food. The fibroid was 'rather larger than a golf ball' but no cancer was found.[122] Afterwards Ray felt 'a bit bruised in the middle' but considered the operation 'amazingly light & trivial'.[123] After a week in hospital, she spent 'a very lazy fortnight' convalescing in 51 Gordon Square before returning to Marsham Street.[124]

Physically she felt well but her intellect was 'muffled & stagnant'.[125] 'I can keep up a more or less intelligent outside, & can make my usual sort of conversation. But there is at the moment nothing behind it'.[126] She assumed it was the result of having 'hopped in one week through the physical changes which normally take several years', and hoped it would pass, 'for it's more fun to be internally active – even though it's sometimes more distressing'.[127] She would need all her energy to cope with Lady Astor (re-elected in a Conservative landslide), and privately admitted dreading the prospect. Disillusion about public life had taken over:

> public affairs look so black, & all sides so stupid that I can't feel the passionate excitement I once knew. It all seems to have got out of hand to such a degree that one is helpless. I find it quite easy to believe that a grand crash is coming upon our civilization. If it does

perhaps things will seem terribly thrilling again. But just now in their tottery state they only look stupid & useless & irrelevant.[128]

But she had little choice about re-entering the familiar arena. At the age of forty-four, an acknowledged expert on women's employment, Ray was about to become an employee for the first time.

PART SIX

Working for Women

CHAPTER FOURTEEN
Hard Times: 1931–1935

…in these hard times bread & butter comes before dreams…[1]

Ray was plunged straight into the whirl of activity which always surrounded Nancy Astor. The problems of the job were clear from the start: spending time on the genuinely interesting matters was threatened by the never-ending flood of routine letters and telephone calls, and by Nancy's erratic working methods. Mastering anything intellectually challenging was hindered by the melée of different subjects: 'Charlie Chaplin, & Swedish Crown Princes & GBS & Gandhi all mixed up with women MPs & the price of bread & nursery schools'.[2] Nevertheless there was an initial unexpected satisfaction from shedding responsibility, leaving Ray 'much less impatient & much less active than in an unpaid job'.[3]

Slacker moments when Lady Astor was away were paid for by turmoil when she returned, with Ray having to pack '10 days' work into 2' on disparate questions such as '1. The politics of the BBC 2. The forthcoming Children's Bill 3. Allotments for the unemployed 4. Nursery schools in various parts of the country 5. Pensions cases from Plymouth 6. Scandals in the police force 7. The Unemployment Anomalies Act & 8. Civil Service Superannuation'.[4] It took time to work out what her employer wanted from her. Lady Astor was 'amazingly clever, & exceedingly attractive' but her failure to concentrate on her political role necessitated a 'grand bluff' involving Ray too.[5] Her employer's continuing capacity for springing surprises was both exasperating and admirable, with her 'impromptu flashes' often more valuable, Ray acknowledged, than her own 'carefully prepared solid stuff'.[6]

The slackening of pressure during the Christmas Parliamentary recess was filled by a family crisis. When Oliver's brother Lytton became ill in December 1931, there was a mass movement of Stracheys to Ham Spray and the Bear Inn, Hungerford. Ray had never been close to Lytton, but hoped to relieve the burden on Pippa, who was doing much of the nursing. As usual, Ray became a practical mainstay to all those involved, taking over the housekeeping from Carrington (and later the funeral arrangements from James). During that grim month before Lytton's death on 21 January, while medical diagnoses (all wrong) succeeded one another and Lytton's condition fluctuated, Ray shuttled between Hungerford and London. Fond though she was of many of Lytton's siblings and friends, she was repelled by 'all those naked emotions & the way they were mixed up & tangled by all the personalities' and suspected emotional self-indulgence.[7] Carrington's 'wild state' was at least genuine – and her suicide a few weeks later was 'too painful' for comment in Ray's diary.[8]

When Pippa left for Roquebrune to recover from her exertions, additional responsibilities in the LNSWS fell on Ray, just as the tempo of her paid work dramatically increased. At home, Oliver succumbed to gastric flu and demanded time and attention. To make matters worse, Ursula was ill; bed-bound and deeply depressed, 'all the awful anxieties of her life came out of their holes & stared at her' and Ray could do nothing to comfort her.[9] Ray dashed home from her office in the Astors' house at 4 St. James's Square to cook Ursula meals twice a day and then to make arrangements for her to recuperate at La Souco.

An even worse worry during these 'very black months' was Mary.[10] Her recovery from an operation in November had been slow and erratic, genuine illness compounded by 'a terribly strong element of hysteria'.[11] Mary, 'the worst invalid in the world', provoked countless scenes; Berenson and Nicky Mariano feared this would be her permanent state.[12] In February Mary came close to death, an episode which had a dramatic effect on her. By the time Ray visited I Tatti at Easter, dreading 'unspeakably' the task which fell to her of making 'a real outspoken attack' on her mother, Mary had 'ceased to want to be ill, & […] had thrown aside all her grudges against BB'.[13] For the time being, Mary became 'a different person – the whole feel of her was back to what it had been before her breakdown in 1917'.[14] For Ray, it was 'a tremendous relief'.[15]

Through this black winter Ray clung onto one source of comfort: she had made a new friend. In a life filled with acquaintances, Ray's only close friend had been Pippa. 'The worst thing about me', Ray admitted, 'is that I don't like enough people – or like people enough.'[16] The tentative early stages of this new friendship ('so enchanting that I think it makes me safe against all but real misfortunes') gave her the consolation, valuable in itself, of 'being fond of someone' even though as yet 'there was precious little objective substance to it'.[17] The firm friendship which developed provided Ray with companionship and mental stimulation – and an alternative to the Strachey view of life.

Mary Agnes ('Molly') Hamilton was Scottish, a Newnham alumna of greater intellectual distinction than Ray, and five years older. She and Ray had crossed paths during the suffrage campaigns, but Molly's left-wing and pacifist political sympathies were at the time rather different from Ray's. Her friendship with Ray started while she was a member of the Royal Commission on the Civil Service, to which Ray had given evidence – they regularly lunched together. Her career as journalist, novelist, biographer and political activist followed a short-lived early marriage. Molly joined the ILP and UDC and was twice an unsuccessful Labour Parliamentary candidate. She was finally elected for Blackburn in 1929, became parliamentary private secretary to Clement Attlee, the postmaster-general, was appointed delegate to the League of Nations and presented the first series of 'The Week in Westminster' for the BBC. After turning against the Labour Party for its failure to deal with unemployment, she lost her seat in October 1931.

Ray's devotion to Pippa was no longer a source of emotional anguish and her reaction to the behaviour of the Strachey family at Hungerford during Lytton's final weeks perhaps provides an indication that she was ready for different influences. Molly disliked the Stracheys' insistence on intellectual values and their fierce criticism of friends – and made her views plain to Ray. Whereas the Stracheys remained huddled round the fire when they visited Fernhurst, Molly proved as ready to offer manual labour on Ray's building projects (often in companionable silence) as constructive criticism of her writing. Molly had a wide range of other friends and the friendship with Ray never became claustrophobic; she appears to have been the only person close to Ray who never needed looking after.

Ray had long hoped to pursue her interest in the anti-slavery movement in pre-Civil War America. In early 1931, with her biography of Millicent Fawcett completed, she suggested to her American publisher a history of the slave trade, in place of outdated contracts for biographies of John Brown and Stonewall Jackson. Slavery was in the news. The League of Nations had been taking a close interest in allegations of slavery in Liberia – the country founded allegedly as a refuge for freed slaves. Ray threw herself into the subject with enthusiasm, rapidly becoming engrossed. She read widely about West Africa (in London and in the League of Nations Library in Geneva); received advice from André Gide, an experienced traveller in Africa; corresponded with people on the spot in West Africa; and talked to the relatively few people she could find with any knowledge of Liberia – from Lord Robert Cecil, Chairman of the League's Liberia committee, through the secretaries of all the relevant League of Nations departments, to various unappealing individuals with strong views about what should be done to or for Liberia. She planned an extended trip along the Slave Coast the following winter, despite the fearful health risks, and hoped for funding either from her publisher, the League of Nations or the Anti-Slavery Society, who were looking for 'trustworthy agents to send out (anonymously)'.[18]

The detailed proposal Ray sent her publisher is remarkable both for its depth and breadth and for what it reveals of Ray's own views on colonialism. An account of the development, impact and abolition of the slave trade, covering West Africa, the West Indies, the United States and Europe, would, she planned, lead to a consideration of the current position in Liberia (and condemnation of the role of the United States). The book would be history, not propaganda; nevertheless its main theme would be that 'the exploitation of a race is not a benefit even to the exploiter'.[19]

When Ray's finances collapsed in late 1931, the trip to Liberia was abandoned and the book deferred, but Ray kept in close touch with League of Nations developments over Liberia and interested Lady Astor in the question. On her behalf Ray received a member of the Kru tribe, a 'poor little fellow', who wanted to spell out his people's grievances against the ruling Americo-Liberian elite to the League of Nations but had run out of money.[20] Ray lent him £7-10/- [£480] to get to Geneva, with an unexpected outcome:

> after some months a draft came to her for the money she had lent and a letter from the man she had helped, signed also by the Chiefs of all the tribes who were suffering at the hands of the Liberian Negroes. They apparently thought that the being that lent their emissary that fabulous sum of money was an enormously rich and important person, and they asked her to be their Queen and to protect them against the Liberians.[21]

The Liberian Government soon took up this idea that Ray was a person of influence. In bed early one night after an exhausting day, Ray was forced to scramble into some clothes by the arrival on the doorstep of 53 Marsham Street of ' "The Sec of State for Liberia" [...] (appropriately named Mr Grimes) – as black as ink, & I think very wicked, but very clever', who expounded the Liberian Government's case.[22] Ray was entertained but bemused: 'What they think I can do stumps me'.[23] When, some years later, Ray gave evidence on behalf of the LNSWS to a Government Committee considering (and ultimately rejecting) the case for allowing women to join the Diplomatic Service ('a set of complete dead heads, stuck in their prejudices, & entirely unaware of what has been going on recently in the world'), she was able to cite the offer to her of a Liberian Crown as evidence that women were not wholly unacceptable in Liberia.[24]

The slavery book was not alone in making no progress beyond a pile of notes. A projected biography of Nancy Astor, for which Ray assembled material during a long journey to Istanbul with her by then ex-employer in 1935, suffered the same fate. But Ray's final attempt at a novel was more substantial.[25] The typescript which survives is incomplete, with sporadic chapters and odd pages missing, but it appears that a complete draft, revised at least once, did at one point exist. Roughly a quarter of the total has since been lost, but it is nevertheless possible to fill in many of the gaps in the story from what remains. Although it is grossly unfair to judge any author's work on an incomplete draft, it does not seem that the world has lost a masterpiece. Nevertheless the manuscript is of absorbing interest as an indicator of Ray's preoccupations and responses to public events in the 1930s.

The untitled novel is set in or soon after 1933, and mainly concerns the efforts of a strongly left wing periodical in London (perhaps based on St Loe Strachey's *Spectator*) to survive financially. Publication of a newly discovered manuscript by a charismatic Marxist writer who died during the war fifteen years previously offers the prospect of financial rescue but causes controversy, as a religious approach has replaced the author's earlier political stance. The novel explores the human need for worship – of a political ideology such as Marxism, of a philosophical approach such as positivism or materialism, or of a religious creed, as well as hero worship of people both living and dead – and the consequent dangers in each of losing touch with reality. The opposition between determinism – both political and scientific – and free will is a central theme, with the final outcome reaffirming Ray's dislike of determinism and her belief in the values of decency and integrity in public life and of friendship as a basis for private relationships. The book also portrays the functioning of a hospital, the financial struggle facing working men and women, the experience of refugees from Nazism, and a somewhat unconvincing love story (Ray's depiction of the workings of committees is far more realistic). As Ray appears to have kept no diary for the late 1930s, we have no evidence as to whether lack of time, questions over the novel's suitability for publication or the advent of war kept it unpublished. One possibility is that Ray was sorting out her own ideas as much as writing for a wider audience.

Despite Ray's characterisation of her working life as 'futile hurly burly', there were occasional topics she considered worthwhile and on which she knew she had made a major contribution.[26] In the autumn of 1932, with Lady Astor away, Ray, 'horribly bored' with her job and on the trail of a possible alternative, plunged into a time-consuming but useful project, a proposal to set up day nurseries for the young children of the unemployed (under the auspices of the Save the Children Fund).[27] On her return Lady Astor, already interested in the nursery school movement, took up the idea with rapture, but Ray retained some autonomy, becoming Chairman, successful fund-raiser and public spokesman of the Emergency Open-Air Nurseries Committee. The project was small-scale, but where a nursery was established, its contribution to the well-being of local families was clear.

Discussions about the future constitution of India, including the extent to which women should be granted the vote, continued throughout 1933 under the direction of Lady Astor's close friend Lord Lothian, the Under-Secretary of State for India. Ray was summoned to give evidence to the Joint Committee on the Indian Constitution in the House of Lords, in the unfamiliar persona of Government-backed troublemaker:

My role was to threaten them with a suffrage agitation in India if they didn't give a reasonable proportion of votes now. The Govt. want to do it, we know, but are being held back by Indian officials, & we got the tip to be rather violent. So I was, & it was great fun. The Chairman (Lord Lothian) was delighted, & told me afterwards that bombs were what they needed, & that I had thrown them.[28]

(Figure 29) The Astors' town house in St James's Square, where Ray had a small office.

More Indian women were enfranchised as a result, though universal suffrage had to wait for independence.

Despite such occasional bright spots, Ray found her job increasingly unbearable. Her skills in organisation, negotiation and drafting were constantly in demand, and she was expected to write everything – 'letters, memoranda, petitions, reports, resolutions, & summaries without number' – no matter how varied the topics.[29] Coaching Lady Astor in her speeches was 'too difficult. No one in the world could do it', and in bulk it reduced Ray to despair.[30] For all her kindness, Lady Astor was a demanding employer. (In August 1933 Ray nearly resigned on the spot when her holiday arrangements were threatened.) £400 [£26,000] a year for what was expected of Ray was slavery, she felt, and the weakening dollar presaged a pay cut. She wondered whether to leave and rely on journalism, but caution, for once, prevailed. She would however resign at the next election, even if financial ruin followed.

Ray's earnings were proving inadequate to maintain her family and, despite sporadic help from Mary, she had to draw on capital. There was barely any time for journalism and none for weightier books. A little extra money trickled in from radio broadcasts, but these were erratic and often last-minute. After Hilda Matheson's departure, the Talks Department was wary of inviting women to give talks; when Molly Hamilton was made a Governor of the BBC in late 1932, Ray hoped for a change in attitude, but an occasional short series of talks – all she was offered – made little difference to the family's financial plight.

Unexpected income tax bills drained Ray's purse, as did the cost of maintaining their decaying house. When Westminster's electricity supply changed from DC to AC in September 1932, the electricity supplier insisted on major rewiring to make the house safe; the damp in the walls from the 1928 floods had interfered with the resistance and 'the fuses blew every hour or so with loud bangs, frightening Oliver nearly to death'.[31] And then there was the bath. It collapsed through the rotten bathroom floor – with Oliver inside. The sight greatly amused Ray, but days without bath and WC ('at an angle of 45°') were not so funny and 'Oliver's complaints rise to heaven'.[32] They were forced to share the lodger's bathroom but 'it was pathetic to see Oliver creeping upstairs in his bath towel, in dread of lodgers. He made me stay to convoy him safely down, thus preventing me from leaving sharp at a quarter to ten'.[33] The repair costs, not met by the landlord, were no joke either – but Ray did succeed in negotiating a lower rent.

Inevitably, Ray was swept into the Astors' extensive social life. She was forced to attend parties in St James's Square and at Cliveden, and to dress more smartly. She lost weight and to her own surprise rather enjoyed her new elegance. But her dislike of parties persisted: 'Night after night I seem to have to dress up in my grand top, & oil my curls & powder my nose & sally forth to smile engagingly at people I just know & never wish to see again. It's a mug's game'.[34] At one party Ray found herself rubbing backs with the Prince of Wales, but she was unimpressed by such company, and anyhow the Royal Family's intellectual deficiencies made extra work for her: a wide-ranging memorandum about juveniles for the Prince and the King (both 'so stupid') had to be 'extremely short, of the simplicity of an alphabet, & yet fully comprehensive!'[35] She supposed it was 'worth while to try & educate the royal family!' but implied that it was an impossible task.[36]

The process which eventually freed Ray from the Astor treadmill was inadvertently started by her employer. The campaigns which Lady Astor, a fervent teetotaller, led against the drink industry came to a head in February 1934 during the Second Reading debate on the Hotels and Restaurants Bill. Lady Astor opposed the Bill as being an unfairly selective implementation of the recommendations of a Royal Commission, and accused unnamed MPs of being in the pay of the drink industry (justifiably, Ray thought). When Douglas Hacking, a Home Office Minister, brandished a letter from Ray to one of Lady Astor's constituents pledging her employer's support for an earlier version of the Bill, Lady Astor laid the blame on Ray: 'that was written by my private secretary, who did not know any of my views about the Bill. [...] The person who wrote that letter did so without my sanction.'[37]

There was general condemnation of this 'disloyal & shabby attitude', and Ray bemoaned her employer's failure to keep her head and deal with the accusation: 'She knew all the facts, & I had reminded her of them only two days before, just so as to be prepared! [...] she doesn't give enough thought or attention to her political work.'[38] It fell to Ray to rescue the position through a loyal, dignified and devastating letter to *The Times*:

> Everybody knows Lady Astor's opinion on the drink trade, and Mr Hacking's attempt to suggest that she tries to deceive her constituents on the matter is hardly worth answering. The facts, however, are simple.
>
> I, like other members of the general public, was temporarily deceived by the misleading statement which appeared on the face of the first Hotels and Restaurants Bill to the effect that it carried out the recommendations of the Royal Commission. These recommendations have Lady Astor's support, and I accordingly wrote to the hon. secretary of the local branch of the Hotels and Restaurants Association the letter which Mr. Hacking quoted in the House of Commons on Friday. Subsequently this mistake was corrected, and the reasons for Lady Astor's opposition to the Bill

(which are based upon its divergence from the recommendations) were explained to the same correspondent.

It would be interesting to know how the first letter to the local branch of the Hotels and Restaurants Association came into the hands of the Parliamentary Under-Secretary for the Home Office, and why he made use of it without notice, and without reference to the subsequent correspondence between that body and Lady Astor.[39]

The Bill got no further.

Lord Astor apologised to Ray, but his wife, with the 'code of [...] a Southern belle', could not grasp what she had done wrong.[40] Ray's offer to resign was rejected, and keen though she was to leave the impossible job, she concluded that 'it wouldn't be dignified or admirable for me to bounce off & leave her in the lurch just because she leaves me in the lurch!'.[41] But changes were inevitable. From then on, Lady Astor, who until then had 'neither seen nor heard of 4/5ths of her correspondence', would have to sign everything, as her correspondents could now never be sure that she would not repudiate a letter signed by Ray.[42]

Within weeks, Lady Astor noticed how much Ray disliked her work and they negotiated a new arrangement. Ray would go part-time (hoping to spend her mornings writing to make up for the reduction in salary). Having admitted to Lady Astor that 'all her Conservative stuff fairly sticks in my throat', Ray would give up 'all the routine stuff about her engagements, & all the strictly political stuff about her constituency & her general Conservative party speeches [...], & all the boring stuff with journalists & beggars & so on', and concentrate on 'the women's things, the social reform things & the difficult letters'.[43] In practice, cutting her workload proved difficult, but in autumn 1934 a crisis over Barbara – and a new opportunity – ended this phase of Ray's life.

Despite Barbara's success in finally buckling down to work at Oxford, she was still in revolt against Ray's intellectual snobbery. Practical activities and emotional experiences were her priorities. Barbara was prone to resort to drastic action when unhappy and 1932, a Leap Year, gave her an opportunity. On 29 February she sent out four carbon copies of a typed marriage proposal to her ex-boyfriend, another close friend, and two dark horses who attracted her. The obviously humorous proposal 'put forward such claims as that my financial encumbrances were insignificant and that my assets included a real taste for darning'.[44] Three replies were equally light-hearted; the fourth was 'a single sheet from one of the dark horses with one word "Yes" on it', accompanied by an invitation to tea.[45]

Wolf Abiram Halpern was three years older than Barbara, born in Germany but educated in England, dark, good-looking, possessed of 'the most complicated and cryptic mind' Barbara had ever encountered, and in rebellion against the suffocating closeness of his Zionist Jewish background.[46] His father, Georg Halpern, a close associate of the Zionist leader Chaim Weizmann, was an insurance broker; his mother, Emily, was English, a Catholic before converting to Judaism. For Wolf, marrying an English gentile offered an escape route from the intensity of Zionism – but it took Barbara several months even to begin to understand his motivation, and for the artificial engagement to develop into a real one. By then Wolf was on the point of leaving Oxford, despatched by his father to join an insurance company in Trieste to learn the business.

Barbara had said nothing to her parents about this strange relationship and only when she stopped talking about her emotional life and started asking about 'cookery schools & the intelligent planning of small house-keeping' did Ray become suspicious.[47] Even so, Barbara's definite announcement (in October 1932) of an engagement took her aback: 'one is so stormy at 20' and Wolf's 'barrage of shyness & selfconsciousness' made him difficult to know.[48] Reassuringly, Barbara accepted that finances precluded an early wedding.

Barbara planned to spend Christmas at I Tatti so as to be able to fit in a visit to Trieste. Ray was forced, reluctantly, to tell her mother of the engagement and to defend Barbara when Mary, hardly a model of propriety herself, put the worst interpretation on her actions: 'I am absolutely convinced that she is not "carrying on" with him, &

that she has no intention of doing so, so that I see no harm in her visiting him in this way.'[49] 'If I were to make a fuss about propriety,' Ray added, 'it would put the whole thing wrong.'[50] When Barbara began to panic about her approaching final examinations, Ray tried to forestall another emotional outbreak with characteristic praise of self-reliance:

> Try not to worry Wolf or Gram or anyone but yourself & me. One has to swallow one's troubles, especially when they come out of one's own character & mental proclivities, as far as it can be done. [...] one has to keep the responsibility for them in one's own hands. No one else can take that anyhow, & it's only agony all round to try & make them do so. [51]

She added the guiding principle which had held her own challenging marriage together: 'No matter how devoted people may be they just simply can't become one person. And it's death to everything precious to refuse to recognize this.'[52]

When Barbara seized upon the idea of training to become a midwife, Ray was torn between relief that Barbara was prepared to put up with hard work and discipline in the cause of a useful and portable career and the belief that 'she'd be so horribly disillusioned with the unintellectual life that she'd see some of her present folly.'[53] The idea was dropped because Wolf did not want to be married to a nurse, after which Ray's puzzled neutrality towards her prospective son-in-law started to harden into dislike: 'if he is the sort of young man who won't allow his wife to do this or that he's certainly no husband for our little Barbara!'[54]

In letters to Barbara, Ray increasingly expressed her concern about the relationship ('nearly everyone does make mistakes about falling in love'), inferring that Barbara was trying to 'make up to him something he has missed. [...] There must be a lot of take as well as a lot of give if it's really going to work.'[55] She even suggested a pretend marriage (until children arrived) to avoid the fuss of a divorce should the relationship fail.

The Easter vacation gave Barbara a chance to recuperate at Fernhurst, to be coached for her approaching Finals (by Veronica Wedgwood), and to discuss her feelings with her anxious parents. After Barbara had sat talking on each of their beds until 3 a.m., Ray and Oliver were both convinced that 'she doesn't really want to marry him' and that she wanted an escape route from an immediate decision.[56] Oliver suggested a trip round the world (which had been the making of him, he believed) to give her the chance to think things through. Barbara jumped at the idea and became 'a different creature, as if a weight had been lifted off her mind'.[57] The trip would be expensive and demand the realisation of capital but, Ray felt, 'we must run to the cost of it somehow'.[58]

Barbara scraped through her exams with a Third and set off to join Wolf in Trieste for 'a sort of trial marriage' before her long voyage.[59] She had kept her promise to Ray to preserve her virginity until she was twenty-one and had left Oxford, but was now determined to lose it. Ray, who had talked the matter over with her at length, was unenthusiastic but resigned: 'So long as she doesn't marry hastily it's as much as we can expect nowadays!'[60] And she made sure that Barbara was well informed about contraception.

Ray visited the young couple herself en route from I Tatti to a long-planned holiday in Greece with Molly Hamilton. Barbara seemed very happy, she reported, and was now 'quite sure that she wants to marry W.H. (but is not quite so sure of his wanting to marry her)'.[61] Wolf struck Ray more favourably than before, but uncertainty over his future location cast even more doubt on whether or when the marriage would take place. The situation would be reviewed in a year's time when Barbara returned. To Barbara, Ray had argued that she 'couldn't see how one could love without Romance', and now confessed that 'I don't at all understand these modern ways of falling in love, & they don't look to me like the real thing at all'.[62] She went on to Greece and Barbara, via I Tatti, back to London to prepare for her own departure, initially to Copenhagen, with Ray's 'somewhat passionate blessing'.[63] Barbara had decided to travel out to Australia as one of the few passengers (at 10 shillings a day) on a Finnish windjammer, *L'Avenir*, travelling out in water ballast to bring back wheat. The ship would not stop en route and had no radio, so mother and daughter would be out of contact for several eventful months.

Ray and Molly had an idyllic few weeks exploring Greece in a borrowed car, living on simple local food, often camping overnight, drinking in the natural and architectural beauties and revelling in the 'fading out process' ('a middle aged joy') which liberated them from the preoccupations of everyday life.[64] Ray returned thoroughly refreshed and longing to repeat the experience when funds were available.

Her optimism did not last long in the face of public events. The Great Depression had spread and intensified since 1931, unemployment had soared worldwide, international negotiations on economic measures and disarmament had failed, social reform had stalled, Hitler and the Nazi Party were rapidly destroying German democracy, and the possibility of major catastrophe – complete economic breakdown or social revolution – seemed ever-present. Ray was soon convinced that 'the world is collapsing piecemeal' and was 'tottering towards ruin'.[65] 'Security has quite gone, & your generation may have the most startling things to face,' she warned Christopher.[66]

The LNSWS had hit another financial crisis in late 1932, necessitating painful sackings and pay cuts. Ray's personal financial position became more and more precarious, but when Bill Glazier, husband of the housekeeper at the Mud House, lost his building job, she felt unable to stand by:

> I found Glazier out of work, & the three of them trying to live on the dole, which is only 25/3 [£80] a week for them all. I couldn't bear that, so I have arranged for him to do 3 days' work a week for me, at the regular wage of £1. This plan enables him still to draw 12/6 dole, so that they now have 32/6 [£103] a week – which isn't much, but is at least more like their usual standard of living, & enables them to keep up their insurance & pay their rent.[67]

On this occasion a cheque from Mary coincidentally saved the day but the dollar slump was further eroding the Berensons' financial position and by late 1933 there was a strong chance they would have to leave I Tatti. Ray's family could expect no more lavish presents from Mary, who would probably be unable to cover even her personal expenses from her own income.

In November Ray started writing a one-sided sequence of letters to her far distant daughter, even though she expected to hear nothing from her before a cable announcing her arrival in Australia some weeks later. Snippets of domestic news – an unexpectedly pleasant evening with Wolf's sister Ika and her husband Rudolf Olden, Ursula's failure to secure an acting job – accompanied gloomy financial forebodings: 'I doubt if I can send you any more except your minimum passage home.'[68] But the inevitable lack of news from Barbara, coupled with her knowledge of her daughter's character, was starting to worry Ray: 'I do wonder what she is up to!'[69]

On 6 January news from the shipping company that Barbara's ship had reached Australia safely came at a dramatic moment. Ray had been struck down by a violent pain in her left side the night before. Ellie Rendel diagnosed kidney trouble and even though the pain disappeared by the time the specialist arrived, Ray was packed off to hospital for tests, which eventually confirmed a kidney stone (and revealed that she had a double kidney). Recovery from the effects of morphia and the 'thoroughly disagreeable' examination, 'rather a shattering affair', demanded a week off work.[70] It was then, on 10 January, that the long-awaited telegram from Barbara herself arrived:

> Delightful voyage have fallen undoubtedly in love Olav Hultin fellow passenger propose marrying here immediately please approve no conceivable misgivings tons love Barbara.[71]

In the ensuing 'complete ferment', it was clear that Ray had little chance of influencing her headstrong and distant daughter.[72] She dashed off a cable:

> Tons of love how can we approve without knowing the nationality age profession income plans & thousand items besides charm would fly out if possible don't be precipitate marriage rather serious business.[73]

'Practically incoherent', Ray poured her reactions into a letter which would certainly reach Barbara far too late.[74] Why was she in such a 'fantastic hurry'?[75] Why not ('at the ends of the earth') have a trial marriage without 'the tiresome legal complications'?[76] Marrying a foreigner meant losing her nationality and being unable to work or train in England. Ray and Oliver could not afford to go on supporting her. Why not come home on the next boat? And what had Barbara done about Wolf (though Ray did not regret the ending of that relationship)? 'Oh Barbara dear, what are you up to! But all the same give my love to your young man.'[77] Ray's inner battle between disquiet and affectionate hopes for the couple's happiness would continue for months. Her one consolation – if Barbara was 'such a goose' as to rush into an imprudent marriage – was that 'in these days, & especially in Scandinavia – there need be nothing irrevocable about marriage.'[78]

Further information was frustratingly slow to arrive and cabling to Australia expensive. A further cable from Barbara shed some light: 'Olav Finn 23 in business income 700 pounds marriage next Tuesday staying Adelaide 3 weeks proceeding Tahiti etc home.'[79] When the Finnish legation in London helpfully identified Professor Arvid Hultin as Head of the University Library in Helsingfors [Helsinki], Ray cabled him:

> have heard by Australian cable my daughter marrying Olav Hultin both passengers L'Avenir can you give Olav's bona fides Barbara's are Oxford graduate granddaughter Mrs Bernard Berenson niece Lytton Strachey father Civil Service no money apologise telegram marriage reported next [sic] feel anxious.[80]

The reply – in German – was hardly encouraging: 'regret Olav unable to marry no assured position no means.'[81] Oliver cabled to Barbara:

Olav's people say he cannot yet marry no assured position no means sorry you must postpone wedding till after trip will help you then be reasonable darling may financially spoil both futures.[82]

Not expecting to influence Barbara, Ray and Oliver tried to convince themselves (and Mary) that all might be well. Olav appeared 'educated, respectable & well connected', and his family might set him up in business with an allowance.[83] The marriage was starting to seem to Ray the least bad outcome:

> I have now become entirely resigned, & indeed almost hope they are marrying tomorrow. I don't want to go through this same game with another young man at Tahiti, San Francisco or Honolulu! Nor do I want to have to stand by B. through a long engagement to a young man in Helsingfors.[84]

The uncertainty was resolved by a further cable. 'Married yesterday finance perfectly sound parents probably biased anyway returning direct to clear everything up happy Barbara.'[85]

Ray and Oliver inserted a discreet announcement of the marriage in *The Times*. But in Australia detailed accounts of the romance and wedding were widespread; to Ray's horror she received 'two very repulsive newspaper cuttings [...] from Australia, saying that B had taken to smoking cigars & actually quoting some of our telegrams.'[86] Julia received the first news of her sister's marriage through watching a Fox Movietone newsreel in a cinema.

While Ray and Oliver made enquiries about their new son-in-law, and waited for letters from Barbara, other relationships demanded their attention. Ursula's engagement was broken by her solid and apparently reliable fiancé, leaving her 'completely knocked out'.[87] Ray was torn between the requirements of her job, overwhelmingly hectic at the time, and the needs of Ursula, who 'weeps, & weeps, can't eat, has palpitations, & is not only wretched but ill & limp'.[88] The unbearable combination of a heavy workload and coming home to Ursula's misery would, Ray complained, 'drive me distracted in no time.'[89] It was a relief when she succeeded in making arrangements for Ursula to recuperate at La Souco again, but even so, after the stress of these weeks (culminating in her repudiation by Lady Astor in the House of Commons), Ray's recently-enlarged skirt became three inches looser.

Then Julia left her 'hysterical and unbalanced' husband, to no-one's surprise or blame.[90] Tommy's behaviour had become increasingly erratic and he made 'such fearful scenes that she can't stand it'.[91] In his grief Tommy turned to Oliver, which was 'hard on Oliver [...] for he's not much given to tears & emotional expressions'.[92] As Ray reflected, 'this house has been the rendezvous of the heartbroken lately, & Oliver's shoulders, & mine, are quite damp with other people's tears'.[93]

Information on Olav trickled in. The Finnish Minister reported that (to Ray's delight) Olav's aunt was an MP and that the family were cultivated and travelled, 'GOOD, SOLID & RELIABLE'.[94] Photos from Olav's parents showed their son looking, Ray thought, 'intelligent & full of mischief, & very very young – not at all a stolid Viking as we had expected'.[95] The accompanying letter (in German), though 'very polite & friendly', was not altogether reassuring.[96] Olav had broken off his studies because of illness but was now recovered; his parents could not imagine how he could support a wife without a job in prospect; fond of the sea and practical with his hands, his idea had been to become a purser on an Atlantic liner. Ray and Oliver were mystified and could 'only suppose that he has had an offer of a job his parents don't know of, or that he is a first class liar'.[97]

Letters from Barbara started to reach other people – Christopher, Nicky Mariano, and Barbara's friend Kathleen (reportedly 122 pages long) – but nothing came to her anxious parents. The ones Ray saw left her uneasy. Olav was, according to Barbara, even crazier than her, melodramatic, romantic and passionate, determined to have his own way, colourfully dressed in clothes he had made himself, multi-talented, and a complete contrast to Wolf – which accounted for much of his attraction. He too had been engaged to someone else before the voyage. He loved shocking people and appeared to have an uncanny ability to read her thoughts, despite their lack of a common language: his command of English was poor and she had no Swedish (his native language). Barbara's 'penny novelette pen' dwelt at length on her emotional state but ignored practicalities like immediate plans and long-term prospects.[98] There was, Ray decided, 'something about these letters that I really don't like, though it's hard to say just what, unless it's frivolity melodrama & heedlessness'.[99]

When in late March a much-delayed long letter from Barbara to Ray eventually arrived, accompanied by Barbara's diary up to her engagement on 29 November, Ray felt no happier. The diary contained nothing but 'sentiment, melodrama & sex'.[100] The letter described Olav's 'big blue eyes, very strange & hypnotic looking – crazy – with a sort of white curtain behind' and gave an equally alarming account of his insulting the Captain while drunk, and being hated by the crew.[101] Barbara claimed Olav's job in a family firm provided a sound financial basis for married life but then described Olav's plans to give it up to join a fashion firm in Paris or Vienna, a 'wild scheme' in Ray's view.[102] The couple appeared to be following Barbara's initial plan of visiting Ray's second cousin Charlie Nordhoff (co-author of *Mutiny on the Bounty*) in Tahiti, then returning via the United States, but even that was not clear.

Confirmation of their route home arrived mid-April in a letter from Barbara with momentous news – she was pregnant. Oliver was delighted, Ray more struck by the magnitude of the change in Barbara's life, 'almost more far reaching in one's personal life than having a husband'.[103] Unable to imagine herself as a grandmother, she was clear about the impact on Barbara; 'the poor dear will have to grow up with a vengeance', she forecast.[104] Olav's financial standing became even more crucial, as Ray and Oliver could certainly not support an entire family.

Barbara's next letter in mid-May struck a different note: Tahiti had been horrible, she was homesick and never wanted to live anywhere but England. Perhaps the result of pregnancy, Ray surmised, but the couple's plans and finances remained incomprehensible. A few days later a transatlantic telephone call from Barbara in San Francisco to Ray at Fernhurst brought disquieting news. Olav (now dubbed Toby by Barbara) was in hospital with suspected measles and Barbara had run out of money (and was on the verge of starvation) – could Ray send some? Barbara never forgot Ray's instantaneous and, 'as usual, absolutely admirable' response.[105] 'I had no time to explain anything except to say that Toby was ill. "How much?" and "Where shall I send it?" were all she needed to say.'[106]

Olav's suspected measles miraculously disappeared once the money arrived. They flew to New York (at great expense) and stayed in the Waldorf Astoria Hotel until money ran out again and a further loan was provided by a cousin in Philadelphia, sufficient to pay their bills and the sea passage back to England. By the time Barbara and Olav reached London on 7 June, her parents' investigations had yielded worrying results. Olav was reported to be 'wild and uncontrollable', a drunkard and a psychotic, who had spent time in a mental hospital and whose previous trip on a windjammer had been arranged to keep him out of trouble.[107] Barbara was clearly ignorant of her husband's true nature and revealing what Ray and Oliver knew and suspected would be traumatic for her. Remembering her own miscarriage after a shock twenty years earlier, Ray was determined to spare Barbara the same fate. Nothing would be said to her until after the baby was born.

This decision left Ray playing a most uncomfortable role for the next six months. As Barbara and Olav moved into Rookhanger (the cottage Ray and Christopher had built in the grounds of the Mud House), acquired a puppy, quarrelled and made up, and made fantastic and expensive plans for the future, Ray tried to fathom the reality behind the outward friendliness and self-confidence of her son-in-law. She and Oliver remained sceptical about his finances but hoped that the young couple's trip to Finland in July would clarify matters. It did not. Barbara was never given the chance to meet his father (who was ill), nor to have any private conversation with his family nor the lawyer who was meant to be transferring Olav's money to England; she returned none the wiser.

Over the next few weeks Olav ran up large debts in the village and within the family, produced endless stories (some plausible) to explain his shortage of cash, and succumbed to convenient illnesses which prevented him visiting the bank whenever it was open. The illnesses disappeared when the bank was closed. With no cash left even for a bus fare, Olav walked the three miles into Haslemere and negotiated for the purchase of a Bentley. Meanwhile Ray's American relative wrote asking for urgent repayment of the substantial sum he had lent Olav and Barbara.

By the end of September it was clear that all Olav's financial claims were fantasy. The Hultin family, once wealthy, had little money left and Olav virtually none. When Karin diagnosed him as a 'violent hysteric' who probably did not 'distinguish truth from lies', Ray agreed: 'No mere villain would face it out so near to the crack of doom.'[108] She stopped his credit at Fernhurst and put Mrs Glazier in charge of the money for food. The next step would be raising the funds to pay off Olav's debts, provide for Barbara's confinement and finance the divorce Barbara would clearly need. If the bank would not help, she would turn to Lady Astor.

Money was not the only problem. Already 'restless & impatient & arbitrary' (in Christopher's view), Olav behaved worse as exposure threatened.[109] His treatment of Barbara had been high-handed from the start. In Tahiti he had threatened her with a knife. Now he insisted that even in late pregnancy she wait on him hand and foot during his alleged illness, and was 'so frightfully exacting & cross that she [couldn't] cope with it'.[110] 'He is a beast,' Ray concluded, 'over & above being a scoundrel & lunatic!'[111] But at least Barbara's growing disenchantment would cushion her eventual shock. 'Poor Barbara's disillusionment & sorrow' would, Ray recognised, be the 'worst feature of the affair'.[112] But there was little they could do about that, except stand by her.

Ray moved the couple into the Mud House and took to ringing every evening to ask if Barbara wanted her to come down: the brief answer 'Yes' or 'No' would give nothing away to Olav. This might be a comfort to Barbara, though hardly to Ray, 'obsessed & knocked flat inwardly' by worry.[114] As she got to grips with the practicalities, Ray was acutely 'aware of the fact that at present, as far as B is concerned, I am the only solid rock on the horizon. So I have got to solidify!'[115]

Ray found the £600 [£39,000] she needed. She sold an acre of the Fernhurst land for £200; Lady Astor gave her £50 towards Barbara's confinement; and the bank agreed to increase her overdraft. When Olav announced that he wanted a holiday in Hamburg before the birth, Ray assumed that if he left he would not return and wondered whether to fund his departure:

> though it would be a great comfort to be rid of him, it seems hardly right to do this without B's knowledge. It is after all her decision, whether to stick to him or not, & she would have some right to be aggrieved if I helped him to vamoose now.[115]

In the end she decided against conniving at Olav's disappearance; Barbara had the right to make her own decision.

By early October, when Barbara did ask her mother to come to Fernhurst, Ray had obtained leave of absence from Lady Astor ('I don't think it's humanly possible to do such an exacting job all through such a fierce domestic crisis') and identified a substitute to cover her work, retaining her half-time salary on a consultation basis.[116] At the Mud House they formed an uncomfortable trio. Olav busied himself with practical tasks – making a Swedish cradle, putting windows in the garage doors which bore witness to the originally intended purpose of the Mud House, putting Christopher's old printing press back into working order; Barbara, whose baby was due at the beginning of November, knitted baby clothes; Ray tried to concentrate on the much delayed book she was writing on careers for women, and escaped for bouts of therapeutic bricklaying whenever possible.

Ironically, during the weeks Ray spent 'standing guard' over Barbara, it was Ray herself who put her daughter at serious risk of death or injury.[117] That summer she and Molly Hamilton had built a brick fireplace in the sitting room, but not tied it into the wall. As Barbara held on to it to pull herself up, it collapsed, and she only just escaped in time. Ray was chastened that her slipshod building methods had nearly caused a tragedy.

During the last week of October Barbara started to get pains. A nurse was installed in the Mud House, but as she advised that the baby would not arrive before 2 November, Ray felt free to spend a night in London tying up loose ends and going to the dentist. It was a relief to be away from the strained situation at Fernhurst: Barbara was increasingly uncomfortable, Olav increasingly bad tempered, and Ray increasingly unable to disguise her dislike of him (only partially relieved when she painted an 'unspeakably unkind' portrait of him).[118] By the time Ray returned on 30 October, Barbara had just given birth to a son. Ray found herself 'instantly & overwhelmingly pleased by being a grandmother'.[119]

Roger Sven Allen Hultin had arrived without undue difficulty, but post-natal complications set in and on 10 November Barbara was taken into Haslemere Hospital for the removal of a clot. Without antibiotics, her condition was serious, even life-threatening – on one visit Olav told her the doctors estimated her chance of survival as one in three. She needed 24-hour nursing care so Ray had to accommodate two nurses at the Mud House and ferry them back and forth for their shifts, as well as visiting Barbara and, with Mrs Glazier's help, caring for the baby. The worst problem was enduring Olav ('it would give me the greatest satisfaction to be able to drown him in the Pond') but the pain she was about to inflict on Barbara made the approaching crisis a 'fresh horror'.[120] Her building site was the only place she could escape her 'loathly incubus' – and it kept raining.[121]

Barbara came home from hospital on 21 November but had to stay in bed for several weeks, with cystitis and kidney problems proving slow to clear. It was time to tackle Olav. Matters came to a head after lunch on 28 November. To Ray's profound gratitude, Oliver took on the task of dealing with Olav while she talked to Barbara. The Glaziers had loathed Olav ever since he had sworn violently at Mrs Glazier, and had had to be let into the secret to avert premature violence. So beefy Bill Glazier, a formidable left-arm bowler, was stationed nearby, pruning bushes, in case of violence from Olav (whose knife had already been removed and hidden). The precautions proved unnecessary. Olav admitted all the charges at once, and, to Oliver's acute embarrassment, wept and fell on his knees saying "Oh, poor Oliver, I am so sorry".[122]

Barbara, who had been in denial about her own suspicions, took the news calmly, but Olav's plausibility remained dangerous. She agreed to the idea of a divorce so that she could regain her nationality and look for work – but did not rule out the possibility of remarriage should Olav find a job in Finland. Oliver escorted Olav to London and the following day saw him onto a cargo boat bound for Finland, his passage arranged by the Finnish Minister. For Ray it was a relief to end the 'long course of deceit'.[123] The previous six months had been 'a complete nightmare' and she hoped never to have to live through such horrors again.[124]

The whole episode represented a battle between Ray's cherished belief in personal freedom and her fear for her daughter's well-being. Olav's mental instability posed a threat to Barbara's physical safety as well as to the family's finances. Barbara had not behaved like a mature adult, and rescuing her from her own folly meant that she had to be treated like a child. When Ray and Oliver effectively frogmarched their son-in-law out of the country, and then pulled strings to ensure he would be refused re-entry, they demonstrated the victory of parental concern over abstract principles.

CHAPTER FIFTEEN

Keeping Calm and Carrying On: 1935–1940

Women's labour is the greatest of the nation's reserves.[1]

The book that Ray wrote on a dressing-table in a tiny bedroom at Mud while guarding her heavily pregnant daughter was, she claimed, 'a utility book' with 'no effort of imagination required'.[2] While true of the factual sections dealing with specific careers, this downplays the general chapters, where sound common sense underlies both Ray's passionately held and robustly expressed personal opinions about how women should approach career choice and her forthright political statements about the injustices suffered by working women – now perhaps self-evident but at the time far from uncontroversial. *Careers and Openings for Women* sets out a personal agenda far more clearly than Ray's rather duller chapter on women's employment in the book of essays on the impact of female suffrage which she edited a year later.[3]

This was no dry impersonal account. Ray's family and friends can be seen in the exemplars: Pippa as the self-sacrificing unmarried daughter tied down to the care of an elderly parent; Barbara as the young woman led astray by romantic novels to dream of marriage instead of a career; Julia, going about her work 'half-heartedly', her 'earnest attention [...] given instead to lipstick and the fashions, and the efficacy of a permanent wave'; Oliver's sister-in-law Margaret as one of 'those women who attempt to devote their whole selves to motherhood' and who are 'liable to make a failure of the task because of their very narrowness of occupation'.[4] Ray's own experience informed the portrayal of the married woman with children trying, with little help, to manage a home as well as a career, and perhaps even the disillusioned wife's discovery of 'the hard and wearing struggle against poverty, dirt, illness and disappointment' where she expected a domestic idyll.[5]

Ray's years of involvement in the LNSWS – and her own work analysing census returns – had given her a detailed understanding of women's employment at all levels, the good and the bad. Her book balanced realism, encouragement and empathy: empathy with the older woman loyally working in a junior position for years who is replaced by someone younger in a reorganization; with the poorly-paid industrial worker; and with the youngster, abandoning education too soon, who works hard as an office girl during the day, then studies shorthand and typing in the evenings, 'with the result that she gets tired and anaemic, [...] and loses the brightness and energy with which she left school'.[6]

Ray's harshest criticisms were reserved for those young women who refused to take employment seriously:

> If they have not, and do not wish to have any interest in their work, and do not intend to spend many years at it, and if they consider it as of no importance in their lives, they need not trouble about selection or training. They can take the first thing which comes to hand, and it will not matter if it is as unsuitable to them as they to it. They will increase the great army of unintelligent workers, and reinforce the popular belief that women are only suitable for, and actually prefer to do, dull work at low wages. They may find themselves, in later life, filled with regrets and grievances. But it will be their own fault, and no one can help those who have no sense.[7]

As Ray later admitted, the pre-war women's movement had unduly glamorised the idea of pursuing a career, attaching 'a value to earning their own livings which that somewhat dreary necessity does not in reality possess'.[8] For all Ray's optimism about what women could and should aim at in their careers, she was brutally realistic about the problems they faced, especially if they attempted to combine a career with marriage: 'there is no advantage in ignoring facts, and no kindness in misstating them'.[9] That married women could be Secretaries of State but not civil servants was only one of many unjust anomalies afflicting married women. While recognising that many women would not marry or remain married – an argument for a careful choice of career – Ray never suggested that a choice should be made between a satisfying professional life and bringing up a family. The effort involved in having two careers at once, the domestic one unpaid, was undoubtedly considerable, but had great compensations.

The book's constant encouragement to girls and parents to take the long-term view on education and career choice reveals how much having an occupation outside the home meant to Ray. In addition to friends, companionship and self-respect,

> the woman who finds work which it interests her to do has a source of happiness of great value, [...] which has the refreshing quality of being impersonal. Women's lives, as a whole, are very closely tied up with the details of human relationships and the adjustments of human beings to each other; and outside interests, which follow from any absorbing work, have therefore a special importance for them as providing mental change and refreshment.[10]

By the end of 1934, tired of dealing with human relationships, Ray needed just such a break from the incessant strains of family life.

The tantalising prospect of a more appealing, and better paid, job hovered just out of reach for most of Ray's time with Lady Astor. The Central Employment Bureau for Women had fostered women's employment for many years before the LSWS became involved during the war. By

1932 those running the Bureau had become elderly, autocratic and increasingly inefficient, with a distressing tendency to regard their own typing courses as an essential prerequisite for women seeking work. Ray had contacts on the Bureau's Council and heard the rumblings of discontent at an early stage. If the old guard could be ousted, there might be a role for her in revitalising this moribund organisation in the area of work which most interested her. 'If I'd been asked to select out of all the world a bit of work of importance I was fitted to carry through I couldn't have found anything better', she enthused, her head 'fairly bursting with schemes for setting the place to rights'.[11] But the rebels underestimated the tenacity of their opponents and in exasperation resigned en masse, frustrating Ray's hopes.[12]

Undeterred, the reformers embarked on creating a new organisation, 'The Women's Employment Federation (National Federation of Organisations concerned with the Training and Employment of Educated Women)', a cumbersome title inevitably abbreviated to WEF. The nucleus of the new body set up in October 1933 was the advisory work on women's employment still being undertaken by the LNSWS (whose role as employment agency had long since ceased for financial reasons). The LNSWS offered WEF accommodation in their premises in Marsham Street, and Pippa became its first Honorary Secretary.

Ray was in the thick of the planning throughout, on an unpaid basis, and the aims and activities of WEF bear her stamp. Within its broad intention 'to assist women and girls of secondary education in their efforts to prepare for and to obtain work', WEF's main purposes were to maintain a clearing-house for information about training and careers; and to encourage co-ordination between (non-commercial) organisations concerned with women's employment.[13] After a year of preparatory work, WEF became fully operational in January 1935. With the financial consequences of Barbara's marriage on her mind, Ray applied for a newly created (part-time) position and was duly appointed joint Organising Secretary of WEF; in August, on the resignation of her co-Secretary, she took on the entire post at a salary of £500 [£32,000] a year.

The Federation prided itself on the wide range of careers it covered: 'from fashion designing to veterinary surgery, police work to salesmanship, advertising to occupational therapy'.[14] It was never an exclusively middle class organisation: intelligence and ambition were not middle class preserves. WEF never refused anyone wanting advice and, in Ray's time, many working class parents, ambitious for their daughters, consulted it (and were considerably easier to deal with than impoverished middle class families not entirely reconciled to the idea of daughters going out to work). Even when WEF introduced fees for services, up to a third of its work was undertaken on a charitable basis.

The Organising Secretary reported to an Executive Committee comprised of representatives of the main subscriber organisations; it was a high-powered group (efficient, serious and democratic according to one member of staff).[15] Supportive though the Committee usually was, Ray did not inevitably get her own way and not all of her bolder plans were approved. Ray's experience, energy and contacts were what fitted her for the role, but her first major task was the part of the job she loathed: fund-raising. The new Federation planned to become self-supporting from subscriptions and fees for services provided, but in its early days had little money and needed donations. By October 1935, it looked very likely that WEF and Ray's job would both disappear by Christmas for lack of funds.

In desperation she turned to a philanthropic organisation which years earlier had helped the LSWS – the Carnegie United Kingdom Trust. The Trust's long-term Secretary, Colonel J. M. Mitchell, had once been prominent in the Men's League for Women's Suffrage, so had sympathies with the women's movement; two of the Trustees, Janet Courtney and Elizabeth Haldane, were also well-known to Ray. The problem was that the Trust was already funding the Central Bureau. Ray's task was to persuade the Trust that the new Federation was a better prospect than the Central Bureau, and that it would soon be the only body in the field.

The technique Ray adopted was characteristic of her professional style, combining a detailed mastery and presentation of facts and figures with an informal approach designed to establish a personal bond with professional contacts. Ray's energy, clear idea of what should be achieved and how to go about it, and personal approachability were effective weapons. She sought advice from likely donors before moving into outright fund-raising, and a personal meeting gave her a chance to charm and convince a potential helper: Colonel Mitchell came away very greatly impressed, as later did his successor James Wilkie. By the time Ray submitted an appeal to the Carnegie Trustees for £2000 [£125,000] in 1936, £1000 in 1937 and £500 in 1938, the Trust's Secretary was ready to argue her case to a not totally sympathetic Board of Trustees.

The decision of the Carnegie Trustees in December 1935 to offer WEF half what Ray had asked for in each year allowed WEF to continue, and even to take on more staff and more space, but it meant that for the next few years much of Ray's attention and energy had to be diverted from the Federation's key work into supplementary fund-raising. Dinners and bazaars took up staff time; charitable donations were elusive and erratic. WEF lived from hand to mouth and more than once Ray feared that she would not be able to pay the staff's salaries. Something always did turn up, but WEF's Micawber-like existence was hard on its Organising Secretary's nerves.

With her children almost off her hands, Ray was able to indulge her self-confessed 'insatiable tendency to overwork'.[16] She was the dynamo powering WEF, as likely to stand over a printer 'like a dragon' to obtain a high-quality pamphlet as to race round the country making speeches at schools, universities, business functions and conferences.[17] Interviewing employees and employers was largely the preserve of her expert staff, but Ray did enough to keep in practice, retaining as her own specialism potential entrants to the Civil Service. She was, Molly Hamilton remembered, 'without exception, the best interviewer I have known'.[18] Even though Ray complained of over-work, running her own organisation was energising, and during a rare lull she champed on the bit, leaving her staff 'in terror lest I shall start some new hares. And of course I shall soon'.[19]

Staff management had its amusements, but Ray felt uncomfortable imposing discipline. Her style was to choose staff well, delegate without intervening, back staff who were active (always preferable to caution in her eyes), share with them the credit for her successes, take the blame on herself when things went wrong, and by her own *joie de vivre* bring such fun and sense of shared commitment to the whole enterprise that the low salaries all had to endure seemed less irksome. As Irene Hilton, who worked for WEF and was one of Ray's successors as Organising Secretary recalled, she 'warmed you by her presence' and her staff rewarded her with their total loyalty.[20]

However chaotic Ray's home life may have sometimes seemed, in the office she was in perfect control. Her paperwork was well organised, her decisions rapid and her efforts unrelenting. She poured out letters: to prospective helpers of all kinds (identified by her 'uncanny sense' amounting almost to second sight in her judgement of people); to those who had helped in any way (often personal letters of warm and exuberant gratitude); to Government departments, employers, schools, universities and more.[21] Once decided on an organisational objective, she 'went hell for leather for it', sticking her neck out and taking calculated risks (invariably after taking advice from Pippa, who was more cautious in temperament).[22] Her battering ram approach was not universally popular.

In dealing with individuals, Ray's approach was very different. Always courteous, friendly and open, if sometimes unpredictable (somewhat American in approach, according to Irene Hilton), Ray masked her essential ruthlessness on behalf of WEF by disarming manipulative charm. Inventively unscrupulous in furthering WEF's ends, Ray would, for instance, suggest to a father reluctant to prolong a daughter's education that her future enhanced earnings might help to fund a younger son. Men in positions of power and influence 'often failed to realize the hand of steel within the velvet glove; the unyielding purpose behind the easy jollity of manner'.[23]

Few people were aware that the impressive public façade hid a very different private person. Irene Hilton saw an underlying shyness and recognised that Ray, essentially honest, regarded with contempt her own ability to switch her charm on and off. Buttering people up revolted her, but the end justified the means. Even though one of the first characterisations of Ray that Irene had heard was as 'someone who takes up lost causes and then they cease to be lost', she came to understand the effort it took Ray to be outgoing and fight in the cause of WEF.[24] Always more interested in causes than people, Ray was not motivated by personal glory (gratifying though it was), power or even money (though being free from constant money worries would have been welcome). Her devotion to WEF was totally selfless.

Under Ray's direction, WEF grew and prospered. It became generally regarded as an efficient and valuable body, much better organised than many Government committees. Organisations kept joining, schools and universities requested speakers, careers mistresses flocked to vacation courses, girls and women came to seek advice. Ray, 'full of schemes & plots of all sorts', was constantly looking for ways to increase WEF's usefulness (and income).[25] Expansion initially increased the financial pressure but eventually, as subscriptions increased and WEF found itself able to charge for some of its services, the position improved. The self-sufficiency which Ray had confidently promised the Carnegie Trustees would follow the three years of support from them looked increasingly achievable.

Virginia Woolf's first openly feminist work, *A Room of One's Own*, had in the name of the fictional Fernham College, fused two of Ray's main passions, Fernhurst and Newnham. Now Virginia, a good friend of Pippa Strachey and a loyal supporter of the LSNWS, paid her own tribute to Ray's work for the Women's Employment Federation: in *Three Guineas* Woolf donated her second guinea to a 'society to help the daughters of educated men to obtain employment in the professions'.[26] Ray reciprocated with overwhelming enthusiasm to the publication of *Three Guineas*: 'your book has given me so much joy that I don't quite know how to express it. It's simply perfect, & if the imbeciles in high places are not now pulverized it will only be because they are so densely stupid'.[27] She had instructed Lady Astor to send a copy 'to all the male devils she knows. As there are some

thousands of them your sales should leap up if she obeys me! I'd like
to see Winston's face while he reads it.'[28]

As with many of her generation, Ray's political views shifted to the
left during the 1930s. 'I've practically become a communist during the
last month. Working in a millionaire's household has that effect', she
admitted in November 1932, and a year later:

> In my inside thoughts I grow more Communist daily: but I can't see
> how to bring it about without the horrors of revolution, & I can't get
> round to approving of that. Meantime I go on moving among the
> ostrich circles of the Conservative party, who really seem to think
> that the present National Government can pull us through – tho'
> Europe gets worse & worse every moment.[29]

'There seems to be nothing to do but keep calm & carry on as best one
can', she concluded, 'so that's what I'm doing'.[30] Nevertheless her public
statements on politics remained centrist. Although journalism can
require the author to subordinate personal beliefs to the requirements
of the newspaper concerned, an article in a series on 'Misgivings about
Socialism' commissioned by a left-wing Sunday paper in 1936 rings
true as a summary of Ray's longstanding political stance:

> most serious people in this country today are prepared to accept the
> view that it is desirable for every human being to have a reasonable
> chance of self development. They want every child and every adult
> to have as much food and shelter and air and space and warmth
> and protection as will secure full health, and they want to add as
> much education and leisure and opportunity as will allow the
> development of individual gifts, in so far as these can be developed
> without impinging on other people. [...] On the whole, I do not
> think that there are many genuine misgivings on this first point; and
> I certainly have none myself. [...]
>   I am not sure that human beings are capable of carrying on
> sustained and disinterested action for the common good. I am not

sure that the motive of self-interest can be successfully subordinated to the interests of the community, or that greed and jealousy can be adequately kept down.

Even if I am wrong about this (as I sincerely hope I am) I still doubt whether state controlled undertakings will be more efficient and more productive than private ones. I fear that inter-departmental struggles may be as damaging to the ordinary consumer as the clash of private profit making, and I fear that state monopolies may fall into slackness and sloth. And over and above this, I doubt whether the planning of Governments is likely to turn out any better for humanity than the unplanned confusions of the past. I am afraid that large-scale mistakes may be planned, which may become hideously difficult to remedy, and in fact my misgivings cover the whole human field.

I admit that the world we live in is bad in a thousand ways, and that the Socialist ideal is magnificent. But I doubt whether human beings are wise enough, steady enough or good enough to create, manage and live in a Socialist state.[31]

Ray's motive in writing for a Socialist paper went some way to proving her point: the irresistible lure of a six guinea fee [£393].

By 1938, Ray was starting to hanker for a rest. Being tied to office hours and subject to formal responsibilities had always been 'black & boring', and she had never enjoyed the constant socialising her job entailed.[32] Now her work remained heavy, but with few new challenges to excite her. (The possibility of succeeding her sister-in-law Pernel as Principal of Newnham College had once attracted her but that post would not fall vacant until 1941.) She longed to 'give up all work & retire into country life & grow vegetables' so as to escape her workaholic tendencies.[33] However the lull between challenges was short-lived.

The Munich crisis of September 1938 dramatically increased the work and reduced the income of WEF. The classification and registration of floods of volunteers for war work was a temporary problem. Far more serious was the sharp reduction in WEF's income from donations, subscriptions and fees, because of continuing fears about the international situation. 'No one feels disposed to help anything but present misery, & tho' our work exists to prevent future misery no one is in the frame of mind to think of that', Ray lamented.[34] She turned again to WEF's guardian angels, the Carnegie Trustees.

The overlap between WEF and the Central Bureau was a continuing source of concern to the Carnegie Trust. In her Report to the Trustees for 1937, Ray admitted that the future funding of WEF was not yet secure; 'gravely concerned at the costs of their overhead expenses', the WEF Executive Committee 'would greatly welcome the advice of the Carnegie Trustees as to the possibilities of sharing these costs with any other organization working with the same material in the same field'.[35] The code was clear. WEF wanted the Carnegie Trustees to put pressure on the Central Bureau to cooperate or amalgamate with WEF. The timing was propitious, as one of the main stumbling blocks, the Secretary of the Central Bureau, had just died. But her husband remained as Treasurer, and the Bureau's formidable President was his staunch defender. As Ray doubtless expected, the Central Bureau ignored or rebuffed subsequent approaches by the Carnegie Trust proposing amalgamation. All parties involved must have recognised that amalgamation was a polite fiction – what was being discussed was a WEF takeover – but by appearing cooperative, Ray and WEF claimed the moral high ground.

As the three years of Carnegie funding ran out in 1938, Ray appealed to the Trustees for four years' further funding to allow the work of WEF to continue on its existing scale and to develop further. Fortunately for Ray, the Trustees' patience with the Central Bureau's financial mismanagement and evasiveness was running out. The Trustees voted narrowly to grant WEF the £2000 [£114,000] for 1939 which Ray had sought, consideration of the later years being deferred until 1939 to await developments over the Central Bureau.

The decision left Ray 'dizzy with relief and joy'; it was entirely her achievement and her Executive Committee gave her a round of applause.[36] WEF swept back into full action, even working in shifts to make best use of space and volunteers. Government preparations for possible war continued, with WEF increasingly receiving official recognition. Ray, infuriated by delays caused by Governmental red tape, was busier than ever ('I do nothing at all but rush from bed to office, & from office to bed'), but for once everything was going well.[37]

In September 1938 WEF made its Joint Placing Register available for Government use, and in early 1939 was authorised to draw up an Emergency Register of women with specialist experience. There were, Ray estimated, 35,000 women of high qualifications and skill eligible for inclusion (from potential ambulance drivers and hospital caterers to linguists and camouflage artists), and each would need a 20 minute interview. WEF needed more space. Ray had long cast covetous eyes at the Central Bureau's offices in Russell Square, but in default took on an 'an old tumbledown shop exactly opposite in Marsham St – so filthy dirty & dilapidated that everyone thought I was crazy'.[38] Her old suffrage friends and their skills at transforming accommodation on a low budget came to the rescue.

The volunteer ex-headmistresses drawing up the Register were less satisfactory; admirable at interviewing, they were lost without their secretaries to deal with the paperwork. 'Careless, inaccurate, offhand, & really stupid at times', they made such a muddle of record-keeping that Ray and three friends were forced to undertake 'a midnight session' to put the records in order while they were not in use.[39] Ray only undertook a few of the interviews herself, but she reviewed the record cards each night and was struck by the difference from 1914: 'Then we saw the same streams of people, none of whom had any experience or special knowledge. The 25 years have actually changed women's lives; if anyone still doubts the results of the vote they must be blind!'[40]

In April Ray snatched a quick break in Nice, where the Bussy family now lived. Flu laid her low while the international situation became more threatening. On her return it felt odd 'to be slaving away for a purpose which everyone concerned profoundly hopes will never be needed!', but it was increasingly likely that the Emergency Register would be put to use.[41] Other contingency plans were necessary too:

where should WEF go if Marsham Street were bombed? For Ray and WEF, it was a summer of hoping for the best and preparing for the worst. 'No one quite expects catastrophe, yet everyone has to take its possibility into account.'[42]

During her years at WEF, Ray kept her public and private lives resolutely separate. Friends such as Pippa and Molly were involved in the running of WEF, but Ray never socialised with her staff outside the office. In consequence, her WEF colleagues found it easy to underestimate the strength of Ray's family ties. WEF was more Ray's baby than Barbara and Christopher had ever been, Irene Hilton believed.[43] She was wrong. However great Ray's professional responsibilities, they never came before her devotion to her family.

Ray started work at WEF only weeks after enforcing the separation of her daughter and son-in-law, and the consequences of Barbara's marriage ran in parallel to Ray's professional activities. Although Barbara recognised that her parents had her best interests at heart, she continued to care for her departed husband, whatever his faults, and was not entirely convinced of the rightness of her parents' action. For her part, Ray believed that Barbara's reluctance to write off her marriage was a defence against accepting that it 'was all the hideous mistake we believe it to have been'.[44]

In the immediate aftermath of the revelation, Barbara was in a 'very unhappy, guilty, humiliated, and above all confused state'.[45] Her attempt at independence and breaking away from her parents' values had been disastrous and she had hurt many other people. Once again her mother had been proved right: it was unbearable. In 53 Marsham Street – now bursting at the seams – she had little privacy from her parents, a particular problem when Wolf Halpern, now working in London, re-entered her life. 'B has had Wolf here all day, I don't know how she can!' Ray reported disapprovingly, her libertarian principles reasserting themselves with difficulty as she added 'But it's her affair'.[46]

Barbara became desperate to get away, first staying with friends, then taking a temporary job at a prep school. Ray was horrified to receive a long letter from her backing away from the idea of a divorce until attempts – perhaps taking years – had been made to cure Olav's mental problems. Barbara argued that, as her parents' well-meaning actions had been taken without her knowledge, 'the thing was a fait accompli & I did not then & have not now agreed in my heart that our marriage is at an end'.[47] Ray's reply appears not to have survived, but apparently dwelt on the financial impossibility of bringing Olav to England for treatment. It proved persuasive. 'Without your letter I don't think I should have been forced to analyse the horror sufficiently to find a way out', Barbara admitted, accepting that 'it is wrong for me to feel responsible for him' and agreeing that the marriage was finally over.[48]

Ray's optimism about the ease with which a divorce could be obtained in Scandinavia proved ill-founded. Under Finnish law, she was advised, divorce had to be on grounds valid in the country of a non-Finnish partner. As adultery was an essential ground for divorce in England, Olav's adultery, either real or fabricated, would have to be one of the grounds. Olav refused to provide manufactured evidence (adultery was a punishable offence in Finland) and there seemed to be a risk that he would again be certified as insane and confined, in which case Barbara could never be divorced. Fortunately it emerged that Barbara could work in Britain even with Finnish nationality. This meant that any delays over the divorce would not matter so much – and would have the advantage of preventing Barbara from rushing into another hasty marriage.

Mary, bored and in fluctuating health, was eager to see her great-grandson. A visit to I Tatti would give Barbara a breathing-space while she considered her future and relieve the dual pressures of space and money at home. Berenson, supported by Nicky Mariano, opposed the idea. Once again Ray's powers of persuasion were successful. The visit took place, with surprising results. Mary's total preoccupation with Roger was predictable, but not the delight the baby caused the rest of the household. Even Berenson, a self-proclaimed 'President of the Herod Club', was enchanted.[49] The eventual decision that Roger should stay at I Tatti for the following winter suited everyone and allowed Barbara time to find work. Ray could certainly not afford to support her and

Roger long-term, and offered advice on likely careers with alacrity.

On Ray's advice, and with her funding, in August 1935 Barbara took a training course in Austria with the photographer E. O. Hoppé, which led to the offer of a job in his firm in London that October, and hence to later posts with a book club and in an advertising agency. When Barbara moved out of 53 Marsham Street, the disruption her marriage had caused to Ray's life significantly reduced. Barbara's private life became more settled too. Ostensibly sharing a flat with a girlfriend from November 1935, she was really living with Wolf Halpern. Despite her lack of enthusiasm for the relationship, Ray gradually came to accept it. In Finland a new lawyer argued for a different interpretation of the divorce legislation and succeeded in obtaining a divorce for Barbara. She regained her British nationality and in September 1937 married Wolf Halpern. Ray and Oliver were among the small group of guests.

Christopher remained one of the main joys of Ray's life. During his school career at Gresham's School in Norfolk, he had matured from an excitable and rather nervous small boy to a self-confident, even abrasive, senior pupil, with (despite her warnings) his mother's tendency to pass 'severe judgments' on others and a conviction that he was 'the only sensible person within 5 miles radius of Holt'.[50] Popularity seems to have meant nothing to him: other boys were wary of him and he was 'regarded as a sort of alarming volcano by his house master, because of his mixture of brains, unconventionality & uncompromisingness'.[51] Ray was torn between anxious amusement at seeing some of her own characteristics reappearing in her son and amazement at these public perceptions of him: 'It's not the way we look at our little Christopher is it!'[52]

Christopher's academic career had been mixed but his brilliance in maths and the sciences, and his contributions to school life as a musician and an actor, made up for his lack of application elsewhere. His success at winning scholarships was a financial relief to Ray and, when he left school in the summer of 1935, equally brilliant academic achievements in mathematics at Kings College, Cambridge, were confidently expected of him. Problems started even before Christopher went up. He developed difficulty in moving his arms and shoulders, eventually diagnosed as the result of an extra rib on each side. An operation in September 1935 dealt with his right side: the other would have to wait until Ray could afford it.

Christopher's first term at Cambridge went well: Oliver reported on his 'bubbling joy & great popularity'.[53] In exams the following summer his results were adequate but disappointing. Over the next year Ray watched her son gradually lose his sparkle and sink into lassitude. Only in July 1937, when Christopher appears to have admitted to her that he needed psychiatric help, did Ray tackle the matter openly. The problem was twofold: Christopher was losing his enthusiasm for maths and he was in sexual turmoil. Ray realised that part of the problem was sexual but initially assumed masturbation was the cause. Her response was unembarrassed, encouraging, affectionate, full of practical suggestions and without a hint of criticism ('I am ready to take any & every step necessary to pull you through. Don't feel that we can't afford things [...] Count on me always for anything that I can do. You know all that, ugly one').[54]

Christopher switched to Natural Sciences for his third year and flung himself into physics, working harder but still 'apathetic & melancholy' and considering whether to undergo psychoanalysis. By then Ray knew that Christopher had doubts about his sexuality. Ray had known many homosexuals – her uncle Logan Pearsall Smith, Oliver's brothers Lytton and, for a time, James, and many of their friends – and she does not seem to have been distressed at the thought of her son joining their number. If she was, she suppressed it. For Christopher's twenty-first birthday she wrote to him:

> As you know I would do anything in the world for you. But as things are it seems as if the only thing I can do is to refrain from all action. You have however my fullest – indeed my most acutely painful sympathy. [...] It doesn't contain any criticism, or sting of any sort: & I shall hold up your hands to the best of my abilities when you decide which ones to hold so to speak.[56]

In January 1938 Christopher was quarantined for several weeks because of measles, a break in his studies which seems to have brought to a head the question of whether he should take some time out from Cambridge. In the end he spent from March to June in America, visiting relatives, touring around in the car he bought there and, presumably, settling his sexual orientation. He was a homosexual for the rest of his life.

When Christopher returned to Cambridge, his zest for life returned and by January 1939 Ray had never known him 'more vigorous & keenly alive'.[57] He broached the idea of becoming a teacher, but, despite her commitment to education, Ray tried to dissuade him, as she saw 'a shocking number of heartbroken teachers in the course of [her] own job, who feel themselves caught up & powerless to do anything worth the doing' and anyhow 'there's a dreadful tendency for teachers to get deadened themselves by the perpetual contact with immature minds'.[58] Even though Christopher was now working hard, he had effectively only spent one year on Natural Sciences so all chance of a brilliant degree and a hoped-for research scholarship had gone. By the time Christopher took his final exams he had already decided to accept a job in the research laboratories of Standard Telephones and Cables in Woolwich, to which his lower second class degree made no difference. He started work in August 1939.

Ray's marriage to Oliver had settled down into a comfortable loving friendship. They were often apart but clearly delighted in spending time together, according to Barbara, with Ray remaining unperturbed by Oliver's habit of noisy complaint: 'all Oliver's shindys are really acting, so that we both break out laughing in the midst of them'.[59] Molly Hamilton was certain that Oliver was 'by long odds, [Ray's] favourite companion'.[60] Oliver often spent weekends at Mud, sometimes bringing a group of friends, occasionally including his current girlfriend.

The couple's London base changed several times during these years – but never left Marsham Street. For all Ray's sporadic efforts to smarten it up, 53 had not recovered from the 1928 flood and the rebuilding around it was intolerably noisy. When in May 1937 the Spanish Relief Company, based at 35 Marsham Street, needed bigger accommodation, Ray shocked even herself by sub-letting 53 to them on the spur of the moment: Oliver was abroad and could not be consulted, and the move had to take place within days. Ray worked frantically to sort out all the family's possessions and decide what should go where. She was, she assumed, the only one 'to feel the smallest pang' about leaving 'that damp smelly bugridden house to which I was so much attached', where they had had '10 very good years'.[61]

The Stracheys moved briefly into the vacated rooms at 35 then, almost immediately, into rooms Ray found and fell in love with on the upper floors of 73 Marsham Street: 'Perfect condition, central heating, electric power & gas, & lovely panelled rooms'.[62] For this decision Ray did wait for Oliver's return and consent. At £150 [£8,900] a year it was quite a saving, and proved a successful base until their departure in September 1938, a move probably forced by demolition and rebuilding. They returned to 35 Marsham Street, effectively a boarding-house, which offered 'one really lovely large sitting room [...] & bedrooms ad lib upstairs, takeable by the night or the week'.[63] As the accommodation at Mud was improved, becoming to Ray's mind 'too smart for its inhabitants', to cope with Mary's needs, the London facilities became totally unsuitable for her : 'the bedrooms are 3 floors up, & the WC on the ground floor, & there is only one bathroom to 10 people. It's very rough & ready, & though our sitting-room is lovely, the living arrangements are thoroughly makeshift'.[64]

The large sitting-room lent itself to entertaining, so Oliver persuaded Ray to give three sherry parties, the first social events they had hosted in London for years. Otherwise Oliver's social life was conducted mainly in the company of his current girlfriend. After Inez Jenkins had a baby in 1930 (not his, Oliver asserted), he had a brief relationship with Helen Anrep (inherited from Roger Fry) and a longer one with Lucy Scott, his acknowledged partner, sometimes even at Mud, for the rest of the decade.

Ray ran Oliver's domestic life and finances, even filling in his tax return and forging his signature on cheques. She was regularly called on to minister to his needs in times of illness and injury, to which Oliver was prone: a prolonged and recurring nosebleed from an abscess in 1935 led to a hospital stay and lengthy recuperation; in 1937, while Ray was arranging their move, Oliver, abroad, fell and cut his head; in 1938 he slipped over in a Westminster street and broke his arm; and he regularly succumbed to flu. Such ailments not only distracted Ray from her professional activities, but, pre-NHS, cost a great deal too.

Oliver's work in the Government Code and Cypher School, breaking diplomatic codes, had been fairly relaxed as he coasted towards retirement, but with international tensions building up, the task assumed a higher priority. Planning began in 1938 when a group of GC&CS staff in the guise of Captain Ridley's shooting party (almost certainly including Oliver) spent some weeks secretly assessing the suitability as a wartime operations centre of the country house acquired for that purpose – Bletchley Park. Ray knew well that if war broke out Oliver would be snatched away to an unknown location. And although Oliver could say little about his work she would have been aware of his gloomy assessment of the international situation, a particular worry to a family with a son of fighting age.

Mary's annual visits to England became increasingly difficult as her age increased and her health declined. Roughing it was not her style, even at Mud. She expected I Tatti-style comfort, importing it when she could ('Silver cream jugs, napkins for tea (!) & all sorts of elegancies') and inconveniencing the other occupants when she could not.[65] Her purchase of a Frigidaire for Mud was welcome but hardly compensated for the disruption caused by her arrival with an entourage of servants. The 'avalanche' of 1936 left Ray 'frazzled' and 'aggravated' and, in October, the final fortnight of Mary's visit proved 'simply crushing' when Mary was ill at the same time as other members of the family, leaving Ray with '5 invalids in 3 houses on my hands'.[66] Mary's departure was a huge relief.

Ray took action to improve matters for 1937. A further bathroom was needed at Mud for Mary's use and Ray could not afford to pay for it. Her supremely diplomatic letter to Berenson secured the promise of funding for the project if Mary could not afford to pay for it herself. Inevitably the building costs exceeded the estimate; but Berenson met them and even made up Ray's loss of salary from taking unpaid leave during Mary's visit.

Mary's 1938 visit was even more demanding. It began with her deep depression and threats of suicide, proceeded via her stay in a nursing home and a return to Mud with an extra nurse in tow (coinciding with an impossible number of visitors at Mud and a crisis when Logan Pearsall Smith became physically and mentally ill on holiday in Iceland), and ended with the very real possibility of Ray being left to deal with her mother in the event of war. As the international crisis approached in September, Ray tried to make contingency arrangements for Mary to return home only to hear from Berenson and Nicky Mariano that they did not want an invalid on their hands in wartime: Mary should go to neutral Switzerland instead. In the end Mary did fly back to Italy on 29 September at the height of the Munich crisis. Ray could not help feeling that she now did not care 'if the skies fall!'[67]

In denial about the possibility of war, Mary insisted on her usual summer visit in 1939. She arrived at the end of July, was bed-bound by illness for most of August, and was still there on 3 September, reduced to a trance-like state by shock at the outbreak of war, but still adamant that she must return to Berenson and I Tatti. Italy had not yet joined the conflict but by the time she was fit to return a permit to travel was required. When this was granted, as Mary recalled, 'there was no longer a direct air-route over France to Milan, so Ray had to make elaborate plans for the difficult journey over Belgium and Holland and across very high alps where passengers could breathe only with the aid of oxygen-producing machines'.[68]

The main advantage of Mary's descents on Mud each summer was that she brought with her Barbara's son Roger, the only 'unmixed blessing' to come from his parents' marriage.[69] Roger spent three

(Figure 30) The grandmother: Ray (with her habitual cigarette) playing with Roger at Mud in August 1936.

winters with the Berensons at I Tatti, largely cared for by Mary's Irish maid Elizabeth. He was a beautiful child and only gradually did his health problems emerge. In 1937 Mary had to return to Italy ahead of Roger, who was in Guy's Hospital having tests. Epileptic fits were originally diagnosed as infantile convulsions (and at I Tatti wrongly suspected as signs of inherited syphilis), to be treated with a plain, low-fat diet and regular doses of the barbiturate luminol. The vigorous three year old was becoming too much for Mary, and Barbara's plans to have him living with her and Wolf from the summer of 1938 met with 'plenty of fuss but no resistance'.[70]

With Roger living in London, Barbara and Ray had greater opportunity to assess his problems. More worrying even than his seizures was the backwardness of his development. His speech was delayed, toilet training went through major reverses and certain behavioural traits (failure to interact with or imitate other people, need for a regular routine, and repetitive actions such as tearing up paper) would now be associated with the autistic spectrum. Barbara explored the most up-to-date approaches to promoting child development; Ray remained somewhat sceptical of them. Inevitably Ray's help was called on during Barbara's domestic crises (but, somewhat unexpectedly, she found that she could rely on Barbara for reciprocal assistance). In April 1939 Roger had a bout of early TB, apparently successfully treated, his convalescence at Mud mainly supervised by his nursery nurse, Mrs Glazier and, in Barbara's absence at work, Ray, who took unpaid leave again that summer to attend to Mary. By the time war broke out, Roger was nearly five but his challenging behaviour meant that he could not be left alone for a minute.

Age and experience had changed Ray's attitude to war. While many of her contemporaries abandoned pacifism to oppose Hitler, Ray, while equally appalled by the Nazi regime, followed the opposite course. 'All my principles have left me, & I think nothing is worth fighting for', she admitted. The Munich agreement she greeted with relief and gratitude, initially refusing to join the backlash against Chamberlain, since 'anything is better than war' and 'while there is peace there is hope, but when there is war it's all at an end – civilization & all'.[72] When all her hopes that war might be avoided were extinguished, and they were 'all caught up in the mad business', Ray followed her usual policy of doing what was needed without fuss: 'it's no good grumbling at the war! There it is, & there's nothing to be done but bear it, & do our best to be useful'.[73]

The family scattered. Oliver was now at the secret location Ray referred to as Whipsnade [Bletchley Park], Barbara, Wolf and Roger in a flat in South Kensington, Christopher lodging in Woolwich (later in Blackheath), his work developing radar a reserved occupation. WEF moved into accommodation in Bedford College, Regent's Park, a safer location for staff and visitors than Westminster. Ray moved in, too, reducing the need to negotiate darkened streets and allowing even longer working hours during the week; weekends she hoped to spend at Fernhurst.

Even before Ray had despatched her mother back to Italy, another family crisis demanded her attention when Christopher went down with acute appendicitis. Surgery was successful but he needed several weeks' convalescence at Mud before returning to his job; Ray and Barbara both had to run around sorting out problems with his lodgings and car. Barbara gave up her job and moved briefly to Fernhurst with Roger; Wolf, already a member of the Territorial Army, became a part-time air-raid warden. Barbara brought in a Viennese child psychologist, Ilse Hellmann, to advise on Roger's treatment. An instant success with all the family, including Roger, Ilse suggested sending him to a Rudolf Steiner nursery school near Maidstone, which specialised in retarded children. Even though Roger settled happily at the school, the diagnosis of the extent of his problems was, Ray admitted, 'a serious trouble both to B. & me'.[74]

Ray and WEF plunged into the wartime activity for which they had been preparing, a repeat of what the Women's Service Bureau of the LSWS had done twenty-five years earlier. They had queues of applicants for jobs, but, initially, few jobs to offer and rapidly diminishing resources. Relations with the Ministry of Labour proved a particular problem, as 'official agencies cannot tolerate unofficial ones'.[75] In November money was so tight that Ray had had to give her whole staff provisional notice and was close to despair. Then her pleas for help to the Carnegie Trust produced a series of short-term grants which met the financial needs of WEF's normal work (Carnegie funds could not be applied to war work) and there seemed a good chance that the Ministry of Labour would fund or take over the war work. By January 1940 Ray's office was 'running so smoothly that it is barely interesting, though its work is going decidedly well'.[76]

The Queen, who had visited WEF in October and demonstrated considerable interest, agreed to become its Patron, a great boost to WEF's morale and reputation. The long delay in extracting a decision from the Ministry of Labour led Ray to conclude that continuing as an independent body had its attractions. When in late February the Ministry finally rejected the idea of taking over WEF's war work, the refusal was 'in some ways [...] disappointing, but in others a great relief'.[77] With the number of available posts rising rapidly, WEF funded the work by charging fees for placements.

Ray added to her already heavy workload by helping to organise a cross-party deputation of women MPs to the Financial Secretary to the Treasury on 15 February. It was a taxing job as the women MPs were 'an awkward party to handle – very hard to get hold of, frightfully hard to pin down as they are trying to take in so many too many things at once – & a very unruly team personally, all pulling different ways'.[78] Fortunately they were 'all quite united about the employment of women business'.[79] Ray was one of four speakers on the deputation to argue that during the war the Government could make much better use of women, particularly those suitable for senior posts.

The platitudes with which the deputation was greeted disappointed Ray but Ellen Wilkinson, with inside knowledge, was not discouraged.

(Figure 31) Bricklaying at the cottage left incomplete at Ray's death (now known as 'the Ruin').

The important thing was that the deputation had been seen, and she expected that the nod would be given for a substantial number of good jobs to be awarded to women. A favourable *Times* leader, derived from Ray's detailed conversation with the editor, strongly reinforced the deputation's message.[80] Ray's suggestion of regular meetings of women MPs to 'hold a watching brief for women, and especially for industrial women, while the war lasts' got nowhere at that time but when in June the women members decided to form a committee to advise on problems affecting the war effort of women, Ray was immediately invited to join it.[81]

The early weeks of 1940 saw heavy snow and bitter temperatures in London. Everything froze, the pipes at Bedford College as well as the lake in Regent's Park, and flu laid low Ray's family and staff. Going out to dine meant braving snowdrifts and the blackout. But it was impossible to look forward to spring given the expected intensification of fighting then. The military campaigns in Scandinavia during April marked the end of the Phoney War. As the momentous events of May 1940 unfolded, Ray managed to snatch some time at Fernhurst and shut out thoughts of war, as far as she could, by concentrating on the sunny weather, the spring flowers, a nightingale in the field, and manual labour – carpentry and bricklaying. At her recently reorganised office, work had reached a plateau and the pressure relaxed slightly.

Nationally, Ray assured Mary, there was 'a tremendous sense of determination, & a drive for increased production'.[82] Ray's family were each contributing, with Barbara, placed by Ray in the Ministry of Information, and Christopher both working long hours. Oliver and his overstretched section at Bletchley Park had just been tasked with breaking an important manual cipher used by the German Intelligence Services, the Abwehr. (Their eventual success in December 1940 contributed significantly to the Double-Cross system which concealed the breaking of the crucial machine-based Enigma code, the old and new approaches to codebreaking forming a war-winning partnership.) On Oliver's brief, infrequent, visits to London Ray could see that he was 'working so very hard & incessantly that he finds life very grim'.[83]

The fall of France threatened the Bussy family in Nice, but more significant was the entry of Italy into the war. The Berensons were now living in an enemy country, protected for the time being by their American nationality, but out of direct contact with England. Although letters could still be sent via relatives in the United States, communication would be slow and uncertain. As the threat of a German invasion of Britain grew, Ray despatched what she knew might be her final farewell to her mother:

> By the time this gets to you, if it does, all the circumstances of all of us may have changed. But whatever happens you know that we've all had enjoyable existences, packed with interest & good things, & even if we all snuffed out now, we should every one of us have had good worthwhile Times, & been glad to have been alive. This sounds very deathbed-like, & I can assure you it's not the way we feel. But life is precarious now, & you might as well be told explicitly that your descendants are grateful for being born![84]

Ray had survived the winter in better health than many around her (apart from a touch of lumbago) and as she approached her fifty-third birthday on 4 June assured her mother that 'I don't feel any older than I did 25 years ago – except perhaps that I have less tolerance for pure theory, & that I'm not so ready to run or climb stairs'.[85] But in June she suffered abdominal pain from another fibroid (unusual after the menopause but not unknown), and was advised to have a gynaecological operation, perhaps just straightforward removal or perhaps a full hysterectomy. As the expected mass employment of women for war work was being frustratingly delayed, it was a less inconvenient moment than many for Ray to be away from WEF. She obtained medical leave of absence and found someone to take over her professional role until her return. Leaving the office, Ray popped her head round Irene Hilton's door and instructed her to 'look after WEF for me'.[86]

Ray assured Christopher that 'I neither expect nor intend to die in the course of the coming operation' but, as it was only rational to simplify business in case she did, she provided detailed information about her financial circumstances and the location of key documents.[87] 'I can't help feeling that nothing can possibly be disentangled without me, but realize actually that this is not so,' she added.[88] She had made a new will a few days earlier, a brief manuscript document witnessed by Pippa and Ellie Rendel, leaving everything to Christopher, the sole executor. Now she explained that he was to 'make an equitable division with B, & between you to provide for O' (and take over responsibility for dealing with Oliver's income tax returns, given his financial incompetence).[89] She hoped that it would be possible to continue paying a surreptitious pension to a former WEF employee without revealing that the source was not WEF.

Ray's attitude to death was habitually matter-of-fact. Fourteen years earlier she had confided to her diary 'life is as it is, & the end of it is part of it just as much as the beginning.'[90] Now she rejected all overt display of emotion: 'Deathbed sentiments are quite uncalled for. Anyhow you know what they would be well enough.'[91] In the event of her death, Christopher and Barbara should send a 'suitably painful' letter to Mary.[92] On Friday 5 July, the day she went into the Royal Free Hospital in Grays Inn Road, Ray wrote again to her mother without mentioning the impending operation. 'Life goes on quite normally,' she asserted and, less truthfully given that there were persistent rumours of an imminent invasion, 'we fully expect this to continue.'[93]

A successful minor operation to remove the fibroid (which confirmed that no cancer was present) unexpectedly left Ray in pain for the next week. Eventually on 14 July the puzzled doctors (depleted by the evacuation of medical students and teaching staff) diagnosed an adhesion causing a blockage in the intestine (a not uncommon complication) and performed a hysterectomy, at the time a major operation with a risk of excessive blood loss. Ray survived the operation, but the next two or three days would be critical. Her condition fluctuated. On 16 July Barbara, whose office was in the nearby Senate House of the University of London, was summoned to give blood, but arrived too late: she was just in time to see her mother die of heart failure.

Epilogue

She impressed one as a happy woman, not because her life had lacked struggle or a knowledge of the world's sorrows, but because her response to all experience had been at once honest and generous.[1]

The tearful cremation at Golders Green on 18 July was attended by Oliver, Barbara, Wolf, Christopher, Karin (terribly overcome), Adrian, Alys, Pippa and her sister Pernel, Molly Hamilton, Ellie Rendel (looking awful, according to Molly) and Mrs Glazier. There was no service: the mourners sat in silence for a while, then stood. Rather grim, Molly thought, but what Ray would have preferred. With the Battle of Britain under way, there was little alternative to following Ray's example and coping without fuss. Oliver returned to Bletchley Park and Christopher took on the administration of Ray's estate and the financial problems the loss of Ray's salary created for the family.

Silence, beloved by Ray, was alien to Barbara. Constrained from expressing her feelings to her stunned family for fear of destroying their 'precarious composure', she poured them out in a letter to Lady Astor: 'I can't imagine or wish to imagine a better mother than she was, not only in every action and decision, but in person. She contrived to be that unique thing, a great woman, a truly wise parent & a very lovable person'.[2] Other letters confirmed Ray's crucial role within her family: she was 'my pride & joy [...] my mainstay & comfort', 'our standby & anchor in our everyday life', 'the centre and the core of very many lives.'[3] 'Everyone asked & took her advice, everyone loved & admired her.'[4] The letters of condolence which inundated the family proved that many others felt the same way, and that she was 'revered & loved by thousands of women'.[5]

Private and public tributes to Ray poured forth. Characterised by apparently genuine feeling rather than conventional platitudes, they stressed her courage, humour, warmth, realism, honesty, dynamic energy, selflessness, inspirational powers of leadership, sense of fun, lack of pettiness or pomposity, and practical kindness. Nesca Robb, a colleague in WEF, remembered Ray's 'idealism without self-deceiving, practical sense without narrowness of vision'.[6] Iris Origo recognised that 'No one could know Ray even slightly [...] without feeling that one was in the presence of a very remarkable human being,'[7]

At a dinner held on 17 July for members of the British Federation of Business and Professional Women to impress on Ernest Bevin, Minister of Labour and National Service, the contribution which women could make to the war effort, the sorrowful minute's silence in Ray's memory observed by 560 guests confirmed the respect and affection Ray had earned in her public life. For *The Times*, Nancy Astor remembered Ray as 'one of the happy warriors who bring joy as well as zest into every campaign, light its incidents with humour, and lift the whole to the plane of high adventure'; her life had been one of 'continuous practical activity, lit by social imagination of a high order, and carried through with organizing genius' demonstrating 'the complete disinterestedness that was the more striking in a personality at once so warm, vivid, and challenging'.[8] 'Of herself or for herself she never thought', Lady Astor wrote; 'she wanted things done; she was not in the least interested in credit or reputation for doing them and was ingenious in handing both elsewhere.'[9]

Molly Hamilton acknowledged that 'in speech, Ray could be highly critical' but stressed that 'in action, her kindness knew no bounds': she could hardly remember a time when Ray 'was not deeply involved in straightening out somebody else's troubles; or any when she suggested she had any of her own'.[10] Ray's 'verbal cynicism' was, thought Molly, merely 'a protective covering for an unexpressed idealism that neither flagged nor faltered, once it had found its mark'.[11] At work Ray was 'an organiser of dynamic power, who never asked of others half the work she asked of herself' with the 'vision to conceive a grand design, and drive and tenacity to carry it through in detail', 'always wholly singleminded, totally disinterested, quite careless of anything less than the cause'.[12] Personally and professionally, Ray was invariably 'the giver, not the taker'.[13]

Virginia Woolf's verdict was harsher. While acknowledging Ray's courage, humanity, competence, good nature, wisdom and cordiality, she discerned disappointment and a sense of failure too:

> Her bitterness at Oliver, whom she had loved, & did love, was perceptible – something tart about her; & as if some of the petals of what she hoped, as a girl, to be so yellow a sunflower – she was ambitious, self confident, was greedy & a little insensitive about 'fame'– as if these petals had withered & she could no longer be confident; was indeed disappointed, a little wounded, embittered; chiefly shown by her immense activity, as if always trying to get what she could not.[14]

As a judgement this seems out-dated: Ray's pain and disappointment during the 1920s had given way to a new confidence as she rebuilt her relationship with Oliver and set up WEF. But it is a valuable corrective to Mary's short-sighted emphasis on Ray's perpetual cheerfulness. Virginia, who judged Ray's life 'much of a scramble & a fight', had mainly met her in social contexts (the setting in which Ray felt least comfortable), and knew little of her in her domestic and professional roles.[15] Nevertheless she rightly surmised that in the office Ray would have been 'very commanding, controlling & masterly'.[16]

Ray's colleagues at WEF saw no hope of keeping the organisation going without her. Horrified at the idea that her mother's work would be wasted, Barbara wrote to all those concerned, stressing how much Ray would have wanted WEF to continue. It did. After fruitless searches for an external replacement, staff selected and inspired by

Ray eventually took on her role: first Dorothy Wise, then Irene Hilton, who ran WEF from 1948 to 1972. With the demise of the Central Bureau in 1941, competition for Carnegie funding eased. WEF lasted, under various names, until 1995, by which time the 'equality of *opportunity*' which Ray had sought for working women had been substantially achieved.[17]

Oliver was sent to Canada in early 1942 for nine months to strengthen the cryptanalytic unit there. A serious heart attack in February 1943 (when he was 68) eventually ended his career. After the war he moved into 51 Gordon Square to join Pippa and Pernel but suffered a long sad decline of physical ailments and self-pity – not helped by over-indulgence in whisky – which ended with his death in a nursing home at the age of 85 in 1960.

Mary died in March 1945, a few months after the liberation of I Tatti and the return of Berenson and Nicky Mariano. Her 'Life of Ray Strachey', largely complete but never published, offers a useful factual record insofar as it reproduces Ray's accounts of her activities but an inadequate portrayal of her personality and a totally misconceived account of the mother-daughter relationship. Mary's lively writing style dangerously conceals her untrustworthiness as a chronicler of Ray's life.

Alys Russell survived until 1951, enduring her brother Logan's increasingly irrational behaviour as his manic depression worsened until his death in 1946, but overjoyed by a final reconciliation with Bertrand Russell. Karin too fell victim to the Pearsall Smith curse of manic depression which spared Ray; she took a fatal overdose of morphine in 1953, five years after her husband Adrian's death. Pippa was, Barbara thought, shattered by Ray's death, but remained as Secretary of the LNSWS until 1951, continuing the fight to improve employment opportunities and conditions for women which she and Ray had waged together for so many years. Despite her fluctuating health, she was the last of the Strachey siblings to die, in 1968, cheerful and friendly to the last despite blindness and physical frailty.

Wolf's conversion to Anglicanism, Barbara's entry into the Roman

Catholic church (a substitute for Ray as a source of moral authority, one friend commented), other relationships on both sides, and Wolf's enrolment in the RAF as a navigator all put Barbara's marriage under increasing strain until Wolf was killed on a training flight in Gloucestershire in 1943. With her son Roger living in a succession of institutions, Barbara went on to have a successful career as a radio producer and planner in the BBC, playing a major role in the development of the World Service. On her retirement to Oxford in 1975, she produced a book of maps to illustrate J.R.R. Tolkien's *The Lord of the Rings*, two books about her family and an edition of Mary Berenson's letters and diaries; she became the keeper and interpreter of the family archive to interested researchers. Barbara died in 1999.

Post-war, Christopher realised the ambition to teach which he had voiced to Ray, first at St Edmund's School, Canterbury, then at Harrow. The new field of computing drew on Christopher's scientific knowledge and his teaching experience. By the time he responded to a radio talk by Alan Turing entitled 'Can digital computers think?' in 1951, he was already working on a draughts-playing program and pondering how to replicate in a machine human processes of grasping and applying relationships between facts. His work as an amateur computer programmer (including a love-letter generator devised with Barbara's enthusiastic collaboration) eventually secured him a post at the National Research Development Corporation, then in 1959 a lucrative career as a computer consultant, working from the home in London he and Barbara shared. Christopher eventually returned to academic life to lead a programming research group at Oxford University, the success of which, particularly in denotational semantics, brought him a personal chair as Oxford's first Professor of Computation. He died in May 1975 at the age of 58 from hepatitis, a known risk to homosexual men. He retained the Mud House throughout his life, a treasured retreat for him as it had been for Ray.

Ray Strachey has been remembered mainly as the author of *The Cause*, still a classic text for students of, and writers about, the Women's Movement in Britain. But her achievement was far wider. An energetic organiser and facilitator, she raised public consciousness of what women could and should achieve as much by her own example of rationality, realism, moderation and sheer competence as by what she said. In her youth, Ray assumed that she would 'stride from peak to peak' (while conceding that she might be 'unusually conceited'), but in later life this arrogance matured into a steady self-confidence which gave Ray both the somewhat illusory appearance of a perpetual optimist and the very real drive to keep fighting for her chosen causes.[18] Even when particular decisions did not go her way, Ray's efforts changed attitudes and paved the way for later successes. She demonstrated that women did not have to choose between family life and a public role. Women of today owe her a great debt.

Figure 32: Ray Strachey is among the suffrage campaigners whose photographs are etched onto the plinth of Gillian Wearing's statue of Millicent Garrett Fawcett in Parliament Square.

APPENDICES

Appendix A: The Whitall and Smith Families

John Mickle Whitall, b. 1800, d. 1877
+Mary Tatum, m. 1830
— **Hannah Whitall,** b. 1832, d. 1911
  +Robert (Pearsall) Smith, b. 1827, m. 1851, d. 1898
    — **Nellie Smith,** b. 1852, d. 1857
    — **Frank Smith,** b. 1854, d. 1872
    — **Mary Pearsall Smith,** b. 1864, d. 1945
      +Benjamin Francis Conn ('Frank') Costelloe, b. 1854, m. 1885, d. 1899
        — **Rachel Pearsall Conn ('Ray') Costelloe,** b. 1887, d. 1940
          +Oliver Strachey, b. 1874, m. 1911, d. 1960
            — **Barbara Mary Strachey,** b. 1912, d. 1999
              +Olav Arvidson Hultin, b. 1910, m. 1934, d. circa 1979
                └── **Roger Sven Allen Hultin,** b. 1934, d. 2017
              +Wolf Abiram Halpern, b. 1909, m. 1937, d. 1943
            — **Christopher Strachey,** b. 1916, d. 1975
        — **Catherine Elizabeth ('Karin') Costelloe,** b. 1889, d. 1953
          +Adrian Stephen, b. 1883, m. 1914, d. 1948
            — **Ann Stephen,** b. 1916, d. 1997
              +Richard Llewelyn-Davies, m. 1938
              +Richard Lawrence Millington Synge, m. 1943
            — **(Karin) Judith Stephen,** b. 1918, d. 1972
              +Nigel Graeme Henderson, m. 1943
      +Bern(h)ard Berenson, b. 1865, m. 1900, d. 1959
    — **(Lloyd) Logan Pearsall Smith,** b. 1865, d. 1946
    — **Alys Pearsall Smith,** b. 1867, d. 1951
      +Bertrand Russell, b. 1872, m. 1894, d. 1970
    — **Rachel 'Ray' Smith,** b. 1868, d. 1880
    └── **(stillborn daughter) Smith,** b. 1873, d. 1873
— **Sarah Whitall,** b. 1833, d. 1880
  +William Nicholson
  └── **Rebecca Morgan Nicholson**
      +Frank Hendrikson Taylor
      └── **William Nicholson ('Willy') Taylor,** b. 1882, d. 1945
└── **Mary Whitall,** b. 1836, d. 1888
  +James Thomas, m. 1854
    — **M(artha) Carey Thomas,** b. 1857, d. 1935
    — **(Mary) Grace Thomas,** b. 1866, d. 1937
      +Thomas Kimber ('Tom') Worthington, m. 1887
        — **Bond Valentine Thomas ('Val') Worthington,** b. 1888, d. 1932
          +Anne Middleton Means, m. 1916
        — **Mary Dorothy Whitall ('Pug') Worthington,** b. 1889, d. 1912
        └── **Harold ('Babe') Worthington,** b. 1890, d. 1978
          +(Sada) Elizabeth Hoyt, m. 1926
          +Helen Woodford Hoffman, m. 1944
    └── **Helen Thomas,** b. 1871, d. 1956
      +Simon Flexner, m. 1903

Appendix B: The Costelloe Family

Thomas Costelloe
+Margaret Kilmartin
└── Martin Richard Costelloe, b. 1812, d. 1879
   +Mary Anne Conn, b. 1819, m. 1853, d. 1897
    ├── Benjamin Francis Conn ('Frank') Costelloe, b. 1854, d. 1899
      +Mary Pearsall Smith, b. 1864, m. 1885, d. 1945
       ├── Rachel Pearsall Conn ('Ray') Costelloe, b. 1887, d. 1940
        +Oliver Strachey, b. 1874, m. 1911, d. 1960
         ├── Barbara Mary Strachey, b. 1912, d. 1999
          +Olav Arvidson Hultin, b. 1910, m. 1934, d. circa 1979
           └── Roger Sven Allen Hultin, b. 1934, d. 2017
          +Wolf Abiram Halpern, b. 1909, m. 1937, d. 1943
         └── Christopher Strachey, b. 1916, d. 1975
       └── Catherine Elizabeth ('Karin') Costelloe, b. 1889, d. 1953
        +Adrian Stephen, b. 1883, m. 1914, d. 1948
         ├── Ann Stephen, b. 1916, d. 1997
          +Richard Llewelyn-Davies, m. 1938
          +Richard Lawrence Millington Synge, m. 1943
         └── (Karin) Judith Stephen, b. 1918, d. 1972
          +Nigel Graeme Henderson, m. 1943
    ├── Thomas John Costelloe, b. 1855, d. 1855
    └── Richard Martin Costelloe, b. 1859, d. 1863

Appendix C: The Strachey Family

Richard Strachey, b. 1817, d. 1908
+Caroline Bowles, m. 1854, d. 1855
+Jane Maria Grant, b. 1840, m. 1859, d. 1928
    ── **Elinor Strachey,** b. 1859, d. 1944
    +James Meadows Rendel, b. 1854, m. 1882, d. 1937
       ── **Elizabeth ('Betty') Rendel,** b. 1883, d. 1923
       ── **Frances Elinor ('Ellie') Rendel,** b. 1885, d. 1942
       ── **Richard Meadows ('Dick') Rendel,** b. 1887, d. 1966
       +Julia Margaret ('Judy') Marshall, m. 1912
       ── **Andrew James Rendel,** b. 1888, d. 1917
       +Gladys Louise Romer, m. 1913
       ── **(William) Vincent Rendel,** b. 1898, d. 1974
       +Margaret Ecila Wilkinson, m. 1928
    ── **Richard John ('Dick') Strachey,** b. 1861, d. 1935
    +Grace Alice Norman, m. 1896
    ── **Dorothea ('Dorothy') Strachey,** b. 1865, d. 1960
    +(Albert) Simon Aimé Bussy, b. 1870, m. 1903, d. 1954
       ── **Jane Simone ('Janie') Bussy,** b. 1906, d. 1960
    ── **Ralph Strachey,** b. 1868, d. 1923
    +Margaret Winifred Severs, b. 1878, m. 1901, d. 1972
       ── **Richard Philip Farquhar ('Dick') Strachey,** b. 1902, d. 1976
       +(Frances) Esmé Rudd, m. 1927
       +Simonette Mary Reynolds Woods, m. 1943
       ── **John Ralph Severs Strachey,** b. 1905
       +Isobel Bertha Leslie, m. 1933
       +Rosemary Mavor, m. 1945
       +Margaret Bainbridge, m. 1973
       ── **Ursula Margaret Strachey,** b. 1911, d. 1999
       +Cyril Charles Wentzel, m. 1939
    ── **Philippa ('Pippa') Strachey,** b. 1872, d. 1968
    ── **Oliver Strachey,** b. 1874, d. 1960
    +Ruby Julia Mayer, b. 1881, m. 1901, d. 1959
       ── **Julia Frances Strachey,** b. 1901, d. 1979
       +Stephen Tomlin, b. 1901, m. 1927, d. 1937
       +Lawrence Gowing, m. 1952
    +Rachel Pearsall Conn ('Ray') Costelloe, b. 1887, m. 1911, d. 1940
       ── **Barbara Mary Strachey,** b. 1912, d. 1999
       +Olav Arvidson Hultin, b. 1910, m. 1934, d. circa 1979
          ── **Roger Sven Allen Hultin,** b. 1934, d. 2017
       +Wolf Abiram Halpern, b. 1909, m. 1937, d. 1943
       ── **Christopher Strachey,** b. 1916, d. 1975
    ── **(Joan) Pernel Strachey,** b. 1876, d. 1951
    ── **(Giles) Lytton Strachey,** b. 1880, d. 1932
    ── **Marjorie Colville Strachey,** b. 1882, d. 1962
    ── **James Beaumont Strachey,** b. 1887, d. 1967
    +Alix Sargant-Florence, b. 1892, m. 1920, d. 1973

NOTES

The vast majority of quotations in this biography are the words of Ray Costelloe/Strachey. Published works cited are by Ray Costelloe/Strachey unless otherwise specified. In quotations from unpublished material, Ray is identified as RC until her marriage on 31 May 1911 and as RS thereafter.

In quotations I have retained Ray's idiosyncratic spellings and habitual use of ampersands but, for the sake of readability, I have silently adjusted some of her punctuation, especially her omission of apostrophes in letters and diaries. Where appropriate, I have also silently adjusted the letter-case at the start of quotations.

Bernhard/Bernard Berenson dropped the Germanic 'h' during the First World War; I refer to him by the spelling in use at the time of mention.

In references to the Hannah Whitall Smith Collection of material in the Lilly Library, University of Indiana, box numbers (for loose leaf items) are indicated by a number (e.g. HWS, 13) and bound volumes by BV and a number (e.g. HWS, BV 32). Quotation from this collection is courtesy of the Lilly Library, Indiana University, Bloomington, Indiana.

Money values adjusted to 2017 prices are shown in square brackets in the text. These figures are approximately based on comparisons of purchasing power calculated by the Measuring Worth website < https://www.measuringworth.com/ppoweruk/>.

Changes to UK legislation in 2014 have considerably extended exceptions to copyright for quotation from material which has been made available to the public. Within this new legislative framework, I have attempted to obtain all necessary permissions from copyright-holders (and should be glad to be notified of any inadvertent omissions).

Preface

1   *The Cause: A Short History of the Women's Movement in Great Britain* (London: G. Bell, 1928; repr. Virago, 1978).

2   Barbara Strachey Halpern, 'Ray Strachey—A Memoir', in Wayne K. Chapman and Janet M. Manson, eds, *Women in the Milieu of Leonard and Virginia Woolf: Peace, Politics and Education* (New York: Pace University, 1998), pp. 76–86 (p. 84).

3   Lilly Library, Indiana University, Bloomington, Indiana, Hannah Whitall Smith papers (henceforward HWS), 14, RS to Barbara Strachey, 19 February 1930.

Prologue

1   The Women's Library @ LSE, Strachey Family Papers, 7BSH/1/1 and 2, Boxes 1 and 2, Mary Berenson MS 'Life of Ray Strachey' (henceforward WL, 'Life of Ray Strachey').

Chapter 1: Divided Loyalties: 1887–1900

1   Barbara Strachey, *Remarkable Relations: The Story of the Pearsall Smith Family* (London: Gollancz, 1980), p. 121 (quoting Hannah Whitall Smith to Mary Costelloe, 3 January 1893).

2   WL, 7BSH/5/2/13, Box 12, typescript copy of letter from F. D. Acland to RS [November 1918].

3   Barbara Strachey, *Remarkable Relations*, p. 78.

4   HWS, 9, Hannah Whitall Smith to Mary Pearsall Smith, 17 and 20 January 1885.

5   Costelloe forecast, perhaps over-optimistically, that in 1885 his total income from a variety of sources was likely to exceed £600 [roughly £60,000 in 2017 prices] (HWS, 1, undated letter to Robert Pearsall Smith).

6   HWS, Box 1, Frank Costelloe to Marion Paterson, [15] June 1887.

7   *All the Good Things of Life: The Diary of Beatrice Webb, Volume Two 1892–*

1905, ed. by Norman and Jeanne MacKenzie (London: Virago in association with the London School of Economics, 1993), p. 34. John Williams Benn (grandfather of Tony Benn) was a LCC councillor and close colleague of Costelloe and Webb.

8   Ernest Samuels, *Bernard Berenson: The Making of a Connoisseur* (Cambridge, MA., and London: Harvard University, 1979), p. 116.

9   Barbara Strachey and Jayne Samuels, eds, *Mary Berenson: A Self-Portrait from her Letters & Diaries*, (London: Gollancz, 1983), p. 32 (Mary Berenson to Alys Pearsall Smith, 14 January 1886).

10   Giovanni Morelli (1816–1891) pioneered a method of attribution of paintings through a detailed analysis of artists' characteristic styles.

11   *The letters of Sidney and Beatrice Webb*, ed. by Norman MacKenzie, 3 vols (Cambridge: Cambridge University Press, 1978), I, *Apprenticeships 1873– 1892*, p. 297 (Sidney Webb to Beatrice Potter, 14 September 1891).

12   Barbara Strachey and Jayne Samuels, p. 46 (Mary Costelloe to Hannah Whitall Smith, 26 August 1891).

13   Barbara Strachey and Jayne Samuels, p. 48 (Mary Costelloe diary, 2 January 1892).

14   WL, 'Life of Ray Strachey', (quoting Mary Costelloe to Hannah Whitall Smith, 6 March 1892).

15   Barbara Strachey and Jayne Samuels, pp. 49–50 (Mary Costelloe diary, 11 April and 25 October 1892).

16   The legal position was that a wife could be divorced for adultery alone, but a wife seeking a divorce needed to prove incest, bigamy, cruelty, unnatural vice or desertion for two years as well as adultery.

17   Samuels, *The Making of a Connoisseur*, p. 162.

18   Barbara Strachey and Jayne Samuels, p. 50 (Mary Costelloe diary, 14 October 1892).

19   Barbara Strachey and Jayne Samuels, p. 66 (Mary Costelloe to Bernhard Berenson, 4 January 1896).

20   Barbara Strachey and Jayne Samuels, p. 66 (Mary Costelloe to Bernhard Berenson, 5 January 1896).

21   Barbara Strachey and Jayne Samuels, p. 51 (Mary Costelloe to Ray Costelloe, 21 January 1893).

22   Ray Strachey, *A Quaker Grandmother: Hannah Whitall Smith* (London: Fleming H. Revell, 1914), p. 43 (quoting Hannah Whitall Smith to unnamed correspondents, 16 March 1897 and 16 December 1896).

23   HWS, 9, Hannah Whitall Smith to Mary Costelloe, 5 May 1893.

24   Ray Strachey, *A Quaker Grandmother*, p. 60 (quoting Hannah Whitall Smith to unnamed correspondent, 17 November 1898).

25   HWS, 9, Hannah Whitall Smith to Mary Costelloe, 7 October 1892.

26   HWS, 1, Frank Costelloe to Mary Costelloe, 25 February 1894.

27   HWS, BV 41, Hannah Whitall Smith to Mary Costelloe, 19 March 1896. It is just possible that Mary misremembered the location of the children's first school. Other evidence suggests St Joseph's, a Catholic school in Chelsea, as an alternative.

28   Ray Strachey, *A Quaker Grandmother*, p. 39 (quoting Hannah Whitall Smith to unnamed correspondent, 5 March 1896).

29   *A Religious Rebel: The Letters of "H. W. S." (Mrs Pearsall Smith)*, ed. by Logan Pearsall Smith, (London: Nisbet, 1949), p. 139 (Hannah Whitall Smith to Olive Seward, 28 March 1898).

30   Samuels, *The Making of a Connoisseur*, p. 198.

31   Barbara Strachey and Jayne Samuels, p. 67 (Mary Costelloe to Bernhard Berenson, 12 June 1899).

32   HWS, BV 43, Hannah Whitall Smith to Mary Costelloe, 24 March 1898.

33   Ray Strachey, *A Quaker Grandmother*, p. 55.

34   'East St. Pancras Election', *Morning Post*, 13 July 1899, p. 5.

35   Barbara Strachey and Jayne Samuels, p. 83 (Mary Costelloe to Bernhard Berenson, 18 July 1899).

36   'Benjamin Francis Conn Costelloe', *New Era*, 23 December 1899, p. 1.

37   HWS, 1, Grace Worthington to Hannah Whitall Smith, 15 September 1899; HWS, 10, Hannah Whitall Smith to Mary Costelloe, 18 September 1899.

38   HWS, 10, Hannah Whitall Smith to Alys Russell, 26 September 1899.

39   HWS, 10, Hannah Whitall Smith to Mary Costelloe, 28 September 1899.

40   HWS, 10, Hannah Whitall Smith to Mary Costelloe, 15 October 1899.

41   HWS, 10, Hannah Whitall Smith to Mary Costelloe, 22 October 1899.

42   HWS, 10, Hannah Whitall Smith to Mary Costelloe, 24 October 1899.

43   HWS, 10, Hannah Whitall Smith to Mary Costelloe, 13 November 1899.

44   'Underfed School Children', *The Times*, 2 November 1899, p. 15.

45   'The London School Board: The School and the Hungry Child', *Schoolmaster*, 18 November 1899, p. 922.

46   Ibid.

47   Barbara Strachey and Jayne Samuels, p. 86 (Mary Costelloe to Bernhard Berenson, 12 December 1899).

48   Will of Benjamin Francis Conn Costelloe, dated 5 October 1899 with codicils dated 5 and 18 October 1899; probate granted 9 February 1900 to Terence Woulfe Flanagan, physician and surgeon, and the reverend William Francis Brown, clerk; value of estate £6582 17s. 10d [£653,700 in 2017 prices].

49   Hannah Whitall Smith, *The Christian's Secret of a Happy Life* (New York: Fleming H. Revell, 1888 and 1916), p. 223.

50   HWS, 10, Hannah Whitall Smith to Alys Russell, 4 January 1900; to Mary
      Costelloe, 20 February 1900; Barbara Strachey, *Remarkable Relations*, p. 194
      (quoting Hannah Whitall Smith to Mary Costelloe, 16 May 1900).

51   *The Letters of Virginia Woolf*, ed. by Nigel Nicolson and Joanne Trautmann,
      6 vols (London: Hogarth Press, 1975–1980), I, *The Flight of the Mind: 1888–
      1912 (Virginia Stephen)* (1975), p. 456 (Virginia Stephen to Vanessa Bell, 6
      April [1911]).

Chapter 2: The New Girl: 1900 –1905

1   WL, 7BSH/2/2/7, Box 3, Ellie Rendel to RC, 26 September [1905].

2   HWS, BV 35, RC diary, 9 January 1904.

3   University College London, Institute of Education archives, GDS13/11
      (prospectus of The Kensington High School, 1900 and 1904).

4   See Sally Mitchell, *The New Girl: Girls' Culture in England 1880–1915* (New
      York: Columbia University Press, 1995).

5   Elizabeth Thomasina Meade (1844–1914), the daughter of an Anglo-Irish
      clergyman from County Cork, horrified her father by moving to London
      at the age of seventeen so as to turn herself into a professional writer. This
      she did, producing nearly three hundred books in various genres, founding
      Atalanta, a magazine for girls, in 1887 and editing it for six years, and in the
      1890s becoming a leading figure in the Pioneer Club for progressive women.
      Alongside this professional activity, she married Alfred Toulmin Smith, a
      solicitor, and had three children.

6   Mitchell, p. 172.

7   Elizabeth Sloan Chesser, M.B., *From Girlhood to Womanhood* (London:
      Cassell, 1913), p. 80.

8   Chesser, p. 97.

9   *A Quaker Grandmother*, p. 92 (quoting Hannah Whitall Smith to Mary
      Costelloe, 21 January 1904).

10   *A Quaker Grandmother*, p. 24.

11   *A Quaker Grandmother*, p. 73.

12   HWS, BV 35, RC diary, [October/November] 1903.

13   HWS, BV 41, Hannah Whitall Smith to Mary Costelloe, 19 December 1896.

14   *A Quaker Grandmother*, p. 73.

15   HWS, BV 34, RC diary, 11 May and 12 June 1902, 1 March and 30 April 1903.

16   HWS, BV 34, RC diary, 24 June 1903.

17   HWS, BV 34, RC diary, frontispiece.

18   HWS, BV 34, RC diary, 3 April 1902.

19   HWS, BV 34, RC diary, 25 May 1902.

20   Ibid.

21   Ibid.

22   Ibid.

23   HWS, BV 34, RC diary, 8 May 1903.

24   Ibid.

25   Ibid.

26   HWS, BV 34, RC diary, 4 July 1903.

27   Ibid.

28   Ibid.

29   Josephine Kamm, *Indicative Past: A Hundred Years of The Girls' Public Day School Trust* (London: George Allen & Unwin, 1971), p. 130.

30   HWS, BV 34, RC diary, 24 July 1903.

31   HWS, BV 34, RC diary, 4 July 1903.

32   HWS, BV 35, RC diary, 11 November 1903.

33   HWS, BV 35, RC diary, 12 September 1904.

34   HWS, BV 35, RC diary, 29 January 1904.

35   Pearsall Smith, *A Religious Rebel*, p. 171 (Hannah Whitall Smith to Mary Berenson, 12 November 1904).

36   HWS, BV 36, RC diary, 20 November 1904.

37   As girls were not officially awarded degrees at Cambridge (a situation which continued until 1948), their results were read out in a separate list with indications as to where each girl would have been placed in comparison to the men. No-one at Newnham would ever be allowed to forget the occasion in 1890 when Philippa Fawcett's outstanding results placed her above the Senior Wrangler.

38   HWS, BV 36, RC diary, 7 February 1905.

39   HWS, BV 36, RC diary, 13 April 1905.

Chapter 3: 'Hurrah for Ray':1905–1906:

1   The respective roles of husband and wife as attributed by Ray to the fictional anti-hero of her first novel. *The World at Eighteen*, (London: T. Fisher Unwin, 1907), p. 45.

2   Barbara Strachey, *Remarkable Relations*, p. 196 (quoting Hannah Whitall Smith to Alys Russell, 27 December 1900).

3   WL, 'Life of Ray Strachey'.

4   HWS, BV 34, RC diary, 21 Dec 1902.

5   Barbara Strachey and Jayne Samuels, p. 122 (Mary Berenson to Hannah Whitall Smith, 9 April 1905).

6   HWS, BV 34, RC diary, 25 July 1900 and 26 May 1902.

7   WL, 'Life of Ray Strachey'; HWS, BV 36, RC diary, 5 January 1905.

8   Barbara Strachey, *Remarkable Relations,* p. 231 (quoting Mary Berenson to Hannah Whitall Smith, 24 April 1905).

9   Ibid.

10 HWS, 13, RC to Karin Costelloe, 28 April 1905.

11 Ibid.

12 HWS, BV 36, RC diary, 22 June 1905.

13 Barbara Strachey and Jayne Samuels, p. 123 (Mary Berenson to Hannah Whitall Smith, 24 April 1905).

14 Ibid.

15 Barbara Strachey and Jayne Samuels, p. 122 (Mary Berenson to Hannah Whitall Smith, 24 April 1905).

16 HWS, BV 36, RC diary, 22 May 1905.

17 HWS, BV 36, RC diary, 4 May 1905; *A Quaker Grandmother*, p. 94 (quoting Hannah Whitall Smith to Mary Berenson, 13 June 1904).

18 HWS, BV 36, RC diary, 4 May 1905.

19 Pearsall Smith, *A Religious Rebel*, p. 176 (Hannah Whitall Smith to Mary Berenson, 22 May 1905).

20 HWS, BV 36, RC diary, 1 June 1905.

21 HWS, BV 36, RC diary, 7 June 1905.

22 Ibid.

23 Barbara Strachey and Jayne Samuels, p. 124 (Mary Berenson to Hannah Whitall Smith, 11 June 1905).

24 HWS, BV 36, RC diary, 2 July 1905.

25 Barbara Strachey and Jayne Samuels, p. 124 (Mary Berenson to Hannah Whitall Smith, 30 June 1905).

26 WL, 'Life of Ray Strachey'.

27 HWS, BV 36, RC diary, 9 July 1905.

28 Barbara Strachey, *Remarkable Relations*, p. 232 (quoting Mary Berenson to Bernhard Berenson, 16 August 1905).

29 *The World at Eighteen*, pp. 13, 114, 133 and 134.

30 *The World at Eighteen*, p. 3.

31 *The World at Eighteen*, p. 28.

32 Sarah Grand, *Babs the Impossible* (London: Hutchinson, 1900).

33 Barbara Strachey, *Remarkable Relations*, p. 232 (quoting Mary Berenson to Hannah Whitall Smith, 14 June 1905).

34 Barbara Strachey and Jayne Samuels, p. 128 (Mary Berenson to Hannah Whitall Smith, 23 March 1906).

35 Barbara Strachey and Jayne Samuels, p. 126 (Mary Berenson, diary, 18 December 1905).

36 Barbara Strachey and Jayne Samuels, p. 129 (Mary Berenson to Hannah Whitall Smith, 1 April 1906).

37 HWS, BV 36, RC diary, 21 June 1906.

38 HWS, BV 36, RC diary, 22 June 1906.

39 HWS, BV 36, RC diary, 21 June 1906.

40 Barbara Strachey and Jayne Samuels, p. 124 (Mary Berenson to Hannah Whitall Smith, 20 September 1905).

41 Dunn, *Geoffrey Scott and the Berenson Circle*, p. 26 (quoting Karin Costelloe to Mary Berenson, 18 March 1906).

42 HWS, BV 36, RC diary, 22 June 1906.

43 Bryn Mawr College Special Collections (via Triptych: The Tri-College Digital Library), diary of Mary Whitall Worthington, Volume 11, 11 August 1908.

44 WL, 'Life of Ray Strachey'.

45 HWS, BV 36, RC diary, 8 September 1906.

46 HWS, BV 36, RC diary, 21 June 1906.

47 Ibid.

48 *The Letters of Geoffrey Scott*, ed. by Richard Dunn ([n.p.]: the editor, 2011), eBook (PDF) <http://www.lulu.com/items/volume_28/440000/440306/1/print/440306.pdf > [accessed 12 November 2015] (Geoffrey Scott to Mary Berenson, 15 August [1906]).

49 D. E. Moggridge, *Maynard Keynes: An Economist's Biography* (London: Routledge, 1992), pp.104–5 (quoting John Maynard Keynes to Lytton Strachey, 15 April 1906).

50 Moggridge, pp. 104–5 (quoting John Maynard Keynes to Lytton Strachey, 15 April 1906).

51 HWS, BV 36, RC diary, 8 September 1906.

52 Barbara Strachey and Jayne Samuels, p. 134 (Mary Berenson to Bernhard Berenson, 11 September and 5 August 1906).

53 HWS, BV 36, RC diary, 8 September 1906.

54 WL, 'Life of Ray Strachey'.

55 Ibid.

56 Ibid.

Chapter 4: Embracing the Cause: 1905–1908

1 *The Cause*, p. 304.

2 *The Cause*, p. 6.

3 *The Cause*, p. 303.

4 *The Cause*, pp. 303–4.

5 Lady Margaret Hall Archives, PRI/3/2/1/1.

6   Ibid.

7   Ibid.

8   Barbara Strachey, *Remarkable Relations*, p. 238 (quoting Ray Costelloe to Hannah Whitall Smith, 10 February 1907).

9   HWS, 13, RC to Family, 17 September 1907.

10   Ibid.

11   Ibid.

12   HWS, BV 36, RC diary, 26 September 1907.

13   HWS, 13, RC to Mary Berenson, 20 September 1907.

14   HWS, BV 36, RC diary, 30 September 1907.

15   WL, 'Life of Ray Strachey' (quoting RC to Family, September/October 1907).

16   HWS, BV 36, RC diary, 26 December 1907.

17   HWS, BV 36, RC diary, 17 December 1907.

18   Later known as the Cambridge University Women's Suffrage Society.

19   HWS, BV 36, RC diary, 17 December 1907.

20   Her stepfather, Bernhard Berenson, who had so far overcome his earlier aversion as to find Ray 'a great joy', came to admire the 'detached yet active and exciting quality of her mind', perhaps because she was so different from her over-emotional mother (*The Letters of Bernard Berenson and Isabella Stewart Gardner 1887–1924: With Correspondence by Mary Berenson*, ed. by Rollin Van. N. Hadley (Boston: Northeastern University Press, 1987) p. 466).

21   WL, 'Life of Ray Strachey' (quoting RC to Family, September/October 1907).

22   Ibid.

23   WL, 7BSH/2/2/3, Box 3, RC to M. Carey Thomas, 24 March 1908.

24   Ibid.

25   WL, 7BSH/2/2/3, Box 3, RC to M. Carey Thomas, 7 June 1908.

26   HWS, 13, RC to Mary Berenson, 1 February 1908.

27   Ibid.

28   WL, 7BSH/2/2/3, Box 3, RC to M. Carey Thomas, 24 March 1908.

29   HWS, 13, RC to Family, 16 June 1908.

30   HWS, 13, RC to Mary Berenson, 23 June 1908.

31   HWS, 13, RC to Family, 2 and 3 July 1908; F. E. Rendel and R. Costelloe, 'The Suffrage Caravan', *Newnham College Club Letter 1908*, p. 22.

32   HWS, 17, folder 42, press cutting from *Kendal Mercury & Times*, 17 July 1908.

33   HWS, 13, RC to Family, 10 July 1908.

34   Rendel and Costelloe, 'The Suffrage Caravan', p. 26.

35   HWS, 17, folder 42, press cutting from *Lakes Herald*, 17 July 1908.

36   HWS, 17, folder 42, press cutting from *Westmoreland Gazette*, 18 July 1908.

37   HWS, 13, RC to Family, 17 and 15 July 1908.

38 HWS, 13, RC to Family, 9 July 1908.

39 HWS, 13, RC to Family, 10 July 1908.

40 Ibid.

41 Ibid.

42 HWS, 13, RC to Family, 16 July 1908. Ellie Rendel's sister Betty had joined the group.

43 HWS, 13, RC to Family, 22 July 1908.

44 Ibid.

45 WL, 'Life of Ray Strachey'.

46 Rendel and Costelloe, 'The Suffrage Caravan', p. 27.

Chapter 5: Apprenticeship: 1908–1910

1 Carolyn G. Heilbrun, *Writing a Woman's Life* (London: The Women's Press, 1989), p. 49.

2 HWS, 13, RC to Hannah Whitall Smith, 21 September 1908; HWS, Volume 32, RC diary, [autumn 1908].

3 Schlesinger Library, Radcliffe Institute, Harvard University, Elinor Rendel (henceforward ER) diary, 25 (sc. 26) September 1908.

4 Ibid.

5 HWS, BV 32, RC diary, [autumn 1908].

6 ER diary, 27 [sc. 28] September 1908.

7 Barbara Strachey and Jayne Samuels, p. 147 (Mary Berenson to Bernhard Berenson, 29 September 1908).

8 HWS, BV 32, RC diary, [autumn 1908].

9 ER diary, 28 [sc.29] September 1908; HWS, BV 32, RC diary, [autumn 1908].

10 ER diary, 23 September 1908.

11 HWS, 13, RC to Family, 8 October 1908, referring to Louise Carey, a relative of Carey Thomas and Grace Worthington who later married a radical Socialist.

12 WL, 7BSH/5/1/1/20, Box 8, Ray Costelloe 'Impressions of America' (typescript with manuscript additions), p. 2.

13 'Impressions of America', pp. 4 and 2. As Ray reported, 'A girl may easily, in her four years at college, study English literature and composition, Philosophy, Physics, History, German, and Law, and then specialize for two years in Greek and Mathematics. To get a degree every student must pass an oral examination in French and German, must take the two years required courses in English and Science, must specialize in some group of subjects. Exercise also is compulsary [*sic*], and so many hours a week have to be registered by every student: strangely enough they must also attend classes in the correct spelling and pronunciation of the English language'. 'Impressions of America', p. 2.

14   'Impressions of America', pp. 2–3.

15   'Impressions of America', p. 2.

16   HWS, BV 36, RC diary, [autumn 1908].

17   ER diary, 17 October 1908.

18   MWW diary, 15 November 1908.

19   ER diary, 20 October 1908.

20   HWS, BV 36, RC diary, [autumn 1908].

21   HWS, 13, RC to Family, 26 October 1908; ER diary, 26 October 1908.

22   HWS, 13, RC to Family, 29 October 1908.

23   Ibid.

24   HWS, 13, RC to Family, 31 October 1908.

25   HWS, 13, RC to Family, 31 October and 3 November 1908.

26   HWS, 13, RC to Family, 3 and 1 November 1908.

27   HWS, 13, RC to Family, 5 November 1908.

28   WL, 7BSH/5/2/07, Box 12, press cutting from *Daily News*, Denver, 4 November 1908.

29   HWS, 13, RC to Family, 5 November 1908.

30   HWS, 13, RC to Hannah Whitall Smith, 27 October 1908.

31   HWS, 13, RC to Hannah Whitall Smith, 14 November 1908.

32   HWS, BV 32, RC diary, [autumn 1908].

33   HWS, 13, RC to Hannah Whitall Smith, 11 February 1909.

34   HWS, 13, RC to Hannah Whitall Smith, 25 January 1909.

35   Ibid.

36   Ibid.

37   HWS, 13, RC to Family, 31 December 1908.

38   WL, 7BSH/5/2/6, Box 12, press cutting of Louise Satterthwaite, 'Bryn Mawr Girl is a Suffragette', *Philadelphia Evening Telegraph*, 4 February 1909.

39   Ibid.

40   Ibid.

41   WL, 'Impressions of America', p. 4.

42   HWS, 13, RC to Family, 16 February 1909.

43   HWS, 13, RC to Family, 21 February 1909.

44   Ibid.

45   HWS, 13, RC to M. Carey Thomas, 25 February 1909.

46   WL, 'Life of Ray Strachey'.

47   HWS, 13, RC to Hannah Whitall Smith, 25 January 1909.

48   Jill Liddington, *Rebel Girls: Their Fight for the Vote* (London: Virago, 2006), p. 212, quoting *Common Cause*, 17 June 1909.

49   WL, 7BSH/5/2/9, Box 12, press cutting from *The Woman's Journal*, Boston, 31 July 1909, p. 121, quoting, without date, letter from Ray Costelloe to Anna Shaw.

50   HWS, 13, RC to Hannah Whitall Smith, 1 April 1909.

51   HWS, 13, RC to Family, 21 April 1909.

52   HWS, 13, RC to Mary Berenson, 9 April 1909.

53   HWS, 13, RC to Family, 24 June 1909.

54   WL, 7BSH/5/2/9, Box 12, *Woman's Journal*, Boston, 31 July 1909, p. 121 (quoting, without date, letter from Ray Costelloe to Anna Shaw).

55   Ibid.

56   HWS, BV 37, RC diary, 18 November 1910.

57   HWS, 13, RC to Family, 21 July 1909.

58   Catherine Marshall, 'Open-air Campaign in Cumberland', *Common Cause*, 29 July 1909, p. 207.

59   WL, 7BSH/2/2/3, Box 3, RC to M. Carey Thomas, 25 July 1909.

60   Ibid.

61   HWS, BV 37, RC diary, 24 September 1909.

62   Ibid.

63   HWS, BV 37, RC diary, 29 November 1909.

64   HWS, BV 37, RC diary, 24 September 1909.

65   HWS, BV 37, RC diary, 24 November 1909.

66   WL, 7BSH/2/2/3, Box 3, RC to M. Carey Thomas, 2 May 1909; HWS, BV 37, RC diary, 9 October 1909.

67   HWS, 13, RC to Mary Berenson, 13 October 1909

68   HWS, BV 37, RC diary, 16 October 1909.

69   HWS, BV 37, RC diary, 23 October 1909.

70   WL, 7BSH/2/2/3, Box 3, RC to M. Carey Thomas, 10 February 1910.

71   HWS, 13, RC to Mary Berenson, 29 December 1909.

72   HWS, BV 37, RC diary, 20 August 1910.

73   Ibid.

74   WL, 'Life of Ray Strachey' (quoting Ray Costelloe [to Mary Berenson], 12 January 1910).

75   Ibid.

76   Ibid.

77   Ibid.

78   Ibid.

79   HWS, 13, RC to Mary Berenson, 18 November 1909; 'zoccoli' is Italian for skirting-boards – presumably an error for the singular 'zoccolo'.

80   WL, 7BSH/3/2, Box 4, RC to Alys Russell, 18 February 1910 (transcribed by Barbara Strachey).

81   Later in 1910 Washington State was to be the next success.

82   HWS, BV 37, RC diary, 20 August 1910.

83   Ibid.

84   University of Virginia, Albert and Shirley Small Special Collections Library, Mary Johnston papers (henceforward MJP), RC to Mary Johnston, 4 May 1910.

85   MJP, RC to Mary Johnston, 21 August 1910.

86   HWS, BV 37, RC diary, 20 August 1910.

87   Ibid.

88   Ibid.

89   Ibid.

90   HWS, BV 37, RC diary, 17 October 1910.

91   HWS, BV 37, RC diary, 4 November 1910.

92   WL, 7BSH/3/2, Box 4, RC to Family, 2 December 1910 (transcribed by Barbara Strachey); HWS, BV 37, RC diary, 13 December 1910.

93   HWS, BV 37, RC diary, 13 December 1910.

94   WL, 7BSH/2/2/1, Box 3, RC to Mary Berenson, 14 November 1910.

95   WL, 7BSH/2/2/ 2, Box 3, RC to Family, 21 December 1910.

96   HWS, BV 37, RC diary, 20 August 1910.

97   HWS, BV 37, RC diary, 30 January 1911.

Chapter 6: Ending and Beginning: 1911

1   HWS, BV 36, RC diary, 26 December 1907.

2   WL, 'Life of Ray Strachey' (quoting Ray Costelloe to Mary Berenson, 11 November 1909).

3   Barbara Strachey, *Remarkable Relations*, p. 247, quoting Hannah Whitall Smith to Mary Berenson (on a letter from Karin Costelloe), 20 March 1910.

4   WL, 'Life of Ray Strachey'.

5   Ibid.

6   Ibid.

7   Ibid.

8   The Women's Library @ LSE, 7BSH/3/5/3, Barbara Strachey, 'Full Measure' (henceforward WL, 'Full Measure'), Chapter 5.

9   WL, 'Full Measure', Chapter 5.

10   British Library, Add. MS 60723, Oliver Strachey to Lady Strachey, 7 May 1903 and 16 March 1899.

11   BL, Add. MS 60723, Oliver Strachey to Lady Strachey, 4 September 1907.

12   It later emerged that Indian divorces of persons domiciled in England were not valid, so that, until the British Government in 1926 hastily passed legislation to allow retrospective validation, Oliver's second marriage was bigamous and his second family illegitimate. Ruby's marriage to Hunter in 1910 was no more successful than her marriage to Oliver and

eventually ended in another divorce, after which she married once again. Many years later, she admitted to Oliver that her daughter and four sons all had different fathers.

13 WL, 9/27/C/47, Oliver Strachey to Pippa Strachey, 19 October 1906.

14 Julia Strachey and Frances Partridge, *Julia: A Portrait of Julia Strachey by Herself and Frances Partridge* (London: Penguin, 1984), pp. 29–33. Julia's account is not fully reliable as a record of events, though it doubtless reflects her own emotions. She claims never to have met her Aunt Elinor Rendel before being deposited in her Kensington house in 1907. But it seems unlikely that she never met the Rendel family during the two summers she had already spent in England, when she stayed at least once with her Strachey grandmother nearby: perhaps she was too young to remember such events clearly in later life. More puzzling are Julia's claims to have parted from her mother for good in Rome soon after the birth of her half-brother and to have been taken by Mabel the nursemaid directly to the Rendel family in Kensington. Julia, whose birthday was in August, was five when the baby was born on 30 January 1907, but later claimed 'The Northern winter was coming on when I arrived in London from India. I was just six years old'. It seems likely that she is conflating her parting from her mother in Rome in early 1907 and her arrival to live with the Rendels the following autumn. The intervening months must have been spent in part with her mother and new half-brother when they arrived in England, given that Ruby's letters suggest that she did not decide for some time whether to return from England to India.

15 Julia Strachey and Frances Partridge, *Julia*, pp. 50 and 42.

16 Julia Strachey and Frances Partridge, *Julia*, p. 31.

17 Julia Strachey and Frances Partridge, *Julia*, p. 21.

18 Julia Strachey and Frances Partridge, *Julia*, p. 31–2.

19 Barbara Strachey, *Remarkable Relations*, p. 253 (quoting Bertrand Russell to Ottoline Morrell, 25 March and 2 April 1911).

20 Barbara Strachey, *Remarkable Relations*, p. 253 (quoting Bertrand Russell to Ottoline Morrell, 1 April 1911).

21 Barbara Strachey, *Remarkable Relations*, p. 253 (quoting Bertrand Russell to Ottoline Morrell, 25 March 1911).

22 HWS, 13, RC to Hannah Whitall Smith, 29 March 1911.

23 Barbara Strachey, *Remarkable Relations*, p. 252 (quoting Karin Costelloe to Mary Berenson, 29 March 1911).

24 *The Letters of Virginia Woolf*, I, p. 457 (Virginia Woolf to Vanessa Bell, 6 April 1911).

25 Ibid., p. 456.

26   Ibid., p. 458.

27   Ibid., p. 456.

28   Ibid., p. 457.

29   Ibid., p. 457. Many years later Oliver angered Virginia by claiming that his preference had been for Vanessa.

30   HWS, 13, RC to Family, 16 April 1911.

31   Ibid.

32   *The Diary of Virginia Woolf, Volume IV: 1931–1935*, ed. by Anne Olivier Bell, assisted by Andrew McNeillie (London: Hogarth Press, 1982), p. 66.

33   HWS, 13, RC to Oliver Strachey, 24 April 1911.

34   Ibid.

35   HWS, 13, RC to Mary Berenson, 23 April 1911. David Pye went on to achieve professional eminence as President of the Institute of Mechanical Engineers, but he is equally well known as the biographer of his close friend and mountain climbing partner George Mallory (briefly a lover of James Strachey).

36   HWS, 13, RC to Oliver Strachey, 27 April 1911.

37   HWS, 13, RC to Mary Berenson, 27 April 1911.

38   HWS, 13, RC to Oliver Strachey, 5 May 1911.

39   Ibid.

40   Ibid.

41   Barbara Strachey, *Remarkable Relations*, p. 257 (quoting Mary Berenson to Bernhard Berenson, 8 May 1911); Barbara Strachey and Jayne Samuels, p. 169 (quoting Mary Berenson to Bernhard Berenson, 6 May 1911).

42   HWS, 13, RC to Oliver Strachey, 11 May 1911.

43   Ibid.

44   HWS, BV 37, RC diary, 1 October 1909.

45   Barbara Strachey, *Remarkable Relations*, p. 257 (quoting Karin Costelloe to Mary Berenson, 16 May 1911).

46   Barbara Strachey and Jayne Samuels, p. 170 (quoting Mary Berenson to Bernhard Berenson, 15 May 1911).

47   Barbara Strachey, *Remarkable Relations*, p. 257 (quoting Mary Berenson to Karin Costelloe, 15 May 1911).

48   WL, 'Life of Ray Strachey'.

49   HWS, 13, Oliver Strachey and Ray Costelloe to Karin Costelloe, 18 May 1911.

50   WL, 'Life of Ray Strachey' (quoting Pippa Strachey to Alys Russell, 18 May 1911).

51   WL, 'Life of Ray Strachey' (quoting Karin Costelloe to Mary Berenson, 19 May 1911).

52   WL, 'Life of Ray Strachey' (quoting Alys Russell to Mary Berenson, 28 May 1911).

53   HWS, 13, Oliver Strachey and Ray Costelloe to Karin Costelloe, 18 May 1911.

54   WL, 'Life of Ray Strachey' (quoting Oliver Strachey to Mary Berenson, 30 May 1911).

55   Ibid.

56   HWS, 13, RC to Oliver Strachey, [24 May] 1911.

57   HWS, 13, RC to Oliver Strachey, 22 May 1911.

58   WL, 'Life of Ray Strachey' (quoting, without date, Ray Costelloe to Grace Worthington).

59   Ibid.

60   WL, 'Life of Ray Strachey' (quoting Karin Costelloe to Mary Berenson, 21 May 1911).

61   HWS, 13, RC to Oliver Strachey, 23 May 1911.

62   WL, 7BSH/2/2/5, Ellie Rendel to Ray Costelloe, undated.

63   Barbara Strachey, *Remarkable Relations*, p. 258 (quoting Oliver Strachey to Ray Costelloe, 24 May 1911).

64   HWS, 13, RC to Oliver Strachey, 25 May 1911, and to Mary Berenson, 8 June 1911.

65   WL, 7BSH/2/2/4, RS to Carey Thomas, 14 July 1911.

66   Ibid.

Chapter 7: Mrs Strachey: 1911–1914

1   HWS, 13, RS to Mary Berenson, 3 November 1911.

2   HWS, 13, RS to Family, 26 August 1911.

3   HWS, 13, RS to Grace Worthington, 23 November 1911; RS to Family, 8 November 1911.

4   HWS, 13, RS to Grace Worthington, 23 November 1911; RS to Family, 13 December 1911.

5   HWS, 14, RS to Family, 18 January 1912.

6   HWS, 14, RS to Family, 26 February 1912.

7   HWS, 14, RS to Family, 12 May 1912.

8   HWS, 14, RS to Mary Berenson, 20 May 1912.

9   Ibid.

10   Ibid.

11   Ibid.

12   Julia Strachey and Frances Partridge, *Julia*, p. 51.

13   HWS, BV 38, RS diary, [14] September 1912.

14   Ibid.

15   HWS, BV 38, RS diary, 26 March 1916.

16   HWS, 14, RS to Family, 13 and [before 16] September 1912.

17   HWS, 14, RS to Family, 29 September 1912.

18   HWS, 14, RS to Family, 6 October 1913.

19   HWS, 14, RS to Family, 23 March 1913.

20   HWS, 14, RS to Family, 29 November 1912.

21   HWS, 14, RS to Family, 28 April 1913; RS to Mary Berenson, 2 May 1913.

22   HWS, 14, RS to Family, 16 September 1912.

23   HWS, 14, RS to Family, 4 September 1912.

24   Ibid.

25   HWS, 14, RS to Mary Berenson, 26 October 1912.

26   HWS, 14, RS to Family, 6 October 1913.

27   Julia Strachey and Frances Partridge, *Julia*, p. 45.

28   HWS, 5, Alys Russell to Mary Berenson, 6 January 1912.

29   Ibid.

30   Ibid.

31   HWS, 5, Alys Russell to Mary Berenson, 18 January 1912.

32   HWS, 14, RS to Family, 28 February 1912.

33   Joan Mary Fry (1862–1955), a committed Quaker, later achieved fame for her wartime pacifist activities and post-war relief work in Germany and Wales.

34   HWS, 14, RS to Family, 30 November 1912.

35   Julia's eventual companion was Elizabeth Ponsonby, daughter of Arthur Ponsonby, MP, a family friend.

36   HWS, 14, RS to Mary Berenson, 4 June 1914.

37   UCL, Julia Strachey papers, Alys Russell to Mary Berenson, 26 February 1913.

38   Barbara Strachey and Jayne Samuels, p. 197 (Mary Berenson to Alys Russell, 29 May 1914).

39   Julia Strachey and Frances Partridge, *Julia*, p. 50.

40   HWS, 14, Ray Strachey to Family, 17 March 1913.

41   HWS, 14, Ray Strachey to Family, 12 May 1913.

42   HWS, 14, Ray Strachey to Family, 27 November 1912.

43   Richard Strachey (ed. Simonette Strachey), *A Strachey Boy* (London: Peter Owen, 1980), p. 58-59.

44   HWS, 14, RS to Family, 15 October 1913.

45   HWS, 14, Alys Russell to Ray Strachey, [16 October] 1913 [note at end of Ray's letter to Family of 15 October].

46   HWS, BV 37, RS diary, 23 November 1914.

47   WL, 'Life of Ray Strachey'.

48 HWS, 14, RS to Family, [11 March] 1913.

49 Ray and Oliver Strachey, *Keigwin's Rebellion (1683–4): An Episode in the History of Bombay,* Oxford Historical and Literary Studies, Volume 6 (Oxford: Clarendon Press, 1916).

50 HWS, 14, RS to Family, 25 November 1912.

51 HWS, 14, RS to Family, 30 May 1913.

52 HWS, 14, RS to Family 10 July 1913.

53 HWS, 14, RS to Family, 25 January 1913.

54 HWS, 14, RS to Family, 26 May 1913.

55 HWS, 14, RS to Family, 24 June 1913.

56 Ibid.

57 Carlisle Archive Centre, Catherine E. Marshall Papers (henceforward CEM), RS (as Hon. Secretary, Hampstead Branch) to members of LSWS, [Nov-Dec 1913].

58 HWS, 14, RS to Family, 18 November 1913; HWS, BV 37, RS diary, 23 November 1914.

59 HWS, 14, RS to Oliver Strachey, 20 January 1914.

60 HWS, 14, RS to Oliver Strachey, 22 January 1914.

61 HWS, 14, RS to Oliver Strachey, 29 January 1914.

Chapter 8: Wars and Peace: 1914–1916

1 MJP, Box 6, RS to Mary Johnston, 13 December 1914 [catalogued as 1916].

2 HWS, BV 37, RS diary, 23 November 1914.

3 HWS, BV 38, RS diary, 26 March 1916.

4 Ibid.

5 Ibid.; HWS, 14, RS to Mary Berenson, 7 June 1914.

6 HWS, 14, RS to Mary Berenson, 7 June 1914; HWS, BV 38, RS diary, 26 March 1916.

7 HWS, BV 38, RS diary, 26 March 1916.

8 WL, 7BSH2/2/2, Box 3, Ray Strachey to Family, 6 July 1914.

9 HWS, 14, RS to Family, 29 July 1914.

10 NUWSS, Executive Committee Minutes, 3 August 1914, quoted in David Rubinstein, *A Different World for Women: The Life of Millicent Garrett Fawcett* (Columbus: Ohio State University Press, 1991), p. 213. The resolution echoed a manifesto signed by members of the International Woman Suffrage Alliance (IWSA), including Mrs Fawcett. By chance, the IWSA had arranged to hold a gathering of its senior officers in London in July 1914 to plan a congress in Berlin the following year; some members were still in London when the possibility emerged of British participation in a European war.

11 Sybil Oldfield, *Spinsters of this Parish: The Life and Times of F. M. Mayor and Mary Sheepshanks* (London: Virago: 1984), p. 179.

12 NUWSS, Executive Committee Minutes, 3 August 1914, quoted in Rubinstein, p. 214.

13 *Common Cause*, 7 August 1914, p. 376.

14 HWS, 14, RS to Family, 9 August 1914.

15 BL, Strachey papers (20th century series). Vol. LXXV, Add MS 60729, RS to Lady Strachey, 27 September 1914; HWS, 14, RS to Mary Berenson, 21 September 1914.

16 HWS, 14, RS to Family, 11 August 1914.

17 HWS, 14, RS to Mary Berenson, 25 September 1914.

18 BL, Add MS 60729, RS to Lady Strachey, 27 September 1914.

19 Ibid. The newly-formed MO5, which Oliver joined, was a section of the Directorate of Military Operations until April 1915, when it was upgraded to sub-directorate as 'The Directorate of Special Intelligence', and became a full Directorate of Military Intelligence in January 1916. Brigadier-General Francis J. Anderson, who recruited Oliver, headed MO5(e) (renamed MO6(b) from April 1915 and MI1(b) after January 1916), which dealt with cryptanalysis. Anderson, a retired officer of the Royal Engineers with a longstanding interest in and experience of cryptography, volunteered his expertise and was tasked with deciphering intercepted German wireless messages, aided by 'J. St. Vincent Pletts of Marconi House', 'a young Cambridge scholar called J. D. Crocker', and Oliver, 'all unusually able young men' (quoted in Peter Freeman, 'MI1(b) and the Origins of British Diplomatic Cryptanalysis', *Intelligence and National Security*, 22 (2007)). The source of this assessment, Malcolm Hay, a Scottish landowner severely wounded at Mons, joined them in December 1915 (and eventually replaced Anderson). After a brief honeymoon of close cooperation between military and naval intelligence, the two services went their own way until much later in the War. Inter-service rivalry played a role. The Admiralty's 'Room 40' had the advantage of captured, jealously guarded, codebooks and soon concentrated on naval messages, deciphered for the benefit of the Navy and the Admiralty.

20 HWS, 14, RS to Mary Berenson, 3 October 1914.

21 HWS, 14, RS to Family, 5 October 1914.

22 During 1915 Oliver worked, with considerable success, on American diplomatic codes; the section then moved on to the codes used by Greek, Swiss and Spanish diplomats, complementing naval intelligence work on German diplomatic codes. During 1916 liaison with the Admiralty's Room 40 was re-established, and both organisations worked on a wide range of diplomatic codes; by the end of the war MI1(b) claimed the solution of fifty-

two diplomatic code books and many more systems of encipherment.

23 MJP, Box 6, RS to Mary Johnston, 13 December 1914 [catalogued as 1916].

24 HWS, 14, RS to Family, 11 August 1914; MJP, Box 6, RS to Mary Johnston, 13 December 1914 [catalogued as 1916].

25 MJP, Box 6, RS to Mary Johnston, 13 December 1914 [catalogued as 1916].

26 Ibid.

27 HWS, 14, RS to Mary Berenson, 1 February 1915.

28 HWS, 14, RS to Family, 11 August 1914; RS to Mary Berenson, 11 November and 21 September 1914.

29 HWS, 14, RS to Mary Berenson, 14 November 1914.

30 HWS, 14, RS to Mary Berenson, 10 March 1915.

31 Ibid.

32 WL, Autograph Letter Collection, 9/27/E/96, RS to Pippa Strachey, 26 March 1915.

33 Michael Holroyd, *Lytton Strachey* (London: Virago, 1995), p. 96 (quoting Lytton Strachey to Lady Strachey 13 April 1904); Peter and Leni Gillman, *The Wildest Dream: Mallory, His Life and Conflicting Passions* (London: Headline, 2000), pp. 66–7; *The Letters of Rudyard Kipling Volume 5 1920–30* ed. by Thomas Pinney (Basingstoke: Palgrave Macmillan, 2004), pp. 274–5 (letter to Elsie Bambridge, 14 February 1926).

34 HWS, 14, RS to Mary Berenson, 3 May 1915.

35 Ibid.

36 Ibid.

37 In particular Kathleen Courtney as Honorary Secretary, Catherine Marshall as Honorary Parliamentary Secretary, and Maude Royden, from April 1913 editor of the NUWSS newspaper.

38 HWS, 14, RS to Oliver Strachey, 29 Jan 1914.

39 Ibid.

40 WL, Autograph Letter Collection, 9/27/E/92, RS to Pippa Strachey, 14 July 1914.

41 'Dame Millicent Fawcett', *Manchester Guardian*, 5 August 1929.

42 HWS, 14, RS to Mary Berenson, 7 December 1914.

43 MJP, Box 6, RS to Mary Johnston, 13 December 1914 [catalogued as 1916].

44 Carlisle Archive Centre, CEM, DMAR/ 3/ 44, 'Questions to be addressed to Candidates for Election to the National Union Executive Committee, Feb. 1915', attached to letter from Ray Strachey to 'Dear Madam', 31 December 1914.

45 Carlisle, CEM, DMAR/ 3/ 44, Oliver Strachey's election address, undated [January 1915].

46 Ibid.

47   HWS, 14, RS to Mary Berenson, 1 and 5 February 1915.

48   HWS, 14, RS to Mary Berenson, 6 February 1915.

49   WL, Autograph Letter Collection, 9/27/E/95, RS to Pippa Strachey, 12 March 1915.

50   HWS, 14, RS to Mary Berenson, 21 April 1915.

51   HWS, 14, RS to Alys Russell, 29 April 1915.

52   Ibid.

53   Ibid.

54   WL, 7BSH/5/3/1/12, Box 13, RS to Millicent Fawcett, 18 February 1918.

55   HWS, 14, RS to Mary Berenson, 20 May 1915.

56   HWS, 14, RS to Mary Berenson, 20 June 1915.

57   HWS, 14, RS to Mary Berenson, 28 June 1915.

58   HWS, 14, RS to Family, 16 October 1915.

59   HWS, 14, RS to Family, 7 December 1915.

60   HWS, 14, RS to Mary Berenson, 28 March 1916.

61   Ibid.

62   HWS, 14, RS to Mary Berenson, 3 July 1915.

63   HWS, 14, RS to Family, 7 December 1915.

64   Ibid.

65   WL, 7BSH5/2/11a, Box 12, unsigned and undated manuscript note on typed letter from Ray Strachey to members of the Executive Committee of the NUWSS, 1 November 1915.

66   HWS, 14, RS to Family, 7 December 1915.

Chapter 9: Triumph! 1916–1918

1   *The Cause*, p. 354, quoting *Observer*, 13 August 1916, p. 6.

2   HWS, 14, RS to Mary Berenson, 19 July 1916.

3   Ibid.

4   Harvard University Center for Italian Renaissance Studies, Florence (Italy), Villa I Tatti, Berenson Library, RS to Family, 7 July 1916.

5   HWS, 14, RS to Family, 22 June 1916.

6   Ibid.

7   HWS, 14, RS to Mary Berenson, 9 January 1916; RS to Alys Russell, 16 March 1916.

8   HWS, 14, RS to Mary Berenson, 9 January 1916.

9   HWS, 14, RS to Family, 11 June 1916.

10   Ibid.

11   HWS, 14, RS to Mary Berenson, 9 May and 22 August 1916.

12   HWS, 2, Oliver Strachey to RS, postmarked 6 October 1916.

13   HWS, 14, RS to Mary Berenson, 26 September 1916.

14   HWS, 14, RS to Oliver Strachey, 18 October [sc. November] 1916.

15   HWS, 14, RS to Oliver Strachey, 20 November 1916.

16   *The Times*, 15 August 1916, p. 10.

17   HWS, 14, RS to Family, 12 August 1916.

18   WL, 7BSH/5/3/1, RS to Millicent Fawcett, 16 August 1916.

19   HWS, 14, RS to Family, 15 August 1916.

20   HWS, 14, RS to Mary Berenson, 8 December 1916.

21   HWS, 14, RS to Mary Berenson, 26 February 1917.

22   Probably 'National Civilian Service', *The Times*, 29 January 1917, p. 7.

23   HWS, 14, RS to Oliver Strachey, 2 February 1917.

24   HWS, 14, RS to Mary Berenson, 7 January 1917.

25   HWS, 14, RS to Mary Berenson, 13 January 1917.

26   Ibid.

27   HWS, 14, RS to Mary Berenson, 26 January 1917.

28   Ibid.

29   *The Cause*, p. 357.

30   HWS, 14, RS to Oliver Strachey, 2 February 1917.

31   WL, 'Life of Ray Strachey' (quoting Alys Russell to Mary Berenson, 3
      February 1917).

32   Ibid.

33   HWS, 14, RS to Oliver Strachey, 2 February 1917.

34   HWS, 14, RS to Mary Berenson, 4 February 1917.

35   Ibid.

36   WL, 'Life of Ray Strachey' (quoting Alys Russell to Mary Berenson, 16
      February 1917).

37   HWS, 14, RS to Mary Berenson, 25 March 1917.

38   HWS, 14, RS to Mary Berenson, 7 January 1917.

39   HWS, 14, RS to Mary Berenson, 1 April 1917.

40   Ibid.

41   HWS, 14, RS to Mary Berenson, 5 April and 9 May 1917.

42   'Representation of the People Bill', *The Times,* 19 June 1918, p. 4.

43   *The Cause*, p. 361.

44   *The Cause*, p. 362.

45   HWS, 14, RS to Family, 14 August 1917.

46   HWS, 14, RS to Family, 1 November 1917.

47   HWS, 14, RS to Family, 23 December 1917.

48   Ibid.

49   HWS, 14, RS to Family, 24 January 1918; Millicent Garrett Fawcett, *What I
      Remember* (London: T. Fisher Unwin Ltd, 1924), p. 245.

50 HWS, 14, RS to Family, 11 February 1918.

51 Ibid.

52 Ibid.

53 Ibid.

Chapter 10: Aftermath: 1918–1920

1 HWS, 15, RS to Barbara Strachey, 22 December 1932.

2 HWS, 14, RS to Family, 3 November 1918.

3 Berenson replaced the Germanic 'Bernhard' by the English 'Bernard' during the war.

4 Ray Strachey, 'The New Paris', *Daily Express*, 21 March 1919, p. 3.

5 WL, 7BSH/5/3/1/13, Box 13, RS to Millicent Fawcett, 20 April 1918; HWS, 14, RS to Alys Russell, 11 April 1918.

6 WL, 7BSH/5/3/1/13, Box 13, RS to Millicent Fawcett, 20 April 1918.

7 HWS, 14, RS to Family, 22 April 1918.

8 BL, Add MSS 60729, RS to Pippa Strachey, 12 April 1918.

9 WL, 'Life of Ray Strachey'.

10 Carlisle, CEM, DMAR/ 3/ 44, Oliver Strachey's election address, undated [January 1915].

11 BL, Add MSS 60723, Oliver Strachey to Lytton Strachey, 18 January 1906.

12 HWS, 2, Oliver Strachey to RS, [April] 1918.

13 HWS, 14, RS to Mary Berenson, 22 January 1915.

14 HWS, 14, RS to Mary Berenson, 14 April 1917.

15 Ibid.

16 The external shareholders were Oliver, Maynard Keynes, Saxon Sydney-Turner and Harry Norton. Carrington's friend Barbara Hiles, like her a former student of the Slade School of Art, volunteered to act as the scheme's treasurer.

17 BL, Add MSS 60723, Oliver Strachey to Lytton Strachey, 16 May 1918. When Virginia Woolf met Inez in November 1918, she was not impressed: 'Oliver's young lady has a thin, disagreeable face' (to Vanessa Bell [13 November 1918]). Her opinion had not changed a few months later: 'Inez is a pert young professional, by no means of the seductive kind, I should have thought; and ill spaced, indeed rather vulgar looking and splotchy in the face' (to Vanessa Bell [16 April 1919]). Inez had 'more wits than Barbara', Virginia thought – perhaps a hint that Oliver had been interested in Barbara Hiles before her marriage in February 1918 to Nick Bagenal – but even though Virginia later conceded that Inez was 'amiable' (to Vanessa Bell, 7 June [1928]), she never seems to have become popular in Bloomsbury circles (*The Letters of Virginia*

Woolf, ed. by Nigel Nicolson and Joanne Trautmann, 6 vols (London: Hogarth Press,1975–1980), II *The Question of Things Happening: 1912-1922*, (1976), pp. 292 and 348; III *A Change of Perspective: 1923-1928* (1977), p. 509).

18 HWS, 2, Oliver Strachey to RS, [16 August 1918].

19 Ibid.

20 Ibid.

21 *A Quaker Grandmother*, p. 28.

22 HWS, 2, Oliver Strachey to RS, [16 August 1918].

23 WL, 7BSH/5/3/1/01, Box 13, RS to Millicent Fawcett, 8 August 1918.

24 WL, 7BSH/5/3/1/14, Box 13, RS to Millicent Fawcett, 15 August 1918.

25 WL, Autograph Letter Collection, 9/27/E/97, RS to Pippa Strachey, 22 August 1918.

26 Ibid. Dame (since 1917) Katharine Furse (1875–1952), daughter of John Addington Symonds and widow of the painter Charles Furse, had been a senior nursing administrator during the war, then director of the newly-formed Women's Royal Naval Service; Katharine Stewart-Murray (1874–1960), Duchess of Atholl since 1917, had for many years been a prominent public figure and Conservative politician (mainly in Scotland), and an anti-suffragist; Dame (since 1917) Edith Lyttelton (1865–1948), widow of Liberal Unionist MP Alfred Lyttelton, was an author, suffragist, imperialist, social reformer and public administrator, with a particular interest in women's employment and a growing commitment to spiritualism.

27 WL, Autograph Letter Collection, 9/27/E/97, RS to Pippa Strachey, 22 August 1918.

28 BL, Add MSS 60723, Oliver Strachey to Lytton Strachey, 28 January 1919.

29 *The Letters of Virginia Woolf*, II, pp. 357–8 (to Vanessa Bell, [18 May 1919]).

30 Postcard to Margaret Llewellyn Davies postmarked 31 August 1915 quoted by Quentin Bell in *Virginia Woolf: A Biography Volume Two: Mrs Woolf 1912-1941* (London: Hogarth Press, 1972), p. 29.

31 *The Letters of Virginia Woolf*, II, pp. 357 (to Vanessa Bell, [18 May 1919]).

32 HWS, 14, RS to Family, 23 October 1918.

33 WL, 7BSH/5/2/13, Box 12, typescript copy of letter from H.A. L. Fisher to RS, 7 November 1918.

34 WL, 7BSH/5/2/13, Box 12, typescript copy of letter from Millicent Garrett Fawcett to Selection Committee, 6 November 1918.

35 WL, 7BSH/5/2/13, Box 12, typescript copy of letter from F. D. Acland to RS [November 1918].

36 HWS, 14, RS to Family, 20 November 1918.

37 HWS, 14, RS to Family, 25 November 1918.

38 Ibid.

39 Imperial War Museum, London, Women at Work Collection [henceforward IWM, WW], Mrs Oliver Strachey's election address, 22 November 1918, S. and P. 14, 10/7.

40 IWM, WW, S. and P. 14, 10/1 and 10/3.

41 HWS, 14, attachment to letter from RS to Family, 3 November 1918.

42 WL, 'Life of Ray Strachey'. Ray's views may have been influenced by her friend Maynard Keynes.

43 *Daily Mail*, 13 December 1918, p. 6.

44 Quoted derisively in Ray's election literature, IWM, S. and P.14, 10/7.

45 HWS, 14, RS to Mary Berenson, 2 January 1919.

46 HWS, 14, RS to Mary Berenson, 1 April 1919. The Government Code and Cypher School was the forerunner of the Government Communications Headquarters (GCHQ).

47 *The Letters of Virginia Woolf*, II, p. 349 (to Vanessa Bell, 16 April 1919).

48 HWS, 14, RS to Mary Berenson, 7 October 1919.

49 HWS, 14, RS to Mary Berenson, 30 January 1922.

50 HWS, 14, RS to Mary Berenson, 8 December 1921 and 30 January 1922.

51 HWS, 14, RS to Mary Berenson, [7] November and 4 October 1921.

52 The economic boost from the ending of the war was short-lived; by the end of 1920 the country faced major financial problems, accompanied by frequent strikes and increasing unemployment.

53 HWS, 14, RS to Mary Berenson, 5 April 1919.

54 Ray Strachey, 'Women and the Industries of the Future', *Common Cause*, 6 June 1919, p. 84.

55 HWS, 14, RS to Family, 2 February 1918.

56 HWS, 14, RS to Family, 24 January 1918.

57 Ibid.

58 Ibid.

59 HWS, 14, RS to Mary Berenson, [July] 1919.

60 HWS, 14, RS to Mary Berenson, 6 June 1919.

61 Ibid.

62 Ibid.

63 'Restoration of Pre-War Practices Bill', *Common Cause*, 6 June 1919, p. 84.

64 Ray Strachey, 'Women and the Industries of the Future', *Common Cause*, 6 June 1919, p. 84.

65 Report of NUWSS Council Meeting, *Common Cause*, 22 March 1918, p. 660.

66 WL, 7BSH/5/3/1/14, Box 13, RS to Millicent Fawcett, 15 August 1918.

67 'Schemes for the Future of the N.U.W.S.S.', *Common Cause*, 21 February 1919, pp. 546–7 (547).

68 HWS, 14, RS to Mary Berenson, 10 March 1919.

69   Ibid.

70   HWS, 14, RS to Mary Berenson, 3 October 1919.

71   HWS, 14, RS to Mary Berenson, 31 October 1919.

72   HWS, 14, RS to Mary Berenson, 7 October 1919.

73   HWS, 14, RS to Mary Berenson, 19 October 1919.

74   HWS, 14, RS to Mary Berenson, 7 October 1919.

75   HWS, 14, RS to Mary Berenson, 6 November 1919.

76   HWS, 14, RS to Mary Berenson, 20 November 1919.

77   Ibid.

78   Ibid.

79   HWS, 14, RS to Mary Berenson, 1 December 1919.

80   Ibid.

81   HWS, 14, to Mary Berenson, [28] February 1920. Nancy's biographer,
      Christopher Sykes, suggested that 'The interior evidence, especially from the
      excellent balance of her early House of Commons speeches, and the only
      occasional appearance of blemishes typical of her, indicates Waldorf's strong
      directing hand' (Christopher Sykes, *Nancy: The Life of Lady Astor* (London:
      Collins, 1972), p. 213). It is perhaps more likely that Ray, as she had intended,
      wrote many of the speeches delivered by Lady Astor in her first months in
      Parliament, which established Nancy as a force to be reckoned with, maverick
      though she remained.

82   HWS, 14, RS to Mary Berenson, 20 November 1919.

83   WL, 7BSH/5/1/1/20, Box 8, 'Lady Astor M.P. and Her Constituency', undated
      MS. [1923].

84   HWS, 14, RS to Mary Berenson, 14 February 1920. In his newspaper *John
      Bull*, Horatio Bottomley (then influential but later imprisoned for fraud)
      made vicious and largely inaccurate attacks on Nancy Astor's conduct during
      and honesty about her divorce from her first husband.

85   HWS, 14, RS to Mary Berenson, 16 June 1920.

Chapter 11: 'A Reckless Woman': 1920–1923

1   HWS, 14, RS to Mary Berenson, 24 May 1920.

2   HWS, 14, RS to Alys Russell, [15] and 13 April 1920.

3   HWS, 14, RS to Mary Berenson, 24 May 1920.

4   Neither Ray nor her friends appear to have played a physical part in the
      original construction of Copse Cottage (the Mud House), nor in its various
      extensions. Ray's later bricklaying activities produced a cottage known as
      Rookhanger down the slope from the main house (so badly built it was later
      condemned by the Local Authority and totally rebuilt on the same site) and a

further cottage unfinished at Ray's death and known locally as 'the Ruin'.

5   HWS, 14, RS to Mary Berenson, 15 January 1921.

6   HWS, 14, RS to Mary Berenson, 29 September 1920.

7   HWS, 14, RS to Mary Berenson, 15 September 1920.

8   HWS, 14, RS to Mary Berenson, 26 October 1920.

9   HWS, 14, RS to Mary Berenson, 12 December 1920.

10   HWS, 14, RS to Bernard Berenson, 18 December 1920.

11   HWS, 14, RS to Bernard Berenson, 5 October 1921.

12   HWS, 14, RS to Mary Berenson, 30 May 1921.

13   HWS, 14, RS to Bernard Berenson, 18 February 1922.

14   HWS, 14, RS to Mary Berenson, 5 March 1922.

15   WL, 7BSH/5/3/1/12, Box 13, RS to Millicent Fawcett, 18 February 1918.

16   Ibid.

17   'B. F. C. Costelloe – 1855–1899', *Schoolmaster*, 30 December 1899, p. 1219.

18   HWS, BV 39, RS diary, 27 September 1926.

19   Michael Bentley, 'Liberal Politics and the Grey Conspiracy of 1921', *Historical Journal*, 20 (1977), 461–478 (462) (quoting Cecil to J. A. Spender 30 August 1921).

20   HWS, 14, RS to Bernard Berenson, 18 February 1922.

21   Ibid.

22   Ibid.

23   Ibid.

24   The Centre Party project eventually foundered on Grey's reluctance to be drawn back into politics, Asquith's unwillingness to cede the Liberal leadership to him, and the broader divide between those like Cecil who saw a Centre Party as a means of uniting progressive thinkers from across the political spectrum and Liberals who saw it as a way of revitalising the Liberal Party by capturing Lord Robert Cecil from the Conservatives.

25   Ray Strachey, *Millicent Garrett Fawcett*, (London: John Murray, 1931), p. 331.

26   HWS, 14, RS to Mary Berenson, 26 June 1921.

27   HWS, 14, RS to Mary Berenson, 8 December 1921.

28   HWS, BV 39, RS diary, 27 September 1926.

29   HWS, 14, RS to Bernard Berenson, 15 May 1921.

30   HWS, 14, RS to Mary Berenson, 14 December 1921.

31   HWS, 14, RS to Mary Berenson, 17 July 1922.

32   HWS, 14, RS to Mary Berenson, 14 September 1922. In *The Dissociation of a Personality* (1906), the American psychologist Morton Prince described a case of multiple personality disorder in one of his patients, referring to one of the woman's personalities as Sally; the name was habitually used in the Pearsall Smith family to denote outspokenness and self-confidence in public appearances.

33   WL, 7BHS/5/2/17, Box 12, RS election letter to voters of Brentford and
     Chiswick, 27 October 1922.

34   Ibid.

35   Ibid.

36   Ibid.

37   Ibid.

38   WL. 7BSH/2/2/1 Box 3, RS to Mary Berenson, 26 October 1922.

39   HWS, 14, RS to Family, 15 March 1923.

40   HWS, 14, RS to Bernard Berenson, 6 March 1923.

41   WL, 'Life of Ray Strachey' (quoting Grace Worthington to Mary Berenson,
     16 February 1923).

42   WL, 'Life of Ray Strachey' (quoting Helen Flexner to Mary Berenson, 15
     February 1923).

43   HWS, 14,RS to Family, 15 February 1923.

44   HWS, 14, RS to Family, 1 March 1923.

45   HWS, 14, RS to Family, 15 March 1923.

46   HWS, 14, RS to Family, 8 April 1923.

47   WL, 7BSH/5/2/15, Box 12, collage of US press comment on Ray with
     manuscript additions by her agent G. Arnold Shaw, spring 1923.

48   HWS, 14, RS to Family, 8 April 1923.

49   HWS, 14, RS to Family, 5 February 1923; Viscount Cecil of Chelwood, *All
     The Way* (London: Hodder and Stoughton, 1949), p. 176.

50   HWS, 14, RS to Mary Berenson, 15 March 1923.

51   HWS, 14, RS to Family, 15 March 1923.

52   HWS, 14, RS to Family, 5 April 1923.

53   HWS, 14, RS to Family, 30 March 1923. Henry Ford (1863–1947), the
     industrialist, and William Borah (1865–1940), a Republican Senator, both
     strongly influenced public opinion.

54   HWS, 14, RS to Family, 30 March 1923.

55   HWS, 14, RS to Mary Berenson, 23 April 1923.

56   HWS, 14, RS to Family, 13 April 1923.

57   Cecil, *All The Way*, p. 176.

58   Cecil, *All The Way*, p. 178.

59   Cecil, *All The Way*, p. 177.

60   HWS, 14, RS to Family, 24 February 1918.

61   HWS, 14, RS to Family, 13 April 1923.

62   HWS, 14, RS to Mary Berenson, 5 May 1923.

63   HWS, BV 39, RS diary, 27 September 1926.

64   Ibid.

65   HWS, BV 39, RS diary, 25 [July] 1924.

66   Ibid.

67   HWS, 14, RS to Mary Berenson, 19 June 1923.

68   WL, 'Life of Ray Strachey'.

69   *Marching On* (New York: Harcourt Brace and London: Cape, 1923).

70   Anna Shaw died in 1919.

71   Isabel Paterson, *New York Tribune,* 7 October 1923, p 22.

72   HWS, 14, RS to Mary Berenson, 17 September 1923.

73   HWS, 14, RS to Mary Berenson, 20 September 1923.

74   Ibid.

75   HWS, BV 39, RS diary, 27 September 1926.

76   HWS, 14, RS to Barbara Strachey, 30 November 1923.

77   Ibid.

Chapter 12: A Mother's Place? 1924–1930

1   *Our Freedom and Its Results by Five Women: Eleanor F. Rathbone, Erna Reiss, Ray Strachey, Alison Neilans, Mary Agnes Hamilton,* ed. by Ray Strachey (London: Hogarth Press, 1936), p. 10.

2   HWS, BV 39, RS diary, 27 September 1926.

3   Ibid.

4   HWS, 14, RS to Mary Berenson, 28 February 1924.

5   HWS, 14, RS to Mary Berenson, 7 March 1924. 'Grunching' is an old Scottish word meaning grumbling or resentful.

6   HWS, BV 39, RS diary, 25 May 1925.

7   HWS, BV 39, RS diary, [before 24] March 1924.

8   HWS, BV 39, RS diary, 24 March 1924.

9   HWS, 14, RS to Mary Berenson, 8 April 1924.

10   *Diary of Virginia Woolf, Volume II 1920-1924*, ed. by Anne Olivier Bell assisted by Andrew McNeillie, (London: Hogarth Press, 1978), p. 324 (entry for 13 December 1924).

11   Julia Strachey and Frances Partridge, *Julia*, p.14.

12   Julia Strachey and Frances Partridge, *Julia*, p. 12.

13   WL, 'Full Measure', Chapter 6.

14   HWS, 14, RS to Mary Berenson, 8 October 1924.

15   HWS, 14, RS to Mary Berenson, 25 October 1925.

16   HWS, 14, RS to Mary Berenson, 3 November 1925.

17   HWS, 14, RS to Mary Berenson, 8 April 1924 and 6 November 1925.

18   HWS, BV 39, RS diary, 27 September 1926.

19   Ibid.

20   Ibid.

21   Ibid.

22   HWS, 14, RS to Mary Berenson, 11 October 1926.

23   HWS, 14, RS to Mary Berenson, 7 December 1926.

24   HWS, 14, RS to Mary Berenson, 8 July 1927.

25   Ibid.

26   WL, 'Full Measure', Chapter 3.

27   HWS, 14, RS to Mary Berenson, 26 February 1924.

28   WL, 'Full Measure', Chapter 2.

29   Ibid.

30   WL, 'Full Measure', Chapter 4.

31   HWS, 14, RS to Mary Berenson, 17 and 11 February 1924.

32   HWS, 14, RS to Mary Berenson, 11 February 1924.

33   HWS, 14, RS to Mary Berenson, 10 February 1924.

34   HWS, 14, RS to Mary Berenson, 6 July 1926.

35   HWS, BV 39, RS diary, 27 September 1926.

36   HWS, 14, RS to Mary Berenson, 7 January 1925.

37   HWS, 14, RS to Mary Berenson, 20 May 1923.

38   HWS, 14, RS to Mary Berenson, 10 March 1924.

39   HWS, BV 39, RS diary, [25 July] 1924.

40   HWS, 14, RS to Mary Berenson, 6 October 1925.

41   HWS, BV 39, RS diary, 19 October 1926.

42   HWS, 14, RS to Mary Berenson, 30 November 1926.

43   HWS, 14, RS to Mary Berenson, 21 December 1927.

44   HWS, 14, RS to Mary Berenson, 8 March 1927.

45   Barbara Strachey, *Remarkable Relations*, p. 284; HWS, 14, RS to Mary
     Berenson, 15 December and 26 February 1924.

46   HWS, 14, RS to Mary Berenson, 26 February 1924.

47   After Ray's marriage, Ellie undertook medical training. During the war she
     worked in Serbia with the Scottish Women's Hospital Unit and afterwards, as
     a doctor in private practice, had many of the Bloomsbury circle among her
     patients.

48   *Bloomsbury/Freud: The Letters of James and Alix Strachey 1924–1925*, ed. by
     Perry Maisel and Walter Kendrick, (London: Chatto & Windus, 1986), pp.
     142-3 (letter of 9 December 1924).

49   HWS, 14, RS to Mary Berenson, 3 November 1924.

50   Ibid.

51   Ibid.

52   HWS, 14, RS to Mary Berenson, 3 June 1925.

53   HWS, 14, RS to Mary Berenson, 9 March 1924.

54   HWS, 14, RS to Mary Berenson, 24 November 1925.

55   HWS, 14, RS to Mary Berenson, 9 December 1925.

56   HWS, 14, RS to Alys Russell, 4 February 1924.

57   WL, 'Full Measure', Chapter 5.

58   HWS, 14, RS to Mary Berenson, 22 September 1925.

59   HWS, 14, RS to Mary Berenson, 9 March 1924.

60   HWS, 14, RS to Mary Berenson, 9 and 24 March 1924.

61   UCL, Julia Strachey papers: James Strachey to Julia Strachey, postmarked 27 May 1929.

62   HWS, 14, RS to Mary Berenson, 8 January 1927.

63   HWS, 14, RS to Mary Berenson, 8 January 1928.

64   HWS, 14, RS to Mary Berenson, 4 May 1926; HWS, BV 39, RS diary, 31 January 1927.

65   HWS, 14, RS to Mary Berenson, 19 May 1927.

66   WL, 'Full Measure', Chapter 7.

67   HWS, 14, RS to Barbara Strachey, 16 June 1927.

68   HWS, 14, RS to Mary Berenson, 18 January 1928.

69   WL, 7BSH/3/1/1, Box 4, Barbara Strachey to RS, undated [from Oxford].

70   HWS, 14, RS to Mary Berenson, 18 January 1928.

71   WL, 7BSH/3/1/1, Box 4, note by Irene Hancock on undated letter from Barbara Strachey to RS.

72   WL, 'Life of Ray Strachey'; HWS, BV 39, RS diary, 2 June 1929.

73   HWS, 14, RS to Barbara Strachey, 4 February 1929.

74   HWS, 14, RS to Mary Berenson, 25 June 1929.

75   Ibid.

76   HWS, 14, RS to Mary Berenson, 15 June 1929.

77   HWS, 14, RS to Mary Berenson, [December 1929].

78   WL, 7 BSH/3/1/2, Box 4, Barbara Strachey to RS, 25, 27 and 30 October 1929.

79   HWS, 14, RS to Barbara Strachey, 28 October 1929.

80   Ibid.

81   Ibid.

82   HWS, 14, RS to Barbara Strachey, 21 November 1929.

83   HWS, 14, RS to Barbara Strachey, 19 February 1930.

84   HWS, 14, RS to Mary Berenson, 24 February 1930; RS to Barbara Strachey, 22 January 1930.

85   HWS, 14, RS to Christopher Strachey, 5 June 1930.

86   HWS, BV 39, RS diary, 1 January 1931; WL, 'Life of Ray Strachey'.

87   HWS, BV 39, RS diary, 1 January 1931.

88   HWS, 14, RS to Mary Berenson, 12 January 1931.

89   Ibid.

90   HWS, 14, RS to Mary Berenson, 31 March and 28 April 1931.

91   HWS, 14, RS to Barbara Strachey, 23 October 1929.

92   HWS, BV 39, RS diary, 27 September 1926 and 30 January 1927.

93   HWS, 14, RS to Mary Berenson, 2 January 1928.

94   HWS, BV 39, RS diary, [before 24] March 1924.

95   HWS, BV 39, RS diary, 27 September 1931.

96   HWS, BV 39, RS diary, [before 24] March 1924.

97   HWS, BV 39, RS diary, 24 March 1924.

98   Ibid.

99   HWS, BV 39, RS diary, 27 September 1926.

100   HWS, BV 39, RS diary, 31 May 1929.

101   Ibid.

102   Ibid.

103   Ibid.

104   Ibid.

105   Ibid.

106   HWS, 14, RS to Mary Berenson, 15 June 1928.

107   Ray Strachey, ed., *Religious Fanaticism: Extracts from the Papers of Hannah Whitall Smith* (London: Faber & Gwyer, 1928).

108   HWS, BV 39, RS diary, 31 May 1929.

109   HWS, 14, RS to Mary Berenson, 7 December 1928.

110   WL, 8SUF/B/186, Barbara Halpern interviewed by Brian Harrison, 18 August 1979.

111   HWS, 14, RS to Mary Berenson, 26 February 1929.

112   HWS, BV 39, RS diary, 31 May 1929.

113   Ibid.

Chapter 13: Fame without Fortune 1927–1931

1   HWS, BV 39, RS diary, 27 September 1926.

2   WL, 8SUF/B/129, Irene Hilton interviewed by Brian Harrison, 24 February 1977.

3   WL, 'Full Measure', Chapter 1.

4   Ibid.

5   HWS, BV 39, RS diary, [before 24] March 1924.

6   HWS, BV 39, RS diary, 30 and 25 July 1924.

7   HWS, BV 39, RS diary, 25 July 1924.

8   HWS, BV 39, RS diary, 30 July 1924.

9   Quoted in HWS, 14, RS to Mary Berenson, 26 April 1925.

10   Faber & Gwyer had already accepted *Midnight*, a detective story to which Ray made a major contribution. Oliver's youngest sister Marjorie Strachey,

Adrian Stephen and his wife Karin, Ray's sister, discussed the plot and wrote alternate chapters, then Ray added 10,000 words to pull the whole work into shape. The pseudonym the four authors adopted, Mark Strange, included an acronym of their Christian names.

11 L. P. Hartley, 'New Fiction', *Saturday Review*, 22 Oct 1927, p. 555.

12 *Shaken by the Wind: A Story of Fanaticism* (London: Faber & Gwyer, 1927).

13 *Shaken by the Wind*, p. 185.

14 *Shaken by the Wind*, pp. 118 and 147.

15 HWS, 14, RS to Mary Berenson, 13 November 1924.

16 HWS, 14, RS to Mary Berenson, 1 December 1925; HWS, BV 39, RS diary, 27 September 1926.

17 HWS, BV 39, RS diary, 26 March 1924.

18 *Women's Suffrage and Women's Service: The History of the London and National Society for Women's Service* (London: London and National Society for Women's Service, 1927); HWS, BV 39, diary, 19 October 1926.

19 HWS, 14, RS to Mary Berenson, 22 May 1927.

20 HWS, 14, RS to Mary Berenson, 12, 27 and 31 May 1927.

21 WL, 7BSH/5/3/1/17, Box 13, RS to Millicent Garrett Fawcett, 10 March 1927.

22 *The Cause*, p. 384.

23 HWS, 14, RS to Mary Berenson, 24 March 1924.

24 Ibid.

25 HWS, BV 39, RS diary, 30 November 1926.

26 Ibid.

27 HWS, BV 39, RS diary, 30 January 1927.

28 HWS, BV 39, RS diary, 5 December 1927.

29 Ibid.

30 Ibid.

31 Ibid. Ida O'Malley proved magnanimous in the end (and eventually wrote a balanced though not uncritical review); the friendship recovered.

32 HWS, BV 39, RS diary, 31 May 1929.

33 HWS, 14, RS to Mary Berenson, 8 January 1928.

34 HWS, 14, RS to Mary Berenson, 29 March 1928.

35 HWS, 14, RS to Mary Berenson, 11 November 1928; RS to Alys Russell, 23 October 1928; Lady Rhondda, 'A New Light on Florence Nightingale', *Time & Tide*, 19 October 1928, pp. 274 and 276.

36 HWS, 14. RS to Mary Berenson, 20 and 29 January 1929.

37 *The Cause*, p. 4 (new preface to 1978 edition by Barbara Strachey).

38 *The Cause*, p. 110.

39 *The Cause*, p. 274. The examples Ray cited included John Stuart Mill; the Cambridge professors who gave up their time to teach and examine women

students; William Booth, whose Salvation Army did not discriminate between the sexes; tried friends of the women's movement like Lord Robert Cecil, Arthur Henderson and David Lloyd George; and former opponents who had the courage to change their minds, like F. D. Maurice over the admission of women to the medical profession and the Contagious Diseases Acts and Walter Long on suffrage.

40   *The Cause*, p. 361.

41   *The Cause*, p. 6.

42   *The Cause*, pp. 305, 303, 304, 306-7.

43   *The Cause*, p. 97.

44   *The Cause*, p. 211.

45   *The Cause*, p. 96.

46   HWS, BV 39, RS diary, 26 March 1924; *The Cause*, pp. 33, 78 and 278.

47   *The Cause*, pp. 41, 85 and 228.

48   *The Cause*, p. 272.

49   *The Cause*, p. 340.

50   BL, Add MS 60729, RS to Pippa Strachey, 18 February 1928.

51   *The Cause*, pp. 315 and 333.

52   *The Cause*, pp. 309, 327 and 313.

53   *The Cause*, p. 311.

54   WL, 7BSH/2/2/4, Box 3, RS to M. Carey Thomas, 2 January 1928.

55   *The Cause*, p. 273, 216 and 307.

56   *The Cause*, p. 214.

57   HWS, 14, RS to Barbara Strachey, 8 July 1931.

58   *The Cause*, pp. 386 and 70–1.

59   *The Cause*, p. 204.

60   *The Cause*, pp. 304 and 390.

61   *The Cause*, p. 390.

62   'Battle of the Ladies', *Sunday Times*, 21 October 1928, p. 10.

63   HWS, 14, RS to Mary Berenson, 26 February 1926.

64   HWS, 14, RS to Mary Berenson, 7 February 1929.

65   Ibid.

66   HWS, 14, RS to Mary Berenson, 16 October 1930.

67   Ibid.

68   HWS, 14, RS to Mary Berenson, 10 June 1930.

69   The female Commissioners were the Duchess of Atholl, Mrs Margaret Wintringham, Mrs Mary Agnes Hamilton, Mrs Ayrton Gould and Mrs E.M. Lowe.

70   HWS, 14, RS to Mary Berenson, 21 December 1927.

71   WL, 7BSH/2/2/4, Box 3, RS to M. Carey Thomas, 3 April 1929.

72   Ibid.

73   HWS, 14, RS to Mary Berenson, 13 February 1929.

74   WL, 7BSH/2/2/4, Box 3, RS to M. Carey Thomas, 3 April 1929. In the early days of radio, broadcasts were live, and scripts had to be approved in advance.

75   WL, 7BSH/5/1/2/3, Box 9, script of broadcast given 10 January 1931.

76   WL, 7BSH/5/1/2/3, Box 9, script of broadcast given 31 January 1931.

77   WL, 7BSH/5/1/2/3, Box 9, script of broadcast given 10 January 1931.

78   WL, 7BSH/5/1/2/3, Box 9, script of broadcast given 24 January 1931.

79   WL, 7BSH/5/1/1/11/16, Box 7, Gladys M. Sunderland to RS, 17 February 1931.

80   HWS, 14, RS to Christopher Strachey, 2 November 1931.

81   HWS, 14, RS to Mary Berenson, 2 January 1931 sc. 1932.

82   Ibid.

83   Kate Murphy, *Behind the Wireless: A History of Early Women at the BBC* (London: Palgrave Macmillan, 2016), p. 240.

84   HWS, 14, RS to Mary Berenson, 10 August 1929.

85   HWS, 14, RS to Mary Berenson, 5 February 1930.

86   HWS, 14, RS to Mary Berenson, 17 February 1930.

87   HWS, 14, RS to Mary Berenson, 24 October 1930.

88   HWS, 14, RS to Mary Berenson, 4 November 1930.

89   HWS, 14, RS to Mary Berenson, 27 December 1930.

90   HWS, BV 39, RS diary, 1 January 1931.

91   HWS, 14, RS to Mary Berenson, 29 December 1930.

92   HWS, 14, RS to Mary Berenson, 2 and 12 January 1931.

93   HWS, BV 39, RS diary, 27 September 1931.

94   Ibid.

95   David Rubinstein, *A Different World for Women: The Life of Millicent Garrett Fawcett* (Columbus: Ohio State University Press, 1991), pp. 18 and xi.

96   HWS, BV 39, RS diary, 1 January 1931.

97   *Millicent Garrett Fawcett* (London: John Murray, 1931), p. 103.

98   *Millicent Garrett Fawcett*, p. 159.

99   *Millicent Garrett Fawcett*, p. 19.

100   HWS, 14, RS to Mary Berenson, 5 January 1928.

101   HWS, 14, RS to Mary Berenson, 7 February 1930.

102   HWS, 14, RS to Mary Berenson, 7 and 19 February 1930; RS to Bernard Berenson, 11 February 1930.

103   According to Ursula's brother Dick, their mother 'felt that love, like everything else, should be kept within conventional limits [...] Naturally one loved one's husband and children. It went without saying. And so it went without feeling' (BL, Add. MS 61730, Richard P. F. Strachey, 'The Story of My Life', 2, p. 140).

104 HWS, BV 39, RS diary, 1 January 1931.

105 Ibid.

106 HWS, 14, RS to Mary Berenson, 17 February 1930.

107 HWS, 14, RS to Mary Berenson, 9 December 1930.

108 HWS, 14, RS to Mary Berenson, 15 July 1931.

109 HWS, 14, RS to Mary Berenson, 3 August 1931.

110 HWS, 14, RS to Mary Berenson, 7 September 1931.

111 HWS, 14, RS to Mary Berenson, 26 September 1931.

112 HWS, 14, RS to Christopher Strachey, 20 September 1931.

113 HWS, 14, RS to Christopher Strachey, 26 September 1931.

114 HWS, BV 39, RS diary, 27 September 1931.

115 HWS, 14, RS to Alys Russell, 28 May 1929; RS to Mary Berenson, 10 July 1929.

116 HWS, 14, RS to Mary Berenson, 3 October 1931.

117 Ibid.

118 HWS, 14, RS to Mary Berenson, 20 September 1931.

119 HWS, BV 39, RS diary, 27 September 1931; WL, 7BSH/2/1, Box 3, manuscript note dated 28 September 1931.

120 WL, 7BSH/2/1, Box 3, manuscript note dated 28 September 1931.

121 HWS, 14, RS to Mary Berenson, 30 September 1931.

122 HWS, 14, RS to Mary Berenson, 14 October 1931.

123 Ibid.; HWS, BV 39, RS diary, 10 November 1931.

124 HWS, BV 39, RS diary, 10 November 1931.

125 Ibid.

126 Ibid.

127 Ibid.

128 Ibid.

Chapter 14: Hard Times: 1931–1935

1   HWS, 15, RS to Mary Berenson, 13 July 1932.

2   HWS, 14, RS to Barbara Strachey, 19 November 1931.

3   HWS, 14, RS to Mary Berenson, 13 November 1931.

4   HWS, 14, RS to Mary Berenson, 8 December 1931.

5   HWS, BV 39, RS diary, 27 May 1932.

6   HWS, 14, RS to Mary Berenson, 25 November 1931.

7   HWS, BV 39, RS diary, 27 May 1932.

8   Ibid.

9   Ibid.

10   Ibid.

11   Ibid.

12   Ibid.

13   Ibid.

14   Ibid.

15   Ibid.

16   Ibid.

17   Ibid.

18   HWS, 15, RS to Mary Berenson, 3 April 1931. The Anti-Slavery Society
      eventually sent the novelist Graham Greene to Sierra Leone and Liberia in
      1936. His long inland trek, the subject of his *Journey Without Maps*, would
      have been far beyond Ray's physical capacities.

19   WL, 7BSH/5/1/3/3, RS to Mr Higham, 8 April 1931.

20   HWS, 15, RS to Mary Berenson, 26 May 1932.

21   WL, 'Life of Ray Strachey'.

22   HWS, 15, RS to Mary Berenson, 15 June 1933.

23   Ibid.

24   HWS, 15, RS to Christopher Strachey, 16 March 1934.

25   WL, 7BSH/5/1/12, Box 7.

26   HWS, 15, RS to Christopher Strachey, 8 November 1932.

27   HWS, 15, RS to Barbara Strachey, 20 September 1932.

28   HWS, 15, RS to Mary Berenson, 28 July 1933.

29   HWS, 15, RS to Mary Berenson, 25 January 1934.

30   HWS, 15, RS to Mary Berenson, 6 February 1934.

31   HWS, 15, RS to Christopher Strachey, 29 September 1932.

32   HWS, 15, RS to Christopher Strachey, 11 May 1933; to Barbara Strachey, 16
      May 1933.

33   HWS, 15, RS to Christopher Strachey, 18 May 1933.

34   HWS, 15, RS to Christopher Strachey, 3 March 1933.

35   HWS, 15, RS to Christopher Strachey, 8 February 1934; to Mary Berenson, 31
      January 1934.

36   HWS, 15, RS to Mary Berenson, 31 January 1934.

37   Hansard, Vol. 285, c. 1534, House of Commons Debate, 9 February
      1934, Second Reading of Hotels and Restaurants Bill < http://hansard.
      millbanksystems.com/commons/1934/feb/09/hotels-and-restaurants-bill>
      [accessed 14 January 2016].

38   HWS, 15, RS to Mary Berenson, 14 February 1934.

39   'Lady Astor and the Hotels Bill', *Times*, 12 February 1934, p. 13.

40   HWS, 15, RS to Mary Berenson, 14 February 1934.

41   Ibid.

42   HWS, 15, RS to Mary Berenson, 16 February 1934.

43   HWS, 15, RS to Mary Berenson, 26 April 1934.

44   WL, 'Full Measure', Chapter 8.

45   Ibid.

46   WL, 'Full Measure', Chapter 9.

47   HWS, 15, RS to Barbara Strachey, 18 October 1932.

48   Ibid.

49   HWS, 15, RS to Mary Berenson, 29 November 1932.

50   Ibid.

51   HWS, 15, RS to Barbara Strachey, 22 December 1932.

52   Ibid.

53   HWS, 15, RS to Mary Berenson, 14 January 1933.

54   HWS, 15, RS to Christopher Strachey, 10 February 1933.

55   HWS, 15, RS to Barbara Strachey, 12 February 1933.

56   HWS, 15, RS to Mary Berenson, 11 April 1933.

57   Ibid.

58   Ibid.

59   HWS, 15, RS to Mary Berenson, 20 June 1933.

60   Ibid.

61   HWS, 15, RS to Mary Berenson, 30 August 1933.

62   WL, 7BSH/3/1/3, Box 4, Barbara Strachey to RS, 31 December 1933 (quoting Ray's earlier advice back to her); HWS, 15, RS to Mary Berenson, 30 August 1933.

63   HWS, 15, RS to Barbara Strachey, 12 September 1933.

64   Ibid.

65   HWS, 15, RS to Christopher Strachey, 13 November 1933; to Barbara Strachey, 19 November 1933.

66   HWS, 15, RS to Christopher Strachey, 13 November 1933.

67   HWS, 15, RS to Mary Berenson, 10 January 1933.

68   HWS, 15, RS to Barbara Strachey, 21 November 1933.

69   HWS, 15, RS to Mary Berenson, 27 November 1933.

70   HWS, 15, RS to Mary Berenson, 8 January 1934; to Alys Russell, 10 January 1934.

71   HWS, 15, RS to Mary Berenson, 11 January 1934 (quoting Barbara's cable).

72   HWS, 15, RS to Barbara Strachey, 10 January 1934.

73   HWS, 15, RS to Mary Berenson, 11 January 1934.

74   HWS, 15, RS to Barbara Strachey, 10 January 1934.

75   Ibid.

76   Ibid.

77   Ibid.

78   HWS, 15, RS to Mary Berenson, 10 January 1934.

79   HWS, 15, RS to Mary Berenson, cable 13 January 1934.

80   HWS, 15, RS to Mary Berenson, 14 January 1934.

81   Ibid.

82   Ibid.

83   Ibid.

84   HWS, 15, RS to Mary Berenson, 15 January 1934.

85   HWS, 15, RS to Mary Berenson, 17 January 1934 .

86   HWS, 15, RS to Christopher Strachey, 27 February 1934.

87   HWS, 15, RS to Christopher Strachey, 23 January 1934.

88   Ibid.

89   Ibid.

90   HWS, 15, RS to Mary Berenson, 6 March 1934.

91   HWS, 15, RS to Christopher Strachey, 4 March 1934.

92   Ibid. When Tommy became seriously ill in 1937, Julia and Oliver spent days
       at his hospital bedside before his death.

93   HWS, 15, RS to Barbara Hultin, 7 March 1934.

94   HWS, 15, RS to Mary Berenson, 8 February 1934.

95   HWS, 15, RS to Mary Berenson, 28 January 1934.

96   HWS, 15, RS to Christopher Strachey, 28 January 1934.

97   Ibid.

98   HWS, 15, RS to Mary Berenson, 2 February 1934.

99   HWS, 15, RS to Mary Berenson, 23 February 1934.

100   HWS, 15, RS to Mary Berenson, 21 March 1934.

101   WL, 7BSH/3/1/3, Box 4, Barbara Strachey to RS, 31 December 1933.

102   HWS, 15, RS to Mary Berenson, 21 March 1934.

103   HWS, 15, RS to Barbara Hultin, 19 April 1934.

104   HWS, 15, RS to Mary Berenson, 19 April 1934.

105   WL, 'Full Measure', Chapter 12.

106   Ibid.

107   Ibid.

108   HWS, 15, RS to Christopher Strachey, 28 September 1934.

109   HWS, 15, RS to Alys Russell, 16 August 1934.

110   HWS, 15, RS to Christopher Strachey, 9 October 1934.

111   Ibid.

112   HWS, 15, RS to Christopher Strachey, 28 September 1934.

113   Ibid.

114   Ibid.

115   Ibid.

116   HWS, 15, RS to Christopher Strachey, 2 October 1934.

117   HWS, BV 39, RS diary, 3 December 1935.

118   HWS, 15, RS to Mary Berenson, 22 [sc. 23] October 1934.

119   HWS, BV 39, RS diary, 3 December 1935.

120   HWS, 15, RS to Christopher Strachey, 15 November 1934.

121   HWS, 15, RS to Christopher Strachey, 21 November 1934.

122   WL, 'Full Measure', Chapter 12.

123   HWS, 15, RS to Christopher Strachey, 29 November 1934.

124   HWS, BV 39, RS diary, 3 December 1935.

Chapter 15: Keeping Calm and Carrying On: 1935–1940

1   National Records of Scotland, papers of the Carnegie (United Kingdom) Trust (henceforward Carnegie), GD281/82/139: Agenda Item 10 for meeting of Executive Committee, Carnegie (UK) Trust, 9 December 1938 (Report from Executive Committee, WEF, signed by G. M. Jebb, Chairman).

2   *Careers and Openings for Women: A Survey of Women's Employment and a Guide for those Seeking Work* (London: Faber and Faber, 1935); HWS, BV 39, RS diary, 3 December 1935.

3   'Changes in Employment' in *Our Freedom and Its Results*, pp. 117–172.

4   *Careers and Openings for Women*, pp. 52 and 50.

5   *Careers and Openings for Women*, p. 57.

6   *Careers and Openings for Women*, p. 101.

7   *Careers and Openings for Women*, pp. 143–44.

8   *Our Freedom and Its Results*, p. 124.

9   *Careers and Openings for Women*, p. 80.

10   *Careers and Openings for Women*, p. 82.

11   HWS, 15, RS to Mary Berenson, 16 December 1932.

12   A note by Colonel J. M. Mitchell of an interview with Ray on 25 October 1935 claims that Ray was among the malcontents and resigned with them, but her private letters strongly suggest that she was not, or was no longer, connected to the Central Bureau during the rebellion. Perhaps a misunderstanding?

13   Carnegie, GD281/82/138, RS to Colonel Mitchell, 29 October 1935.

14   WL, 6CFW/F/2/01, Box 8 (WEF information leaflet). WEF's main activities were maintaining an up-to-date centre of information on women's employment; publishing and distributing advisory material; advising schools, universities and individuals about employment possibilities, training, grants and loans, and other sources of advice; providing specific advice on career choice to individuals, by interview or correspondence; operating a Joint Placing Register so that employers with vacancies at £300 a year and above could be offered lists of suitable candidates; co-ordinating Loan Funds for training; and fostering Insurance schemes specifically designed for working women.

15   WL, 8SUF/B/141, Irene Hilton interviewed by Brian Harrison, 23 March 1977.

16   HWS, 15, RS to Christopher Strachey, 21 June 1935.

17   HWS, 15, RS to Mary Berenson, 14 May 1936.

18   Mary Agnes Hamilton, *Remembering My Good Friends,* (London: Jonathan Cape, 1944), p. 276.

19   HWS, 15, RS to Christopher Strachey, 5 May 1937.

20   WL, 8SUF/B/129, Irene Hilton interviewed by Brian Harrison, 24 February 1977.

21   Ibid.

22   Ibid.

23   Mary Agnes Hamilton, *Remembering My Good Friends*, p. 276.

24   WL, 8SUF/B/129, Irene Hilton interviewed by Brian Harrison, 24 February 1977, quoting Helen Darbishire, Principal of Somerville College, Oxford.

25   HWS, 15, RS to Mary Berenson, 23 April 1936.

26   Virginia Woolf, *Three Guineas* (London: Hogarth Press, 1938); repr. in *Selected Works of Virginia Woolf* (Ware: Wordsworth Editions, 2005), p. 812.

27   WL, 7BSH/2/3/1, RS to Virginia Woolf, 4 June 1938.

28   Ibid.

29   HWS, 15, RS to Christopher Strachey, 1 November 1932; to Barbara Strachey, 19 November 1933.

30   HWS, 15, RS to Barbara Strachey, 19 November 1933.

31   'My Independence –and Your Socialism: A Woman's View', *Reynolds's Illustrated News*, 26 January 1936, p.2.

32   HWS, 15, RS to Mary Berenson, 7 December 1936.

33   HWS, 15, RS to Christopher Strachey, 19 May 1938.

34   HWS, 15, RS to Mary Berenson, 17 November 1938.

35   Carnegie, GD281/82/138, Second Report of WEF to Carnegie Trustees, attached to RS to Colonel Mitchell, 1 November 1937.

36   Carnegie, GD281/82/139, RS to Colonel Mitchell, 12 December 1938; HWS, 15, RS to Mary Berenson, 15 December 1938.

37   HWS, 15, RS to Mary Berenson, 2 February 1939.

38   HWS, 15, RS to Mary Berenson, 8 March 1939.

39   HWS, 15, RS to Mary Berenson, 29 March 1939.

40   HWS, 15, RS to Mary Berenson, 30 April 1939.

41   HWS, 15, RS to Mary Berenson, 19 April 1939.

42   HWS, 15, RS to Mary Berenson, 30 April 1939.

43   WL, 8SUF/B/141, Irene Hilton interviewed by Brian Harrison, 23 March 1977.

44   HWS, 15, RS to Christopher Strachey, 8 March 1935.

45   WL, 'Full Measure', Chapter 12.

46   HWS, 15, RS to Christopher Strachey, 4 February 1935.

47   WL, 7BSH/3/1/3, Box 4, Barbara Hultin to RS, 6 March 1935.

48   WL, 7BSH/3/1/3, Box 4, Barbara Hultin to RS, 9 March 1935.

49   WL, 'Full Measure', Chapter 12.

50   HWS, 15, RS to Christopher Strachey, 31 January 1935.

51   HWS, 15, RS to Barbara Hultin, 31 March 1935.

52   Ibid.

53   HWS, 15, RS to Mary Berenson, 3 December 1935.

54   HWS, 15, RS to Christopher Strachey, 16 July 1937.

55   HWS, 15, RS to Mary Berenson, 17 November 1938.

56   HWS, 15, RS to Christopher Strachey, 15 November 1937.

57   HWS, 15, RS to Mary Berenson, 30 January 1939.

58   HWS, 15, RS to Christopher Strachey, 7 November 1938.

59   HWS, 15, RS to Mary Berenson, 31 January 1936.

60   Mary Agnes Hamilton, *Remembering My Good Friends*, p, 269.

61   HWS, 15, RS to Christopher Strachey, 29 May 1937; to Mary Berenson, 27 May 1937.

62   HWS, 15, RS to Christopher Strachey, 29 May 1937.

63   HWS, 15, RS to Christopher Strachey, 25 May 1937.

64   HWS, 15, RS to Christopher Strachey, 31 May 1937; to Mary Berenson, 27 March 1939.

65   HWS, 15, RS to Christopher Strachey, 27 August 1936.

66   HWS, 15, RS to Christopher Strachey, 14 July, 27 and 12 October 1936.

67   BL Add MS 81956, RS to Pippa Strachey, 29 September 1938.

68   WL, 'Life of Ray Strachey'.

69   HWS, 15, RS to Mary Berenson, 16 February 1937.

70   HWS, 15, RS to Christopher Strachey, 25 April 1938.

71   HWS, 15, RS to Christopher Strachey, 19 May 1938.

72   HWS, 15, RS to Mary Berenson, 3 and 5 October 1938.

73   HWS, 15, RS to Bernard Berenson, 11 September 1939; to Mary Berenson, 3 April 1940.

74   HWS, 15, RS to Mary Berenson, 15 April 1940.

75   HWS, 15, RS to Mary Berenson, 24 November 1939.

76   HWS, 15, RS to Mary Berenson, 11 January 1940.

77   HWS, 15, RS to Mary Berenson, 21 February 1940.

78   HWS, 15, RS to Mary Berenson, 7 February 1940.

79   Ibid.

80   'Women and the War Effort', *The Times*, 15 February 1940, p. 9.

81   WL, 6WEF/07/18, Box FL494, RS to Ellen Wilkinson, 17 February 1940.

82   HWS, 15, RS to Mary Berenson, 25 May 1940.

83   HWS, 15, RS to Mary Berenson, 10 April 1940.

84   HWS, 15, RS to Mary Berenson, 18 June 1940.

85   HWS, 15, RS to Mary Berenson, 1 June 1940.

86   Harrison, *Prudent Revolutionaries,* p. 178.

87   HWS, 15, RS to Christopher Strachey, 3 July 1940.

88   Ibid.

89   Ibid.

90   HWS, BV 39, RS diary, 27 September 1926.

91   HWS, 15, RS to Christopher Strachey, 3 July 1940.

92   Ibid.

93   HWS, 15, RS to Mary Berenson, 5 July 1940.

Epilogue

1   Nesca A. Robb, *An Ulsterwoman in England 1924–1941* (Cambridge: Cambridge University Press, 1942), p. 96.

2   University of Reading Special Collections, Nancy Astor Papers, MS 1416/1/1/1685, Barbara Halpern to Nancy Astor, 29 July 1940.

3   HWS, 8, Alys Russell to Mary Berenson, 23 July 1940; ibid., Alys Russell to Mrs Shapley, 30 July 1940; HWS, 5, Mary Berenson to Lina Waterfield, 29 July 1940; HWS, 2, Dorothy Bussy to Mary Berenson, 15 November 1940.

4   HWS, 5, Mary Berenson to Lina Waterfield, 29 July 1940.

5   HWS, 8, Alys Russell to Mary Berenson, 30 July 1940.

6   Robb, p. 95.

7   WL, 'Life of Ray Strachey'. The originals of many of the letters referred to by Mary Berenson appear to have been lost, probably victims of wartime bombing.

8   Nancy Astor, 'Mrs Oliver Strachey: An Appreciation', *The Times*, 1 August 1940, p. 7.

9   Ibid.

10   WL 7BSH/5/2/2, Box 11, transcript of 'Mrs Strachey (A broadcast by Mrs Mary Agnes Hamilton, at 1.55 on Thursday July 25, 1940, in the Home Service programme "Calling All Women.")'; WL, 7BSH/3/3, Box 5, M.A.H. [Mary Agnes Hamilton] 'Rachel Conn Strachey' (Newnham College booklet, [early 1941]), p. 7.

11   Hamilton, 'Rachel Conn Strachey', p. 4.

12   Hamilton, transcript of 'Mrs Strachey'.

13   Ibid.

14   *The Diary of Virginia Woolf,* ed. Anne Olivier Bell, Volume Five: 1936–1941

(San Diego: Harcourt Brace Jovanovich, 1984), entry for 24 July 1940, p. 304.

15 Ibid., p. 305.

16 Ibid.

17 Ray Strachey, 'What Women Still Want', *Spectator*, 20 July 1934, pp. 81–82. WEF became the National Advisory Centre on Careers for Women in 1971, then Careers for Women in 1991.

18 WL, 'Life of Ray Strachey' (quoting RC to Mary Berenson, 29 December 1909).

SELECT BIBLIOGRAPHY

ARCHIVES

The major archival sources relating to Ray Strachey are:

in the Lilly Library at the Bloomington campus of Indiana University, the Hannah Whitall Smith Collection; in the Women's Library @ LSE, the Autograph Collection, the Strachey Family papers, the papers of the National Union of Women's Suffrage Societies, the London Society for Women's Suffrage and its successors and the Women's Employment Federation, and oral evidence on the suffragette and suffragist movements (the Brian Harrison interviews); in the British Library, the Strachey papers, Richard Strachey's Autobiography and India Office Records and Private Papers; Ray Strachey's paintings and family photograph albums held by the National Portrait Gallery, London; Berenson family correspondence and photographs held by Harvard University Center for Italian Renaissance Studies, Florence (Italy), in the Berenson Library, Villa I Tatti; papers of the Carnegie (United Kingdom) Trust in the National Records of Scotland, Edinburgh; Bryn Mawr College Special Collections, which include the diary of Mary Whitall Worthington; the Catherine E. Marshall papers at Carlisle Archive Centre; Elinor Rendel's diary held by the Schlesinger Library, Radcliffe Institute, Harvard University; Lynda Grier's papers in the Lady Margaret Hall Archives, Oxford; Mary Agnes Hamilton's diaries in the Churchill Archives Centre, Cambridge; the Women at Work Collection in the Imperial War Museum, London; in the National Archives, Kew, Chancery records and evidence to the Royal Commission on the Civil Service (1929–30); Newnham College Archives, Cambridge; the records of Kensington High School at the Institute of Education, University College London; the papers of Julia Strachey in University College London, Special Collections, Strachey papers; the papers of Nancy Astor held by University of Reading, Special Collections; and the papers of Mary Johnston in the Albert and Shirley Small Special Collections, University of Virginia Library, Charlottesville.

WORKS BY RAY STRACHEY

Fiction
(as Ray Costelloe)

The World at Eighteen (London: T. Fisher Unwin, 1907)

(as Ray Strachey)

Marching On (London: Cape, 1923)

Midnight (London: Faber & Gwyer, 1927) (written with Karin Stephen, Adrian
Stephen and Marjorie Strachey, under the joint pseudonym Mark Strange)

Shaken by the Wind: A Story of Fanaticism (London: Faber & Gwyer, 1927)

Biographies
Frances Willard: Her Life and Work (London: T. Fisher Unwin, 1912)

Millicent Garrett Fawcett (London: John Murray, 1931)

A Quaker Grandmother: Hannah Whitall Smith (New York: Fleming H. Revell, 1914)

Women's Movement
*Careers and Openings for Women: A Survey of Women's Employment and a Guide for
those seeking Work* (London: Faber & Faber, 1935)

The Cause: A Short History of the Women's Movement in Great Britain (London: G.
Bell, 1928; repr. Virago, 1978)

Chronological List of leading Events in the Women's Movement in Great Britain
(Leiden: Internationaal Archief voor de Vrouwenbeweging, 1938)

(ed.) *Our Freedom and Its Results by Five Women: Eleanor F. Rathbone, Erna Reiss,
Ray Strachey, Alison Neilans, Mary Agnes Hamilton* (London: Hogarth Press,
1936)

*Women's Suffrage and Women's Service: The History of the London and National
Society for Women's Service* (London: London and National Society for Women's
Service, 1927)

Other
(with Oliver Strachey) *Keigwin's Rebellion (1683–4): An Episode in the History of
Bombay*, Oxford Historical and Literary Studies, Volume 6 (Oxford: Clarendon,
1916; repr. Charleston: BiblioLife, [2010])

(ed.) *Religious Fanaticism: Extracts from the Papers of Hannah Whitall Smith*
(London: Faber & Gwyer, 1928); repr. as *Group Movements of the Past and
Experiments in Guidance* (London: Faber and Faber, 1934)

The Unemployed and the Children: Emergency Open-Air Nurseries (London: The
Emergency Open-Air Nurseries Committee, [n.d.])

SECONDARY WORKS, BOOKS AND BOOKLETS

The Costelloe, Pearsall Smith and Strachey families

Berenson, Bernard, *Rumor and Reflection: 1941–1944* (London: Constable, [1952])

—— *Sketch for a Self-Portrait* (London: Constable, [1949])

—— *Sunset and Twilight: From the Diaries of 1947–1958* ed. by Nicky Mariano (London: Hamish Hamilton, 1964)

Caine, Barbara, *Bombay to Bloomsbury: A Biography of the Strachey Family* (Oxford: Oxford University Press, 2005)

Cohen, Rachel, *Bernard Berenson: A Life in the Picture Trade* (New Haven: Yale University Press, 2013)

Flexner, Helen Thomas, *A Quaker Childhood* (New Haven: Yale University Press, 1940)

Flexner, James Thomas, *An American Saga: The Story of Helen Thomas and Simon Flexner* (Boston: Little, Brown,1984)

Griffin, Nicholas, ed., *The Selected Letters of Bertrand Russell*, 2 vols, (London: Routledge, 1992–2001) II *The Public Years 1914–1970*)

Hadley, Rollin van N., ed., *The Letters of Bernard Berenson and Isabella Stewart Gardener, 1887–1924, with correspondence by Mary Berenson* (Boston: Northeastern University Press, 1987)

Holroyd, Michael, *Lytton Strachey* (London: Chatto & Windus, 1994)

Horowitz, Helen Lefkowitz, *The Power and Passion of M. Carey Thomas* (New York: Alfred A. Knopf, 1994)

Levy, Paul, and Penelope Marcus, eds, *The Letters of Lytton Strachey* (London: Viking, 2005)

McComb, A. K., ed., *The Selected Letters of Bernard Berenson* (London: Hutchinson, 1965)

MacGibbon, Jean, *There's the Lighthouse: A Biography of Adrian Stephen* (London: James & James, 1997)

Monk, Ray, *Bertrand Russell*, 2 vols, (London: Cape, 1996–2000) I *The Spirit of Solitude*

Moorehead, Caroline, *Bertrand Russell: A Life* (London: Sinclair-Stevenson, 1992)

Russell, Bertrand, *The Autobiography of Bertrand Russell*, 3 vols (London: Allen and Unwin, 1967–69) I *1872–1914*

Samuels, Ernest, *Bernard Berenson: The Making of a Connoisseur* (Cambridge, MA., and London: Harvard University, 1979)

——with the collaboration of Jayne Newcomer Samuels, *Bernard Berenson: The Making of a Legend* (Cambridge, MA., and London: Harvard University, 1987)

Secrest, Meryle, *Being Bernard Berenson: A Biography* (Harmondsworth: Penguin, 1980)

Smith, Hannah Whitall, *Child Culture: Or The Science of Motherhood*, 3rd edn (New York: Fleming H. Revell, 1899; repr. LaVergne, TN: Kessinger Publishing, 2011)

Smith, Logan Pearsall, ed., *A Religious Rebel: The Letters of "H.W.S."* (*Mrs Pearsall Smith*) (London: Nisbet, 1949)

—— *Unforgotten Years* (London: Constable, 1938)

Strachey, Barbara, *Remarkable Relations: The Story of the Pearsall Smith Family* (London: Gollancz, 1980)

—— and Jayne Samuels, eds, *Mary Berenson: A Self-Portrait from her Letters & Diaries* (London: Gollancz, 1983)

Strachey, Julia, and Frances Partridge, *Julia: A Portrait of Julia Strachey by Herself and Frances Partridge* (London: Gollancz, 1983; Harmondsworth: Penguin, 1984)

Strachey, Richard, *A Strachey Boy* (London: Peter Owen, 1980)

—— *A Strachey Child* (Oxford: Simonette Strachey, 1979)

Weaver, William, *A Legacy of Excellence: The Story of Villa I Tatti* (New York: Harry N. Abrams, 1997)

Biography, Autobiography, Memoirs, Letters

Bell, Anne Olivier, ed., *The Diary of Virginia Woolf*, 5 vols, I *1915–19* (London: Hogarth Press, 1977; Harmondsworth: Penguin, 1979); II *1920–1924* (London: Hogarth Press, 1978); III *1925–1930* (London: Hogarth Press, 1980); IV *1931–1935* (London: Hogarth Press, 1982); V *1936–1941* (London: Hogarth Press; San Diego: Harcourt Brace Jovanovich, 1984)

Bell, Quentin, *Bloomsbury* (London: Weidenfeld & Nicolson, 1986)

——*Virginia Woolf: A Biography*, 2 vols (London: Hogarth Press, 1972), II *Mrs Woolf 1912–1941*

Berry, Paul, and Mark Bostridge, *Vera Brittain: A Life* (London: Chatto & Windus, 1995)

Brittain, Vera, *Testament of Youth: An Autobiographical Study of the Years 1900–1925*, (London: Gollancz, 1933; Virago, 1978, 2004)

Carney, Michael, *Stoker: The Life of Hilda Matheson OBE 1888–1940* (Llangynog: the author, 1999)

Cecil, Viscount, of Chelwood, *All the Way* (London: Hodder and Stoughton, 1949)

Cella, C. Ronald, *Mary Johnston* (Boston: Twayne Publishers, 1981)

Chisholm, Anne, *Frances Partridge: The Biography* (London: Weidenfeld & Nicolson, 2009)

Clarke, Ethne, *An Infinity of Graces: Cecil Ross Pinsent, an English Architect in the Italian Landscape* (New York: W. W. Norton, 2013)

Davenport-Hines, Richard, *Universal Man: The Seven Lives of John Maynard Keynes* (London: William Collins, 2015)

Dunn, Richard M., *Geoffrey Scott and the Berenson Circle* (Lewiston: Edwin Mellen, 1998)

——, ed., *The Letters of Geoffrey Scott* ([n.p.]: the editor, 2011), eBook (PDF) <http://www.lulu.com/shop/richard-dunn/the-letters-of-geoffrey-scott/ebook/product-17528757.html> [accessed 12 November 2015]

Eoff, Shirley M., *Viscountess Rhondda: Equalitarian Feminist* (Columbus: Ohio State University Press, 1991)

Fawcett, Millicent Garrett, *The Women's Victory – and After: Personal Reminiscences 1911–1918* (London: Sidgwick & Jackson, 1920)

—— *What I Remember* (London: T. Fisher Unwin, [1924])

Fernhurst Society, The, *Voices of Fernhurst* (Fernhurst: The Fernhurst Society, 2006)

Fort, Adrian, *Nancy: The Story of Lady Astor* (London: Cape, 2012)

Hamilton, Mary Agnes, *Remembering My Good Friends* (London: Cape, 1944)

—— *Sidney and Beatrice Webb: A Study in Contemporary Biography* (London: Sampson Low, Marston, 1932)

—— *Up-hill All the Way: A Third Cheer for Democracy* (London: Cape, 1953)

Hession, Charles H., *John Maynard Keynes: A Personal Biography of the Man Who Revolutionized Capitalism and the Way We Live* (London: Collier Macmillan, 1984)

John, Angela V., *Turning the Tide: The Life of Lady Rhondda* (Cardigan: Parthian Books, 2013)

Johnson, Gaynor, *Lord Robert Cecil: Politician and Internationalist* (Farnham: Ashgate, 2013)

Lee, Hermione, *Virginia Woolf* (London: Chatto & Windus, 1996)

Lee, Hugh, ed., *A Cézanne in the Hedge and other memories of Charleston and Bloomsbury* (London: Collins & Brown, 1992)

Light, Alison, *Mrs Woolf and the Servants* (London: Penguin, 2008)

Lumsden, Linda J., *Inez: The Life and Times of Inez Milholland* (Bloomington: Indiana University Press, 2004)

MacKenzie, Norman, ed., *The letters of Sidney and Beatrice Webb*, 3 vols (Cambridge: Cambridge University Press, 1978), I *Apprenticeships 1873–1892* and II *Partnership 1893–1912*

—— and Jeanne MacKenzie, eds, *All the Good Things of Life: The Diary of Beatrice Webb, Volume Two 1892–1905*, (London: Virago in association with the London School of Economics, 1993).

Mariano, Nicky, *Forty Years with Berenson* (London: Hamish Hamilton, 1966)

Marler, Regina, ed., *Selected Letters of Vanessa Bell* (London: Bloomsbury, 1993)

Moggridge, D. E., *Maynard Keynes: An Economist's Biography* (London: Routledge, 1992)

Nicolson, Nigel, and Joanne Trautmann, eds, *The Letters of Virginia Woolf*, 6 vols

(London: Hogarth Press,1975–1980), I *The Flight of the Mind: 1888–1912 (Virginia Stephen)* (1975); II *The Question of Things Happening: 1912–1922* (1976); III *A Change of Perspective: 1923–1928* (1977); IV *A Reflection of the Other Person: 1929–1931* (1978); V *The Sickle Side of the Moon: 1932–1935* (1979); VI *Leave the Letters Till We're Dead: 1936–1941* (1980)

Oldfield, Sybil, *Spinsters of This Parish: The Life and Times of F. M. Mayor and Mary Sheepshanks* (London: Virago, 1984)

Origo, Iris, *Images and Shadows: Part of a Life* (London: Century, 1984)

Partridge, Frances, *A Pacifist's War* (London: Hogarth Press, 1978)

—— *Life Regained: Diaries January 1970 – December 1971* (London: Weidenfeld & Nicolson, 1998)

—— *Memories* (London: Gollancz 1981)

Pedersen, Susan, *Eleanor Rathbone and the Politics of Conscience* (New Haven: Yale University Press, 2004)

Rickman, John, *The Land of Lod* ([n.p.]: Peggy Rickman, 1998)

Robb, Nesca A., *An Ulsterwoman in England 1924–1941* (Cambridge: University Press, 1942)

Roiphe, Katie, *Uncommon Arrangements: Seven Portraits of Married Life in London Literary Circles 1910–1939* (London: Virago, 2008)

Rose, Kenneth, *The Later Cecils* (London: Weidenfeld and Nicolson, 1975)

Rosenbaum, S. P., ed., *The Bloomsbury Group: A Collection of Memoirs, Commentary and Criticism*, (London: Croom Helm, [1975]); revised ed. *The Bloomsbury Group: A Collection of Memoirs and Commentary*, (Toronto: Toronto University Press, 1995)

Rubinstein, David, *A Different World for Women: The Life of Millicent Garrett Fawcett* (Columbus: Ohio State University Press, 1991)

Seymour, Miranda, *Ottoline Morrell: Life on the Grand Scale* (London: Hodder & Stoughton, 1992)

Spalding, Frances, *The Bloomsbury Group* (London: National Portrait Gallery, 2005)

—— *Vanessa Bell* (London: Weidenfeld and Nicolson, 1983)

Stocks, Mary, *My Commonplace Book* (London: Peter Davies, 1970)

—— [as Mary D. Stocks] *Eleanor Rathbone: A Biography* (London: Gollancz, 1949]

—— *Still More Commonplace* (London: Peter Davies, 1973)

Strachey, Lytton, *Eminent Victorians* (London: Chatto & Windus, 1918; repr. Penguin, 1986)

Sykes, Christopher, *Nancy: The Life of Lady Astor* (London: Collins, 1972)

Taylor, D. J., *Bright Young People: The Lost Generation of London's Jazz Age* (New York: Farrar, Strauss and Giroux, 2010)

Tharp, Louise Hall, *Mrs Jack: A Biography of Isabella Stewart Gardner* (Boston: Little, Brown, [1965])

Contemporary Culture

Bingham, Adrian, *Gender, Modernity, and the Popular Press in Inter-War Britain* (Oxford: Clarendon Press, 2004)

Chesser, Elizabeth Sloan, *From Girlhood to Womanhood* (London: Cassell, 1913)

Marcus, Sharon, *Between Women: Friendship, Desire and Marriage in Victorian England* (Princeton: Princeton University Press, 2007)

Mitchell, Sally, *The New Girl: Girls' Culture in England 1880–1915* (New York: Columbia University Press, 1995)

Murphy, Kate, *Behind the Wireless: A History of Early Women at the BBC* (London: Palgrave Macmillan, 2016)

Nicholson, Virginia, *Among the Bohemians: Experiments in Living 1900–1939* (London: Penguin, 2003)

Rees, Rosemary, ed., *Britain 1890–1939*, Heinemann Advanced History (London: Heinemann, 2003)

Tosh, John, *A Man's Place: Masculinity and the Middle-Class Home in Victorian England* (New Haven: Yale University Press, 1999)

'A Work Worthy of the University': A Centenary History of Cambridge University Careers Service (Cambridge: University Careers Service, 2002) <http://www.careers.cam.ac.uk/stuart/cucshistory.pdf> [accessed 12 November 2015]

Women's Movement

Alberti, Johanna, *Beyond Suffrage: Feminists in War and Peace, 1914–28* (Basingstoke: Macmillan, 1989)

Ardis, Ann L., *New Women, New Novels: Feminism and Early Modernism* (New Brunswick: Rutgers University Press, 1990)

Banks, Olive, *The Biographical Dictionary of British Feminists*, 2 vols, (Brighton: Wheatsheaf Books, 1985–90), I *1800–1930*

Bartley, Paula, *Votes for Women 1860–1928* (London: Hodder & Stoughton, 2009)

Bausum, Ann, *With Courage and Cloth: Winning the Fight for a Woman's Right to Vote* (Washington, DC: National Geographic Society, 2004)

Black, Naomi, *Virginia Woolf as Feminist* (Ithaca: Cornell University Press, 2004)

Bland, Lucy, *Modern Women on Trial: Sexual Transgression in the Age of the Flapper* (Manchester: Manchester University Press, 2013)

Bruley, Sue, *Women in Britain since 1900* (Basingstoke: Palgrave, 1999)

Crawford, Elizabeth, *The Women's Suffrage Movement: A Reference Guide 1866–1928* (London: Routledge, 2001)

Frost, Elizabeth, and Kathryn Cullen-DuPont, *Women's Suffrage in America: An Eyewitness History* (New York: Facts On File, 1992)

Garner, Les, *Stepping Stones to Women's Liberty: Feminist Ideas in the Women's Suffrage Movement 1900–1918* (London: Heinemann, 1984)

Gottlieb, Julie V., and Richard Toye, eds, *The Aftermath of Suffrage: Women, Gender, and Politics in Britain, 1918–1945* (Basingstoke: Palgrave Macmillan, 2013)

Harrison, Brian, *Prudent Revolutionaries: Portraits of British Feminists between the Wars* (Oxford: Oxford University Press, 1987)

—— *Separate Spheres: The Opposition to Women's Suffrage in Britain* (London: Croom Helm, 1978)

Harrison, Patricia Greenwood, *Connecting Links: The British and American Woman Suffrage Movements, 1900–1914* (Westport, Connecticut: Greenwood Press, 2000)

Heilbrun, Carolyn G., *Writing a Woman's Life* (London: The Women's Press, 1989)

Heilmann, Ann, *New Woman Strategies: Sarah Grand, Olive Schreiner, Mona Caird* (Manchester: Manchester University Press, 2004)

Hollis, Patricia, *Ladies Elect: Women in English Local Government 1865–1914* (Oxford: Clarendon Press, 1987)

Holton, Sandra Stanley, *Feminism and Democracy: Women's Suffrage and Reform Politics in Britain 1900–1918* (Cambridge: Cambridge University Press, 1986)

—— *Suffrage Days: Stories from the Women's Suffrage Movement* (London: Routledge, 1996)

Hume, Leslie Parker, *The National Union of Women's Suffrage Societies, 1897-1914* (New York & London: Garland, 1982).

John, Angela V., and Claire Eustance, eds, *The Men's Share?: Masculinities, Male Support and Women's Suffrage in Britain, 1890-1920* (London: Routledge, 1997)

Kamm, Josephine, *Indicative Past: A Hundred Years of The Girls' Public Day School Trust* (London: George Allen & Unwin, 1971)

Kent, Susan Kingsley, *Sex and Suffrage in Britain, 1860–1914* (Princeton: Princeton University Press, 1990)

Law, Cheryl, *Women, A Modern Political Dictionary* (London: I. B. Tauris, 2000)

—— *Suffrage and Power: The Women's Movement 1918–1928* (London: I. B. Tauris, 2000)

Liddington, Jill, *Rebel Girls: Their Fight for the Vote* (London: Virago, 2006)

—— and Jill Norris, *One Hand Tied Behind Us: The Rise of the Women's Suffrage Movement* (London: Virago, 1978)

Pugh, Martin, *The March of the Women: A Revisionist Analysis of the Campaign for Women's Suffrage 1866–1914* (Oxford: Oxford University Press, 2000)

—— *Women and the Women's Movement in Britain*, second ed. (Basingstoke: Macmillan, 2000)

—— *The Pankhursts: The History of One Radical Family* (London: Vintage, 2008)

Purvis, June, and Sandra Stanley Holton, eds., *Votes for Women* (London, Routledge, 2000)

Robinson, Jane, *Hearts and Minds: The Untold Story of the Great Pilgrimage and How Women Won the Vote* (London, Doubleday, 2018)

Sharp, Ingrid, and Matthew Stibbe, eds, *Aftermaths of War: Women's Movements and Female Activists, 1918-1923* (Leiden: Brill, 2011)

Smith, Angela K., *Suffrage Discourse in Britain during the First World War* (Aldershot: Ashgate, 2005)

Smith, Harold L., *The British Women's Suffrage Campaign, 1866-1928* (Harlow: Longman, 1998)

Symonds, Richard, *Inside the Citadel: Men and the Emancipation of Women, 1850–1920* (Basingstoke: Macmillan, 1999)

Vellacott, Jo, *From Liberal to Labour with Women's Suffrage: The Story of Catherine Marshall* (Montreal: McGill-Queen's University Press, 1993)

—— *Pacifists, Patriots and the Vote: The Erosion of Democratic Suffragism in Britain during the First World War* (Basingstoke: Palgrave Macmillan, 2007)

Walton, Mary, *A Woman's Crusade: Alice Paul and the Battle for the Ballot* (New York: Palgrave Macmillan, 2010)

Woolf, Virginia, *A Room of One's Own* (London: Hogarth Press, 1929); repr. in *Selected Works of Virginia Woolf* (Ware: Wordsworth Editions, 2005)

—— *Three Guineas* (London: Hogarth Press, 1938); repr. in *Selected Works of Virginia Woolf* (Ware: Wordsworth Editions, 2005)

War, Codebreaking, Pacifism

Atkin, Jonathan, *A War of Individuals: Bloomsbury Attitudes to the Great War* (Manchester: Manchester University Press, 2002)

Batey, Mavis, *Dilly: The Man who Broke Enigmas* (London: Biteback, 2010)

Birch, Frank, *The Official History of British Sigint 1914–19* ed. by John Jackson, The Bletchley Archive 3, 2 vols, I (part 1) (Milton Keynes: Military Press, 2002)

Braybon, Gail, *Women Workers in the First World War: The British Experience* (London: Croom Helm, 1981)

Castle, Ian, *London 1914–17: The Zeppelin Menace*, Campaign 193 (Oxford: Osprey, 2009)

—— *London 1917–18: The Bomber Blitz*, Campaign 227 (Oxford: Osprey, 2010)

Ceadel, Martin, *Semi-detached Idealists: The British Peace Movement and International Relations, 1854-1945* (Oxford: Oxford University Press, 2000)

Denniston, Robin, *Thirty Secret Years: A. G. Denniston's Work in Signals Intelligence 1914–1944* (Clifton-upon-Teme: Polperro Heritage Press, 2007)

Fussell, Paul, *The Great War and Modern Memory* (Oxford: Oxford University Press, 1975, 2000)

Goodall, Felicity, *We Will Not Go to War: Conscientious Objection during the World Wars* (Stroud: History Press, 2010; first published as *A Question of Conscience: Conscientious Objection in the Two World Wars*, Stroud: Sutton Publishing, 1997)

Hinsley, F. H., and Alan Stripp, editors, *Codebreakers: The Inside Story of Bletchley Park* (Oxford: Oxford University Press, 1993).

Hynes, Samuel, *A War Imagined: The First World War and English Culture* (London: Pimlico, 1992)

Hanson, Neil, *First Blitz: The Secret German Plan to Raze London to the Ground in 1918* (London: Corgi, 2009)

Lukacs, John, *Five Days in London, May 1940* (New Haven: Yale University Press, 2001)

McKay, Sinclair, *The Lost World of Bletchley Park: An Illustrated History of the Wartime Codebreaking Centre*, (London: Aurum Press, 2013)

—— *The Secret World of Bletchley Park: The WWII Codebreaking Centre and the Men and Women Who Worked There* (London: Aurum Press, 2010)

Marshall, Catherine, C. K. Ogden and Mary Sargant Florence, *Militarism Versus Feminism: An Enquiry and a Policy Demonstrating that Militarism involves the Subjection of Women* (London: Allen & Unwin, 1915), republished as *Militarism Versus Feminism: Writings on Women and War*, ed. by Margaret Kamester and Jo Vellacott (London: Virago, 1987)

Oldfield, Sybil, *Women against the Iron Fist: Alternatives to Militarism 1900–1989* (Oxford: Blackwell, 1989)

Smith, Michael, *Station X: The Codebreakers of Bletchley Park* (London: Channel 4 Books, 1998)

Trevor-Roper, Hugh, ed. by Edward Harrison, *The Secret World: Behind the Curtain of British Intelligence in World War II and the Cold War* (London: I. B. Tauris, 2014)

West, Nigel, *GCHQ: The Secret Wireless War 1900-86* (London: Weidenfeld and Nicolson, 1986)

Wiltsher, Anne, *Most Dangerous Women: Feminist Peace Campaigners of the Great War* (London: Pandora, 1985)

Woollacott, Angela, *On Her their Lives Depend: Munitions Workers in the Great War* (Berkeley: University of California Press, 1994)

Zühlsdorff, Volkmar, *Hitler's Exiles: The German Cultural Resistance in America and Europe*, trans. by Martin H. Bott (London: Continuum, 2004)

Politics, Social Reform

Davis, John, *Reforming London: The London Government Problem 1855–1900* (Oxford: Clarendon Press, 1988)

Saint, Andrew (ed.), *Politics and the People of London: The London County Council 1889–1965* (London: Hambledon Press, 1989)

Scotland, Nigel, *Squires in the Slums: Settlements and Missions in Late-Victorian London* (London: I. B. Tauris, 2007)

League of Nations

Birn, Donald S., *The League of Nations Union, 1918–1945* (Oxford: Clarendon Press, 1981)

McCarthy, Helen, *The British People and the League of Nations: Democracy, Citizenship and Internationalism, c.1918–45* (Manchester: Manchester University Press, 2011)

India

Brendon, Vyvyen, *Children of the Raj* (London: Phoenix, 2006)

de Courcy, Anne, *The Fishing Fleet: Husband-Hunting in the Raj* (London: Weidenfeld & Nicolson, 2012)

Liberia

Butcher, Tim, *Chasing the Devil: The Search for Africa's Fighting Spirit* (London: Chatto & Windus, 2010)

Dunn, D. Elwood and Svend E. Holsoe, *Historical Dictionary of Liberia*, African Historical Dictionaries 38 (Metuchen, N.J. & London: Scarecrow Press, 1985)

Greene, Barbara, *Too Late to Turn Back: Barbara and Graham Greene in Liberia* (London: Settle Bendall, 1981)

Greene, Graham, *Journey without Maps* (Harmondsworth: Penguin, 1971)

Building

Duncan, Ronald, *Home-Made Home* (London: Faber and Faber, 1947)

Great Britain Building Research Board, *Building in Cob and Pisé de Terre: A Collection of Notes from Various Sources on the Construction of Earth Walls*, Special Report 5 (London: HMSO, 1922)

Swenarton, Mark, *Building the New Jerusalem: Architecture, Housing and Politics 1900–1930* (Bracknell: HIS BRE Press, 2008)

Fiction

Grand, Sarah, *Babs the Impossible* (London: Hutchinson, 1900)

Wells, H. G., *Ann Veronica* (London, T. Fisher Unwin, 1909; repr. Virago, 1990)

—— *The New Machiavelli*, (London: Bodley Head, 1911; repr. Everyman, 1994)

Articles

Alberti, Johanna, 'Striking Rock: The Letters of Ray Strachey to Her Family, 1929–1935' in Trev Lynn Broughton and Linda Anderson, eds, *Women's Lives/ Women's Times: New Essays on Auto/Biography* (Albany: State University of New York Press, 1997), pp. 73–93

Bentley, Michael, 'Liberal Politics and the Grey Conspiracy of 1921', *Historical Journal*, 20 (1977), 461–478 <http://www.jstor.org/stable/2638540>

Brink, Andrew, 'Mariechen's Self-knowledge', *Russell: The Journal of Bertrand Russell Studies*, 4 (1984), 313–320 <http://dx.doi.org/10.15173/russell.v4i2.1624>

Caine, Barbara, 'Mothering Feminism/Mothering Feminists: Ray Strachey and *The Cause*', *Women's History Review*, 8 (1999) 295-310 <http://dx.doi.org/10.1080/09612029900200199>

— 'A Feminist Family: The Stracheys and Feminism, c.1860–1950', *Women's History Review*, 14 (2005), 385–404

Chaudhuri, Nupur, 'Bloomsbury Ancestry: Jane Maria Strachey, Feminism, and Younger Strachey Women' in Wayne K. Chapman and Janet M. Manson, eds, *Women in the Milieu of Leonard and Virginia Woolf: Peace, Politics and Education* (New York: Pace University, 1998), pp. 58–75

Clemson, Janet M. Manson, 'Practical Idealist: The League of Nations and the 1923 American Tour of Lord Robert Cecil and Ray Strachey', *Newsletter (Society for Historians of American Foreign Relations)*, 32 (June 2001), 12-27

DiCenzo, Maria, 'Justifying Their Modern Sisters: History Writing and the British Suffrage Movement', *Victorian Review*, 31 (2005), 40–61 <http://www.jstor.org/stable/27793564>

Dodd, Kathryn, 'Cultural Politics and Women's Historical Writing: The Case of Ray Strachey's *The Cause*', *Women's Studies International Forum*, 13 (1990), 127–137

Freeman, Peter, 'MI1(b) and the Origins of British Diplomatic Cryptanalysis', *Intelligence and National Security*, 22 (2007), 206–228 <http://dx.doi.org/10.1080/02684520701553550>

Gilmore, Myron P., 'The Berensons and I Tatti', *Proceedings of the American Philosophical Society*, 120 (1976), 7–12

Gordon, Ann D., 'Shaw, Anna Howard', *American National Biography Online* (February 2000) <http://www.anb.org/articles/15/15-00615.html> [accessed 12 November 2015]

Halpern, Barbara Strachey, 'Ray Strachey—A Memoir', in Wayne K. Chapman and Janet M. Manson, eds, *Women in the Milieu of Leonard and Virginia Woolf: Peace, Politics and Education* (New York: Pace University, 1998), pp. 76–86

Hannam, June, 'Women's History, Feminist History', *Making History* <http://www.history.ac.uk/makinghistory/resources/articles/womens_history.html> [accessed 12 November 2015]

Harrison, Brian, 'Women in a Men's House: The Women M.P.s, 1919–1945', *Historical Journal*, 29 (September 1986), 623–654 <http://www.jstor.org/stable/2639051>

Lee, J. A. N., 'Christopher Strachey', in *Computer Pioneers* (Los Alamitos, CA: IEEE [Institute of Electrical and Electronics Engineers] Computer Society Press, 1995), pp. 644–652; revised version at <http://history.computer.org/pioneers/strachey.html> [accessed 13 November 2015]

Mayhall, Laura Nym, 'Creating the 'Suffragette Spirit': British Feminism and the Historical Imagination', *Women's History Review*, 4 (1995), 319–344 <http://dx.doi.org/10.1080/09612029500200088>

McCarthy, Helen, 'Pacifism and Feminism in the Great War', *History Today* <http://www.historytoday.com/helen-mccarthy/pacifism-and-feminism-great-war> [accessed 12 November 2015]

Meneghel, Meg A., ' "Dear Mother": Ray Strachey's Role in Feminism and the League of Nations as Seen from the Lilly Library' in Wayne K. Chapman and Janet M. Manson, eds, *Women in the Milieu of Leonard and Virginia Woolf: Peace, Politics and Education* (New York: Pace University, 1998), pp. 87–95

Oakley, Ann, 'Millicent Garrett Fawcett: Duty and Determination (1847–1929)' in *Feminist Theorists: Three Centuries of Women's Intellectual Traditions* ed. by Dale Spender (London: The Women's Press, 1983), pp. 184–202

Pugh, Martin D., 'Politicians and the Woman's Vote 1914–1918', *History*, 59 (October 1974), 358–374

Smith, Harold L., 'British Feminism and the Equal Pay Issue in the 1930s', *Women's History Review*, 5 (1996), 97-110 <http://dx.doi.org/10.1080/09612029600200102>

Smith-Rosenberg, Carroll, 'The Female World of Love and Ritual: Relations between Women in Nineteenth-Century America', *Signs*, 1 (Autumn, 1975), 1-29 < http://www.jstor.org/stable/3172964>

Strachey, Barbara, 'Logan's Letters', *Russell: The Journal of Bertrand Russell Studies*, 5 (1985), 82–84 <http://digitalcommons.mcmaster.ca/russelljournal/vol5/iss1/11> [accessed 22 February 2010]

——'The Life of Julia Strachey', *Russell: the Journal of Bertrand Russell Studies*, 3 (1983), 177–79 <http://digitalcommons.mcmaster.ca/russelljournal/vol3/iss2/9> [accessed 22 February 2010]

Workman, Joanne, 'Wading Through the Mire: An Historiographical Study of the

British Women's Movement Between the Wars', *University of Sussex Journal of Contemporary History*, 2 (2001) <https://www.sussex.ac.uk/webteam/gateway/file.php?name=2-workman-wading-through-the-mire&site=15> [accessed 11 November 2015]

Vickery, Amanda, 'Golden Age to Separate Spheres? A Review of the Categories and Chronology of English Women's History', *Historical Journal*, 36 (1993), 383–414 <http://www.jstor.org/stable/2639654>

INDEX

Illustrations within the text are shown in italics.
Plates are shown in bold.

Acland, F. D., 5, 174, 179
Alexandria, 155
Allahabad, India, 106
Amalgamated Society of Engineers (ASE), 178
Amsterdam, 69
Anderson, Brigadier-General Francis J., 139
Anrep, Helen, 301
Ansermet, Ernest, 189
Anthony, Susan B., 80
Anti-Slavery Society, 262, 357 n. 18
Anti-Waste Campaign, 189
Apostles (Cambridge Society), 54
Ashby, Margery Corbett, 5
Asheham, 136–7
Asquith, Herbert Henry, 67–8, 91, 132, 157, 164, 192, 241, 347 n. 24
Astor, Nancy, Viscountess Astor: elected to the House of Commons (1919), 182–4; assisted by Ray, 183–4; unparliamentary approach, 183, 268–9; maiden speech, 183, 346 n. 81; attacked by Horatio Bottomley, 346 n. 84; commitment to temperance, 183, 268–9; and women's employment, 191; re-elected, 196, 253, 254; and equal franchise for women, 235; employs Ray as political secretary, 253, 259–60, 268–9; and Liberia, 263; and the nursery school movement, 265; and political entertaining, 267; and *Three Guineas*, 291; financial assistance to Ray, 280–1; Ray's views on, 184, 253, 259–60, 266, 268; Ray's

planned biography of, 264; tributes to Ray, 311–12. **Plate 23**
Astor, Waldorf, Viscount Astor, 182, 269, 346 n. 81
Atalanta (magazine), 325 n. 5
Atholl, Duchess of, 173, 344 n. 26, 354 n. 69
Attlee, Clement, 261
'Aunt Loo', *see* Alys Russell
Australia, 274–6
Ayles, Walter, 150

Bagenal, Barbara *see* Hiles, Barbara
Bagenal, Nick, 343 n. 17
Bagley Wood (Russell home), 66, 104
Baker, Philip Noel, 198
Baldwin, Stanley, 235
Balfour, Arthur, 164
Balliol College, Oxford, 6, 7, 105
Barnett, Henrietta, 8
BBC *see* broadcasting
Bedales School, 127, 128, 130
Bedford College, Regent's Park, 305, 307
Bell, Vanessa, 110–11, 137, 171, 335 n. 29
Belsize Park Gardens, Hampstead, 103, 104, 126, 171, 182
Benn, John Williams, 10, 322–3 n.7
Benn, Tony, 6
Bennett, Geoffrey Thomas, 68
Berenson, Bernard (*previously* Bernhard): background and education, 10; begins relationship with Mary, 10; dislike of Mary's children, 12; as art expert, 41–2, 74, 83; marriage to Mary, 42, 44, 55, 94, 156, 167, 168–70, 251,

261, 303; at Villa I Tatti, 41, 46–8, 94, 94–5, 297; enthusiasm for motoring, 46; admires Ray's mind, 329 n. 20; relationship with Belle da Costa Greene, 94, 167, 168; disapproval of Oliver Strachey, 121; financial support for Ray, 121, 130, 176, 190, 251–2, 303; hatred of pacifism, 146, 155; name change, 343 n. 3; in Paris during First World War, 167–9; relationship with Lady Sybil Cutting, 168; affair with French Baroness, 168; refusal to support Oliver, 176; declines to invest in Ray's company, 188–9; avoidance of Ray's children, 218; critical of Ray's writing style, 240; desire to leave I Tatti to Harvard, 251; unpopular with Bloomsbury Group, 251; relationship with Nicky Mariano, 218; worsening financial position, 251–2, 274, changing attitude to Roger, 297; during Second World War, 1, 303, 308, 314; irascibility, 48, 94, 167, 251. **Plates 3 and 39**

Berenson, Mary (*née* Smith *then* Pearsall Smith, *formerly* Costelloe), *8*, *16*; appearance, 1, 7, 32, 167; background and childhood, 6–7; marriage to Frank Costelloe, 7–8; birth of her children, and mental breakdown, 9; follows Berenson to Florence, 10–12; preference for Ray over Karin, 11, 12, 14, 21, 34; separation from Frank Costelloe, 12–13; conflict between children and intellectual life, 13–14; idealised by Ray, 16; illnesses, 19, 42, 170, 218, 223, 260–1, 297, 302; relationships with younger men, 19, 55, 167; and death of Frank Costelloe, 24; custody battle for daughters, 24–6; as art critic, 41, 42; marriage to Berenson, 42, 55, 113, 117, 156, 167–70, 251; attempts to improve Ray's appearance, 43–4, 78, 118; encourages Ray to flirt, 43–5, 53; introduces Ray to motoring, 46–8; pays for publication of Ray's

novel, 49; at Villa I Tatti, 42–5, 50–3, 94–5; entertaining character of, 51; introduces Ray to smoking, 53; relationship with Geoffrey Scott, 53, 56, 94, 167–8; introduces Ray to USA, 74–6, 83; buys Ray a car, 86–7; and Ray's engagement and marriage to Oliver, 113–18, 121; financial support for Ray, 122, 125, 174, 176, 187, 190, 218, 251, 253, 266, 274; treatment of grandchildren, 128, 214, 218, 225, 270; resentment of Stracheys, 129; on suffrage Pilgrimage, 133; nervous breakdown, 168–70; burdensome visits to England, 170, 172, 173, 218, 302–3; provides home for Roger Hultin, 297–8, 303–4; during Second World War, 1–2, 303, 308; and Ray's death, 2, 363 nn. 3 & 4; death, 314; 'Life of Ray Strachey,' 2, 313, 314; personal characteristics, 7, 9 10, 41, 43, 156, 200, 214, 218–9, 314. **Plates 1 and 26**

Bermondsey, 91–2

Bex (Switzerland) *see* École Nouvelle

Bevin, Ernest, 312

Birmingham, Alabama, 96

Bletchley Park, 302, 305, 308, 311

Bloomsbury Group, 99, 170–2, 208, 221, 223, 227, 251, 343 n. 17, 350 n. 47

Boone, Iowa, 80

Booth, Catherine, 242

Booth, William, 353–4, n. 39

Borah, William, 199, 348 n. 53

Boston, USA, 10, 80, 84–5

Bottomley, Horatio, 184, 346 n. 84

Breckinridge, Sophonisba, 79

Brentford and Chiswick constituency, 174–6, 195–6, 203

British Federation of Business and Professional Women, 312

broadcasting: BBC, 245–7, 259, 261, 267, 315, 355 n. 74, 363 n. 10; Ray's broadcasts, 245–7, 250, 253, 267

Brown, Miss (earth-rammer), 187

Brown, William Francis, 324 n. 48

Browning, Elizabeth Barrett, 'How do I

love thee?', 117

Bryn Mawr college, Philadelphia, 74–7, 79, 82, 198, 217

Buckley, Winnie, 38, 42, 91

Buckmaster, Stanley Buckmaster, 1st Viscount, 163

Buffalo, New York, 78

Bussy, Dorothy (*née* Strachey), 37, 120, 141, 227, 311–2, 363 n. 3. **Plate 41**

Bussy family, 295, 308

Bussy, Janie (daughter of Dorothy and Simon), **Plate 43**

Bussy, Simon, 37, 120, 141, 231. **Plate 42**

Butler, Josephine, 242

Calcutta, 119–20

Cambridge, 113, 117, 121, 248; University of, 29, 39, 51, 55, 68, 77, 109, 118, 225, 243, 299, 300, 326 n. 37, 339 n. 19, 353 n. 39; woman's suffrage at, 66–8, 329 n. 18. *See also* individual colleges

Cambridge University Women's Appointments' Board, 243

Cambridge University Women's Society for Women's Suffrage, 66, 329 n. 18

Cambridge University Women's Suffrage Society, 329 n. 18

car driving *see* motoring

caravan tours, 69–73, *71*, 86, 239

Carey, Louise, 330 n. 11

Carnegie United Kingdom Trust, 288–9, 291, 294, 306, 314

Carrington, Dora, 171, 260, 343 n. 16

'Cat and Mouse Act' (Prisoners [Temporary Discharge for Ill-Health] Act) (1913), 132

Catt, Carrie Chapman, 69

Cavalière, France, 228–9

Cecil, Lord Robert: background and character, 190–1, 194; support for women's suffrage, 138, 190, 353–4 n. 39; anger at NUWSS call for peace, 138; support for Ray's election campaign (1918), 174; attempt to set up Centre Party, 191–2, 347 n. 24; commitment to League of Nations, 191, 192–4, 197, 198–9, 202, 235, 262;

funding of Ray's election campaign (1922), 195; visit to USA (1923), 197, 198–9; Ray's admiration for, 190–1, 192, 194, 198–9, 202, 221, 228, 232. **Plate 22**

Central Employment Bureau for Women, 286–8, 294, 314, 360 n. 12

Central Technical College, London, 109

Centre Party, attempt to establish, 191–2, 347 n. 24

Chamberlain, Austen, 164

Chamberlain, Neville, 158, 305

Chaplin, Charlie 259

Charlwood, Surrey, 64–5

Chicago, USA, 79, 82, 95

Chilling, Hampshire, 163, 181

Churchill, Winston, 244, 292

Civil Service, women in the, 177, 244–5, 263–4, 289. *See also* Royal Commission on the Civil Service

Clack's End, Pangbourne, 137

Clarke, Miss (earth-rammer), 186

Cliveden, 267

Clough, Athena, 158, 163

Cobbold Richard, *The History of Margaret Catchpole*, 246

Cobden, Richard, 63

Cobden-Sanderson, Anne, 63

codebreaking, 139–40, 155, 176, 302, 308, 339 nn. 19 & 22

Colorado, USA, female suffrage in, 78, 81–2

Colson, Peggy, 70, 89

Colville, Elinor, 104

Common Cause (newspaper), 149, 176–7, 179

Conan Doyle, Arthur, 246

Contagious Diseases Acts (1864–9), 353–4 n. 39

Copenhagen, Denmark, 119, 272

Copse Cottage *see* Mud House

Corfe Castle, Dorset, 111

Corfu, 202

Costelloe, Benjamin Francis Conn ('Frank'), *8*; background, 6; political ambitions, 6, 21; income, 322 n. 5; Catholicism, 6, 7, 10, 13, 20, 21, 25,

242; journalism, 6, 20, 21, 25; marriage to Mary Pearsall Smith, 6–9; and the women's movement, 7, 59, 61, 191; and the Vigilance Association, 8, 191; elected to LCC, 9–10, 12, 19; naiveté over Mary's relationship with Berenson, 10–11; separates from Mary and retains custody of children, 13; and Hannah Whitall Smith, 15, 25–7; and Ray's upbringing, 15, 17–19, 21, 22; poor health of, 19, 21, 22–4; on the London School Board, 20–1, 23–4, 191; loses East St Pancras by-election, 21; death, 24–5; will, and provision for his children, 25–7; tributes to, 191, and Ray's later political life, 98, 191. **Plate 2**
Costelloe, Mary Anne (née Conn), 15, 19, 29. **Plate 2**
Court Place, Iffley, 39, 90, *90*, 98, 112–13, 117, 127
Courtney, Janet, 288
Courtney, Kathleen, 146, 160, 340 n. 37
Coutts, Angela Burdett, 241
Crocker, J. D., 339 n. 19
Cumberland, suffrage campaigns in, 71–2, 88–9
Curzon, George, 1st Marquess Curzon of Kedleston, 163
Cutting, Lady Sybil, 168

Daily Chronicle, 21, 176
Daily Express, 176, 343 n. 4
Daily Mail, 176
Daily News, 176
Darbishire, Helen, 361 n. 24
Davison, Emily Wilding, 132
Defoe, Daniel, 246
Denver, Colorado, 81–2
Depression (economic), 252, 273
Despard, Charlotte, 5
Dinapore, India, 119–20
divorce: grounds for in Finland, 297–8; grounds for in UK, 323 n. 16; validity of Indian divorces, 333 n. 12
Durbins (Roger Fry's home), 127–8, 152–3, *153*

Duveen, Joseph, 42, 251

Earls Court (amusement park), 136–7
East India Company, 130–1
East India Railway, 103, 105, 119
East St Pancras constituency, 21, 98
École Nouvelle (Bex, Switzerland), 202, 213, 222, 228
Election Fighting Fund (EFF), 149–51
Eliot, T. S., 233
Elizabeth, Queen (consort of George VI), 306
Emergency Open-Air Nurseries Committee, 265
employment: 121, 186, 261, 273, 345 n. 52; of men, 178; of women, 60, 161, 169, 177–9, 180, 238, 252, 284–6, 306, 309, 314, 344 n. 26; of women in wartime, 138–9, 148–9, 153, 158–9, 295, 306–7, 312. *See also* Women's Employment Federation
'endowment of motherhood' (family allowance), 180
Erskine Childers, Robert, 246
Eton, 104
Ewing, Mrs Juliana, 20
Exervis (company), 186

Faber & Gwyer (publishers), 232, 352 n. 10
Fawcett, Millicent Garrett, *236*; in Vigilance Association, 191; as President of NUWSS, 61, 68, 138, 146, 160, 181; and WSPU militancy, 61, 63; and the 'Mud March' (1907), 64; international role of, 69, 193, 338 n. 10; links with LSWS, 133; and the NUWSS during First World War, 138, 142, 146, 159, 190; reliance on Ray, 160–1; and the Representation of the People Act (1918), 162, 164; support for Ray's election campaign (1918), 174; retirement from NUWSS, 181; opposition to 'endowment of motherhood', 180; death, 247; Ray's admiration for, 190, 221; Ray's biography of, 164, 247–50; statue of, 316
Fawcett, Philippa, 68, *236*, 326 n. 37
feminism, interpretations of, 143, 180, 194

Ferguson, Inez *see* Jenkins, Inez (*née* Ferguson)

Fernden Preparatory School, 215

Fernhurst, Sussex, 15–8, 54, 109, 127, 185, 189, 210, 211, 214–5, 220, 222, 228, 231, 272, 280, 281, 282, 291, 305, 307 *See also* Friday's Hill Cottage, Friday's Hill House *and* Mud House

Fielden, Mary, 86

First World War: breaks out, 137–8; suffrage organisations in, 138–9, 156–62; public mood, 140, 142–3, 146, 152, 167; air raids, 140, 156, 163; women workers in, 138–9, 148, 153, 158–9, 161, 172–3, 177–9; conscription and conscientious objection, 154–5; in France and Italy, 141, 147, 168–9; inflation during, 152; post-war economy, 345 n. 52 *See also* codebreaking, LSWS, NUWSS *and* pacifism

Fisher, H. A. L., 174

Flanagan, Terence Woulfe (doctor and Trustee), 20, 26, 324 n. 48

Flexner, Helen, 197

Florence, Italy, 1–2, 10–12, 26, 41–3, 46, 94, 141, 168. *See also* Villa I Tatti

Ford, Henry, 199, 348 n. 53

Ford, Isabella, 86, 88–9

Ford Place, Arundel, 123–4, 128, 129

Foreign Policy Association (USA), 198

Fosdick, Raymond, 197

Freshfield, Sir Douglas, 181

Friday Club, 99. *See also* Bloomsbury Group

Friday's Hill Cottage, 15, 17, 185

Friday's Hill House, 17, 21, 39, 53

Fry, Joan, 127–8, 337 n. 33

Fry, Pamela, 128

Fry, Roger, 127, 128, 152, 153, 301. **Plate 33**

Fürholzer, (Fraülein) Therese ('Terry', governess), 20, 22–3, 25, 27, 33, 35

Furse, Charles, 344 n. 26

Furse, Dame Katharine, 173, 344 n. 26

Gandhi, Mahatma, 259

Gardner, Emilie, 70, *71*, 87, 89

Gardner, Isabella Stewart, 42, 75, 76, 84

Garrett, Agnes, *236*

Garrett, Mary, 97, 217

Garrison, William Lloyd, 240

Gaskell, Elizabeth, 246

Gawthorpe, Mary, 66

general elections: (1885), 7; (1892), 12–13, (1895), 21, (1910), 92–4, 98; (1918), 5, 173–6; (1922), 194–6, *196*; (1923), 203; (1924), 234; (1929), 253; (1931), 246–7; overdue in 1916, 156–7

George, Miss (Ray's secretary), 183, 190

Gide, André, 248, 262

Girls' Public Day School Company, 29

Girton College, Cambridge, 61, 66, 67, 68

Gladstone, Henry, 192

Gladstone, Herbert, 192

Gladstone, William Ewart, 61, 240

Glazier, Bill, 273, 282

Glazier, Mrs (Clarrie), 212, 273, 280, 282, 304, 311

Gloag, John, 247

Glossop, 72–3

Gordon, Anna Adams, 95

Gordon Square, Bloomsbury, 182, 189–90, 208, 210–11, 229, 230, 254, 314

Gould, Mrs (Barbara) Ayrton, 354 n. 69

Government Code and Cypher School (GC&CS), 176, 302, 345 n. 46

Government Communications Headquarters (GCHQ), 345 n. 46

Grand, Sarah, *Babs the Impossible*, 50

Grant, Duncan, 126

Grant Morden, Walter, *see* Mordern, Walter Grant

'Great Pilgrimage' (1913), 133

Greece, 202, 234, 272–3

Green, Thomas Hill, 6

Greene, Belle da Costa, 94, 167

Greene, Graham, *Journey Without Maps*, 357 n. 18

Gresham's School, Holt, 222, 298

Grey, Edward, 1st Viscount Grey of Fallodon, 192, 347 n. 24

Grier, Lynda, 62, 223

Grimes, Louis Arthur, 263

Grosvenor Road, 6, 7–8, 16, 25, 39, 220

Hacking, Douglas, 268-9
Hague, The, International Women's
Congress (1915), 146–7
Haldane, Elizabeth, 288
Halpern, Barbara (*née* Strachey,
formerly Hultin): xiv; birth, 123–5;
childhood, 128, 140, 153, 162, 163,
181, 212–14, *212*, 232; during Ray's
election campaign (1922), 196, *196*;
education, 202, 213, 221–2, 223–4;
on Julia Strachey, 209; on Oliver,
219; in Vienna, 222–4; at Oxford
University, 225–6; relationship with
Wolf Halpern, 269–72, 296; trip to
Australia, 272–3, 274; marriage to
Olav Hultin, 274–83, 296–7; gives
birth to Roger, 282; divorce, 283, 296–
7, 298; marries Wolf Halpern, 298;
trains with E. O. Hoppé, 298; wartime
work, 307–8; and Ray's death, 310; on
Ray, xiv, 311–12; converts to Roman
Catholicism, 314–15; widowed, 315;
career in the BBC, 315; retirement
activities and death, 315; personal
characteristics, 212–14, 221, 222, 223,
224, 225, 269, 284. **Plates 26 and 30**
Halpern, Georg and Emily, 270
Halpern, Wolf Abiram, 270–2, 274, 275,
277, 296, 298, 304, 305, 311, 314–15.
Plates 28 and 34
Hamilton, Mary Agnes ('Molly'): career,
261; friendship with Ray, 261–2;
member of Royal Commission on
Civil Service, 245, 354 n. 69; attitude
to Strachey family, 262; made
Governor of the BBC, 267; holiday in
Greece with Ray, 272, 273; involved in
WEF, 296; bricklaying with Ray, 262,
281; on Ray as interviewer, 289; on
Ray and Oliver, 300; at Ray's funeral,
311; tribute to Ray, 312–13. **Plate 24**
Hampstead, 122, 128, 129, 156, 185;
suffrage society, 131, 133, 135; in war,
138, 140, 141. *See also* South Hill Park
and Belsize Park Gardens

Hancock, Irene, 222
Harcourt Brace (publishers), 197, 232
Harrison, Brian (interviews), 352, nn. 110
& 2, 361 nn. 15, 20, 24 & 43
Hartley, L. P., 233
Harvard Annex, 7
Harvard University, 10, 44, 84, 251
Haslemere, 280, 282
Hay, Malcolm, 339 n. 19
Haywood, William, 175, 203
Hellmann, Ilse, 305
Henderson, Arthur, 353–4 n. 39
Hiles, Barbara, 343 nn. 16 & 17
Hills, John Waller ('Jack'), 174
Hilton, Irene, 290–1, 296, 309, 314,
361 n. 24
Hitler, Adolf, 273, 305
Home, Ethel, 28, 37
Hope, Anthony, 246
Hoppé, E. O., 298
Hotels and Restaurants Bill (1936), 268–9
Houghton, Edmund, 46
Houghton, Mary, 46
House, Colonel Edward, 197
Housing (Additional Powers) Act (1919),
185
Hubback, Eva, 235
Hultin, Arvid, 275, 279
Hultin, Barbara *see* Halpern, Barbara
Hultin, Olav, 274–83, 297. **Plate 27**
Hultin, Roger (*later* Halpern), 282, 297–8,
303–4, *304*, 305, 315. **Plates 26 and 28**
Hunter, James de Graaff, 107–8, 333 n. 12
Hyde Park, London, 63, 69, 133, 193

I Tatti *see* Villa I Tatti
India: Stracheys in, 37, 61, 103, 104, 105–8,
129, 334 n. 14; Ray in, 119–21, 127;
research in India Office, 121, 128,
130–1, 170, 194; divorce in, 333 n. 12;
female suffrage in, 265–6
Indianapolis, 82
Inter-Allied Suffrage Conference (1919),
193
Interdepartmental Committee on
the Admission of Women to the
Diplomatic and Consular Services

(Schuster Committee), 263–4

International Woman Suffrage Alliance (IWSA), 69, 109, 184, 338 n. 10

International Women's Congress (1915), 146–7

Irving, Washington, *A History of the Life and Voyages of Christopher Columbus*, 246

Istanbul, Turkey, 264

Jacobs, Herbert, 98

James, William, 84–5

Jarrett, Rebecca, 8

Jenkin, Professor Charles Frewen, 98

Jenkins, Frederick, 220

Jenkins, Inez (*née* Ferguson), 171–2, *172*, 173, 181, 189, 219, 220, 227, 301, 343 n. 17

Jersey, Lady, 36–7

John Murray (publisher), 247

Johnston, Mary, 96–7, 143

Joint Committee on the Indian Constitution, 265

Jowett, Benjamin, 6

Kendal, 71–2

Kenney, Annie, 61

Kensington High School, 28–9, *30*, 32, 33, *33*, 36–7, 38, 39–40

Keswick, Cumbria, 71–2

Keynes, John Maynard, 50–2, *52*, 53–6, 137, 343 n. 16, 345 n. 42

Kingsway Hall, London, 138

Kipling, Rudyard, 141

Kirkby Lonsdale, 71-2

La Souco, Roquebrune, France, 120, 141, 210, 213, 227, 247, 260, 277

Labouchere, Henry, 60

Labour Party, commitment to women's suffrage, 142, 149–51, 177

Ladies Home Journal, 197

Lakes Herald, 70

Lamb, Henry, 111

Lancaster Gate, 104

Langham Place girls, 239

L'Avenir (ship), 273

Lawless, Emily, *Maria Edgeworth*, 246

League of Nations, 191, 192–4, 195, 197, 198–9, 202, 262–3

League of Nations Union (LNU), 193–4, 202, 234–5

Liberia, and the anti-slavery movement, 262–4, 357 n. 18

Lippmann, Walter, 197

Lloyd George, David, 157–8, 161, 174, 192, 193, 353–4 n. 39

Logan, Mary (pseudonym), 41

London and National Society for Women's Service (LNSWS), 228, 230, 244, 247, 260, 263, 273, 287, 314

London County Council (LCC), 9, 12, 19, 20, 21, 25, 191, 322–3 n. 7

London School Board, 20–1, 23–4, 191

London Society for Women's Service (LSWS), 191, 207, 288

London Society for Women's Suffrage (LSWS), 91–4, 133–4, 135, 138, 145, 147, 148–9, 158–9, 177, 179, 306; Women's Service Bureau training school for women welders, 148–9, *149*, 153

Long, Walter, 353–4 n. 39

Lothian, Philip Kerr, 11th Marquess of (Lord Lothian), 265

Lowe, Mrs E. M., 354 n. 69

Lyttelton, Alfred, 344 n. 26

Lyttelton, Dame Edith, 172–3, 344 n. 26

Lytton, Lady Constance, 241

Lytton, Victor Bulwer-Lytton, 2nd Earl of (Lord Lytton), 163

Macarthur, Mary, 5

MacCarthy, Dermod, 214

MacCarthy, Desmond, 163

MacCarthy, Molly, 163

Macnamara, T. J., 191

Mallory, George, 141, 335 n. 35

Margesson, Kitty, 88

Mariano, Nicky, 1, 168, 218, 261, 277, 297, 303, 314

Marie Curie Hospital, 254

Markham, Violet, 158

Markievicz, Countess Constance, 175

Marshall, Catherine, 71–2, 88–9, 146, 150, *150*, 151, 340 n. 37

Marshall, Frances *see* Partridge, Frances

Marsham Street, Ray and family in, 211, 219, 229, 230, 248, 252, 254, 263, 267, 296, 298, 300–1; flooding of, 220; LNSWS in, 244, 287; WEF in, 296

Mary, Queen, 148–9

Matheson, Hilda, 184, 245, 246, 267

Maurice, F. D., 242, 353–4 n. 39

Mayer, Ruby *see* Strachey, Ruby (*née* Mayer, *later* Hunter)

Meade, L. T., 20, 30, 325 n. 5

Megantic (ship), 155

Men's League for Women's Suffrage, 98, 288

militancy, suffrage *see* Women's Social and Political Union

Mill, John Stuart, 60, 61, 353–4 n. 39

Millbank prison, 7–8

Mitchell, Colonel J. M., 288, 289, 360 n. 12

Moore, G. E., 109, 137

Morden, Walter Grant, 174–5, 195–6, 203

Morelli, Giovanni, 10, 323 n. 10

Morning Post (newspaper), 324 n. 34

Morpeth Mansions, Westminster, 38

Morrell, Ottoline, 109

motoring, 46–8, 51, 86–7, 88–9, 97, 141, 158, *158*, 252, 273, 300

Mud House, Fernhurst: construction of, 185–7, *187*, 188, 218, 220, 252, 279, 301, 303, 346–7 n. 4; occupation of, 187, 189, 211–12, *212*, 231, 248, 253, 262, 273, 279, 280–2, 284, 300, 302–3, 304, 305, 315

'Mud March' (march for women's suffrage, 1907), 64

multiple personality disorder, 347 n. 32

Munich Crisis (1938), 293, 303, 305

Murray, Gilbert, 192

Murray, John *see* John Murray (publisher)

Mussolini, Benito, 202

National American Woman Suffrage Association (NAWSA), 78, 80, 95

National College Equal Suffrage League, 78, 84

National Council Against Conscription

(NCAC), 154

National Federation of Women's Institutes, 181

National Insurance Act (1911), 121

National League for Opposing Woman Suffrage, 163

National Union of Societies for Equal Citizenship (NUSEC), 181, 234, 235, 244

National Union of Women's Suffrage Societies (NUWSS): formed in 1897, 60; reaction to WSPU, 61; and the 'Mud March' (1907), 63–4; suffrage procession (1908), 68; caravan tours to spread the message, 69, 86; distances itself from WSPU, 87, 91; and Asquith's Reform Bill (1913), 132; conflict with the LSWS, 133–4; and male members, 135; relationship with Labour Party, xiii, 142, 149–51; split between 'patriots' and 'pacifists' over response to war, xiii, 138, 142–8, 338 n. 10; contribution to war effort, 138; and the Representation of the People Act (1918), 157, 159–62, 163–4; Inez Ferguson in, 171, 181; support for Ray's election campaign (1918), 174; dissension over future role, 180–1; renamed the National Union of Societies for Equal Citizenship, 181. See also *Common Cause*

Nazi Party, 273

New Era (Catholic newspaper), 324 n. 36

'New Girl' culture, 29–31, 54, 89

'New Woman,' 30

New York Evening Post, 197

Newnham College, Cambridge, 37, 38, 261, 291, 326 n. 37; Ray and, 39, 50, 62–3, 66, 67, 68, 74, 88, 89; different from Bryn Mawr, 77; suffrage caravan, 69–73; Principalship, 243, 293

Nice, France, 295, 308

Nightingale, Florence, 242

Nordhoff, Charlie, 278

Northcliffe, 1st Viscount (Alfred Harmsworth), 154

Northern Polytechnic Institute, 130

Norton, Harry, 343 n. 16

Observer, 161, 176
Olden, Ika, 274
Olden, Rudolf, 274
O'Malley, Ida, 177, 236–7, 353 n. 31
Orient Express, 217
Origo, Iris, 312
Our Lady of Sion School, Chepstow Villas, 18, 29
Oxford, 6, 7, 29, 51, 52, 73, 98, 105, 171, 248; Barbara and, 221–2, 223, 225–6, 250, 270, 272, 315; Christopher and, 315

pacifism, and the women's movement, xiii, 138, 142–8, 261, 305, 337 n. 33
Pankhurst, Adela, 63
Pankhurst, Christabel, 5, 60, 176
Pankhurst, Emmeline, 60, 88, 132, 161, 238, 241
Pankhurst, Sylvia, 238
Paris, France: circle of lesbians, 48; visited in the First World War, 168, 169, 171, 173, 343 n. 4; Inter-Allied Suffrage Conference (1919), 193; Women War Workers Conference in (1918), 173; Paris Peace Conference (1919), 193; Julia and Stephen Tomlin in, 211; Ray and Carey Thomas in, 217
Parliament: female candidates for, 5, 174, 175–6, 196; female MPs, 182–4, 196, 259–60, 261, 277, 306–7
See also Astor, Nancy
Partridge, Frances (*née* Marshall), 108, 123, 181–2, 209
Paterson, Isabel, 201–2, 349 n. 71
Paterson, Marion, 322 n. 6
Perry, Rachel (née Berenson), 84
Perry, Ralph Barton, 84
Pethick-Lawrence, Emmeline, 5
Philadelphia Evening Telegraph, 84
Pinsent, Cecil, 94, 167–8
Pioneer Club, 325 n. 5
pisé de terre, 186–8
Pletts, J. St Vincent, 339 n. 19
Ponsonby, Arthur, 337 n. 35

Ponsonby, Elizabeth, 337 n. 35
Poplar, 93
Portogruaro, Italy, 47
Prince, Morton, 347 n. 32
Prince of Wales (future Edward VIII), 267
Prynne, Miss (Blanche), 181, 232
Pye, David, 112, 115, 335 n. 35

Quaker speech, 8
Queen (magazine) 176-7
Quigley, Janet, 247

Radcliffe College, 7
Radical Liberals (Progressives), 6, 9
Rammed Earth Houses Ltd (company), 188–9
Rathbone, Eleanor, 142, 180, 181, 196
Reform Bill: (1867), 60; (1912), 132
Rendel, Betty, 72, 330 n. 42
Rendel, Edith, 69
Rendel, Elinor (*née* Strachey), 37, 61–2, 107
Rendel family, 55, 64
Rendel, Frances Elinor ('Ellie'): family, schooldays and start of friendship with Ray, 37–8; at Newnham College, 62–3, 66, 67; and women's suffrage, 62– 6, 67, 68–9, 87, 88, 91–2, 94; on suffrage caravan tour, 69–73, *71*; accompanies Ray to Bryn Mawr college, 75–7, 82; involvement in American suffrage movement, 78–82, 84–5, *80*; hated by Anna Shaw, 97; at Corfe Castle with Ray, 111; distress at Ray's engagement, 117; visits Ray's family, 137; as medical doctor, 216, 218, 274, 350 n. 47; witness to Ray's will, 309; at Ray's funeral, 311. **Plate 6**
Rendel, James Meadows, 37, 62
Representation of the People Act (1918), 160–4
Representation of the People (Equal Franchise) Act (1928), 235–6
Restoration of Pre-War Practices Act (1919), 178–9
Reynolds's Illustrated News (newspaper), 292, 361 n. 31
Rhondda, Lady, 174, 238

Rider Haggard, H., 246
Robb, Nesca, 312
Rookhanger, 279, 346–7 n. 4
Roosevelt, Theodore, 95
Roquebrune, France, *see* La Souco
Royal Commission on the Civil Service,
    244–5, 248, 261
Royal Free Hospital, 309–10
Royden, Maude, 133, 340 n. 37
Rubinstein, David, 249
'Ruin, the', *307*, 346–7, n. 4
Russell, Alys (*née* Smith *then* Pearsall
    Smith; 'Aunt Loo'), *16*; childhood, 6;
    helps make Ray and Karin Wards of
    Court, 26; and Ray's childhood, 26,
    49, 128; opposes publication of Ray's
    first novel, 49; despairs over Ray's
    unsociability, 90–1; marriage with
    Bertrand Russell, 55, 109–10, 112,
    117; suffrage activity, 63, 69, 73, 87,
    133, 151; on Oliver Strachey, 115;
    at Ford Place, 123, 128; care of Julia
    Strachey, 127–30; dislike of Stracheys,
    129; on Ray, 151, 160–1; has breast
    cancer, 162; at Chilling, 163, 181; care
    of Ray's children, 181, 198; financial
    support of Julia, 208, 209, 211; at Ray's
    funeral, 311; tributes to Ray, 311–2,
    363 nn. 3 & 5; reconciled with Russell
    and final years, 314. **Plate 7**
Russell, Bertrand: on Hannah Whitall
    Smith, 20; helps make Ray and Karin
    Wards of Court, 26; marriage with
    Alys Pearsall Smith, 55, 109–10, 112,
    117; prepares Ray for Cambridge
    Entrance Exam, 39; tutors Karin for
    Cambridge Finals, 109, 110; dislike of
    Ray, 110; on Executive Committee of
    NUWSS, 135; visits Ray's family, 137;
    reconciled with Alys, 314. **Plate 7**

'Sally' (in multiple personality disorder),
    195, 347–8 n. 32
Satterthwaite, Louise, 331 n. 38
Schoolmaster, 191, 324 n. 45, 347 n. 17,
Scott, C. P., 50
Scott, Geoffrey, 50–6, *52*, 94, 167–8

Scott, Lucy, 301
Selborne, Countess of, 175
Sex Disqualification (Removal) Act (1919),
    177
Shaw, Anna, 78–80, *80*, 82, 85, 95–8, 109,
    118, 201, 349 n. 70
Shaw, G. Arnold, 197
Shaw, George Bernard (GBS), 259
Sidney-Turner, Saxon, 343 n. 16
Silcox, Lucy, 221
Slade School of Art, 182, 208, 343 n. 16
Smith, Alfred Toulmin, 325 n. 5
Smith, Hannah Whitall, *16*; attitude to
    childcare, 6; religious activities, 6, 26–
    7, 38; hostility to Frank Costelloe, 7,
    25–7; moves to London, 8; joins Mary
    in Florence, 12; reaction to Mary's
    behaviour, 14–15, 53; involvement in
    Ray's upbringing, 14–20; attitude to
    education, 18, 28–9, 31–2; response
    to her husband's death, 19–20; gains
    custody of Ray and her sister, 26–7;
    preference for Ray over Karin, 34;
    enthusiasm for infatuations between
    schoolgirls, 38; decline in health, 38,
    218; opposes publication of Ray's
    first novel, 49; funds caravan trip,
    69; despairs over Ray's unsociability,
    90–1; death, 112; attitude to dress,
    43; views on men, 44, 55 on women's
    superiority, 59; on jealousy, 172;
    vehemence, 214; Ray's devotion to, 27,
    112–3, 120, 221; Ray's memoir of, 120,
    131; fictional counterpart, 233. **Plate 4**
Smith, Logan Pearsall, 6, *16*, 39, 48, 123,
    163, 299, 303, 314
Smith, Robert Pearsall, 6–9, 10, 15 *16*,
    19–20, 233
Society of Women Welders, 153, 178
South Hill Park, Hampstead, 122, 125, *126*,
    188, 189–90
Speaker's Conference (1916–17), 158, 159
Spectator, 154, 186. 264
St Augustine, *Confessions*, 246
St Felix School, Southwold, 221
St Francis of Assisi, *Little Flowers*, 246
St James's Square, 260, *266*, 267

St Joseph's School, Chelsea, 324 n. 27
St Mary's Infants' School, Lambeth, 18
State Children's Association, 20
Stead, W. T., 8
Stephen, Adrian, 154, 216, 311, 314, 352 n. 10. **Plates 8, 36 and 37**
Stephen, Ann, 158, 216
Stephen, Judith, 216
Stephen, Karin (*née* Costelloe), *16, 18, 33*; childhood, 9, 11–12, 17–19, 21, 22, 24–7, 29, 42: at Kensington High School, 28, 32; unequal treatment of, 11, 12, 21, 34; deafness, 50, 74; at I Tatti, 42, 51–3, 168; on Keynes, 52; at Newnham College, Cambridge, 74, 109–10, 118; attends Bryn Mawr college, 74–5; tutored by Russell, 109–10; on Oliver Strachey, 110, 113–15, 121; on Ray in love, 116; witness at Ray's wedding, 117; accompanies Ray and Oliver to India, 119–20; on the Strachey family, 129; marries Adrian Stephen, 154–5; and her children, 158, 216–17, 220; revisits Fernhurst, 185; in Bloomsbury, 189; medical qualifications, 216; separates from Adrian, 216; Berenson's financial support of, 251; on Olav Hultin, 280; at Ray's funeral, 311; death, 314; co-author of detective story, 352 n. 10; personal characteristics, 27, 32, 33, 39, 42, 126. **Plates 8, 14 and 35**
Stevenson, Robert Louis, 246
Strachey, Barbara *see* Halpern, Barbara
Strachey, Christopher: birth, 156; childhood, 163, 212, 214–16, 222–3, 232; during Ray's election campaign (1922), 196, *196*; and Oliver, 219; schooling, 222, 251, 253, 298; as Ray's confidant, 253, 273, 309; on Olav Hultin, 280; health problems, 299, 300, 305; sexuality, 299, 300, 315; at Cambridge University, 298–300; war work, 305, 308; executor to Ray's will, 309; career as teacher, 315; career in computing, 315; death, 315; personal characteristics, 212–13, 214–16, 298

Strachey, James, 103–4, 111, 117, 126, 137, 154, 189, 216, 220, 260, 299, 335 n. 35
Strachey, Jane Maria, Lady (*née* Grant): family, 37–8; President of Women's Local Government Society, 61; suffrage activity, 61–2, 63–4; relaxed manners of, 104; and Julia Strachey, 108; on Oliver's marriage to Ray, 114; disapproval of Oliver and Ray's financial arrangements, 121; in Gordon Square, 182, 189; decline and death, 229, 230
Strachey, John, 129, *212*, 216
Strachey, John St Loe, 186
Strachey, Julia, *see* Tomlin, Julia
Strachey, Lytton, 54, 103–4, 111, 113, 117, 137, 154, 170, 171, 246, 260, 299. **Plate 32**
Strachey, Margaret, 129, 252, 285, 355–6 n. 103
Strachey, Marjorie, 37, 140, 214, 252, 352 n. 10
Strachey, Oliver: childhood and education, 104–5; musical interests, 105, 126, 128; works for East India Railway, 105–6; first marriage, and divorce, 103, 106–8; meets and marries Ray, 109–18; trip to India, 119–20; failure of job application, 121; plan to write history of British India with Ray, 121, 130–1; and the women's suffrage movement, 135, 142, 144–7, 157, 180–1; in the First World War, 139–40, 154, 155–6, 163; relationship with Ray, 170–1, 173, 219–20, 300–2; relationship with Inez Ferguson, 171, 173, 181, 189, 220; works in Government Code and Cypher School, 176, 302, 305, 308; relationship with his children, 127–8, 182, 208, 210, 219; atheism, 232; illnesses, 260, 302; and Barbara's marriage to Olav Hultin, 275–6, 282–3; relationships with other women, 301; life after Ray's death, 314; personal characteristics, 105, 107, 108, 113, 122–3, 126, 130–1, 170, 208,

219; *Keigwin's Rebellion*, 131. **Plates 9, 25 and 29**

Strachey, Pernel, 37, 243, 293, 311, 314

Strachey, Philippa ('Pippa'): dedication to suffrage activity, 61; and the 'Mud March' (1907), 64; Secretary to the LSWS, 92, 133; visits India, 105; relationship with Ray, 92, 114, 117, 127,129, 221, 227–30, 261, 262; Pearsall Smith dislike of, 129, 230; 'Great Oriental Bazaar,' 131; at I Tatti and La Souco with Ray, 141; and women's work during the war, 158; and Ralph Strachey's death, 200; ill-health, 228, 230; in France with Ray, 228–9; mother's carer, 229–30, 284; and Lytton Strachey's death, 260; mainstay of family, 284; honorary secretary to WEF, 287, 290; strategic skills, 290; witness to Ray's will, 309; and Ray's death, 311, 314; secretary to LNSWS, 314; later life, 314; personal characteristics, 92, 129, 227, 229. **Plate 10**

Strachey, Ralph, 120, 129, 181, 188–9, 200, 232, 252. **Plate 12**

Strachey, Ray (*née* Costelloe, Rachel Pearsall Conn), xiii–xv, *16, 18, 33, 71, 80, 158, 182, 196, 236, 304, 307, 316*

Life events: birth, 6, 9; mother's favourite as a child, 11, 12, 14, 21; in Florence with mother, 11–12; in London and Sussex, 15–17; childhood illnesses, 19–20; custody battle after death of father, 25–6; diary, 33, 34–6, 208, 227; preferential treatment of, 34–5; lack of privacy, 34–5; adolescence, 35–7; need for a cause, 36, 59, 90–1; move to Morpeth Mansions, 38–9; move to Court Place, Iffley, 39; attends her mother's wedding to Berenson, 42; visits to I Tatti, 42–56, 94–5, 119, 121, 141, 260–1; encounters male chauvinism, 44–5; learns to drive, 46–8; sketches accident, *47*; writes first novel, 46, 48–50; takes up smoking,

53, 91; visits USA (1908–9), 74–86; owns her first car, 86–7; visits USA (1910), 95–7; takes Anna Shaw on motor tour round England, 97; meets Virginia Stephen, 98; gets to know Strachey family, 103–4; has her hair cut short, 109; meets and falls in love with Oliver Strachey, 104, 109–17; death of her grandmother, Hannah Whitall Smith, 112–13; engagement and marriage to Oliver Strachey, 113, 114–18; accompanies Oliver to India, 119–20; first pregnancy, 119–20; plans to write history of British India with Oliver, 121, 130–1; personal finances, 121–2, 125–6, 176, 190, 250–3, 266–7, 273–4, 281; sets up home in Hampstead, 122, 125–6; gives birth to Barbara, 123–5; as stepmother to Julia Strachey, 126–9, 130; pregnancy and miscarriage, 136–7; phantom pregnancies, 140–1, 145; visits to La Souco, 120, 141–2, 213, 227, 247; pregnancy and birth of Christopher, 156; health problems, 162, 218, 248, 253–4, 274, 308–9; goes to Paris to rescue her mother, 169–70; cares for Mary during her breakdown, 170, 172, 173; and her husband's affair, 171–2, 173; builds 'Mud House' in Fernhurst, Sussex, 185–7; sets up 'Rammed Earth Houses Limited,' 188–9; lodges in Gordon Square, 189–90; visit to USA (1923), 197–200; death of Ralph Strachey, 200; moves to Marsham Street, 211, 219–20; at the Mud House, 211–12, 214, 307; care for extended family, 216–7, 252, 260, 261, 276, 302, 303; death of Lytton Strachey, 260; trip to Athens with Carey Thomas, 217; and Barbara's education, 221–222, 223, 225; holiday in Greece with Molly Hamilton, 272, 273; and Barbara's marriage to Olav Hultin, 274–83, 296–7; becomes a grandmother, 282; writes 'farewell' letter to her mother, 308;

final operation and death, 2, 308–10; funeral, 311; tributes to, 311–13, 363 nn. 7 & 10; Mary's biography of, 2, 314; legacy, 315–16

Education: primary schools, 18–19; Kensington High School, 28–33, 35–40; takes the Cambridge entrance exam, 39; at Newnham College, Cambridge, 62–3, 66, 68; attends Bryn Mawr, 74–7, 82–3; studies engineering, 98, 109, 113, 116; evening classes in electricity, 130

Relationships: with her mother, 2, (in childhood) 11, 12, 13–14, 16, 19, 21, 34, 41, 42–5, 48, 50, 53, (pre-marriage) 74, 75, 78, (as an adult) 129, 169–70, 173, 200, 218, 260–1, 302, 303, 308, 314, 363 nn. 3 & 4; with her father, 17–18, 21, 22, 25, 27; with her grandmother Hannah Whitall Smith, 27, 112–13, 120; with Ellie Rendel, 37–8, 62–3, 64–5, 75, 79, 117; with John Maynard Keynes, 54–6; with Anna Shaw 97, 109, 118, 201; with Oliver, 110–11, 113–14, 115–17, 122–3, 126, 134–5, 145, 171–2, 173, 181, 208, 219–20, 300, 302; with Julia, 123, 126–9, 130, 181–2, 208–11; with her children, 213, 217, 221–2, (Barbara) 124–5, 214, 224–5, 271, 272, 274–83, 297, 304, 311, (Christopher) 156, 214–16, 253, 273, 298–300, 309; with Pippa Strachey, 92, 104, 141, 227–30; with Molly Hamilton, 261–2; isolation, 33, 35, 49, 226–7

Interests: bricklaying, 212, 226–7, 281, 307, 346 n. 4; cars, 46–8, 86–7, 125; cross-stitch, 226; education, 68, 77, 84, 213, 222, 223, 225, 226, 286, 300; electricity, 76, 98, 130; foraging, 212, 226; gardening, 125, 212, 213, 226; mathematics, 39, 55, 63; music, 223, 226, 248; playing patience, 63, 226, 248; portrait painting, 227, 282; reading, 20, 226, 245–6; swimming, 17, 96, 187, 226

Work and Political Life: takes part in the 'Mud March' (1907), 63–4; holds suffrage meetings in Charlwood, Surrey, 64–5; in demand as suffrage speaker, 65–6, 66–7; founds Cambridge University Women's Society for Women's Suffrage, 66, 68; attitude to the WSPU, 66, 69, 87–8, 91, 238, 241–2, 250; attends IWSA Congress in Amsterdam, 69; takes part in 'Women's Sunday', 69; caravan trips to promote woman's suffrage, 69–73, 86; involvement in American suffrage movement, 77–85; addresses suffrage meetings in the Midlands (1909), 87; suffrage tour in Cumberland (1909), 88–9; decision to suspend suffrage work, 89–90; work for the LSWS/ LNSWS, 91–4, 98, 133–4, 148–9, 153, 158–9, 234, 244, 260; brief membership of NUWSS Executive Committee, 94, 98; accompanies Anna Shaw on US speaking tour, 95–6; and Hampstead Society for women's suffrage, 131; 'mobbed' at Greenwich, 132; and the Great Pilgrimage (1913), 133; NUWSS relief work in war, 138–9, 141; role in NUWSS split, 143–7; election as Parliamentary Secretary of NUWSS, 147; battle over EFF, 149–51; President of the Society of Women Welders, 153, 178; lobbies the Government over the Representation of the People's Bill, 160–2; and removal of grille from Ladies' Gallery, 162; attends Women War Workers Conference, 172–3; stands in general election (1918), 5–6, 173–6; journalism, 176–7, 179, 197, 212, 292–3; lobbies Parliament over Restoration of Pre-War Practices Bill, 179; and NUSEC, 180–1, 234, 235; assists first woman MP, 182–4; involved in attempt to set up Centre Party, 191–2; and the League of Nations, 191–4, 197–9, 202, 234–5; lectures in the US, 197–8; stands

in general elections, (1922) 194–6,
196, (1923) 203; sets up Women's
Appointments Board for Cambridge
graduates, 243, campaigns for
women in the Civil Service, 244–5;
broadcasting career, 245–7, 267;
political secretary to Nancy Astor,
253, 259–60, 265–6, 267–9; interest in
Liberia, 262–4; Emergency Open-Air
Nurseries Committee, 265; Secretary
of the Women's Employment
Federation, 286–92, 293–6, 306, 309;
organises deputation of women MPs
on women's employment, 306–7

Opinions: on America, 75, 77, 81–2, 86,
195, 199–200, 330 nn. 13, 14 & 15;
on the Bloomsbury Group, 98–9,
208, 221; on clothes, 43–4, 125; on
colonialism, 263; on death, 309; on
England, 120, 147; on exercise, 32, 91,
210, 308; on feminism 59, 180, 194,
235; on free will, 225, 264; on India,
120; intellectual snobbery, 140, 269;
on money, 122, 176, 218 , 247; moral
values, 28, 36, 44, 190–1, 199–200,
207, 224–5, 243, 246, 249, 271; on
parenting, 123–5, 129, 213, 216, 217,
218–19, 221–2, 279, 280, 283, 299;
on politics, 66, 86, 92, 142, 154, 157,
174–5, 183, 190–2, 194, 195, 200, 202,
207, 234, 240, 250, 254–5, 264, 273,
292–3, 305; on privacy, 34–5, 98, 226;
on religion, 18, 55, 91, 232, 242, 264;
on the Royal Family, 267; on servants
125, 216; on silence 35, 52–3, 311; on
social life, 52–3, 83, 170–1, 211, 267;
on the vote, 70, 83–4, 194, 295; on
war, 140, 144, 147, 167, 305; on work,
68, 84, 122, 159, 176, 177, 194, 226,
284–6, 306–7

Personal characteristics: 2, 194, 214, 312–
13; appearance, 32, 43, 70, 173, 231,
267, 277; caustic comments, 227, 249;
concern for others, 216–17, 227, 228,
229, 250, 252, 260, 273, 309, 312–13;
depressive tendencies, 45–6, 49, 54,
55, 208, 226, 230, 253; disregard for

personal appearance, 43–4, 91, 114,
125, 194; drama, enjoyment of, 51,
72–3, 90, 132, 242; duty, sense of, 123,
131, 161, 269; emotional reticence,
xv, 27, 227, 249–50; empathy with
men, xv, 5–6, 130, 178, 238, 289,
290; energy, 161, 288, 289, 312;
extravagance, 79, 190, 218; financial
naivety, 66, 121–2, 125; generosity,
79, 263, 273, 279, 309; hero worship,
190, 228, 242; leadership, 32, 38,
290–1, 312; moral sense, strong, 28,
35, 36, 123, 190, 194, 224–5, 243,
246; observation, powers of 45, 66,
99, 110; organisational abilities, 32,
38, 110, 184, 312; outspokenness in
public, 195, 227, 240, 284; paradoxes,
xiv–xv; professional skills, 288–90,
294, 313; rationality, 214, 242, 309,
316; realism, 114, 145, 285–6, 312;
self-confidence, 33–4, 35, 36, 131,
316; selflessness, 2, 291, 312–13;
sentimentality, dislike of, 38, 123, 128,
242; sexuality 54, 110, 230; shyness,
32, 79, 290; speaking style, 70, 80, 175,
198, 231; temperament, 27, 32, 35,
36,151, 290; unsociability, 35, 52–3,
83, 170–1, 211, 267; writing style, 111,
131, 240–1

Writings: *Careers and Openings for
Women* (1935), 281, 284–6; *The
Cause: A Short History of the Women's
Movement in Great Britain* (1928),
59, 62, 164, 212, 236–43; *Frances
Willard: her life and work* (1912),
90, 95, 98, 109–12, 131; *Keigwin's
Rebellion (1683–4): An Episode in the
History of Bombay* (1916; joint author
with Oliver), 131; *Marching On*
(1923), 95, 109, 137, 142, 197, 201–2;
Midnight (1927; joint author under
pseudonym Mark Strange) 352 n.
10; *Millicent Garrett Fawcett* (1931),
164, 247–50; projected book on the
anti-slavery movement, 262–4; (ed.)
*Our Freedom and Its Results by Five
Women: Eleanor F. Rathbone, Erna*

Reiss, Ray Strachey, Alison Neilans,
Mary Agnes Hamilton (1936), 284;
A Quaker Grandmother (1914), 120,
131; *Religious Fanaticism: Extracts*
from the Papers of Hannah Whitall
Smith (1928), 228–9; *Shaken by the*
Wind: A Story of Fanaticism (1927),
211, 231–4; unpublished novel,
264–5; *Women's Suffrage and Women's*
Service: The History of the London and
National Society for Women's Service
(1927), 234; *The World at Eighteen*
(1907), 46, 48–50
Plates 1, 2, 13–21, 26, 44–46

Strachey, (Lieutenant-General Sir)
Richard, 37, 61, 104
Strachey, Richard ('Dick', brother of
Oliver), 139
Strachey, Richard ('Dick', son of Ralph),
129–30, 355–6 n. 103
Strachey, Ruby (*née* Mayer, *later* Hunter),
106–8, 333–4 n. 12, 334 n. 14
Strachey, Ursula, 129, 181, 183, 216, 252,
254, 260, 274, 276–7, 355 n. 103
'Strange, Mark' (pseudonym), 352 n. 10
suffrage, female, in UK: early pressure for,
59–61, 62; 'Mud March' (1907), 63;
later stages of campaign for, 86, 132,
156–7, 159–61; legislation for, (1918)
162–4, (1928) 235–6. *See also* LSWS,
NUWSS and WSPU
suffrage, male, 60, 157
suffragettes *see* Women's Social and
Political Union
Summerfield Preparatory School, Oxford,
104
Swanwick, Helena, 134
Sykes, Christopher, 346 n. 81
Symonds, John Addington, 344 n. 26

Tahiti, 275, 276, 278, 280
Taylor, William Nicholson ('Willy'), 44–9
Tewkesbury, 87
Thomas, M(artha) Carey: as President of
Bryn Mawr, 74, 75, 76, 82; campaigns
for female suffrage, 78, 79, 84; favours

life of culture, 76, 89, 98; travels, 97,
217. **Plate 5**
Tidmarsh Mill, Pangbourne, 171-3, 343
n. 16
Times, The, 158, 162, 175, 247, 268–9, 276,
307, 312
Tolstoy, Leo, 234, 246; *War and Peace*, 85
Tomlin, Julia (*née* Strachey, *later* Gowing):
childhood, 106–8, 123, 126–9, 130,
140, 163; at the Slade School of Art,
182; difficult behaviour of, 181–2,
208–11, 221, 222, 284–5; marries
Stephen Tomlin, 211, 228; and
Barbara's first wedding, 276; leaves
Stephen Tomlin, 277; widowed, 359 n.
92; unreliable account of childhood,
334 n. 14. **Plates 11 and 31**
Tomlin, Stephen ('Tommy'), 211, 277, 359
n. 92
Tomlin, Thomas, Lord Tomlin, 211, 244
Townley, Annie, 150

Union of Democratic Control (UDC), 145,
154, 261
Upton-on-Severn, 87
USA: politics in, 81, 82, 85–6, 199–200;
suffrage movement in, 77–80, 82, 85,
95; university education in, 77, 84

Vann Bridge Cottage, Fernhurst, 109
Vaughan, Cardinal, 24
Venice, Italy, 46, 48
Versailles, Treaty of, 193
Vienna, 105, 189, 222–3
Vigilance Association, 8, 191
Villa I Tatti, nr. Florence, *43*; Berenson's
leasing of, 42; purchase of, 94;
renovations to, 94–5, 167; Ray's visits
to, 42–5, 50, 52–3, 56, 119, 121, 141,
261, 272; in the First World War, 168;
children's visits to, 181, 218, 248, 270,
272, 297; Berenson plans to leave to
Harvard University, 251; Berensons
forced to contemplate leaving, 274;
Roger cared for at, 297, 303–4; Mary
determined to return to, 303; in the
Second World War, 1–2, 314

Villiers de l'Isle-Adam, Auguste de, *Le chapeau chinois*, 52

Wace, Margery, 246–7
War Office, 139, 158–9. *See also* codebreaking
Ward, Mrs Humphry, 159
Warm Springs, Virginia, 96
Washington, 95
Washington (state), 332 n. 81
Wearing, Gillian, 316
Webb, Beatrice, 9
Webb, Sidney, 9–10, 11
Wedgwood, Veronica, 272
'Week in Westminster, The' (radio programme), 261
Weizmann, Chaim, 270
Westminster *see* Grosvenor Road *and* Marsham Street
Widener family, 83
Wilkie, James, 289
Wilkinson, Ellen, 306
Willard, Frances, 90–1, 95, 98, 131
Williams, Gwen, 70, *71*
Williams-Ellis, Clough, 186
Wilson, Woodrow, 193, 197
Wintringham, Mrs Margaret, 196, 354 n. 69
Wise, Dorothy, 314
Woman's Journal (Boston), 331 n. 49, 332 n. 54
Woman's Leader (newspaper), 177
Women War Workers Conference, 172–3
Women's Army Auxiliary Corps, 159
Women's Emancipation Bill, 177
Women's Employment Federation (WEF), 287–91, 293–6, 305, 306, 307, 309, 313–14, 360 n. 14, 364 n. 17
Women's Freedom League, 87

Women's Liberal Association, 8
Women's Local Government Society, 61
women's movement, development of, 13, 59–62, 212, 236, 238–243, 248–9; split between egalitarian and social welfare approaches, 180–1, 235, 244. *See also* suffrage, female
Women's Royal Naval Service, 344 n. 26
Women's Service Bureau *see* London Society for Women's Suffrage
Women's Social and Political Union (WSPU): early years, 60–1, 62, 63, 68, 69, 77, 86; militancy by, 87–8, 91, 132; attempt to take over LSWS, 134; attitude to men, 135; financial accounting by, 238; withdraws from suffrage campaigning during war, 156; Ray's attitude to, 66, 91, 241–2
'Women's Sunday' (21st June, 1908), 69
Women's Temperance Crusade, 95
Wood, Major Samuel Hill, 179
Woolf, Leonard, 136
Woolf, Virginia (*née* Stephen): on Inez Ferguson, 343 n. 17; on Julia Strachey, 209; on Oliver Strachey, 111, 176; on Ray, 110–11, 173, 313; Ray's friendship with, 27, 54, 98–9, 136, 170; related to Ray by marriage, 154; Vanessa preferred by Oliver, 111, 335 n. 29; *A Room of One's Own*, 291; *Three Guineas*, 291–2. **Plate 38**
Worthington, Grace, 17, 22, 55, 75, 116, 133, 197, 199. **Plate 40**
Worthington, Mary ('Pug'), 17, 53, 74–6
Wych Cross, Ashdown Forest, 181, 232

Yonge, Charlotte M., 234